D0186661

Adobe
Illustrator CS4

Steve Johnson

Perspection, Inc.

PEARSON
Prentice Hall

Harlow, England • London • New York • Boston • San Francisco • Toronto
Sydney • Tokyo • Singapore • Hong Kong • Seoul • Taipei • New Delhi
Cape Town • Madrid • Mexico City • Amsterdam • Munich • Paris • Milan

IT / Photoshop

Pearson Education Limited
Edinburgh Gate
Essex CM20 2JE
England

and Associated Companies throughout the world

Visit us on the World Wide Web at:
www.pearsoned.co.uk

Original edition, entitled ADOBE® ILLUSTRATOR CS4 ON DEMAND, 1ˢᵗ edition, 0789738384 by JOHNSON, STEVE; PERSPECTION, INC., published by Pearson Education, Inc., publishing as Que/Sams. Copyright 2009 Perspection, Inc.

This edition is manufactured in the USA and available for sale only in the United Kingdom and Europe.

The right of Steve Johnson to be identified as author of this work has been asserted by him in accordance with the Copyright, Designs and Patents Act 1988.

ISBN: 978-0-273-72268-7

British Library Cataloguing-in-Publication Data
A catalogue record for this book is available from the British Library

10 9 8 7 6 5 4 3 2 1
12 11 10 09 08

Printed and bound in the United States of America

The publisher's policy is to use paper manufactured from sustainable forests.

Brilliant Guides

What you need to know and how to do it

When you're working on your computer and come up against a problem that you're unsure how to solve, or want to accomplish something in an application that you aren't sure how to do, where do you look?? Manuals and traditional training guides are usually too big and unwieldy and are intended to be used as an end-to-end training resource, making it hard to get to the info you need right away without having to wade through pages of background information that you just don't need at that moment – and helplines are rarely that helpful!

Brilliant guides have been developed to allow you to find the info you need easily and without fuss and guide you through the task using a highly visual, step-by-step approach – providing exactly what you need to know when you need it!!

Brilliant guides provide the quick easy-to-access information that you need, using a detailed index and troubleshooting guide to help you find exactly what you need to know, and then presenting each task on one or two pages. Numbered steps then guide you through each task or problem, using numerous screenshots to illustrate each step. Added features include "See Also…" boxes that point you to related tasks and information in the book, whilst "Did you know?…" sections alert you to relevant expert tips, tricks and advice to further expand your skills and knowledge.

In addition to covering all major office applications, and related computing subjects, the *Brilliant* series also contains titles that will help you in every aspect of your working life, such as writing the perfect CV, answering the toughest interview questions and moving on in your career.

Brilliant guides are the light at the end of the tunnel when you are faced with any minor or major task!

Acknowledgements

Perspection, Inc.

Brilliant Adobe Illustrator CS4 has been created by the professional trainers and writers at Perspection, Inc. to the standards you've come to expect from Que publishing. Together, we are pleased to present this training book.

Perspection, Inc. is a software training company committed to providing information and training to help people use software more effectively in order to communicate, make decisions, and solve problems. Perspection writes and produces software training books, and develops multimedia and Web-based training. Since 1991, we have written more than 80 computer books, with several bestsellers to our credit, and sold over 5 million books.

This book incorporates Perspection's training expertise to ensure that you'll receive the maximum return on your time. You'll focus on the tasks and skills that increase productivity while working at your own pace and convenience.

We invite you to visit the Perspection Web site at:

www.perspection.com

Acknowledgements

The task of creating any book requires the talents of many hard-working people pulling together to meet impossible deadlines and untold stresses. We'd like to thank the outstanding team responsible for making this book possible: the writer, Steve Johnson; the editor, Toni Bennett; the production editors, James Teyler and Beth Teyler; proofreader, Toni Bennett; and the indexer, Sharon Shock.

At Que publishing, we'd like to thank Greg Wiegand and Laura Norman for the opportunity to undertake this project, Cindy Teeters for administrative support, and Sandra Schroeder for your production expertise and support.

Perspection

About The Author

Steve Johnson has written more than 45 books on a variety of computer software, including Adobe Photoshop CS3 and CS2, Adobe Flash CS3, Dreamweaver CS3, Microsoft Office 2007 and 2003, Microsoft Windows Vista and XP, Microsoft Office 2008 for the Macintosh, and Apple Mac OS X Leopard. In 1991, after working for Apple Computer and Microsoft, Steve founded Perspection, Inc., which writes and produces software training. When he is not staying up late writing, he enjoys playing golf, gardening, and spending time with his wife, Holly, and three children, JP, Brett, and Hannah. Steve and his family live in Pleasanton, California, but can also be found visiting family all over the western United States.

Contents

Introduction   *xvii*

1   Getting Started with Illustrator CS4   1

    Installing Illustrator   2
    Getting Started   4
    Viewing the Illustrator Window   6   **New!**
    Showing and Hiding Panels   7
    Working with Panels   8   **New!**
    Using the Tools and Control Panel   10
    Opening a Document   12
    Opening a Document with Adobe Bridge   14
    Inserting Images in a Document   16
    Using the Status Bar   17
    Working with Document Windows   18   **New!**
    Checking for Updates Online   20
    Getting Help While You Work   22   **New!**
    Saving a Document   24
    Finishing Up   26   **New!**

2   Creating and Viewing a Document   27

    Creating a New Document   28
    Creating a New Document Using Presets   29
    Creating a New Document from a Template   30
    Setting Up a Document   32
    Using Multiple Artboards   34   **New!**
    Working with Multiple Artboards   36   **New!**
    Changing the Display View   38
    Changing the View with the Navigator Panel   40
    Customizing the Navigator Panel   42
    Changing the Screen Display Mode   43
    Changing the View with the Zoom Tool   44

Viewing and Using Rulers 46
Using the Guides 48
Using Smart Guides 50 **New!**
Using the Grid 52
Moving Around with the Hand Tool 53 **New!**
Using Crop Marks 54
Working with the Info Panel 55
Creating and Selecting Workspaces 56 **New!**
Using Undo and Redo 58

3 Working with Objects 59

Understanding Vector and Raster Graphics 60
Understanding Paths 61
Creating Rectangles and Ellipses 62
Creating Polygons and Stars 64
Creating Line Segments 65
Creating Arcs and Spirals 66
Creating Grids 68
Understanding Selections 70
Using the Selection Tool 71
Using the Direct Selection Tool 72
Using the Lasso Tool 73
Using the Magic Wand Tool 74
Selecting and Grouping 76
Selecting Similar Objects 78
Saving and Editing Selections 80
Moving Objects 81
Duplicating Objects 82
Aligning and Distributing Objects 84 **New!**
Transforming Objects 85
Using the Free Transform Tool 86
Rotating and Scaling Objects 88
Reflecting and Shearing Objects 89
Applying Multiple Transformations 90
Reshaping Objects with Envelopes 91

4 Working with Color 93

Changing Color Settings 94
Changing Color Profiles 96
Working with Color Modes 97

Changing Color Modes 98
Applying Colors 99
Working with the Color Panel 100
Working with the Swatches Panel 102
Working with Swatch Libraries 104
Adding Colors Using the Kuler Panel 106 **New!**
Replacing Colors 108
Inverting Colors 110
Using the Color Guide Panel 111
Applying Color with the Color Panel 112
Editing Colors with Live Color 114
Proofing Colors on the Screen 116

5 **Applying Fills, Strokes, and Gradients** 117

Applying Fill and Stroke Colors 118
Changing Stroke Attributes 120
Using the Eyedropper Tool 122
Using Patterns as Fills 124
Blending Fill Colors 126
Creating Blends Automatically 127
Applying Blend Options 128
Creating Blends with the Blend Tool 129
Modifying Blend Objects 130
Setting Transparency Options 131
Controlling Transparency Effects 132
Using the Transparency Grid 133
Applying Gradients 134 **New!**
Creating Gradients 135 **New!**
Editing Gradients 136 **New!**
Using the Gradient Tool 137 **New!**
Creating a Gradient Mesh 138

6 **Working with Points and Paths** 139

Drawing with the Pen Tools 140
Setting Anchor Point Preferences 142
Moving Points and Segments 143
Converting Points 144
Adding and Deleting Points 146
Aligning and Joining Points 148
Reshaping Paths 150

Splitting and Dividing Paths	152	
Merging Paths	154	**New!**
Working with Shape Mode	156	
Working with Pathfinder	157	
Creating a Compound Path	158	
Creating a Clipping Set	160	**New!**
Editing a Clipping Set	162	**New!**
Erasing to Reshape Paths	164	

7 Working with Layers — **165**

Understanding the Layers Panel	166
Setting Layers Panel Options	167
Creating Layers	168
Selecting Layers	170
Deleting Layers	171
Selecting Objects with Layers	172
Arranging Layers and Objects	174
Duplicating Layers and Objects	176
Locking Layers and Objects	177
Showing and Hiding Layers and Objects	178
Merging Layers and Groups	179
Moving Objects to a Layer	180
Flattening Layers	182
Locating Objects in the Layers Panel	183

8 Working with Type — **185**

Using Type Tools	186
Creating Type	187
Creating Type in a Text Box	188
Creating Area Type	189
Creating Path Type	190
Modifying Type on a Path	192
Importing Text	193
Selecting Type	194
Copying or Moving	196
Working with Overflow Type	198
Changing Fonts	200
Changing Font Size	202
Leading Type	203
Kerning Type	204

Tracking Type 205
Scaling Type 206
Rotating Type 207
Aligning Paragraphs 208
Indenting and Spacing Paragraphs 209
Setting Tabs 210
Working with Hyphenation 211
Working with Type Styles 212
Using Smart Punctuation 214
Working with Glyphs 215
Wrapping Type Around an Object 216
Creating Type Outlines 217

9 Working with Graphics 219

Opening Graphics 220
Placing Graphics 221
Placing Graphics from Adobe Bridge 222
Linking Graphics 224
Managing Linked Graphics 226
Tracing Raster Graphics 228
Converting Tracing to Paths 230
Applying Graphic Styles 231 **New!**
Creating Graphic Styles 232
Editing Graphic Styles 234 **New!**
Applying Appearance Attributes 236 **New!**

10 Manipulating Artwork with Effects 239

Applying Illustrator Effects 240
Applying the Convert to Shape Effect 242
Applying the Scribble Effect 243
Applying the Inner or Outer Glow Effect 244
Applying the Drop Shadow Effect 245
Applying 3D Effect 246
Changing Raster Effects Settings 248
Working with the Effect Gallery 250
Using the Gaussian Blur Effect 252
Using the Unsharp Mask Effect 253
Applying Multiple Effects 254
Controlling Effects Using Selections 255
Viewing Various Effects 256

11 Drawing and Painting   259

Using Pencil Tool   260
Creating Live Paint Groups   262
Setting Live Paint Bucket Tool Options   264
Using the Live Paint Bucket Tool   266
Using the Live Paint Selection Tool   268
Modifying Live Paint Groups   270
Selecting Gap Options   272
Using the Brushes Panel   273
Using the Paintbrush Tool   274
Creating and Editing Scatter Brushes   276
Creating and Editing Calligraphic Brushes   278
Creating and Editing Art Brushes   280
Creating and Editing Pattern Brushes   282
Working with Brushes   284
Working with Liquify Tools   286

12 Using Symbols   287

Using the Symbols Panel   288
Using Symbol Libraries   289
Working with Symbols   290
Duplicating and Editing Symbols   292
Breaking Symbol Links   294
Using the Symbol Sprayer Tool   296
Using the Symbol Shifter Tool   298
Using the Symbol Scruncher Tool   299
Using the Symbol Sizer Tool   300
Using the Symbol Spinner Tool   301
Using the Symbol Stainer Tool   302
Using the Symbol Screener Tool   303
Using the Symbol Styler Tool   304
Expanding Symbol Instances   305

13 Automating the Way You Work   307

Examining the Actions Panel   308
Building a New Action   310
Controlling the Playback of a Command   311
Adding a Stop to an Action   312
Inserting a Non-Recordable Command into an Action   313
Adding a Command to an Action   314

Deleting a Command from an Action 315
Working with Batch File Processing 316
Opening and Using Scripts 318
Defining and Editing Data Variables 320
Creating a Data Graph 322

14 Proofing and Printing Documents 323

Using Spell Check 324
Using Custom Dictionaries 325
Finding and Replacing Text and Elements 326
Finding and Changing Fonts 328
Printing a Document 330
Printing with Presets 331
Setting General Print Options 332
Setting Marks and Bleed Options 334
Setting Graphics Options 336
Previewing Color Separations 337 **New!**
Setting Output Options 338
Setting Advanced Options 340
Setting Color Management Options 342
Checking for Print Problems 343
Inserting File Information 344
Using the Document Info Panel 346

15 Exporting a Document 347

Exporting a Document 348 **New!**
Understanding Export File Formats 349
Exporting as a Bitmap 350
Exporting as a TIFF 351 **New!**
Exporting to Photoshop 352
Exporting with Presets 353
Exporting as a Flash Movie 354 **New!**
Saving as Adobe PDF 356 **New!**
Saving as EPS 358 **New!**
Saving as Adobe Flex 360 **New!**
Saving a Document for Microsoft office 361
Saving as a Template 362

16 Designing for the Web and Devices 363

Saving for the Web 364
Working with Save For Web Options 366

Optimizing a Image to File Size 367
Working with Web File Formats 368
Optimizing a JPEG Document 370
Optimizing a GIF Document 372
Optimizing a PNG-8 Document 374
Optimizing a PNG-24 Document 376
Optimizing a WBMP Document 377
Slicing Images the Easy Way 378
Working with Slices 380
Arranging Slices 382
Saving a Sliced Image for the Web 384
Adding HTML Text or URL Link to a Slice 386
Optimizing SWF or SVG for the Web 388

17 Customizing the Way You Work 389

Setting General Preferences 390
Setting Selection & Anchor Display Preferences 392
Setting Type Preferences 394
Changing Units & Display Performance Preferences 396
Setting Slices and Hyphenation Preferences 397
Selecting Plug-ins 398
Selecting Scratch Disks 399
Setting User Interface Preferences 400
Setting File Handling & Clipboard Preferences 401
Working with Appearance of Black Preferences 402
Defining Keyboard Shortcuts 403
Using Drawing Tablets 404

18 Working Together with Adobe Programs 405

Exploring Adobe Programs 406 **New!**
Exploring Adobe Bridge 407 **New!**
Getting Started with Adobe Bridge 408
Getting Photos from a Digital Camera 409 **New!**
Working with Raw Images from a Digital Camera 410 **New!**
Working with Images Using Adobe Bridge 412
Setting Preferences in Adobe Bridge 414
Applying Image Adjustments 416
Creating a Web Photo Gallery 417 **New!**
Automating Tasks in Adobe Bridge 418
Sharing My Screen 419 **New!**

Managing Files Using Adobe Version Cue   420
Working with Adobe Drive   421   **New!**
Exploring Adobe Device Central   422
Checking Content Using Adobe Device Central   423
Using Adobe Extension Manager   424

W **Workshops: Putting It All Together**   525

Project 1: Creating and Using Multiple Artboards   525
Project 2: Using Live Trace and Live Paint   428
Want More Projects   430

New Features   *431*   **New!**
Adobe Certified Expert   *435*
Index   *441*

Introduction

Welcome to *Brilliant Adobe Illustrator CS4*, a visual quick reference book that shows you how to work efficiently with Illustrator. This book provides complete coverage of basic to advanced Illustrator skills.

How This Book Works

You don't have to read this book in any particular order. We've designed the book so that you can jump in, get the information you need, and jump out. However, the book does follow a logical progression from simple tasks to more complex ones. Each task is presented on no more than two facing pages, which lets you focus on a single task without having to turn the page. To find the information that you need, just look up the task in the table of contents or index, and turn to the page listed. Read the task introduction, follow the step-by-step instructions in the left column along with screen illustrations in the right column, and you're done.

What's New

If you're searching for what's new in Illustrator CS4, just look for the icon: **New!**. The new icon appears in the table of contents and throughout this book so you can quickly and easily identify a new or improved feature in Illustrator. A complete description of each new feature appears in the New Features guide in the back of this book.

Keyboard Shortcuts

Most menu commands have a keyboard equivalent, such as Ctrl+P (Win) or Command+P (Mac), as a quicker alternative to using the mouse. A complete list of keyboard shortcuts is available on the Web at *www.perspection.com*.

i

How You'll Learn

How This Book Works

What's New

Keyboard Shortcuts

Step-by-Step Instructions

Real World Examples

Workshops

Adobe Certified Expert

Get More on the Web

Step-by-Step Instructions

This book provides concise step-by-step instructions that show you "how" to accomplish a task. Each set of instructions includes illustrations that directly correspond to the easy-to-read steps. Also included in the text are time-savers, tables, and sidebars to help you work more efficiently or to teach you more in-depth information. A "Did You Know?" provides tips and techniques to help you work smarter, while a "See Also" leads you to other parts of the book containing related information about the task.

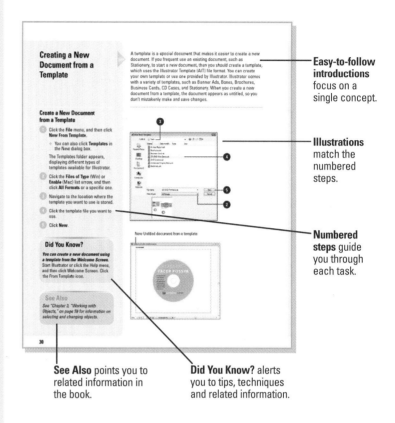

Easy-to-follow introductions focus on a single concept.

Illustrations match the numbered steps.

Numbered steps guide you through each task.

See Also points you to related information in the book.

Did You Know? alerts you to tips, techniques and related information.

Real World Examples

This book uses real world example files to give you a context in which to use the task. By using the example files, you won't waste time looking for or creating sample files. You get a start file and a result file, so you can compare your work. Not every topic needs an example file, such as changing options, so we provide a complete list of the example files used throughout the book. The example files that you need for project tasks along with a complete file list are available on the Web at *www.perspection.com*.

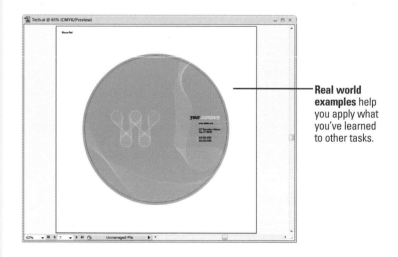

Real world examples help you apply what you've learned to other tasks.

Workshops

This book shows you how to put together the individual step-by-step tasks into in-depth projects with the Workshop. You start each project with a sample file, work through the steps, and then compare your results with a project results file at the end. The Workshop projects and associated files are available on the Web at *www.perspection.com.*

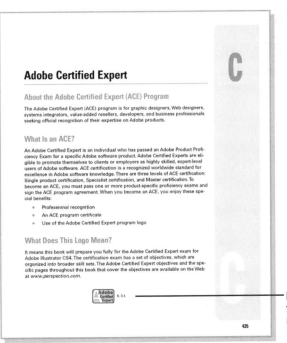

The **Workshop** walks you through in-depth projects to help you put Illustrator to work.

Logo indicates a task fulfills one or more Adobe Certified Expert objectives.

Adobe Certified Expert

This book prepares you fully for the Adobe Certified Expert (ACE) exam for Adobe Illustrator CS4. Each Adobe Certified Expert certification level has a set of objectives, which are organized into broader skill sets. To prepare for the certification exam, you should review and perform each task identified with a Adobe Certified Expert objective to confirm that you can meet the requirements for the exam. The Adobe Certified Expert objectives are available on the Web at *www.perspection.com.*

Get More on the Web

In addition to the information in this book, you can also get more information on the Web to help you get up-to-speed faster with Illustrator CS4. Some of the information includes:

Transition Helpers

◆ **Only New Features.** Download and print the new feature tasks as a quick and easy guide.

Productivity Tools

◆ **Keyboard Shortcuts.** Download a list of keyboard shortcuts to learn faster ways to get the job done.

More Content

◆ **Photographs.** Download photographs and other graphics to use in your Illustrator documents.

◆ **More Content.** Download new content developed after publication.

You can access these additional resources on the Web at *www.perspection.com.*

Keyboard Shortcuts

Adobe Illustrator CS4

If a command on a menu includes a keyboard reference, known as a keyboard short-cut, to the right of the command name, you can perform the action by pressing and holding the first key, and then pressing the second key to perform the command quickly. In some cases, a keyboard shortcut uses three keys. Simply press and hold the first two keys, and then press the third key. Keyboard shortcuts provide an alter-native to using the mouse and make it easy to perform repetitive commands.

If you're searching for new keyboard shortcuts in Illustrator CS4, just look for the letter **N**. The **N** appears in the Keyboard Shortcuts table so you can quickly and eas-ily identify new or changed shortcuts.

Keyboard Shortcuts		
Command	Windows	Macintosh
Selecting Tools		
Artboard tool	Shift + O	Shift + O
Selection tool	V	V
Direct Selection tool	A	A
Magic Wand tool	Y	Y
Lasso tool	Q	Q
Pen tool	P	P
Blob Brush tool	Shift + B	Shift + B
Add Anchor Point tool	+ (plus)	+ (plus)
Delete Anchor Point tool	- (minus)	- (minus)
Convert Anchor Point tool	Shift + C	Shift + C
Type tool	T	T
Line Segment tool	\ (backslash)	
Rectangle tool	M	M
Ellipse tool	L	L

Additional content is available on the Web.

Getting Started with Illustrator CS4

1

Introduction

Adobe Illustrator CS4 is a graphics design and drawing program that runs seamlessly on both Windows and Macintosh platforms. Adobe Illustrator CS4 is a stand-alone program, but it's also part of Adobe's Creative Suite of professional programs that work together to help you create designs in print, on the Web, or on mobile devices. All Creative Suite 4 programs also include additional Adobe programs—Bridge, Version Cue, Device Central, and Extension Manager—to help you manage and work with files.

Creative artists from Hollywood, brochure designers, as well as casual users turn to Illustrator for its proven ability to create top-of-the-line vector artwork and complex graphic designs. Illustrator's ability to manipulate illustrations for use in books, brochures, multimedia presentations, or on the Web, has made Illustrator the undisputed leader in the graphics industry. When it comes to vector illustration, Illustrator is literally the best software the computer industry has to offer.

With Illustrator, you can create anything from simple icons to multilayered illustrations, as well as manipulate text. And Illustrator's ability to work with other programs allows you to import Excel data for graph building, export Illustrator files directly to QuarkXPress and Adobe InDesign, as well as open layered Illustrator files in Photoshop, making it a snap to move back and forth between programs as you design.

What You'll Do

Install and Start Illustrator

View the Illustrator Window

Show and Hide Panels

Work with Panels

Use the Tools and Control Panel

Open a Document

Open a Document with Adobe Bridge

Insert Images in a Document

Work with Document Windows

Use the Status Bar

Check for Updates and Patches

Get Help While You Work

Save a Document

Finish Up

Installing Illustrator

To perform a standard program install, insert the Illustrator CS4 DVD into the DVD player on your computer or download the software online and start the setup program, following the onscreen instructions. Make sure to have your serial number handy because you'll be asked to enter it during the installation process. If you're updating from a previous version of Illustrator, you'll be required to verify the older version by instructing Illustrator where to find the previous version on your hard drive, or by inserting the previous version's install disk. Adobe, in an attempt to thwart software piracy, now requires online or phone activation of the program. The process can be postponed for 30 days. However, at the end of 30 days, the Illustrator program will shut down if it has not been properly activated. You can't blame Adobe for attempting to protect their products, since some surveys suggest there are more pirated than purchased versions of Illustrator in use.

Install Illustrator CS4 in Windows

1. Insert the Illustrator CS4 DVD into your DVD ROM drive, or download the software online to your hard disk.

2. If necessary, double-click the DVD icon or open the folder with the downloaded software, and then double-click the setup icon.

3. Follow the onscreen instructions.

IMPORTANT *During the installation process, Illustrator requires you to activate the program. Activation (using the Internet or by phone), must be accomplished within 30 days of installation, or Illustrator will cease to function.*

Did You Know?

The DVD comes with bonus content. The Resources and Extras DVD included with Adobe CS4 products includes bonus content and files in the Goodies folder. Check it out! For more free online resources, go to *www.adobe.com* and visit Adobe Exchange.

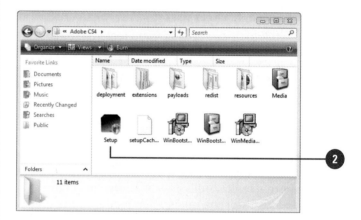

Install Illustrator CS4 in Macintosh

1 Insert the Illustrator CS4 DVD into your DVD ROM drive, or download the software online to your hard disk.

2 If necessary, double-click the DVD icon or open the folder with the downloaded software, and then double-click the setup icon.

3 Follow the onscreen instructions.

Did You Know?

You can create a shortcut on the Macintosh. Drag and drop the Illustrator program to the bottom of the monitor screen, and then add it to the shortcuts panel.

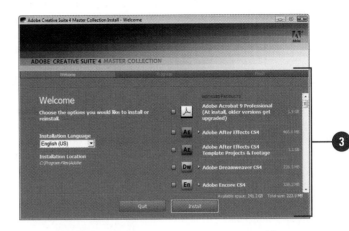

Illustrator CS4 System Requirements

Hardware/Software	Minimum (Recommended)
WINDOWS	
Computer Processor	2.0 GHz or faster processor
Operating System	Microsoft Windows XP SP2 (3) or Vista SP1
Hard Drive	2 GB of available space
Available RAM	512 MB (1 GB recommended)
Video Card	16-bit (GPU-equipped video card for OpenGL features)
Monitor Resolution	1024 x 768 (1280 x 800 or dual monitors)
DVD-ROM drive	Any type
MACINTOSH	
Computer Processor	Power PC G4 or G5 or multi-core Intel-based Macs
Operating System	Macintosh OS X 10.4.11 or higher
Hard Drive	2 GB of available space
Available RAM	512 MB (1 GB recommended)
Video Card	16-bit (GPU-equipped video card for OpenGL features)
Monitor Resolution	1024 x 768 (1280 x 800 or dual monitors)
DVD-ROM drive	Any type (SuperDrive for DVD burning)
Additional	
QuickTime 7.2	Required for multimedia features

Getting Started

You can start Illustrator in several ways, depending on the platform you are using. When you start Illustrator, the software displays a Welcome screen and then the Illustrator window. When you start a new Illustrator session or close all documents, a Welcome screen appears in the Illustrator window, providing easy access links to open a file, open a recent file, create a new file, and create a new file from a template. You can also use the Extend links to access help information, such as Getting Started and New Features, and online resources, such as the Adobe Illustrator Exchange web site, where you can download additional applications and information and Adobe TV, where you can view video tutorials.

Start Illustrator CS4 in Windows

1. Click **Start** on the taskbar.

2. Point to **All Programs** (which changes to Back).

3. Point to an Adobe Collection CS4 menu, if needed.

4. Click **Adobe Illustrator CS4**.

5. If you're starting Illustrator CS4 for the first time, perform the following:

   ◆ Enter your serial number, and then click **OK** to continue.

   ◆ Click **OK** to complete the activation process.

   ◆ Fill in the registration form, click **Register Now**.

Did You Know?

You can create and use a shortcut icon on your desktop to start Illustrator (Win). Click Start on the taskbar, point to All Programs, right-click Adobe Illustrator CS4, point to Send To, and then click Desktop (Create Shortcut). Double-click the shortcut icon on your desktop to start Illustrator.

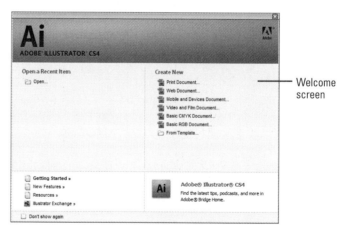

Welcome screen

Start Illustrator CS4 in Macintosh

1. Open the **Applications** folder (located on the main hard drive).

2. Double-click the **Adobe Illustrator CS4** folder.

3. Double-click the **Adobe Illustrator CS4** program icon.

4. If you're starting Illustrator CS4 for the first time, perform the following:

   ◆ Enter your serial number, and then click **OK** to continue.

   ◆ Click **OK** to complete the activation process.

   ◆ Fill in the registration form, click **Register Now**.

Did You Know?

You can create a shortcut on the Macintosh. Drag and drop the Illustrator application to the bottom of the monitor screen, and then add it to the dock.

You can create and use a keyboard shortcut to start Illustrator (Win). Click Start on the taskbar, point to All Programs, right-click Adobe Illustrator CS4, and then click Properties. In the Shortcut Key box, type or press any letter, number, or function key, such as P, to which Windows adds Ctrl+Alt. Click OK to create the keyboard shortcut. From anywhere in Windows, press the keyboard shortcut you defined (Ctrl+Alt+P) to start Illustrator.

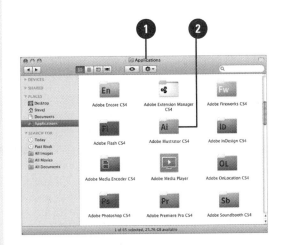

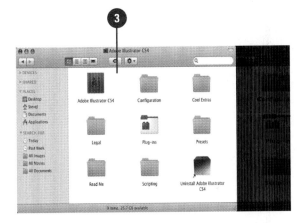

Shortcut for Illustrator CS4

Viewing the Illustrator Window

Adobe Certified Expert   IL 1.5

When you start Illustrator, the program window displays several windows of varying types you can use to work with graphics and illustrations. In Illustrator, windows appear in the workspace in panels. A **panel** is a window you can collapse, expand, and group with other panels, known as a panel group, to improve accessibility and workflow. A panel group consists of either individual panels stacked one on top of the other or related panels organized together with tabs to navigate from one panel to another.

The **Tools panel** contains a set of tools you can use to create shapes, such as lines, rectangles, rounded rectangles, and ellipses. You can fill shapes and text with a color, pattern, or custom tile. When you select a tool, additional options appear on the **Control panel**.

A **menu** is a list of commands that you use to accomplish specific tasks. A **command** is a directive that accesses a feature of a program. Illustrator has its own set of menus, which are located on the Application bar (**New!**) along the top of the Illustrator window. Next to the menu options on the Application bar, are new options for changing the document layout.

The **Document window** displays open Illustrator documents. Illustrator includes tabs to make it easier to switch back and forth between documents and a close button to quickly close a document (**New!**).

Document Window
Displays open Illustrator documents.

Application bar
Displays buttons and menus to change the document layout.

Control Panel
Displays options for the currently selected tool.

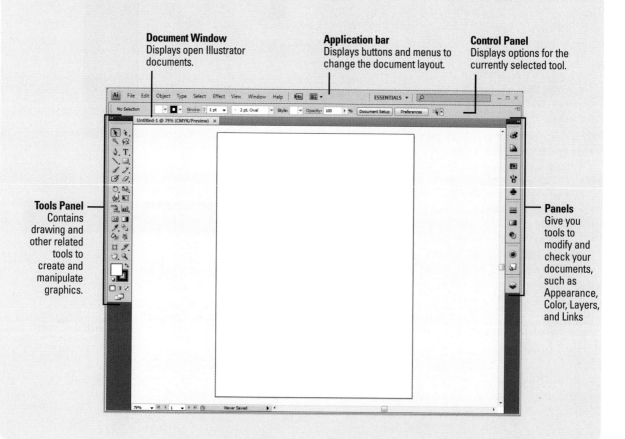

Tools Panel
Contains drawing and other related tools to create and manipulate graphics.

Panels
Give you tools to modify and check your documents, such as Appearance, Color, Layers, and Links

Showing and Hiding Panels

Panels give you easy access to many task-specific commands and operations from color control to vector path information. By default, the main panel display is located along the right side of your window. You can use the Window menu or click a panel tab within a group to display it, and then select options on the panel or choose panel-specific commands from the Panel Options menu to perform actions. Instead of continually moving, resizing, or opening and closing windows, you can use the header bar with the panel tabs to collapse or expand individual panels within a window to save space.

Open and Close a Panel

1 Click the **Window** menu.

2 Click a panel name, such as Color, Layers, Navigator, or Type.

> TIMESAVER To close a panel, or a single tab, right-click (Win) or control-click (Mac) a panel tab, and then click Close Tab Group or Close (for a single tab). On the Mac, you can also click the Close button on the panel.

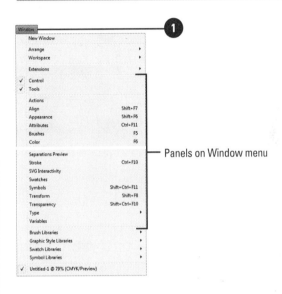

Panels on Window menu

Collapse or Expand a Panel

1 To collapse or expand an open panel, click the dark gray area or double-click a title tab on the header bar of the panel.

If the panel is in icon mode, click on the icon to expand or collapse it. To reduce the panel back to icon mode, click on the double right-facing arrows in the dark gray area. To expand from icons to panels, click on the double left facing arrows.

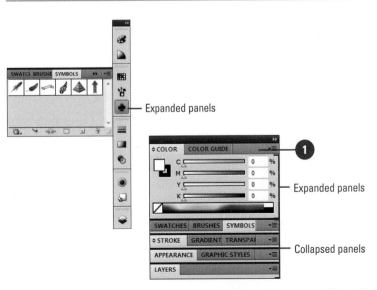

Expanded panels

Expanded panels

Collapsed panels

Working with Panels

IL 1.5

The movable panels are organized into groups, such as Color/ Color Guide and Actions/Links, to save screen space and help with workflow. You can also dock (add) or undock (subtract) specific panels within a group to customize your workspace. A panel appears with a header, which includes the tab titles and three options: the Collapse to Icons or Expand Panels button, the Close button, and an Options menu. The Options menu provides you with panel commands. The entire set of panels includes a double arrow at the top you can use to collapse and expand the entire panel back and forth between icons and full panels.

Dock a Panel

1. Select a panel; click on a named panel, or click the **Window** menu, and then click a panel name.

2. Drag the window away from the panel to a panel.

   ◆ **Add to Panel.** Drag to a panel until a blue rectangle appears around the panel.

   ◆ **Append to Panel.** Drag to a panel until a blue line appears along the side of the panel.

Undock a Panel

1. Select a panel; click on a named panel, or click the **Window** menu, and then click a panel name.

2. Drag the panel out of the group.

3. Drop it onto the Illustrator window.

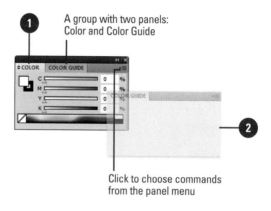

A group with two panels: Color and Color Guide

Click to choose commands from the panel menu

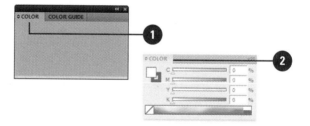

Did You Know?

You can dock and undock panels to a docking channel. You can dock and undock, panels or panel groups in docking channels. A docking channel is a region located on the left and right side of the Illustrator window to which you can attach and detach panels. When you drag a panel over a dockable area, a blue line appears.

Collapse and Expand the Panel Set Between Icons and Panels

◆ To collapse the panel set to icons with text, click the double arrow pointing right (Collapse to Icons) at the top of the panels.

◆ To expand the panel set from icons with text to full panels, click the double arrow pointing left (Expand Panels) at the top of the panels.

◆ To have an expanded panel icon automatically collapse or hide when you click away, right-click (Win) or Control-click (Mac) a panel, and then click **Auto-Collapse Iconic Panels** or **Auto-Show Hidden Panels (New!)**.

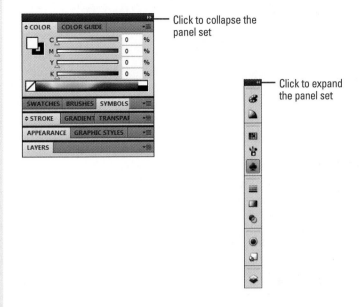

Click to collapse the panel set

Click to expand the panel set

Use the Panel Options Menu

① Open or expand a panel.

② Click the **Options** button on the right side of the panel header bar.

③ Click a command from the list (commands vary).

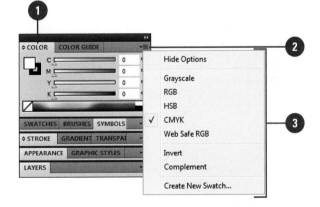

Using the Tools and Control Panel

Illustrator has an abundance of tools that give an Illustrator designer tremendous control over any creative designing problems that may crop up. For example, the Illustrator toolbox contains a variety of different tools: selection tools (you can never have enough selection tools), painting or shape tools, type tools, and other tools dedicated to creating artboards, working with slices and transforming and viewing illustrations. Add to that collection, slicing, sampling, and viewing tools and you have all the tools you need to do any job.

When you work on a document, it's important to know what tools are available, and how they can help in achieving your design goals. Illustrator likes to save space, so it con-solidates similar tools under one button. To access multiple tools, click and hold on any Tools panel button that contains a small black triangle, located in the lower right corner of the tool button. Take a moment to explore the Illustrator toolbox and get to know the tools.

The Illustrator Tools panel contains the tools needed to work through any Illustrator job, but it's not necessary to click on a tool to access it. Simply using a letter of the alphabet can access all of Illustrator's tools. For example, pressing the P key switches to the Pen tool, and pressing the T key switches to the Type tool. In addition, if a button has more than one tool available, clicking the arrow on the right side of the tool menu displays all the tools in a small panel for easy access. When

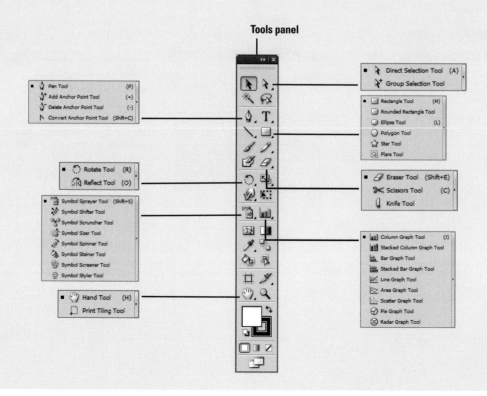

Tools panel

■ ◊ Pen Tool (P)
◊⁺ Add Anchor Point Tool (+)
◊⁻ Delete Anchor Point Tool (-)
⌐ Convert Anchor Point Tool (Shift+C)

■ ↖ Direct Selection Tool (A)
↖⁺ Group Selection Tool

■ ▭ Rectangle Tool (M)
▭ Rounded Rectangle Tool
○ Ellipse Tool (L)
○ Polygon Tool
☆ Star Tool
◎ Flare Tool

■ ○ Rotate Tool (R)
⊙ Reflect Tool (O)

■ ◢ Eraser Tool (Shift+E)
✂ Scissors Tool (C)
∅ Knife Tool

■ ⬚ Symbol Sprayer Tool (Shift+S)
Symbol Shifter Tool
Symbol Scruncher Tool
Symbol Sizer Tool
Symbol Spinner Tool
Symbol Stainer Tool
Symbol Screener Tool
Symbol Styler Tool

■ ⅲ Column Graph Tool (J)
Stacked Column Graph Tool
Bar Graph Tool
Stacked Bar Graph Tool
Line Graph Tool
Area Graph Tool
Scatter Graph Tool
Pie Graph Tool
Radar Graph Tool

■ ✋ Hand Tool (H)
⎙ Print Tiling Tool

10

you display the small panel, you can click the arrow on the right edge to change the menu to a panel, which stays open. You can click the Close button to dismiss it. You can refer to Adobe Illustrator CS4 Keyboard Shortcuts (available for download on the Web at *www.perspection.com*) for more information on all the letter assignments for the various tools. To really get efficient in Illustrator, you need to learn to use both hands. Use one hand for your mouse or drawing tablet, and the other on the keyboard to make quick changes of tools and options. Think of playing Illustrator like playing a piano—you need to use both hands.

Using the Control Panel

The Control panel displays the options for the currently selected tool. For most tools, your options include Selection, Stroke Width, Brush panel, Graphic Style panel, Opacity, Document Setup, Preferences, and Select Similar Objects. When working with the Text tool, additional options include Character panel, Paragraph panel, Align Left, Align Center, and Align Right. The important thing to remember is that the Control panel is customized based on the tool you have selected.

Control panel

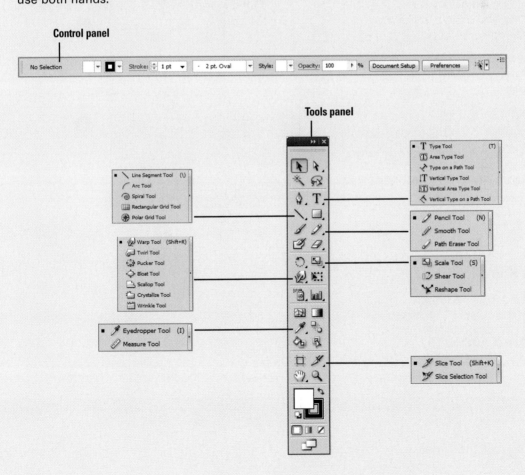

Tools panel

Opening a Document

Illustrator lets you open image files created in different formats, such as TIFF, JPEG, GIF, and PNG, as well as Illustrator documents in the AI format. If you want to simply open an image or Illustrator document, the Welcome Screen or Open dialog box are the most efficient way. However, if you need to manage, organize, or process files, Adobe Bridge is the way to go. You open an existing Illustrator document or image file the same way you open documents in other programs. In Windows Explorer (Win) or Finder (Mac), you can double-click an Illustrator document to open the Illustrator program and the document. When you open a document, a tab appears across the top of the Document window, with the document title. You can click the tab at any time to display that particular document.

Open an Existing Document

① Click the **File** menu, and then click **Open** to display all file types in the file list of the Open dialog box.

② Click the **Files of Type** (Win) or **Enable** (Mac) list arrow, and then select a format.

③ Navigate to the drive or folder location with the document you want to open.

④ Click the image file you want to open.

> **TIMESAVER** *Press and hold the Shift key to select multiple contiguous files to open while in the Open dialog box.*

⑤ Click **Open**.

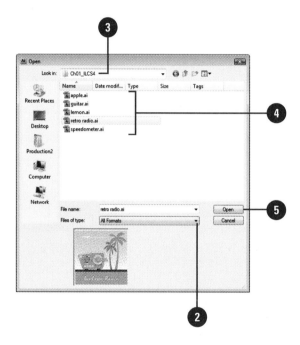

Did You Know?

You can delete a file in a dialog box (Win). In the Open or Save As dialog box, right click the file you want to delete, and then click Delete.

Open a Recently Opened Document

1 Click the **File** menu, and then point to **Open Recent Files**.

2 Click the document you want to open.

Did You Know?

You can open a recent file quickly from the Start menu (Win). Click the Start button, point to Recent Items (Vista) or My Recent Documents (XP), and then click the file name you want to open.

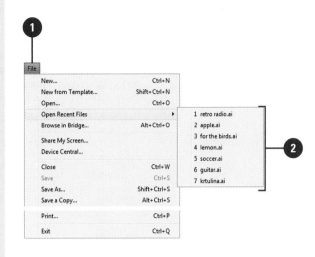

Open a Document from the Welcome Screen

1 Start Adobe Illustrator or click the **Help** menu, and then click **Welcome Screen**.

2 Click a document from the Open a Recent Item list.

3 To open a document not in the list, click **Open**, select a document, and then click **Open**.

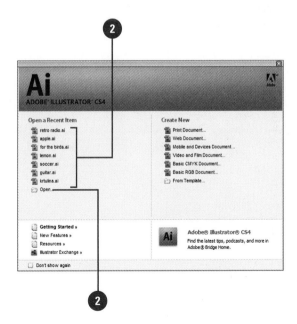

Opening a Document with Adobe Bridge

With Adobe Bridge, you can drag assets into your layouts as needed, preview them, and add metadata to them. Bridge allows you to search, sort, filter, manage, and process files one at a time or in batches. You can also use Bridge to create new folders; rename, move, delete and group files (known as stacking); edit metadata; rotate images; and run batch commands. You can also view information about files and data imported from your digital camera.

Browse and Open Documents with Adobe Bridge

1. Click the **Go to Bridge** button on the Application bar or click the **File** menu, and then click **Browse in Bridge**.

2. In Bridge, select a specific workspace to view your files the way you want.

3. Navigate to the drive or folder where the file is located.

4. To open an image in Illustrator, use any of the following:

   ◆ Double-click on a thumbnail to open it in the default program.

   ◆ Drag the thumbnail from the Bridge into an open Adobe application

   ◆ Select a thumbnail, click the **File** menu, point to **Open With**, and then click **Adobe Illustrator CS4**.

   ◆ Select a thumbnail, click the **File** menu, point to **Place**, and then click **In Illustrator**.

5. To return to Illustrator, click the **File** menu, and then click **Return to Adobe Illustrator**.

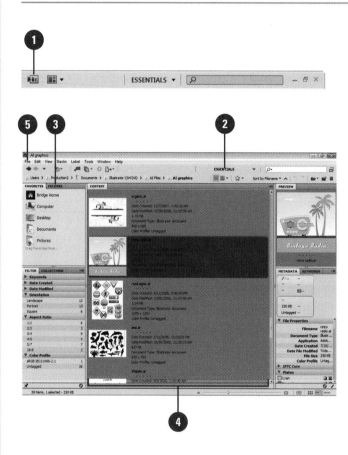

Work with Files Using Bridge

1. Click the **Go to Bridge** button on the Application bar or click the **File** menu, and then click **Browse in Bridge**.

2. Click the **Folders** tab and choose a folder from the scrolling list.

3. Click the **Favorites** tab to choose from a listing of user-defined items, such as Pictures.

4. To narrow down the list of images using a filter, click the criteria you want to use in the Filter panel.

5. Click an image within the preview window to select it.

6. Click the **Preview** tab to view a larger thumbnail of the selected image. Multiple images appear when you select them.

7. Drag the **Zoom** slider to increase or decrease the thumbnail views.

8. Use the file management buttons to rotate or delete images, or create a new folder.

9. Double-click on a thumbnail to open it in the default program, or drag the thumbnail from the Bridge into an open Adobe application.

Did You Know?

You can reveal a document in Adobe Bridge from Illustrator. Open a document in Illustrator, click the black triangle on the Status Bar, and then click Reveal in Bridge.

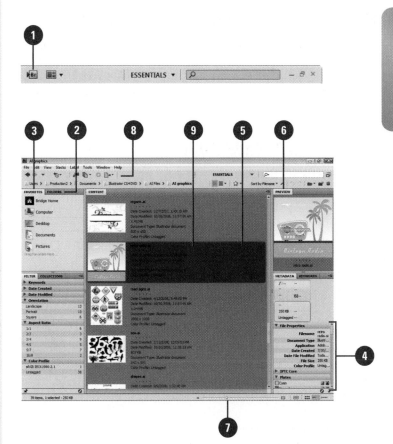

Inserting Images in a Document

IL 7.1

You can use Illustrator's Place command to insert artwork into an open document. To increase your control of the new image information, Illustrator places the new image into a separate layer. Illustrator lets you place files saved in Illustrator AI, Adobe PDF, Photoshop PSD, BMP, JPEG, EPS, PNG, TIFF, and TXT, DOC, or RTF formats to name a few. When you first place a vector-based image into Illustrator, you have the ability to modify the width, height, and rotation while retaining the vector format of the file.

Insert an Image in a Document Using the Place Command

1 Open an Illustrator document.

2 Click the **File** menu, and then click **Place**.

3 Navigate to the drive or folder location with the image, and then select the image you want to place into the active document.

4 Select any of the following options:

◆ **Link.** Places a screen version of the image and links the document to the image file. Deselect to embed a copy of the image in the document.

◆ **Template.** Places a dimmed version of the image on a template layer.

◆ **Replace.** Replaces the current image.

5 Click **Place**.

6 If an addition dialog box appears, specify the Place options that you want, and then click **OK**.

Illustrator places the image in the active layer, and then encloses it within a transformable bounding box.

7 Control the shape by manipulating the corner and side nodes of the freeform bounding box.

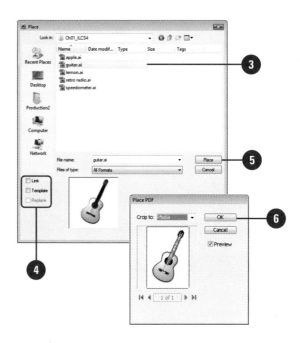

Using the Status Bar

To work efficiently in Illustrator you need information about the active document. Details about the document's color profile can help in the design and preparation of the final document. You can display the current tool, date and time, the number of undos, and Version Cue status. Illustrator displays current information about the active document through the Status Bar, located at the bottom of the document window. From the Status Bar, you can also switch between artboards and change the view size percentage.

Use the Status Bar

1 Click the **black triangle** near the Status bar info box, point to **Show**, and then select from the following options:

- ◆ **Version Cue Status.** Indicates whether Version Cue file management has been enabled.

- ◆ **Current Tool.** Displays the current tool.

- ◆ **Date and Time.** Displays the current date and time.

- ◆ **Number of Undos.** Displays the current number of undos.

- ◆ **Document Color Profile.** Displays the current document color profile.

2 To switch between artboards, use any of the following:

- ◆ **First or Last.** Displays the first or last artboard.

- ◆ **Previous or Next.** Displays the previous or next artboard.

- ◆ **Artboard Navigation.** Displays the specified artboard.

3 To change the view size, click the **View Size** list arrow, and then select a view percentage or **Fit On Screen**.

Working with Document Windows

When you open multiple documents, you can use the Arrange Documents (**New!**) or Window menu or tabs at the top of the Document window to switch between them. You can click a tab name to switch to and activate the document. By default, tabs are displayed in the order in which you open or create documents. When you want to move or copy information between documents, it's easier to display several document windows on the screen at the same time and move them around. However, you must make the window active to work in it. Each tab also includes a Close button (**New!**) to quickly close a document. If the document view is too small or large, you can change it to suit your needs.

Work with Multiple Documents

1 Open more than one document.

2 Click a tab name to switch to the document.

TIMESAVER *Press Ctrl+Tab or Ctrl+Shift+Tab to cycle to the tab you want.*

◆ You can also click the **Window** menu, and then click a document name at the bottom of the menu.

3 To move a document window around, do any of the following:

◆ To rearrange the order of tabbed documents (**New!**), drag a window's tab to a new location.

◆ To switch to another document when dragging a selection (**New!**), drag the selection over the document's tab.

4 Undocked floating document window

Arrange Multiple Documents

① Open more than one document.

② Click the **Arrange Documents** menu (**New!**) on the Application bar.

③ On the menu, select an arrangement button icon:

◆ **Consolidate All.** Displays all active documents as tabs.

◆ **Tile All In Grid.** Displays all open documents in a grid pattern on the screen.

◆ **Tile All Vertically.** Displays all open documents vertically on the screen.

◆ **Tile All Horizontally.** Displays all open documents horizontally on the screen.

◆ **2-Up, 3-Up, 4-Up, 5-Up, or 6-Up.** Displays the number of documents in the selected pattern (in the menu icon) on the screen.

④ To dock or undock a document window (**New!**), drag the window's tab out of the group or into the group.

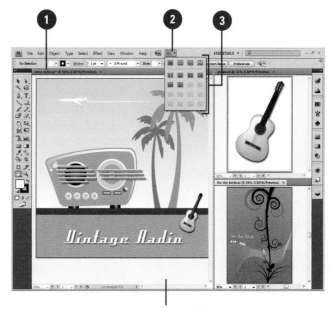

Arranged documents

Checking for Updates Online

As time passes, Illustrator—like any other program—will change. There are two types of changes to a program: updates and patches. Updates are improvements to a program such as a new feature, option, or command. Patches are software fixes for problems discovered after the public release of the program. The good news is that both updates and patches are free, and once downloaded, are self-installing. Adobe gives you two ways to check for changes. You can check manually by going to the Adobe web site, or automatically through the Adobe Updater. The Adobe Updater Preferences dialog box allows you to set update options for Illustrator and other installed Adobe products, such as Bridge. You can set the update preferences to check for updates monthly or weekly and automatically download them, or have Adobe Updater ask before performing the download.

Check for Updates Directly from the Internet

1. Open your Internet browser.

2. Go to the following Web address: *www.adobe.com/downloads/updates/*

3. Click the list arrow, and then click the **Illustrator - Macintosh** or **Illustrator - Windows**.

4. Click **Go**.

   Any updates or patches appear in a list.

5. Based on your operating system, follow the onscreen instructions to download and install the software.

   IMPORTANT *Checking on your own requires a computer with a connection to the Internet. Since some of the updates can be rather large, it's recommended you have high-speed access; 56k is good, but DSL or cable modem is better.*

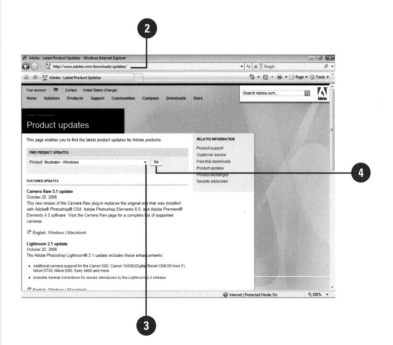

Check for Updates from the Illustrator Help Menu

1. Start Adobe Illustrator, if necessary.

2. Click the **Help** menu, and then click **Updates**.

   Illustrator automatically connects you to the Internet, and checks for updates.

3. If there are any updates available, click **Download and Install**.

   IMPORTANT *Remember, these files can be quite large. So, if your Internet connection speed is slow, you might want to perform downloading files at a low traffic time. Also, by making sure you don't have other programs running, you can maximize your system's resources for the downloading of files.*

   When the check or download is complete, the Adobe Updater dialog box opens.

4. To change Adobe Updater preferences, click **Preferences**, select the **Automatically Check For Adobe Updates** check box, select the update and program options you want, and then click **OK**.

5. Click **Quit**.

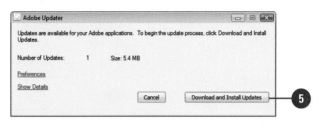

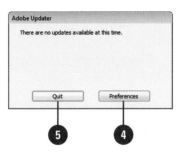

Select to update an application.

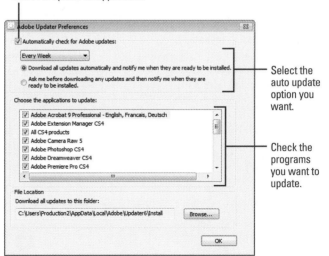

Select the auto update option you want.

Check the programs you want to update.

Getting Help While You Work

At some time, everyone has a question or two about the program they are using. Illustrator Help uses a Community Help site (**New!**) on the web at *adobe.com* (which is updated regularly) to help you find the information you need. When you start Illustrator Help, your browser opens, displaying a web site with Illustrator help categories and topics. You can search the Illustrator Help site by using keywords or phrases or browsing through a list of categories and topics to locate specific information. When you perform a search using keywords or phrases, a list of possible answers is shown to you from adobe.com, with the most likely answer to your question at the top of the list. Along with help text, some help topics include links to text and video tutorials. In addition, comments and ratings from users are available to help guide you to an answer.

Get Help Information

1 Click the **Help** menu, and then click **Illustrator Help**.

> TIMESAVER *Press F1.*

Your browser opens, displaying Illustrator Help from the Web. An Internet connection is required.

2 Click the **Illustrator help (web)** link to access online help.

3 Click Help categories (plus sign icons) until you display the topic you want.

4 Click the topic you want.

5 Read the topic, and if necessary, click any hyperlinks to get information on related topics or definitions.

6 When you're done, close your browser.

Did You Know?

You can get resource help with Illustrator on the Web. Click the Help menu, click Welcome Screen, and then click Resources or Illustrator Exchange to display Illustrator help resources from all over the Web.

Search for Help Information

1 In Illustrator, on the Application bar, type one or more keywords in the Search box, and then press Enter (Win) or Return (Mac).

◆ You can also click the **Help** menu, and then click **Illustrator Help** to open Help and use the Search box.

Your browser displays an Adobe web site with a list of topics that match the keywords you entered in the Search box.

2 Click the link to the topic you want from the search list of results.

3 Read the topic, and then if you want, click any hyperlinks to get information on related topics or definitions.

4 When you're done, close your browser.

Keyword to search

Did You Know?

You can find out what's new in Illustrator. Click the Help menu, click Illustrator Help, click the plus sign (+) next to Resources, and then click What's New.

You can print out the selected Help topic. Open the Help screen in your browser, select the Help topic you want to print, select the Print command, specify print options, and then click Print (Win) or OK (Mac).

You can move backward and forward between help topics. Click the Previous or Next button on the right side of the Help web page.

For Your Information

Participating in Adobe Product Improvement

You can participate in the Adobe Product Improvement Program. (**New!**) Click the Help menu, click Adobe Product Improvement Program, and then follow the on-screen instructions. This is an opt-in program that allows you to test Adobe products and make suggestions for future products. This program enables Adobe to collect product usage data from customers while maintaining their privacy.

Saving a Document

 IL 1.3

When you finish working on your Illustrator document, you need to save it before you close the document or exit Illustrator. While this may seem like a simple task, there are questions that must be asked before saving a file, like *What is the intended final output of the image?* Each output device, whether monitor or paper-based, requires a specific format, and it's best to know this information at the beginning of the creation process. Knowing the eventual destination of an image helps you create the design with the output in mind. A file type specifies the document format (for example, a template) as well as the program in which the file was created (for example, Illustrator). You might want to change the type if you're creating a custom template or sharing files with someone who doesn't have the Adobe Illustrator program.

Save an Illustrator Document

1. Click the **File** menu, and then click **Save As**.

2. Enter a name for the file.

3. Click the **Save as Type** list arrow (Win) or **Format** popup (Mac), and then click **Adobe Illustrator (*.AI)**.

4. Navigate to the drive or folder location where you want to save the document.

5. Click **Save**.

6. Select from the available options:

   ◆ **Version.** Specify an Illustrator version in which to save.

   ◆ **Fonts.** Specify when to embed the entire font or characters.

   ◆ **Create PDF Compatible.** Select to save a PDF in the file.

   ◆ **Include Linked Files.** Select to include linked files.

   ◆ **Embed ICC Profiles.** Select to embed the color profiles.

   ◆ **Use Compression.** Select to compress the file.

   ◆ **Transparency.** Specify options for transparent objects.

7. Click **OK**.

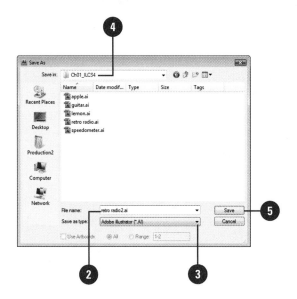

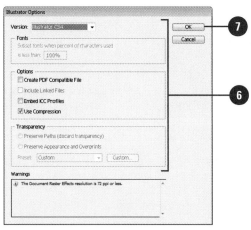

Save a Document in Other Formats

1. Click the **File** menu, and then click **Save As**.

2. Click the **Save as Type** list arrow (Win) or **Format** popup (Mac), and then select a format.

   - ◆ **Adobe PDF.** Creates a PDF (Portable Document Format) document.

   - ◆ **FXG.** Creates a FXG (Adobe Flex) graphics file.

   - ◆ **Illustrator EPS.** Creates an Illustrator- based EPS image file.

   - ◆ **SVG or SVG Compressed.** Creates a SVG (Scalable Vector Graphics) image file.

3. Enter a name for the file.

4. Navigate to the drive or folder location where you want to save the document.

5. Click **Save**.

6. Specify the options that you want for the file type (options vary), and then click **OK**.

   - ◆ For help, point to an option to display a description at the bottom of the dialog box.

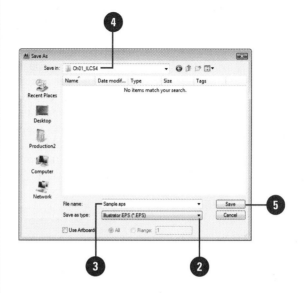

Did You Know?

You can save a copy of an Illustrator document. Open the document that you want to save as a copy, click the File menu, click Save a Copy, specify a name and location, click Save, specify Illustrator options, and then click OK.

You can revert to the last saved version. Click the File menu, and then click Revert.

Finishing Up

After you work on a document, you can finish up by closing the document or by exiting Illustrator. You should save the document before closing it. Exiting Illustrator closes the current document and the Illustrator program and returns you to the desktop. You can use the Exit command on the File menu (Win) or Quit Illustrator command on the Illustrator menu (Mac) to close a document and exit Illustrator, or you can use the Close button on the Illustrator Document tab (**New!**). If you try to close a document without saving your final changes, a dialog box opens, asking if you want to do so.

Close a Document

1 Click the **Close** button on the Document tab, or click the **File** menu, and then click **Close**.

> **TIMESAVER** Press Ctrl+W *(Win) or* ⌘+W *(Mac) to close a document.*

2 If necessary, click **Yes** to save any changes you made to your open documents before the program quits.

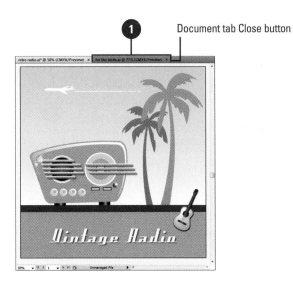

Document tab Close button

Exit Illustrator

1 Choose one of the following:

◆ Click the **Close** button, or click the **File** menu, and then click **Exit** (Win).

◆ Click the **Illustrator** menu, and then click **Quit Illustrator** (Mac).

> **TIMESAVER** Press Ctrl+Q *(Win) or* ⌘+Q *(Mac) to exit Illustrator.*

2 If necessary, click **Yes** to save any changes you made to your open documents before the program quits.

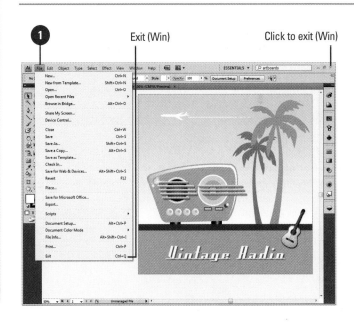

Exit (Win)   Click to exit (Win)

Creating and Viewing a Document

Introduction

You can either open an existing document or create a new one to work on in Illustrator. When you create a new document, you can create one from scratch or use one of the built-in profiles, such as print, web, film, video, or for use on a mobile device. The built-in profiles make it easy to create documents for specific purposes without the hassle of specifying individual settings. However, if you know the individual settings you want, you can create a new document from scratch.

At the same time you create a new document, you can also create multiple artboards. Artboards are regions of a document that contain printable artwork. Multiple artboards are useful for creating documents with different sizes, creating and organizing artwork elements in different places within the same document, and creating multiple page PDFs.

Having problems squinting at the small details of an image? Using the Navigator panel or Zoom tool is a great way to get you focused where you need to be. Zooming into a specific section of a document makes touching up the fine details just that much easier.

Illustrator's navigation and measurement systems—rulers, grid, guides, smart guides—are more than just information; they represent control of the document and control of the creative process. In addition, the Info panel gives you up-to-date information on the exact position of the cursor inside the document, as well as detailed color information that can be indispensable in preparing your designs

What You'll Do

Create a New Document

Create a New Document Using Document Presets

Create a Document from a Template

Set Up a Document

Use and Work with Multiple Artboards

Change the Display View

Change the View with the Navigator Panel

Customize the Navigator Panel

Change the Screen Mode

Change the View with the Zoom Tool

View and Use Rulers

Use Guides and Smart Guides

Use the Grid

Move Around with the Hand Tool

Use Crop Marks

Work with the Info Panel

Create and Select Workspaces

Use Undo and Redo

Creating a New Document

IL 1.1

Creating a new Illustrator document requires more thought than creating a new word processing document. For example, there are bleed, color mode, and raster effect considerations to keep in mind. You can create as many new documents as you need. However, since opening more than one document takes more processing power, it's probably best to work on only one new document at a time. Once a new document is created, you have access to all of Illustrator's design and manipulation tools to create anything you can imagine.

Create a New Document

1. Click the **File** menu, and then click **New**.

2. Type a name for the document.

3. Click the **New Document Profile** list arrow, and then select a preset, or choose your own options to create a custom document.

   ◆ **Number of Artboards.** Specify a number, and then select options for arrangement and spacing.

   ◆ **Size.** Select from the various sizes, such as Letter, Legal, or Tabloid.

   ◆ **Width and Height.** Select from various measurements, such as points, centimeters, or inches.

4. Click the **Advanced** button (if necessary), and then select the advanced options you want:

   ◆ **Color Mode.** Select a color mode, such as RGB or CMYK for color and Grayscale for black/white.

   ◆ **Raster Effects.** Select the resolution for raster effects.

   ◆ **Preview Mode.** Sets the default preview mode. The default displays artwork in vector view. The pixel preview displays artwork with a rasterized look, and Overprint displays an ink preview.

5. Click **OK**.

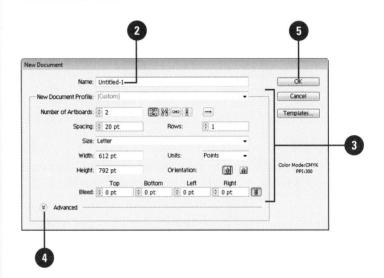

For Your Information

Selecting a Color Mode

A **color mode**, also known as **color space**, determines how Illustrator displays and prints an image. You choose a different color mode (based on models used in publishing) for different tasks. You can choose a color mode when you create a new document or change a color mode for an existing document. The common color modes include: **Grayscale**. Best for printing black-and-white and duotone images. This mode uses one channel and has a maximum of 256 shades of gray. **RGB (Red, Green, and Blue)**. Best for online and multimedia color images. Red, green, and blue are also the primary colors on a monitor. **CMYK (Cyan, Magenta, Yellow, and Black)**. Best for commercial printing of color images.

Creating a New Document Using Presets

 IL 1.1

When you create documents for specific purposes, such as print, web, film, video, or for use on a mobile device, you know the importance of creating documents that will perfectly match the output requirements of the intended file destination. The preset file sizes available in the New Document Profile menu let you create images at a size and pixel aspect ratio that compensate for scaling when you incorporate them into various output modes. When you work with the New Document Profile menu, the guesswork involved in creating compatible photo, web, mobile device, film and video documents in Illustrator is a thing of the past.

Create a New Document Using Presets

1. Click the **File** menu, and then click **New**.

   ◆ You can also click a preset from the Welcome screen.

2. Click the **Preset** list arrow, and then select from the available presets:

   ◆ **Print Document**

   ◆ **Web Document**

   ◆ **Mobile and Devices Document**

   ◆ **Video and Film Document**

   ◆ **Basic CMYK Document**

   ◆ **Basic RGB Document**

   ◆ **Custom**

3. Click the **Size** list arrow, and then select the preset you want. The options vary depending on the type of document you want to create.

   ◆ **Print.** For example, Letter or Legal.

   ◆ **Web.** For example, 640 x 480.

   ◆ **Mobile & Devices.** For example, 176 x 208.

   ◆ **Video & Film.** For example, HDTV 1080.

4. If you want, adjust the available options.

5. Click **OK**.

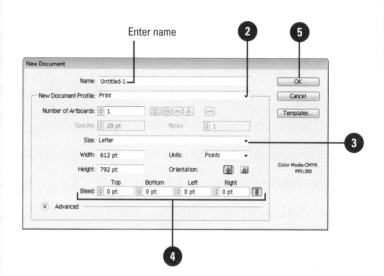

Enter name

Creating a New Document from a Template

 IL 1.2

A template is a special document that makes it easier to create a new document. If you frequently use an existing document, such as Stationery, to start a new document, then you should create a template, which uses the Illustrator Template (AIT) file format. You can create your own template or use one provided by Illustrator. Illustrator comes with a variety of templates, such as Banner Ads, Boxes, Brochures, Business Cards, CD Cases, and Stationery. When you create a new document from a template, the document appears as untitled with the extension AI, so you don't mistakenly make and save changes over the template file.

Create a New Document from a Template

1. Click the **File** menu, and then click **New From Template**.

   ◆ You can also click **Templates** in the New dialog box.

   The Templates folder appears, displaying different types of templates available for Illustrator.

2. Click the **Files of Type** (Win) or **Enable** (Mac) list arrow, and then click **All Formats** or a specific one.

3. Navigate to the location where the template you want to use is stored.

4. Click the template file you want to use.

5. Click **New**.

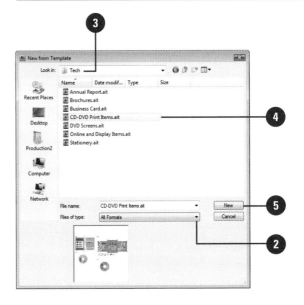

Did You Know?

You can create a new document using a template from the Welcome Screen. Start Illustrator or click the Help menu, and then click Welcome Screen. Click the From Template icon.

See Also

See "Chapter 3, "Working with Objects," on page 59 for information on selecting and changing objects.

New Untitled document from a template

Create a Template Document

1. Open a new or existing document.

2. Create a custom document.

3. Click the **File** menu, and then click **Save As Template**.

    The Templates folder appears, displaying different types of templates available for Illustrator.

4. Type a name for the new template.

5. Click the **Files of Type** (Win) or **Enable** (Mac) list arrow, and then click **Illustrator Template (*.AIT)**, if necessary.

6. Navigate to the location where you want to store the template.

7. Click **Save**.

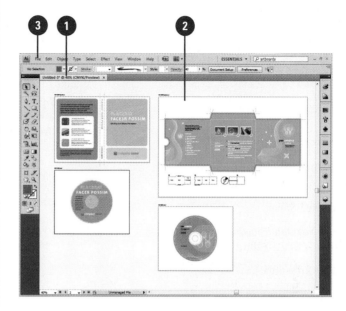

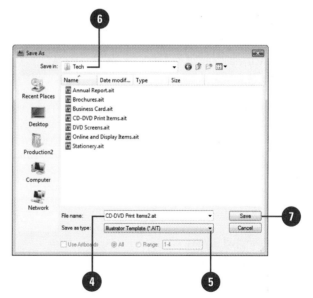

Setting Up a Document

 IL 1.1

After you create a document, you can use the Document Setup command on the File menu to change your document's default options. In the Document Setup dialog box, you can change options for bleed and view, transparency, and type. For Bleed and View, you can change the units of measure and bleed size, view images in Outline mode and highlight substituted fonts and glyphs. For Transparency, you can change the transparency grid size and color. For Type, you can change the document language, double and single quotes styles, superscript and subscript settings, and export options.

Change Document Options

① Click the **File** menu, and then click **Document Setup**.

② Select from the following Bleed and View Options settings:

◆ **Edit Artboards.** Click to close the dialog box and use the Artboard tools to edit artboards.

◆ **Units.** Specify measurement units for the document.

◆ **Bleed.** Specify the amount of bleed around the edges of the document.

◆ **Show Images in Outline Mode.** Select to show image in Outline mode.

◆ **Highlight Substituted Fonts.** Select to highlight unavailable fonts that are substituted for existing fonts on your computer.

◆ **Highlight Substituted Glyphs.** Select to highlight unavailable type glyphs that are substituted for existing glyphs on your computer.

③ Select from the following Transparency settings.

◆ **Grid Size.** Specify a size (Small, Medium or Large) for the transparency grid.

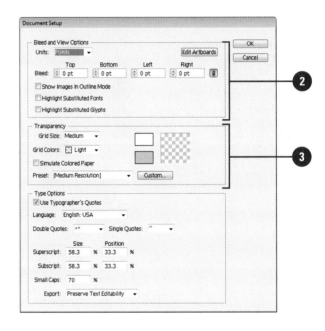

- **Grid Colors.** Specify an intensity and color (Light, Medium, Dark, Red, Orange, Green, Blue, or Purple) for the transparency grid.

- **Simulate Colored Paper.** Select if you plan to print on colored paper. This option replicates the effect of colored paper. This is shown when the transparency grid is not visible.

- **Preset.** Specify a resolution preset (High, Medium, or Low) or select a custom setting. The resolution depends on your output device.

4 Select from the following Type Options settings.

- **Use Typographer's Quotes.** Select to use curly quotes instead of straight ones.

- **Language.** Specify the language for the document.

- **Double Quotes.** Specify the character for double quotes.

- **Single Quotes.** Specify the character for single quotes.

- **Superscript.** Specify the size and position (as a percentage) for text that appears higher than the text line.

- **Subscript.** Specify the size and position (as a percentage) for text that appears lower than the text line.

- **Small Caps.** Specify the size (as a percentage) for small cap text.

- **Export.** Specify an option to preserve text editability or appearance.

5 Click **OK**.

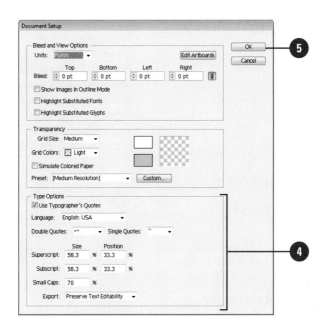

Using Multiple Artboards

Artboards are regions of a document that contain printable artwork. You can use artboards as crop areas for printing or placement. They are useful for working with multiple artwork elements. In CS4, you can create multiple artboards (1 to 100) at different sizes and position them anywhere on the screen (**New!**). You can create multiple artboards by using the New dialog box or the Artboard tools in the Tools panel. Multiple artboards are useful for creating documents at different sizes, creating and organizing artwork elements in different places within the same document, and creating multiple page PDFs.

Create an Artboard

1. Select the **Artboard** tool on the Tools panel.

2. To use a preset dimension, click the **Preset** list arrow on the Control panel, and then select a preset.

3. Drag in the workspace (outside an artboard) to create a new artboard.

   ◆ To create an artboard within an artboard, hold down Shift and then drag.

4. To duplicate an existing artboard, click to select the artboard, click the **New Artboard** button on the Control panel, and then click to place the duplicated artboard.

   ◆ To create multiple duplicates, Alt-click instead as many times as you want.

5. To navigate between artboards, use the Navigation buttons on the Status bar.

6. To exit the artboard editing mode, press Esc or click a different tool.

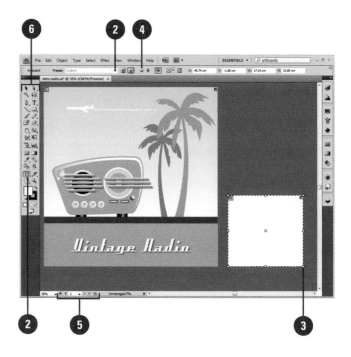

See Also

See "Creating a New Document" on page 28-29 for information on creating artboards along with a new document.

Change Artboard Options

1. Select the **Artboard** tool on the Tools panel.

2. Select from the options below in Step 3 on the Control panel, or click the **Artboard Options** button on the Control panel to open the Artboard Options dialog box.

3. Select from the following options:

   ◆ **Preset.** Specify artboard dimensions using predefined measurements.

   ◆ **Width and Height.** Specify the size of the artboard.

   ◆ **Orientation.** Specify a portrait or landscape orientation.

   ◆ **Constrain Proportions.** Keeps the artboard size proportional.

   ◆ **X and Y Position.** Specifies the position of the artboard.

   ◆ **Show Center Mark.** Displays a point in the center of the artboard.

   ◆ **Show Cross Hairs.** Displays cross hair lines through the center of each artboard side.

   ◆ **Show Video Safe Areas.** Displays guides inside the the video viewable area.

   ◆ **Ruler Pixel Aspect Ratio.** Specify the aspect ratio for artboard rulers.

   ◆ **Fade Region Outside Artboard.** Displays the area outside the artboard in a darker shade.

   ◆ **Update While Dragging.** Displays the area outside the artboard darker as you drag to resize the artboard.

   ◆ **Artboards.** Displays the current number of artboards.

4. Click **OK** to close the dialog box.

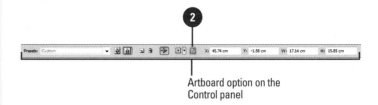

Artboard option on the Control panel

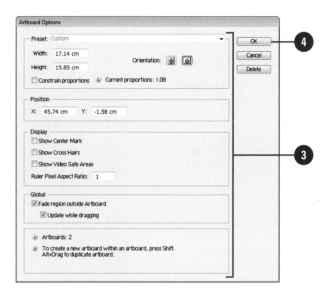

Working with Multiple Artboards

IL 1.11

After you create one or more artboards, you can edit and work with them to display your artwork. You can view all of your artboards by using Artboard Navigation on the Status bar. Each artboard is numbered so you can quickly switch between them (**New!**). In order to work with an artboard, you need to activate it first. You can only active one artboard at a time. After you activate an artboard, you can perform the following artboard operations: change the view (outline or preview), resize, move the artboard with or without its contents, rotate, and delete. In addition, you can also change the display for artboard rulers, center mark, cross hairs, and video safe areas.

Work with Multiple Artboards

◆ **Activate.** Select the **Artboard** tool on the Tools panel, and then click an artboard.

◆ **View as Outline.** Right-click the artboard, and then click **Outline**.

To preview the artboard, right-click the artboard, and then click **Preview**.

◆ **Resize.** Select the **Artboard** tool on the Tools panel, point to the edge or corner (cursor changes to a double-arrow), and then drag to resize the artboard.

◆ **Move with Contents.** Select the **Artboard** tool on the Tools panel, click to select the **Move/Copy Artwork With Artboard** button on the Control panel, and then drag the artboard.

◆ **Move without Contents.** Select the **Artboard** tool on the Tools panel, click to deselect the **Move/Copy Artwork With Artboard** button on the Control panel, and then drag the artboard.

◆ **Rotate.** Select the **Artboard** tool on the Tools panel, press Alt (Win) or Option (Mac), and then press an arrow key to rotate between selected artboards.

◆ **Delete.** Select the **Artboard** tool on the Tools panel, click the artboard to activate it, and then click the **Delete** button on the Control panel or press Delete.

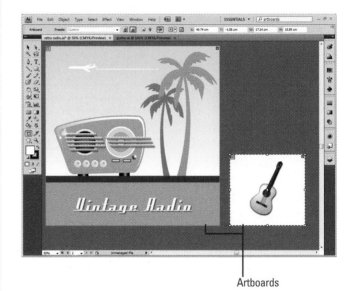

Artboards

Switch Between Artboards

◆ **Switch to a Specific Artboard.**
Click the **Artboard Navigation** list
arrow on the Status bar, and then
select an artboard by number.

◆ **First and Last Artboard.** Click the
First or **Last** button on the Status
bar.

◆ **Previous and Next Artboard.** Click
the **Previous** or **Next** button on the
Status bar.

Switch between artboards

Work with Artboard Display Options

◆ **Rulers.** Click the **View** menu, and
then click **Show Artboard Rulers**
or **Hide Artboard Rulers**.

◆ **Center Mark.** Select the **Artboard**
tool on the Tools panel, click the
Display Options list arrow on the
Control panel, and then click **Show
Center Mark**.

◆ **Cross Hairs.** Select the **Artboard**
tool on the Tools panel, click the
Display Options list arrow on the
Control panel, and then click **Show
Cross Hairs**.

◆ **Safe Area.** Select the **Artboard**
tool on the Tools panel, click the
Display Options list arrow on the
Control panel, and then click **Show
Show Video Safe Areas**.

Artboard display options

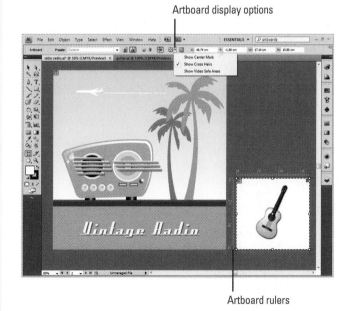

Artboard rulers

Changing the Display View

 IL 1.8

Illustrator uses two main views: Preview and Outline. Preview displays your artwork in color as it appears on the screen, while Outline displays your artwork as an outline, or paths. Outline view speeds redraws for complex artwork. If your artwork doesn't fit on a printed page, you can use tiling options in the Print dialog box to print it. If you want to see how it will print, you can change the view to show print tiling. You can also view your artwork as it will appear in final output, either printed or viewed on the Web or a mobile device. If you like a certain view with different options than the Preview or Outline views, you can also create and work with custom views.

Change the Display View

- **Preview View.** Click the **View** menu, and then click **Preview**.

- **Outline View.** Click the **View** menu, and then click **Outline**.

  To view all artwork in a layer as outlines, Ctrl-click (Win) or Command-click (Mac) the eye icon for the layer in the Layers panel.

  To view all items in unselected layers as outlines, Alt-Ctrl-click (Win) or Option-Command-click (Mac) the eye icon for the layer in the Layers panel.

- **Show Print Tiling.** Click the **View** menu, and then click **Show Print Tiling**. To hide print tiling, click the Show Print Tiling command again.

- **Create a New View.** Set up the view the way you want, click the **View** menu, click **New View**, enter a name, and then click **OK**.

- **Rename or Delete a View.** Click the **View** menu, click **Edit View**, select a view, rename it or click **Delete**, and then click **OK**.

- **Switch Between Custom Views.** Click the **View** menu, and then select a view by name.

Show Print Tiling

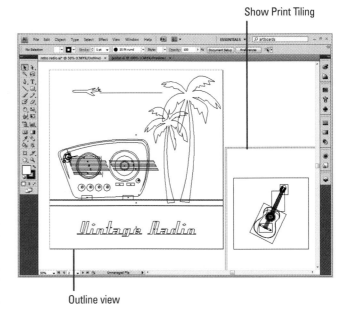

Outline view

New view

Displaying Output Views

◆ **Overprint Preview Mode.** Displays an ink preview with blending, transparency, and overprinting in color separated output. Click the **View** menu, and then click **Overprint Preview**.

◆ **Separations Preview Mode.** Displays separations as they print. Click the **Window** menu, and then click **Separations Preview**.

◆ **Pixel Preview Mode.** Displays the artwork as it's rasterized and viewed on the web. Click the **View** menu, and then click **Pixel Preview**.

◆ **Flattener Preview Mode.** Displays and highlights artwork areas that are flattened when saved or printed. Click the **Window** menu, and then click **Flattener Preview**.

◆ **Soft Proofs.** Displays your artwork as it will appear on a monitor or output device. Click the **View** menu, point to **Proof Setup**, and then select a proof.

◆ **Device Central.** Click the **File** menu, and then click **Device Central**. Displays your artwork as it will appear on a mobile device.

Overprint preview

Separations Preview panel

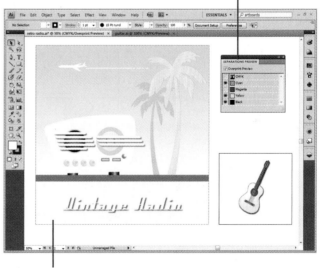

Separations preview

Changing the View with the Navigator Panel

Illustrator's Navigator panel gives you an overall view of the image and the ability to navigate through the document or change the zoom size. Viewing images at different sizes gives you the ability to focus on small elements of the design without actually changing the image in any way. Once small areas of an image are enlarged, it's easier for you to make minute changes. The Navigator panel contains a thumbnail view of the image, and under the thumbnail are easy-to-use controls that let you adjust the zoom of the image. In addition, changes made in the Navigator panel are immediately viewable in the active document window (what you see is what you get). The Navigator panel gives you a visible approach to changing the viewable area of the image. The view box in the Navigator panel represents the visible boundaries of the active document window, which is the viewable area of the image.

Change the View Size with the Navigator Panel

1 Select the **Navigator** panel.

2 Use one of the following methods to change the view size:

- ◆ Drag the triangular slider to the right to increase the zoom or to the left to decrease the zoom.

- ◆ Click the small and large mountain icons, located to the left and right of the triangular slider, to decrease or increase the zoom.

- ◆ Enter a value from .33% to 1600% into the Zoom box.

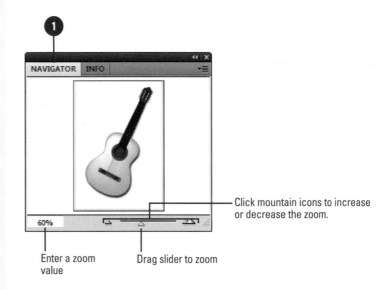

Click mountain icons to increase or decrease the zoom.

Enter a zoom value

Drag slider to zoom

Did You Know?

There are additional ways to zoom in using the Navigator panel. In the View box, hold down the Ctrl (Win) or Command (Mac) key, and then drag to resize the active document.

You can constrain the view box to drag horizontally or vertically. Hold down the Shift key, and then drag the view box horizontally or vertically.

Change the View Area with the Navigator Panel

1. Select the **Navigator** panel.

2. Drag the view box in the thumbnail of the active image.

3. Click within the thumbnail.

   The position of the view box changes, which also changes the viewable area of the image in the document window.

Did You Know?

You can change the Zoom size of an image using the Navigator thumbnail. Hold down the Ctrl key (Win) or the ⌘ key (Mac), and then drag in the thumbnail. When you release your mouse, the selected area expands. It's just like using the Zoom tool, except you're dragging in the Navigator's thumbnail. Conversely, if you drag a second time (this time using a larger rectangle), the image zooms out.

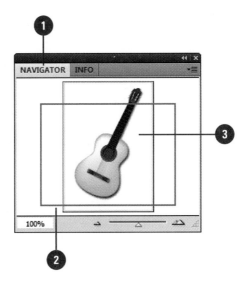

For Your Information

Navigator Panel Shortcut

You can control the view of the document through a great shortcut. Simply click once in the Zoom input box on the Navigator panel, and then use the Up/Down arrow keys to increase or decrease the zoom value of the document 1% at a time. Not fast enough for you? Then hold down the Shift key, and use the Up/Down arrow keys to change the zoom size 10% at a time.

Customizing the Navigator Panel

The colored box in the Navigator panel (proxy preview area) defines the viewable area of the image. It's important for the colored lines of the view box to stand out clearly against the image. The default color of the view box is a light red; however, some documents contain elements that are predominantly the same color as the colored lines of the viewable area, making the viewing area difficult to identify. By changing the color of the lines, you can make sure they stand out against the image. This may seem like a small thing, but choosing a color that contrasts with my image significantly cuts down on my frustration level when I'm attempting to identify the viewable area.

Change the View Box Color

1. Select the **Navigator** panel.

2. Click the **Navigator Options** button, and then click **Panel Options**.

3. Click the **Color** list arrow, and then click a predefined color, or click **Custom** to select a color from the Color Picker dialog box.

4. Specify a **Greeking** value (in point) to set a size approximation for text characters on the screen.

5. Select the **Draw dashed lines as solid lines** check box to display dashed lines as solid to make them easier to view.

6. Click **OK**.

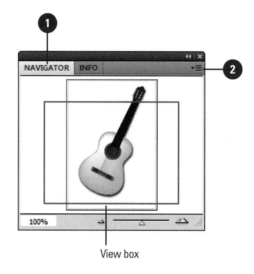

View box

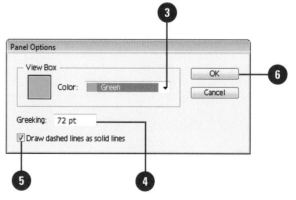

Changing the Screen Display Mode

In Illustrator, the Screen Display mode determines the background displayed behind the active image. For example, you can choose a Screen Mode that hides all the panels, title bar, or menu bar. Since monitor backgrounds, combined with Illustrator's panels, add distracting colors to your workspace, changing the Screen Mode gives you a chance to isolate your image against a solid color background. Viewing your images against a gray background helps your eyes identify the true colors within an image.

Change the Screen Mode

1. Click **Change Screen Mode** button to toggle between screen modes, and then select the mode you want:

   ◆ **Normal Screen Mode.** Displays the artwork in a standard window. All menus, panels, and scroll bars are visible.

   ◆ **Full Screen Mode with Menu Bar.** Displays the artwork full screen. All menus, panels, and scroll bars are visible.

   ◆ **Full Screen Mode.** Displays the artwork full screen. No title bar, menus, or panels are visible.

   TIMESAVER *Press F to toggle between the screen modes.*

Did You Know?

You can temporarily hide all of Illustrator's panels and Tools panel. Press the Tab key to hide the panels. Press the Tab key a second time to display the hidden panels. Hold down the Shift key, and then press the Tab key to hide the panels, but not the Tools and Control panels.

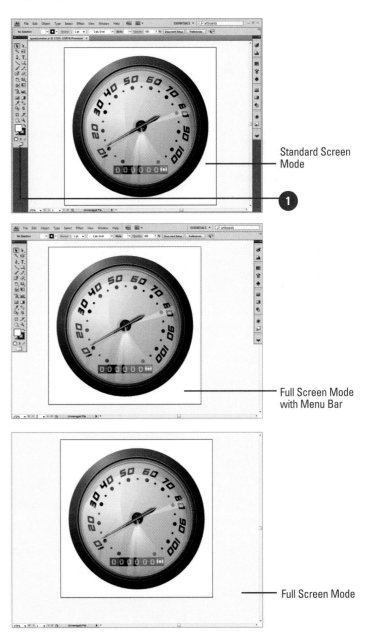

Standard Screen Mode

Full Screen Mode with Menu Bar

Full Screen Mode

Changing the View with the Zoom Tool

Working with the Zoom tool gives you one more way to control exactly what you see in Illustrator. Just like the Navigator panel, the Zoom tool does not change the active image, but allows you to view the image at different magnifications. The Zoom tool is located towards the bottom of Illustrator's Tools panel, and resembles a magnifying glass. The maximum magnification of an Illustrator document is 6400%, and the minimum size is 3.13%. Increasing the magnification of an image gives you control over what you see and gives you control over how you work. Large documents are difficult to work with and difficult to view. Many large documents, when viewed at 100%, are larger than the maximum size of the document window, requiring you to reduce the zoom in order to view the entire image.

Zoom In the View of an Image

1. Select the **Zoom** tool on the Tools panel.

2. Use one of the following methods:

   ◆ **Click on the document.** The image increases in magnification centered on where you clicked.

   ◆ **Drag to define an area with the Zoom tool.** The image increases in magnification based on the boundaries of the area you dragged.

   ◆ **Set a specific view size.** Click the View Size on the Status bar, and then select a specific percentage size magnification.

   ◆ **Fit in Window.** Click the View menu, and then click Fit All In Window or Fit Artboard In Window.

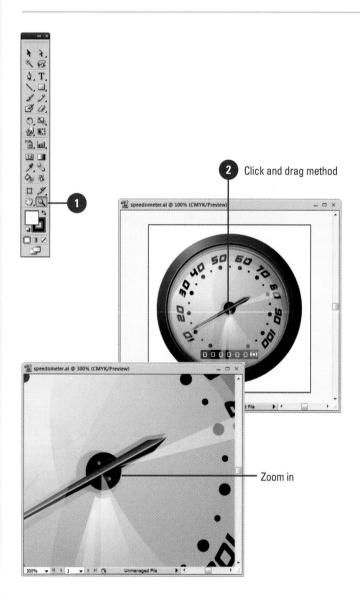

2 Click and drag method

Zoom in

44

Zoom Out the View of an Image

1. Select the **Zoom** tool on the Tools panel.

2. Hold down the Alt (Win) or Option (Mac) key, and then click on the screen to reduce the zoom of the active document.

   The zoom reduction centers on where you click on the active document.

   IMPORTANT *The best way to really see what the printed results of your artwork will look like is to view the image (even if it is too big for the screen) at 100%.*

Did You Know?

You can zoom in or out using shortcut keys regardless of what tool you're currently using. To zoom in, press Ctrl+Spacebar (Win) or ⌘+Spacebar (Mac) and click or drag to define an area. To zoom out, press Ctrl+Spacebar+Alt (Win) or ⌘+Spacebar+Option (Mac) and click or drag to define an area.

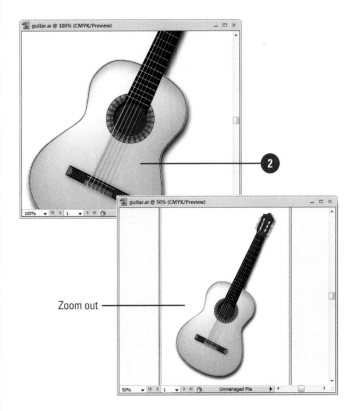

Zoom out

Viewing and Using Rulers

Carpenters know that precise measurements are essential to making things fit, so they have a rule: Measure Twice, Cut Once. The designers of Illustrator also know that measurements are essential and give you several measuring systems—among them are the rulers. Rulers are located on the top and left sides of the active document window, and serve several purposes. They let you measure the width and height of the active image, they let you place guides on the screen to control placement of other image elements, and they create markers that follow your cursor as you move. As you can see, rulers are critical in the design of a document by helping you correctly align image design elements. As a matter of fact, if you're not working on a flat screen or LCD monitor, the curvature of your monitor can give you a false impression of the vertical and horizontal measurements. The default measurement is in points, which you can change in preferences.

Change Ruler Options

1. Click the **Edit** (Win) or **Illustrator** (Mac) menu, point to **Preferences**, and then click **Units & Display Performance**.

2. Click the **General** list arrow, and then select a measurement from the available options.

3. Click **OK**.

> **IMPORTANT** *If the Rulers are not visible in the active document, click the View menu, and then click Rulers.*

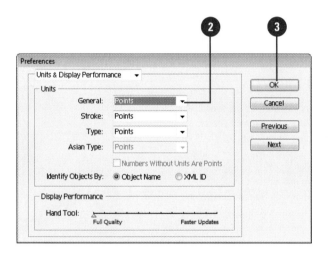

Work with Rulers

◆ **Show or Hide Rulers.** Click the **View** menu, and then click **Show Rulers** or **Hide Rulers**.

◆ **Show or Hide Artboard Rulers.** Click the **View** menu, and then click **Show Artboard Rulers** or **Hide Artboard Rulers**.

◆ **Change Measurement Units.** Right-click (Win) or Option-click (Mac) a ruler, and then select a unit of measure.

◆ **Change Ruler Origin.** Point to the upper-left corner where the rulers intersect, and then drag the pointer to where you want the new ruler origin.

◆ **Reset Ruler Origin.** Double-click the upper-left corner where the rulers intersect.

Did You Know?

You can switch guides on the fly. If you're dragging a vertical or horizontal guide onto the document window, when in fact you wanted the opposite guide, press the Alt (Win) or Option (Mac) key, while still dragging the guide. Vertical guides become horizontal, and horizontal guides become vertical.

Horizontal Ruler bar

Vertical Ruler bar

Using the Guides

A guide is a vertical or horizontal line that helps you align text and graphic objects. With the Snap to Guide command, you can align an object to a guide. When the object's edge comes within 2 pixels of a gridline, it snaps to the guide point. You can use Guides & Grid preferences to set guides settings, such as color and style. To create and use guides, the rulers must first be visible.

Change Guides Preferences

1 Click the **Edit** (Win) or **Illustrator** (Mac) menu, point to **Preferences**, and then click **Guides & Grid**.

2 Select from the following options:

◆ **Color.** Specify a grid color.

◆ **Style.** Specify a grid style, either Lines or Dots.

3 Click **OK**.

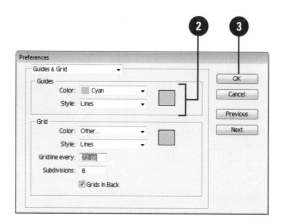

Work with Guides

◆ **Show or Hide Guides.** Click the **View** menu, point to **Guides**, and then click **Show Guides** or **Hide Guides**.

◆ **Lock Guides.** Click the **View** menu, point to Guides, and then click **Lock Guides**.

◆ **Snap Object to Guides.** Click the **View** menu, and then click **Snap To Point**.

When you drag an object near a guide or anchor point, the object snaps to it.

Guide   Snap to guide

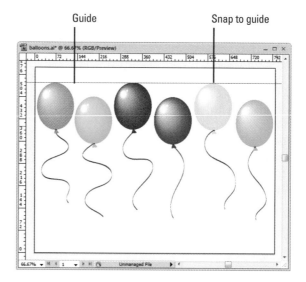

Create and Remove Guides

① Click the **View** menu, and then click **Rulers** to display the ruler bars within the document window.

② Move to the vertical or horizontal Ruler bar, and then click and drag into the document.

③ Return to the Ruler bar and continue to drag until you have all your guides properly set.

④ Click the **View** menu, point to **Guides**, and then click **Lock Guides** to lock the existing guides in place, or click **Clear Guides** to remove all guides.

⑤ Click the **Selection** tool on the Tools panel to drag existing guides to a new position (make sure Lock Guides is not selected).

Did You Know?

You can convert a vector object to a guide. Select the object, click the View menu, point to Guides, and then click Make Guides. To convert it back, click the View menu, point to Guides, and then click Release Guides.

You can remove one guide at a time. Make sure Lock Guides is clear, select the guide, and then press Backspace (Win) or Delete (Mac), or choose Edit/Cut or Edit/Clear.

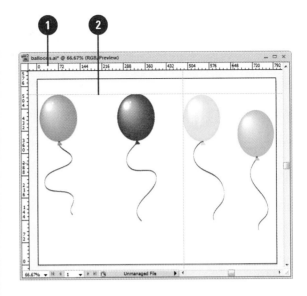

Guide commands

Using Smart Guides

IL 1.5

Illustrator gives you the ability to use Smart Guides to help align shapes, slices, and selections as you draw. They appear automatically as you draw a shape or create a selection or slice, and then disappear after the shape is drawn. They enable you to visually align one object to another with a minimum of effort. Smart Guides also display alignment and measurement information (**New!**), such as distances between objects and angles of rotation, to make alignment even easier. Smart Guides are automatically turned on by default. You can use Smart Guide preferences to set color and information display options to customize your Smart Guides.

Use Smart Guides

① Open or create a multi-layered document.

② To turn Smart Guides on and off, click the **View** menu, and then click **Smart Guides**.

③ Select the **Selection** or **Direct Selection** tool, and drag the object.

◆ Press Ctrl (Win) or Command (Mac) to use the center point or edge of one object or artboard.

As you move the object, Smart Guides appear to help you align the objects.

④ Release the mouse and the guides disappear.

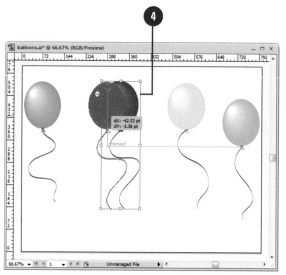

Change Smart Guide Preferences

1. Click the **Edit** (Win) or **Illustrator** (Mac) menu, point to **Preferences**, and then click **Smart Guides**.

2. Select from the following options:

   ◆ **Color.** Specify a guide color.

   ◆ **Alignment Guides.** Select to display guides along the center and edges of objects, artboard, and bleeds.

   ◆ **Anchor/Path Labels.** Select to display path intersection and anchor point information.

   ◆ **Object Highlighting.** Select to highlight objects below the pointer as you drag.

   ◆ **Measurement Labels.** Select to display tool or object location information.

   ◆ **Transform Tools.** Select to display information when you scale, rotate, and shear objects.

   ◆ **Construction Guides.** Select to display guides as you draw new objects. Specify guide angles for anchor points.

   ◆ **Snapping Tolerance.** Specify how close the object must be (measured in number of points) before it snaps to the guide.

3. Click **OK**.

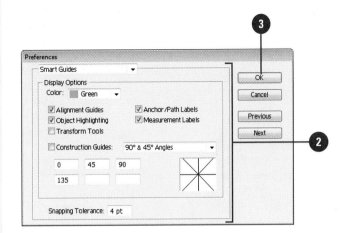

Preferences

Smart Guides

Display Options
Color: Green

☑ Alignment Guides   ☑ Anchor/Path Labels
☑ Object Highlighting ☑ Measurement Labels
☐ Transform Tools

☐ Construction Guides   90° & 45° Angles

0   45   90
135

Snapping Tolerance: 4 pt

OK
Cancel
Previous
Next

Using the Grid

IL 1.5

A grid is a checkerboard display that you can use to help you align text and graphic objects. The grid appears behind your artwork, so it doesn't get in the way. With the Snap to Grid command, you can align an object to a grid line. When the object's edge comes within 2 pixels of a gridline, it snaps to the gridline point. You can use Guides & Grid preferences to set grid settings, such as color, style, and spacing.

Change Grid Preferences

1. Click the **Edit** (Win) or **Illustrator** (Mac) menu, point to **Preferences**, and then click **Guides & Grid**.

2. Select from the following options:

   ◆ **Color.** Specify a grid color.

   ◆ **Style.** Specify a grid style, either Lines or Dots.

   ◆ **Gridline Every.** Specify a measurement for the interval of gridlines. The default is 72 points.

   ◆ **Subdivision.** Specify the number of grid subdivisions.

   ◆ **Grids In Back.** Select to display grids in back of your artwork.

3. Click **OK**.

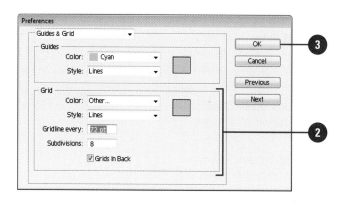

Work with the Grid

◆ **Show or Hide Grid.** Click the **View** menu, and then click **Show Grid** or **Hide Grid**.

◆ **Snap Object to Gridline.** Click the **View** menu, and then click **Snap To Grid**.

   ◆ If the current view is set to Pixel Preview, the Snap To Grid command changes to Snap To Pixel.

   When you drag an object near a gridline, it snaps to the gridline.

Grid

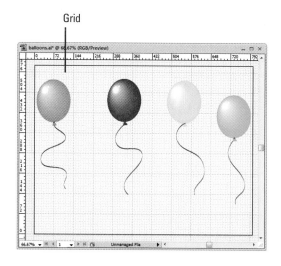

Moving Around with the Hand Tool

One of those little used, but handy, tools is Illustrator's Hand tool. The Hand tool (so named because it resembles an open hand) lets you quickly move the active image within the document window without ever using the scroll bars. For example, you've zoomed the image beyond the size that fits within the document window and you need to change the visible portion of the document. It's a simple operation, but a handy one to know.

Move an Element Around in the Document Window

1 Select the **Hand** tool on the Tools panel.

2 Drag in the active document to move the image.

Did You Know?

You can quickly access the Hand tool whenever you need it. Hold down the Spacebar to temporarily change to the Hand tool. Drag in the active document to the desired position, and then release the Spacebar. You're instantly returned to the last-used tool. It's important to note that you cannot use the Spacebar to access the Hand tool if you are currently using the Type tool.

You can move more quickly between tools in CS4 using Spring-loaded keys (New!). Rather than go back to the Tools panel when you want to switch tools, just hold down the shortcut letter key for the new tool, use the tool, and then let go of the shortcut key and you'll be back using the first tool.

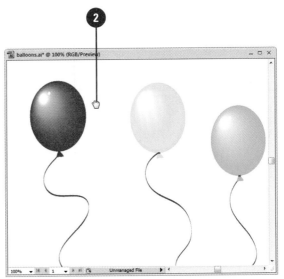

Using Crop Marks

Crop marks indicate where you want a printer to cut the printed page. They are printed with black registration lines so when separations are printed, the printer can align the pages. You can create and display multiple crop marks, which are also useful for trimming or aligning objects on an artboard. If you no longer need or want crop marks, you can delete them by selecting Crop Marks in the Appearance panel and using the Delete Selected Item button at the bottom of the panel.

Create and Delete Crop Marks Around an Object

1. Select one or more objects.

2. Click the **Effect** menu, and then click **Crop Marks**.

3. To delete crop marks, select **Crop Marks** in the Appearance Panel, and then click the **Delete Selected Item** button.

Did You Know?

You can change the registration color. The registration color is used for crop marks and other marks used by commercial printers to align printing plates. If you need to change the registration color so it stands out from the colors used in your document, you can click the Registration swatch in the Swatches panel, and then move the Tint slider on the Color panel.

Crop marks

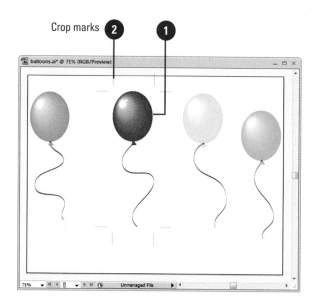

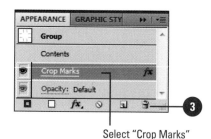

Select "Crop Marks"

Working with the Info Panel

 IL 9.1

Illustrator's Info panel gives you a wealth of data on the current document. The Info panel displays information on the x and y (horizontal/vertical) position of your mouse cursor within the active document window. In addition, when you're using one of Illustrator's drawing, measuring, or transformation tools, the Info panel gives you up-to-date information on the size of the object you're creating. When an object is selected, the Info panel display the x and y position, width (w) and height (h). If you select multiple objects, only information that is the same for all selected objects appears in the Info panel. When you're using the Zoom tool, the Info panel displays the magnification factor and the x and y position. The Info panel also displays color information when you choose to show options.

Create a Specific Size Object

1. Select the **Info** panel.

2. Select a drawing tool on the Tools panel.

3. Drag in the document window to create a shape.

4. Release the mouse when the Info panel displays the correct dimensions.

5. To display color fill and stroke information and the name of any pattern gradient or tint for a selected object, click the **Options** menu, and then click **Show Options**.

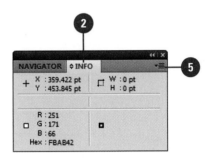

Did You Know?

You can measure the distance between objects. Select the Measure tool in the Tools panel, and then click two points, or click the first point and drag to the second point. Use Shift-drag to constrain the tool to multiples of 45 degrees. The Info panel displays the distances from the x and y axes, the absolute horizontal and vertical distances, the total distances, and the angle measured.

Creating and Selecting Workspaces

IL 1.6

As you work with Illustrator, you'll open, close, and move around windows and panels to meet your individual needs. After you customize the Illustrator workspace, you can save the location of windows and panels as a workspace, which you can display by using the Workspace menu on the Applications bar (**New!**) or the Workspaces submenu on the Window menu. You can create custom workspaces, or use one of the workspaces provided by Illustrator, which are designed for space and workflow efficiency. The built-in workspaces include Essentials, Automation, or Like Photoshop (**New!**). If you no longer use a custom workspace, you can remove it at any time. You can also rename a custom workspace to improve recognition.

Create a Workspace

1. Open and position the panels you want to include in a panel set.

2. Click the **Workspace** menu on the Application bar (**New!**) (the menu name displays the current workspace), and then click **Save Workspace**.

   ◆ You can also click the **Window** menu, point to **Workspace**, and then click **Save Workspace**.

3. Type a name in the Name box.

4. Click **OK**.

   The panel set and its location is now saved.

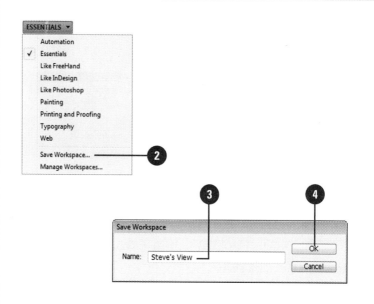

Display a Workspace

1. Click the **Workspace** menu on the Application bar (**New!**) (the menu name displays the current workspace), and then select a panel option:

   ◆ **Custom panel name.** Displays a custom panel layout that you created.

   ◆ **Essentials, Automation, Painting, Typography, or Web.** Displays panel layouts created by Adobe for specific purposes in Illustrator (**New!**).

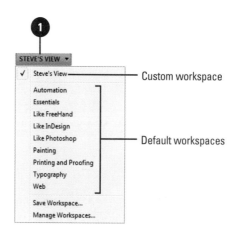

Custom workspace

Default workspaces

Delete a Workspace

1 Click the **Window** menu, point to **Workspace**, and then click **Manage Workspaces**.

The Manage Workspaces dialog box opens.

2 Select the workspace you want to delete.

3 Click **Delete**.

4 Click **OK**.

The workspace is now deleted.

Did You Know?

You can hide a panel. Click the Window menu, and then click a panel Panels to remove the check mark.

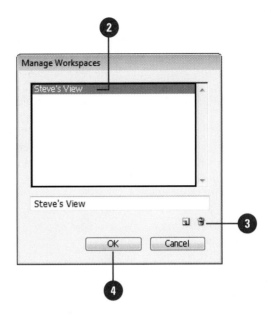

Rename a Workspace

1 Click the **Window** menu, point to **Workspace**, and then click **Manage Workspaces**.

The Manage Workspaces dialog box opens.

2 Select the workspace you want to rename.

3 Type a new name.

The workspace is now renamed.

4 Click **OK**.

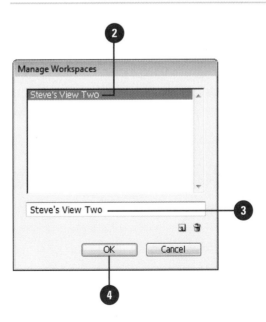

Using Undo and Redo

Probably one of the greatest inventions of the computer industry is the ability to Undo, and Redo. Now, if we could just figure out how to give real life an undo feature... that would be something. Illustrator gives us the ability to undo our past mistakes, and redo something we wished we had not undone.

Undo or Redo One Action at a Time

◆ Click the **Edit** menu, and then click **Undo** to reverse your most recent action, such as typing a word or formatting a paragraph.

   TIMESAVER *Press Ctrl+Z (Win) or ⌘+Z (Mac) to undo.*

◆ Click the **Edit** menu, and then click **Redo** to restore the last action you reversed.

   TIMESAVER *Press Shift+Ctrl+Z to redo your undo.*

Click to Undo or Redo the previous command or action.

Working with Objects

3

Introduction

Adobe Illustrator is an application that gives you great control over vector graphics, which include vector shapes and vector objects. Vector graphics are created using mathematical shapes, not pixels, and that's why vector shapes are considered resolution-independent. When you draw a vector object, you create one or more lines called a path. A path is made up of one or more curved or straight line segments. The start and end points for a line segment is known as an anchor point, which you can drag to change and move.

Illustrator provides drawing tools on the Tools panel that you can use to create a variety of shapes, including rectangles, rounded rectangles, ellipses, polygons, stars, flares, lines, arcs, spirals, rectangle grids, and polar (circular) grids. After you draw an object, you can use Illustrator selection tools to modify it. The two main selection tools are the Selection tool and the Direct Selection tool. The Selection tool allows you to select entire objects, while the Direct Selection tool allows you to select paths and segments. In addition to these tools, you can also use the Select menu. The Select menu provides a variety of powerful selection commands for you to use in a document or artboard. For example, you can select objects whose attributes (including Appearance, Blending Modes, Fill & Stroke, Opacity, and Stroke Color) are similar to the current or last selection.

After you select one or more objects, you can move, align, group, and transform them. The transformation tools allow you to rotate, scale (resize), reflect (mirror image), or shear (slant) an object.

What You'll Do

Understand Vector and Raster Images

Understand Paths

Create Rectangle and Ellipses

Create Polygons and Stars

Create Line Segments

Create Arcs and Spirals

Create Grids

Understand Selections

Use the Selection Tool

Use the Direct Selection Tool

Use the Lasso Tool

Use the Magic Wand Tool

Select and Group

Select Similar Objects

Save and Edit Selections

Move and Duplicate Objects

Align and Distribute Objects

Transform Objects

Rotate, Scale, Reflect, or Shear Objects

Apply Multiple Transformations

Reshape Objects with Envelopes

Understanding Vector and Raster Graphics

Illustrator is an application that gives you great control over vector graphics, which include vector shapes and vector objects. Vector graphics are created using mathematical shapes, not pixels, and that's why vector shapes are considered resolution-independent. For example, if you enlarge a vector image to 100 times its original size, Illustrator merely changes the mathematical formulas to reflect the new size, and since vector shapes are constructed of mathematical data instead of pixels, file sizes are extremely small.

Raster graphics, such as bitmaps and photographs, are images creating using individual pixels that identify one piece of color information. The reason raster images are considered resolution-dependent is that once the image is created or scanned, any enlargement of the image forces Illustrator to enlarge and average the existing color information in the document. This process, called **interpolation**, is what causes enlarged raster images to become blurred, or pixelated.

Vector Image

Close up shows lines

Raster Image

Close up shows pixels

Understanding Paths

When you draw an object, you create one or more lines called a **path**. A path is made up of one or more curved or straight lines, known as **segments**. The start and end points for a segment is called an **anchor point**. An anchor point is a bending point to modify the line segment. A path can be open or closed. An open path has open-ended endpoints, such as a line, while a closed path has connected endpoints, such as a circle. Paths can have two types of anchor points: smooth points or corner points. A smooth point connects two curved segments to create a smooth line, while a corner point connects two straight or curved segments to create a path direction change. You can draw a path using both smooth and corner points. The outline of a path is called a stroke, which you can format with different characteristics. You can specify stroke weight (thickness), color, or a dashed pattern. The interior of an open or closed path is called a fill, which you can also format with a color or gradient.

You can change the shape of a path by dragging its anchor point. A selected anchor point or endpoint appears as a solid square, while an unselected one appears as a white square. When you select an anchor point with a curved segment, a direction line appears with direction points on each end, which you can drag to change the shape of the path. When you change the shape of a smooth point with curved segments on each side, both segments get changed. When you change a shape of a corner point, the corner is maintained, but adjusted based on the change.

Working with Anchor Points

In Illustrator, you can show or hide anchor points, direction lines, and direction points by choosing the **View** menu, and then choosing **Show Edges** or **Hide Edges**. If you want to show or hide direction lines for selected anchor points, select the **Direct Selection** tool, select the anchor point that you want, and then click **Show Handles For Multiple Selected Anchor Points** or **Hide Handles For Multiple Selected Anchor Points** button in the Control panel.

You can specify options in the Selection & Anchor Display preferences to always show handles when multiple anchor points are selected (this option is turned off by default).

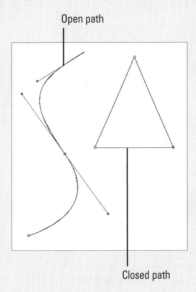

Open path

Closed path

Creating Rectangles and Ellipses

The Illustrator Tools panel includes several tools for quickly creating simple geometric vector shapes. They are easy to use; you just click and drag on the Stage to create the shapes. The Rectangle tool creates rectangles with square or rounded corners. The Ellipse tool creates circular shapes such as ovals and circles. These shapes can be comprised either of Strokes, which are lines that surround and define the shape, or Fills, which can be a color or texture inside the shape, or both.

Draw an Ellipse or Circle

1. Select the **Ellipse** tool on the Tools panel.

   TIMESAVER *Press L to select the Ellipses tool.*

2. Select a **Stroke** and **Fill Color** from the Colors area of the Tools panel.

3. Click and drag on the artboard, and then release the mouse.

   TIMESAVER *Press and hold Shift while you drag to create a circle.*

4. To create an oval or circle with a specific width and height, click on the artboard where you want the top left corner, enter width and height values, and then click **OK**.

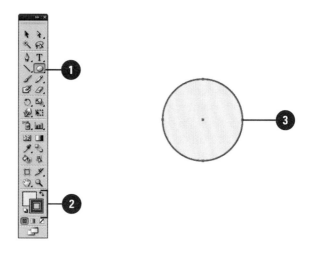

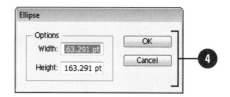

Did You Know?

You can enter values ranging from 0 to 100 points in the Rounded Rectangle Settings dialog box. A value of zero gives you a straight-sided-square. Higher numbers produce squares with more rounded sides.

You can draw shapes without a stroke or a fill. Set either of these properties to No Fill in the Colors section of the Tools panel or in the Color panel.

Draw a Rectangle or Rounded Rectangle

1. Click the **Rectangle** or **Rounded Rectangle** tool on the Tools panel.

   TIMESAVER *Press M to select the Rectangle tool.*

2. Select a **Stroke** and **Fill** color from the Colors area of the Tools panel.

3. Click and drag on the artboard, and then release the mouse.

   TIMESAVER *Press and hold Shift while you drag to create a square.*

4. To create a square, rectangle, or rounded rectangle with a specific width and height, click on the artboard where you want the top left corner, enter width and height values, and then click **OK**.

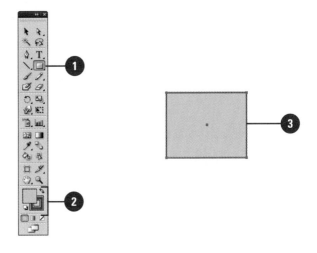

Did You Know?

You can change the corner radius for a rounded rectangle. While you drag a rounded rectangle, press the Up Arrow or Down Arrow key. To create square corners, press the Left Arrow key. To create corners with maximum roundness, press the Right Arrow key.

You can draw shapes with no stroke or fill. If you want to draw an oval or a rectangle without a stroke or fill, you can set either of these options to No Fill in the Colors area of the Tools panel or in the Color Mixer.

You can create a flare shape using the Flare tool. Select the Flare tool on the Tools panel, click and drag on the artboard, and then release the mouse.

Creating Polygons and Stars

The Polygon and Star tools work in much the same way as the Ellipse and Rectangle tools do to allow you to easily create complex vector shapes. You can use these tools to create either polygons and stars. Polygons are shapes based on a center radius and a number of sides, while stars are shapes based on two center radiuses: one for the distance from the center of the star to the innermost points, and another for the distance from the center to the outermost points. Experiment with several options to get the kind of shape you want.

Draw a Polygon or Star Shape

1 Select the **Polygon** or **Star** tool on the Tools panel.

The pointer becomes a crosshair that you can drag anywhere on the artboard.

2 Select a **Stroke** and **Fill** color from the Colors area of the Tools panel.

3 Click and drag on the artboard, and then release the mouse.

TIMESAVER *Press and hold Shift while you drag to create a proportional shape.*

4 To create a shape with a specific radius and number of sides or points, click on the artboard where you want the center of the shape, enter the following values, and then click **OK**.

◆ **Polygon.** Enter a radius and number of sides for the polygon. To create a triangle, enter 3 sides.

◆ **Star.** Enter radius 1 for the distance from the center of the star to the innermost points and enter radius 2 for the distance from the center to the outermost points.

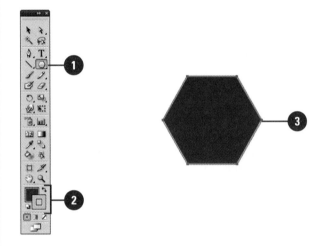

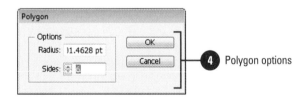

Polygon options

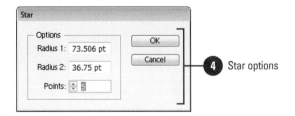

Star options

Creating Line Segments

The Line Segment tool draws perfectly straight lines in any direction you drag your mouse. In Illustrator, a line is called a stroke and there is a variety of thicknesses, styles, colors, and fills that can be applied to it. You can also create your own line style for specific types of dashed, dotted or artistic lines. You can constrain the path a line draws to 45-degree angles or create closed shapes by intersecting the lines you draw.

Draw a Line Segment

1. Click the **Line Segment** tool on the Tools panel.

    The pointer becomes a crosshair that you can drag on the artboard.

    TIMESAVER *Press \ to select the Line tool.*

2. Select a **Stroke** color from the Colors area of the Tools panel.

3. Click and drag on the artboard, and then release the mouse when the line is the length you need.

    TIMESAVER *Hold down the Shift key, and then drag to draw a 45, 90, or 180 degree line.*

4. To create a line with a specific length and angle, click on the artboard where you want the line to begin, enter length and angle values, select the **Fill Line** check box to fill the line with the current fill color, and then click **OK**.

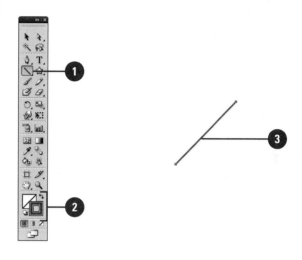

Creating Arcs and Spirals

The Arc and Spiral tools make it easy to create unique and interesting shapes. These tools draw curved lines to create an individual arc or a Spiral wind. An arc consists of an x and y axis length, open or closed path, arc direction (known as the Base Along), arc slope, and arc fill (optional). A Spiral consists of a radius from the center to the outermost point in the Spiral, decay (the amount each wind decreases), number of segments for the spiral, and Spiral style. Each full wind of a Spiral consists of four segments.

Draw an Arc

1. Click the **Arc** tool on the Tools panel.

   The pointer becomes a crosshair that you can drag on the artboard.

2. Select a **Stroke** color from the Colors area of the Tools panel.

3. Click and drag on the artboard, and then release the mouse when the arc is the length you need.

4. To create an arc with specific settings, click on the artboard where you want the arc to begin, enter x and y lengths, specify type (open or closed), arc direction (Base Along) and slope options, select the **Fill Arc** check box to fill the arc with the current fill color, and then click **OK**.

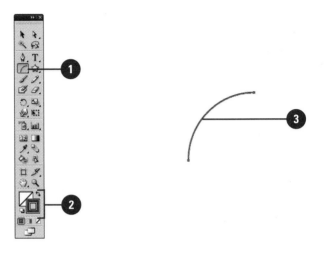

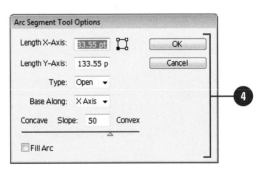

Draw a Spiral

① Click the **Spiral** tool on the Tools panel.

The pointer becomes a crosshair that you can drag on the artboard.

② Select a **Stroke** color from the Colors area of the Tools panel.

③ Click and drag on the artboard, and then release the mouse when the Spiral is the length you need.

④ To create a Spiral with specific settings, click on the artboard where you want the Spiral to begin, enter a radius (distance) from the center to the outermost point, decay percentage (amount of the wind decreases), the number of segments, and style options, and then click **OK**.

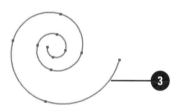

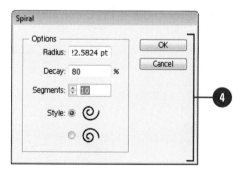

Creating Grids

The grid tools on the Tools panel allow you to create a rectangular or circular polar grid. The Rectangular Grid tool creates rectangular grids of a specified size and number of horizontal and vertical dividers. The Polar Grid tool creates concentric circles of a specified size and specific number of concentric and radial dividers.

Draw Rectangle Grids

1 Click the **Rectangle Grid** tool on the Tools panel.

The pointer becomes a crosshair that you can drag on the artboard.

2 Select a **Stroke** color from the Colors area of the Tools panel.

3 Click and drag on the artboard, and then release the mouse when the grid is the size you need.

4 To create a grid with specific settings, click on the artboard where you want the grid reference point, enter a width and height for the grid, specify the number of horizontal and vertical dividers, select the **Use Outside Rectangle As Frame** check box to replace individual segments with a separate rectangle object, select the **Fill Grid** check box to fill the grid with the current fill color, and then click **OK**.

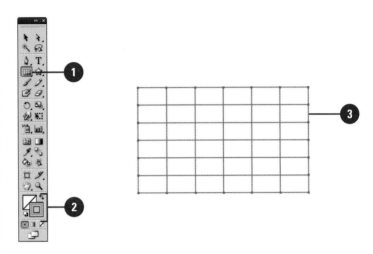

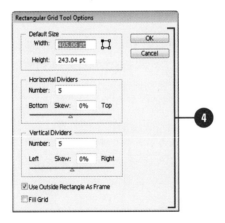

Draw Circular Polar Grids

1. Click the **Polar Grid** tool on the Tools panel.

   The pointer becomes a crosshair that you can drag on the artboard.

2. Select a **Stroke** color from the Colors area of the Tools panel.

3. Click and drag on the artboard, and then release the mouse when the grid is the size you need.

4. To create a grid with specific settings, click on the artboard where you want the grid reference point, enter a width and height for the grid, specify the number of concentric and radial dividers, select the **Create Compound Path From Ellipses** check box to replace circles with separate compound paths, select the **Fill Grid** check box to fill the grid with the current fill color, and then click **OK**.

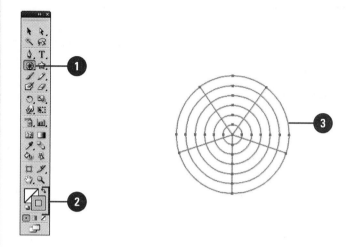

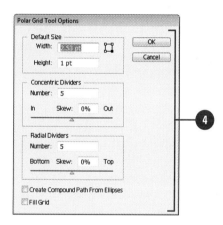

Understanding Selections

IL 2.8

When you create vector graphics in Illustrator, they are comprised of distinct segments that can be selected separately or as a whole with a variety of selection tools. The type of editing you need to perform determines which tool you use. For example, a simple rectangle is comprised of four line segments that surround the contour of the shape and one fill in the center. Each of these parts can be selected as a group with the **Selection** tool or individually with the **Direct Selection** tool. To select an object using the fill, you need to deselect the Object Selection by Path Only check box in Selection & Anchor Display preferences.

In addition to the Selection and Direct Selection tools, you can also use the **Group Selection** tool to select all the anchor points on a single path. With the Group Selection tool, click to select an object, click twice to select the object's group, and click three times to select the group within the group (if available). The Group Selection tool is useful for working with multiple objects. If you want to work with an individual object without affecting other objects, it's better to use Isolation Mode.

The **Lasso** tool is a classic selection tool that allows you to select path points and segments by dragging a freeform marquee around them.

The **Magic Wand** tool allows you to select objects of the same or a similar fill color, stroke color, stroke weight, opacity, or blending mode.

Selection preferences

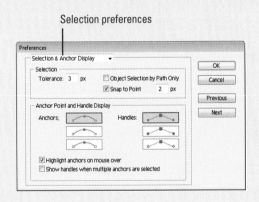

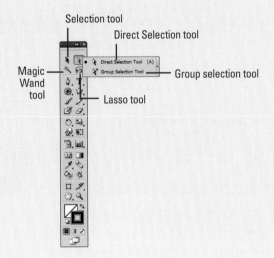

Selection tool
Direct Selection tool
Magic Wand tool
Group selection tool
Lasso tool

Using the Selection Tool

 IL 2.8

There are several ways to select objects in Illustrator. With the Selection tool, you can select an object's stroke or fill. You can only select an object using the fill if the path appears in Preview mode, and the Object Selection by Path Only check box is deselected in Selection & Anchor Display preferences. After you select one or more objects, you can add or subtract objects to/from the selection. In addition, you can use the Selection tool and drag a marquee to select parts of the object or drag over a portion of it to create a selection rectangle.

Select an Object with the Selection Tool

1. Click the **Selection** tool on the Tools panel.

   The pointer becomes an arrow.

   TIMESAVER *Press V to select the Selection tool.*

2. Position the arrow on the edge of the object, and then click it.

   ◆ You can also drag a marquee across all or part of the object to select the entire path.

   ◆ If the path has a color fill, appears in Preview mode, and the Object Selection by Path Only check box is deselected in Selection & Anchor Display preferences, you can also click the fill to select the object.

3. To add or subtract objects from the selection, hold down the Shift key, and then click unselected objects to add or click selected objects to subtract them from the selection.

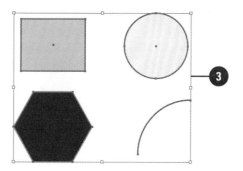

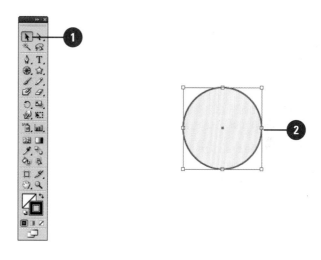

Using the Direct Selection Tool

Select Anchor Points and Segments with the Selection Tool

1 Click the **Direct Selection** tool on the Tools panel.

The pointer becomes an arrow.

TIMESAVER *Press A to select the Direct Selection tool.*

2 Position the arrow on the edge of the path and click to select a segment, and then click an anchor point to select it.

◆ You can also select an anchor point directly. Pass the pointer over a path and then point to an anchor point and then click it.

◆ You can also drag a marquee across all or part of the object to select the entire path.

3 To add or subtract anchor points or segments from the selection, hold down the Shift key, and then click unselected items to add them or selected items to subtract them from the selection.

With the Direct Selection tool, you can select individual points and segments of a path. After you select one or more individual points and segments, you can add or subtract items to/from the selection. In addition, you can also use the Direct Selection tool and drag a marquee to select parts of the path or drag over a portion of it to create a selection rectangle.

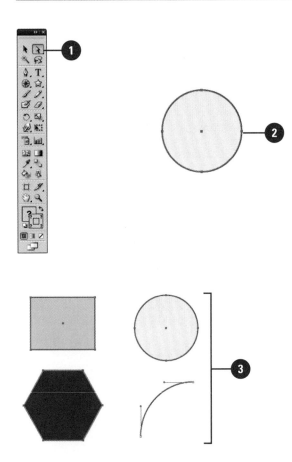

Using the Lasso Tool

IL 2.8

Use the Lasso tool when you want to select shapes that are very close to shapes you don't want to select. This tool allows you to draw around the shape, selecting everything contained within the drawn area. When you draw a selection, you can drag across a path to include it in the selection instead of dragging completely around it. This selection tool is useful when you are working with overlapping paths.

Select with the Lasso Tool

1. Click the **Lasso** tool on the Tools panel.

2. Draw around the shapes you want to select.

3. To complete the selection, return to the point where you started.

Did You Know?

You can select single or multiple objects. Holding the Shift key adds line segments and fills them. Shift-clicking selected items deselects them.

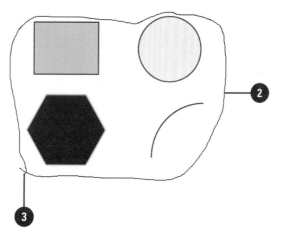

Using the Magic Wand Tool

 IL 2.8

The Magic Wand tool (so named since it looks like a magic wand) is unique in the fact that you do not drag and select with this tool; you simply click. The Magic Wand tool creates a selection based on the shift in brightness ranges within an image. If there is a definable shift in the brightness of the pixels, it can be a very powerful tool for the selection of odd-shaped areas. To use the Magic Wand, click on the Magic Wand Tool button on the Tools panel.

Select Options for the Magic Wand Tool

1. Double-click the **Magic Wand** tool on the Tools panel.

   ◆ You can also click the **Window** menu, and then click **Magic Wand** to display the panel.

2. Click the **Options** menu, and then select the **Show Stroke Options** and **Show Transparency Options** (if necessary) to display them in the Magic Wand panel.

   ◆ You can also click the double-arrow next to the Magic Wand title to display options.

3. Select the check box for the attributes that you want the Magic Wand to select. The options include: **Fill Color**, **Stroke Color**, **Stroke Weight**, **Opacity**, or **Blending Mode**.

4. Enter a Tolerance value (0 to 255). The higher the value, the more information the Magic Wand tool selects.

5. To select objects on all layers, click the **Options** menu, and then select **Use All Layers** to check it. Select it again to select objects only on the current layer.

6. To reset all fields in the Magic Wand panel, click the **Options** menu, and then click **Reset**.

Use the Magic Wand Tool

1. Select the **Magic Wand** tool on the Tools panel.

2. Click an object area to make a selection.

   Depending on the options you selected in the Magic Wand panel, other objects with the same or similar attributes (fill color, stroke color, stroke weight, opacity, or blending mode) are selected.

3. To add to the selection, hold down the Shift key, and then click another unselected object.

   To subtract from the selection, hold down the Alt (Win) or Option (Mac) key, and then click a selected object.

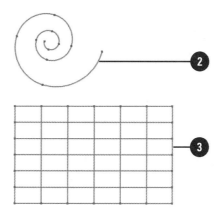

Selecting and Grouping

 IL 2.4, 2.8

Selecting and grouping objects makes it easier to work with multiple objects as if they were a single object. You can easily select, isolate, cut, copy, paste, move, recolor, and transform a grouped object. You can group all types of objects, yet still edit individual objects within the group as needed without having to ungroup them first by using Isolation Mode. Illustrator places a grouped object on the top level of the top object in the group and uses the same selection color. If you no longer need to group objects, you can ungroup them.

Create a Group

1. Select the **Selection** tool on the Tools panel.

2. Use a selection method to select the objects that you want in the group.

3. Click the **Objects** menu, and then click **Group**.

   ◆ You can use the Group command again to group objects already in a group; this is known as a nested group.

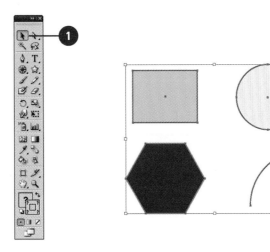

Ungroup Objects

1. Select the **Selection** tool on the Tools panel.

2. Select the grouped objects that you want to ungroup.

3. Click the **Objects** menu, and then click **Ungroup.**

   ◆ If you have nested groups within an object, you can use the Ungroup command again to ungroup it.

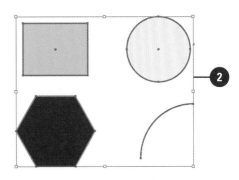

Use Isolation Mode to Work with Groups

① Select the **Selection** tool on the Tools panel.

② Double-click a grouped object.

◆ You need to click the **Isolate Selected Group** button on the Control panel or select the **Double-click to Isolate** check box in General preferences.

A gray bar appears with the name of the group at the top of the document window. All objects outside the group are dimmed out and uneditable. The words "Isolation Mode" also appear on the Layers panel.

③ Edit individual objects or add new objects to the group.

④ To exit Isolation Mode, click the gray bar.

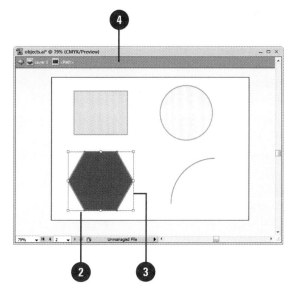

Selecting Similar Objects

 IL 2.8

The Select menu provides a variety of powerful selection commands for you to use in a document or artboard. In addition to the common commands, such as All, Deselect, and Inverse, you can also select objects whose attributes (including Appearance, Blending Modes, Fill & Stroke, Opacity, and Stroke Color) are similar to the current or last selection. For more selection power, you can select objects based on the object type (including All on Same Layers, Direction Handles, Brush Strokes, Clipping Masks, Stray Points, Text Objects).

Use the Select Menu to Select Objects

1 Click the **Select** menu.

2 Select the command that you want:

◆ **All.** Selects all objects in the document.

◆ **All in Active Artboard.** Selects all objects in the active artboard.

◆ **Deselect.** Deselects all objects in the document.

◆ **Reselect.** Reselects the most recent selection.

◆ **Inverse.** Inverses the current selection.

◆ **Next Object Above.** Selects the next object above the current selection.

◆ **Next Object Below.** Selects the next object below the current selection.

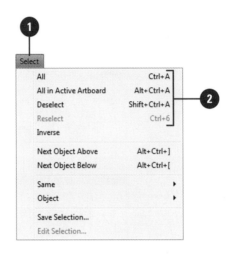

Select Similar Objects or Object Attributes

① Select an object on which to base the new selection or deselect all objects to base the new selection on the last selected object.

② Click the **Select** menu, and then point to **Same** or **Object**.

③ Choose the command that you want to use to make a selection.

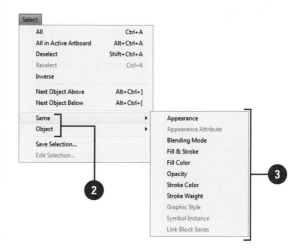

Select Objects in the Layers Panel

① Open the Layers panel.

② Click the expand/collapse triangle to display the layer that you want to select.

③ Click the selection area on the right side of the layer in the Layers panel that has the object that you want to select.

◆ You can also click the **Select** menu, point to **Object**, and then click **All on Same Layers** to select all on a layer.

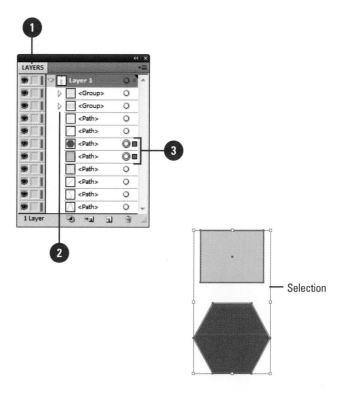

Selection

Saving and Editing Selections

If you frequently select the same elements in a document, you can save yourself some time by saving the selection with a name of your choice. After you save a selection, the saved selection name appears as a menu command at the bottom of the Select menu. When you need to make the same selection, simply choose the command. When you no longer use a saved selection, you can delete it.

Save and Use a Selection

① Make the selection that you want to save.

② Click the **Select** menu, and then click **Save Selection**.

③ Enter a name for the selection.

④ Click **OK**.

⑤ Click the **Select** menu, and then click the name of the saved selection at the bottom of the menu.

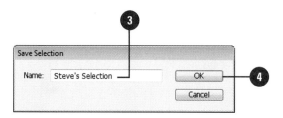

Edit a Saved Selection

① Click the **Select** menu, and then click **Edit Selection**.

② Select the saved selection that you want to rename or delete.

③ To delete a saved selection, click **Delete**.

④ To rename a saved selection, change the name in the Name box.

⑤ Click **OK**.

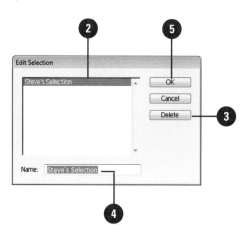

Moving Objects

Moving an object or group of objects is very easy. The simplest way is to drag the edge of an object in Outline or Preview view. If you want to constrain the movement of the object in multiples of 45 degrees, then use the Shift key as you drag. While you drag an object, Smart Guides appear automatically to make it easier for you to align objects with other objects.

Move an Object

1. Select the **Selection** tool on the Tools panel.

2. Select one or more objects that you want to move.

3. Drag the edge of an object.

   ◆ To constrain the movement of the object to multiples of 45 degrees or the current angle in General preferences, hold down the Shift key as you drag.

   ◆ If the path has a color fill, appears in Preview mode, and the Object Selection by Path Only check box is deselected in Selection & Anchor Display preferences, you can also click the fill to select the object.

Did You Know?

You can delete an object. Select the object that you want to delete, and then press Delete, or click the Edit menu, and then click Clear.

See Also

See "Using Smart Guides" on page 50 for more information on setting Smart Guide preferences and using Smart Guides.

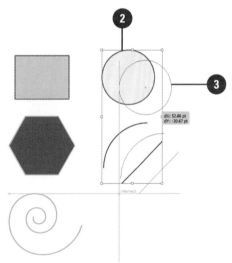

Duplicating Objects

Duplicating objects can be a powerful way of creating geometrical art-work. You can duplicate one or more selected objects by dragging them, using Arrow keys, copying to and pasting from the Clipboard, or using the Offset Path command. The Offset Path command duplicates a path (along with fill and stroke attributes) and places it on the artboard based on the offset distance specified in the Offset Path dialog box. The duplicate path is reshaped to fit around the original path.

Duplicate Objects

1. Select the **Selection** tool on the Tools panel.

   ◆ If the object is in a group, select the Direct Selection tool on the Tools panel.

2. Use any of the following methods:

   ◆ **Same Document.** Hold down Alt (Win) or Option (Mac), and then drag the edge or fill of the object.

   ◆ **Different Documents.** Open the documents side by side, and then drag the edge or fill of the object from one document to another.

   ◆ **Clipboard.** Select the object, click the **Edit** menu, and then click **Copy**. Click in the target document or artboard, click the **Edit** menu, and then click **Paste**, **Paste in Front**, or **Paste in Back**.

   ◆ **Keyboard.** Select the object, press Control (Win) or Command (Mac) key, and then use one of the Arrow keys to move the duplicated object in the direction you want. The duplicate object moves away from the original object based on the current keyboard increment value in General preferences.

dX: 270.08 pt
dY: 13.06 pt

Duplicate Objects Using an Offset

1. Select the **Selection** tool on the Tools panel.

2. Select an object.

3. Click the **Object** menu, point to **Path**, and then click **Offset Path**.

4. Enter the distance you want to offset the duplicate path from the original object.

5. Click the **Joins** list arrow, and then select a bend style: **Miter** (pointed), **Round** (circular), or **Bevel** (square-cornered)

6. You can set a limit (1-500) to determine when a mitered corner changes into a beveled corner. A low number creates a more beveled corner, while a high number creates a sharper corner.

7. Click **OK**.

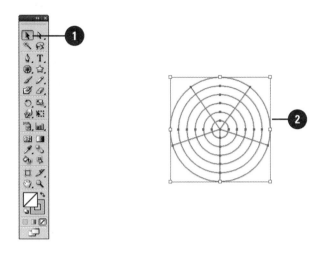

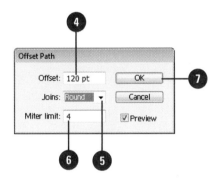

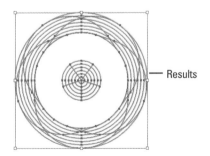

Results

Aligning and Distributing Objects

In addition to using grids and guides to align objects to a specific point, you can align a group of objects to each other. The Align panel buttons make it easy to align two or more objects relative to each other or to the page. To evenly align several objects to each other across the document, either horizontally or vertically, select them and then choose a distribution option. Before you select an align command, specify how you want Illustrator to align the objects. You can align the objects in relation to the document or to the selected objects. If you want to align all the objects to another object, you can select and use a key object (**New!**), before you select an alignment option.

Align or Distribute Objects

1. Select the **Selection** tool on the Tools panel.

2. Select two or more objects to align them or select three or more objects to distribute them.

3. Select the **Align** panel or click **Align** on the Control panel.

4. Click the **Options** menu, and then click **Use Preview Bounds**. A checked option uses he object's stroke weight and any applied effects when aligning or distributing.

5. If you want to align objects along the edges of the artboard, click the **Align To** menu on the Align or Control panel, and then click **Align to Artboard**. Objects are moved on the artboard based on the alignment or distribution command to the closest edge (top and bottom, or left and right).

6. If you want to align objects to a key object, click an object to make it the key object (a thick blue outline appears and the **Align To Key Object** option is selected in the Align and Control panel).

7. Use the alignment and distribution buttons on the Align or Control panel.

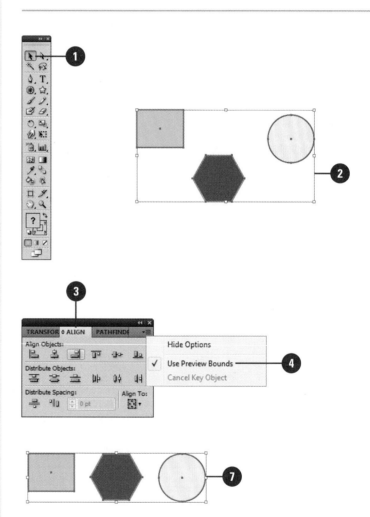

Transforming Objects

 IL 2.9

Transform an Object with the Bounding Box

1. Click the **View** menu, and then click **Show Bounding Box** to display it.

2. Select the **Selection** tool on the Tools panel.

3. Select one or more objects to transform.

4. Use any of the following methods:

   ◆ Scale. Drag a corner handle to scale along two axes; drag a side handle to scale along one axis; Shift-drag to scale proportionally; hold down Alt (Win) or Option (Mac), and then drag to scale from the center. Also hold down Shift to scale from the center proportionally.

   ◆ Reflect. Drag a side handle all the way across the object to the other side.

   ◆ Rotate. Point slightly outside a corner handle (pointer changes to a double arrow), and then drag in a circular motion.

   To rotate an object 180 degrees, drag a corner handle diagonally all the way across the object.

The easiest way to transform an object is to use the bounding box. With the bounding box, you can quickly scale (resize), reflect (mirror), and rotate an object. However, you cannot copy an object or move the reference point. As you drag to transform an object, you can use keyboard keys to alter the results of a transformation. Experiment with the different options to create some new results.

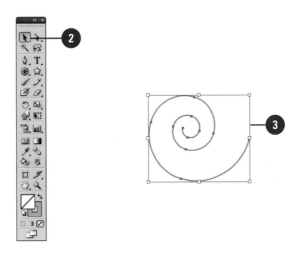

Scale

W: 409.67 pt
H: 183.01 pt

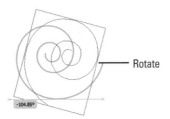

Rotate

-104.85°

Using the Free Transform Tool

 IL 2.9

The Free Transformation tool allows you to rotate, scale (resize), reflect (mirror image), or shear (slant) an object. In addition, you can apply perspective and distortion to an object. However, you cannot copy an object or move the reference point. As you drag to transform an object, you can use keyboard keys to alter the results of a transformation. To help you align the results the way you want, you can use Smart Guides to make it easier.

Transform an Object with the Free Transform Tool

1. Select the **Free Transform** tool on the Tools panel.

2. Select one or more objects to transform.

3. Use any of the following methods:

   ◆ **Scale.** Drag a corner handle to scale along two axes; drag a side handle to scale along one axis; Shift-drag to scale proportionally; hold down Alt (Win) or Option (Mac), and then drag to scale from the center. Also hold down Shift to scale from the center proportionally.

   ◆ **Reflect.** Drag a side handle all the way across the object to the other side.

   ◆ **Rotate.** Point slightly outside a corner handle (pointer changes to a double arrow), and then drag in a circular motion. To rotate in 45 degree increments, Shift-drag.

   To rotate an object 180 degrees, drag a corner handle diagonally all the way across the object.

   ◆ **Shear.** Drag a side handle and then hold down Ctrl (Win) or Command (Mac) as you continue to drag. To constrain the movement, also press Shift. To shear from the center, also press Alt (Win) or Option (Mac).

Shear

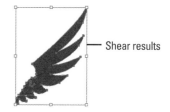

Shear results

- **Perspective.** Drag a side handle and then hold down Ctrl+Alt+Shift (Win) or Command+Option+Shift (Mac) as you continue to drag.

- **Distort.** Drag a corner handle and then hold down Ctrl (Win) or Command (Mac) as you continue to drag.

4 To use Smart Guides as you transform an object:

- Select the **Transform Tools** check box in Smart Guides preferences.

- Click the **View** menu, and then click **Smart Guides** to display them.

- As you drag to transform an object, smart guides appear in your document, which you can use to align the transformed object.

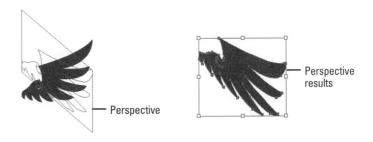

Perspective

Perspective results

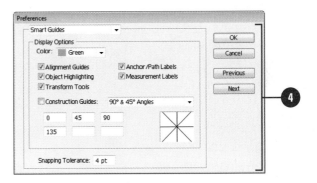

Rotating and Scaling Objects

IL 2.9

After you create an object, you can change its orientation by rotating it or change its size by scaling it. For a freeform rotation, when you want to rotate the object in other than 90 or 180 degree increments, you can use the Rotate tool. To resize an object, either smaller or larger, you can use the Scale tool. With either tool, you can transform the object from its center or the reference point. To rotate or scale an object using exact values or percentages, use the Transform panel, which is available on the Control panel or Window menu.

Rotate or Scale an Object

1. Select the **Selection** tool on the Tools panel.

2. Select one or more objects to transform.

3. Select the **Rotate** or **Scale** tool on the Tools panel.

4. To move the reference point, click a new point.

5. Use the appropriate method:

   ◆ Rotate. Drag in a circular motion. To rotate in 45 degree increments, Shift-drag.

   ◆ Scale. Drag away from or toward the object. Shift-drag to scale proportionally; hold down Alt (Win) or Option (Mac), and then drag to scale from the center. Also hold down Shift to scale from the center proportionally.

   ◆ Scale and Flip. Drag across the entire object.

   ◆ Scale and Copy. Hold down Alt+Shift (Win) or Option+Shift (Mac), and then drag.

6. To rotate or scale an object using exact values or percentages, use the Transform panel. If the Transform panel is not visible, select it from the Window menu.

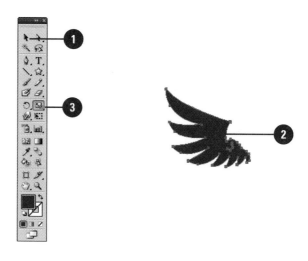

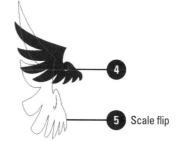

5 Scale flip

Reflecting and Shearing Objects

IL 2.9

The Reflect and Shear tools on the Tools panel allow you to be creative as you transform an object. The Reflect tool creates a mirror image of an object, while the Shear tool creates a slanted image of an object. To reflect or shear an object using exact values or percentages, open the Transform panel, which is available on the Control panel or Window menu.

Reflect or Shear an Object

1. Select the **Selection** tool on the Tools panel.

2. Select one or more objects to transform.

3. Select the **Reflect** or **Shear** tool on the Tools panel.

4. To move the reference point, click a new point.

5. Use the appropriate method:

   ◆ **Reflect.** Click to establish a reference point, and then click again to establish the axis of reflection.

   ◆ **Shear.** Drag away from the object.

6. To reflect or shear an object using exact values or percentages, use the Transform panel.

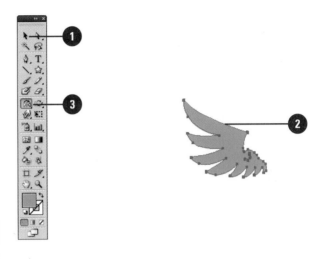

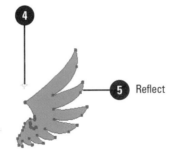

Reflect

Applying Multiple Transformations

IL 2.9

The Transform Each command allows you to transform multiple objects relative to their individual reference points instead of a single reference point. With the Transform Each command, you can scale or move objects horizontally or vertically, rotate objects by a specific angle, and create a mirror reflection of the objects. If you want to create a unique effect, you can also have Illustrator apply random transformations. You can also use the Transform Effect command to create similar effects, which you can modify.

Use the Transform Each Command

1. Select the **Selection** tool on the Tools panel.

2. Select one or more objects to transform.

3. Click the **Object** menu, point to **Transform**, and then click **Transform Each**.

4. Select the **Preview** check box to view your changes on the selected object.

5. Do any of the following:

   ◆ **Scale Horizontal or Vertical.** Drag the slider or enter a percentage to scale objects from their reference point.

   ◆ **Move Horizontal or Vertical.** Drag the slider or enter a percentage to move objects left or right and up or down.

   ◆ **Rotate Angle.** Enter a rotate angle or drag the dial.

   ◆ **Reflect X or Y.** Select to create a mirror reflection of the objects.

   ◆ **Reference Point.** Click a square to change the reference point.

   ◆ **Random.** Select to apply random transformations using the values in the dialog box.

6. Click **OK** or **Copy** (creates a copy and applies the transformation).

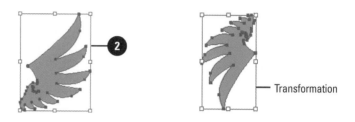

Transformation

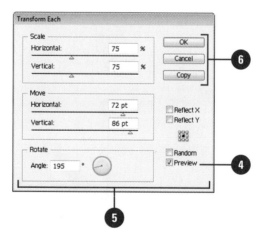

90

Use the Transform Effect

1. Select the **Selection** tool on the Tools panel.

2. Select one or more objects to transform.

3. Click the **Effect** menu, point to **Distort & Transform**, and then click **Transform**.

4. Select the **Preview** check box to view your changes on the selected object.

5. Do any of the following:

   ◆ **Scale Horizontal or Vertical.** Drag the slider or enter a percentage to scale objects from their reference point.

   ◆ **Move Horizontal or Vertical.** Drag the slider or enter a percentage to move objects left or right and up or down.

   ◆ **Rotate Angle.** Enter a rotate angle or drag the dial.

   ◆ **Copies.** Enter the number of copies you want.

   ◆ **Reflect X or Y.** Select to create a mirror reflection of the objects.

   ◆ **Reference Point.** Click a square to change the reference point.

   ◆ **Random.** Select to apply random transformations using the values in the dialog box.

6. Click **OK**.

7. To edit the transformation, select the object, and then click **Transform** on the Appearance panel.

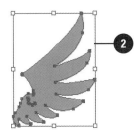

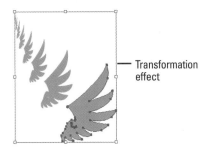

Transformation effect

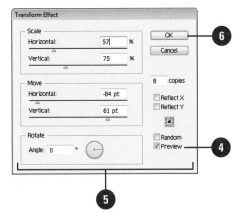

For Your Information

Repeating a Transformation

The Transform Again command allows you to quickly repeat the last transformation with the last-used values on a selected object. To use the command, transform and select an object or group, click the Object menu, point to Transform, and then click Transform Again or press Ctrl+D (Win) or Command+D (Mac).

Reshaping Objects with Envelopes

IL 6.2, 6.7

Envelopes are objects you can use to reshape other objects, except graphs, guides, or linked objects. You can use one of the built-in envelopes or create your own out of an existing object. The built-in envelopes use warp shapes or a mesh grid as the object. After you apply an envelope, you can edit the original object or the envelope (anchor points), separately, using the Selection and Mesh tools on the Tools panel.

Distort Objects with an Envelope

1. Select the **Selection** tool on the Tools panel.

2. Select one or more objects to reshape.

3. Click the **Object** menu, point to **Envelope Distort**, and then click one of the following:

   ◆ **Make With Warp.** Uses a preset warp shape.

   ◆ **Make with Mesh.** Uses a rectangle grid.

   ◆ **Make With Top Object.** Uses an object as the shape of the envelope. The object needs to be at the top of the stacking order.

4. Specify the options you want for the envelope type; select the **Preview** check box to view your changes on the selected object.

5. Click **OK**.

6. Do any of the following:

   ◆ **Reshape.** Select the **Selection** or **Mesh** tool, and then drag any anchor points.

   ◆ **Delete Anchor Points.** For a mesh grid, Select the **Selection** or **Mesh** tool, select an anchor point, and then press Delete.

   ◆ **Add Anchor Points.** For mesh grid, select the **Mesh** tool, and then click on the grid.

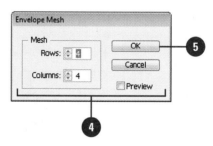

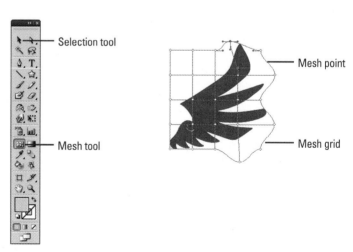

Selection tool

Mesh tool

Mesh point

Mesh grid

Working with Color

4

Introduction

When you create or open a document, Illustrator creates or looks for a color profile, which specifies color usage in the document. Color modes define the colors represented in the active document. Although you can change the color mode of a document, it is best to select the correct color mode when you create a document. Illustrator's main color modes are RGB (Red, Green, and Blue) for onscreen and web projects and CMYK (Cyan, Magenta, Yellow, and Black) for commercial printing projects.

Illustrator provides several panels (Tools, Color, Swatches, Color Guide, and Kuler) for you to use to work with color and apply color to one or more objects. For example, the Color panel lets you create colors using different sliders and spectrum color selectors. Illustrator not only lets you select virtually any colors you desire, it also lets you store those colors for future use in the Swatches panel. Along with the panels, Illustrator also provides the Live Color dialog box, which you can use to change multiple colors in your artwork at the same time by editing and applying color groups. This makes it easy to recolor your artwork.

As you start to use color in your document, it's important to view how your document will actually appear with your current color settings. With Illustrator, you can view a soft proof on your screen to quickly see a simulation of how your colors will appear based on your output device.

What You'll Do

Change Color Settings

Change Color Profiles

Work with Color Modes

Change Color Modes

Apply Colors

Work with the Color Panel

Work with the Swatches Panel

Work with Swatch Libraries

Add Colors Using the Kuler Panel

Replace or Invert Colors

Use the Color Guide Panel

Apply Color with the Color Guide Panel

Edit Color with Live Color

Proof Colors on the Screen

Changing Color Settings

 IL 3.1

Illustrator does its best to manage color for you. However, sometimes there are color conflicts or you have specific color requirements that you want to use. When you create or open a document, Illustrator creates or looks for a color profile, which specifies color usage in the document. The Color Settings dialog box allows you to specify color settings and select options to deal with conflicts. The two main color settings are Working Space and Color Management Policies. Working Space controls how RGB and CMYK colors are used in a document that doesn't have an embedded profile, while Color Management Policies controls how Illustrator works with color when opening files that don't have a color profile or one that doesn't match your current color settings from the RGB and CMYK menus. If you need to convert colors between color spaces, use Advanced mode.

Change Color Settings

1. Click the **Edit** menu, and then click **Color Settings**.

2. Click the **Settings** list arrow, and then select from the following preset color settings:

   ◆ **Monitor Color.** Useful for video and on-screen content. Sets the RGB working space to your current monitor space.

   ◆ **North America General Purpose 2.** Useful for screen and print content in North America.

   ◆ **North America Prepress 2.** Useful for common printing conditions in North America. The default RGB color space is set to Adobe RGB.

   ◆ **North America Web/Internet.** Useful for non-print content on the Web in North America.

3. Click **OK** to use the defined settings, or select your own custom settings:

   ◆ **Working Spaces.** Controls how RGB and CMYK colors are used in a document that doesn't have an embedded profile.

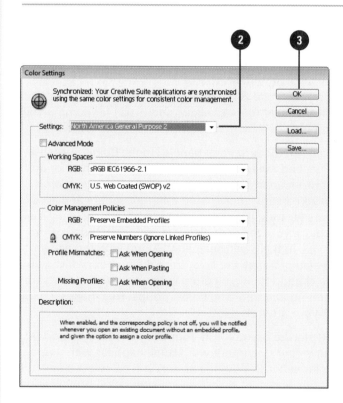

Select **Monitor RGB** for onscreen output; **Adobe RGB** for photo inkjet printers (converts RGB images to CMYK images); **ProPhoto RGB** for inkjet printers; and **sRGB IEC61966-2.1** for web output.

◆ **Color Management Policies.** Controls how Illustrator works with color when opening files that don't have a color profile or one that doesn't match your current color settings from the RGB and CMYK menus.

Select **Off** to prevent the use of color management, **Preserve Numbers** to preserve the document color profile for CMYK documents, **Preserve Embedded Profiles** to preserve links to color profiles, or **Convert to Working Space** to use the working space color (useful for the web).

Select the appropriate check boxes to choose if and when Illustrator will warn you of profile mismatches (no warning, when opening the file, or when pasting) or missing profiles (when opening a file or no warning).

④ Click **OK**.

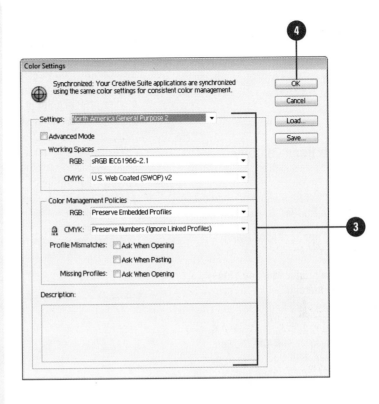

For Your Information

Synchronizing Color Settings Using Bridge

If you're using Adobe Creative Suite, you can use Adobe Bridge to synchronize your color settings for all programs in the suite. When you synchronize your color settings, you can avoid color profile conflicts. In Adobe Bridge, click the Edit menu, and then click Creative Suite Color Settings, select one of the settings, and then click Apply.

Changing Color Profiles

IL 3.1

When you create or open a document, Illustrator creates or looks for a color profile, which specifies color usage in the document. If a document's profile doesn't match the current working color space or is missing an assigned color profile, you can use the Assign Profile dialog box to change or remove a profile to avoid conflicts. When you change a color profile, color in your document may shift to match the new color profile.

Change or Remove Color Profiles

1. Click the **Edit** menu, and then click **Assign Profile**.

2. Select one of the following options:

   ◆ **Don't Color Manage This Document.** Select to remove a color profile from your document.

   ◆ **Working RGB/CMYK.** Select when your document doesn't have an assigned profile or its profile is different from the current working space.

   ◆ **Profile.** Select to assign a different profile to your document.

3. Click **OK**.

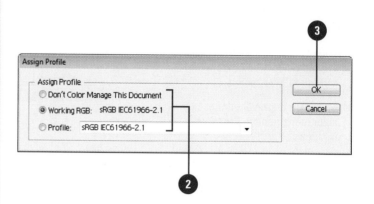

Working with Color Modes

Color modes define the colors represented in the active document. Although you can change the color mode of a document, it is best to select the correct color mode at the start of the project. Illustrator's main color modes are RGB (Red, Green, and Blue) and CMYK (Cyan, Magenta, Yellow, and Black).

Color modes determine the number of colors and the file size of an image. For example, an RGB image has at least three colors (like a printing plate), one for red, green, and blue color information. Color modes not only define the working color space of the active document, they also represent the color space of the output document. It's the document output (print, press, or monitor) that ultimately determines the document color mode. Color modes do not just determine what colors the eye sees; they represent how the colors are mixed, and that's very important because different output devices use different color mixes.

Therefore, when selecting a color mode, know the file format of the document and where it will be used. An image taken with a digital camera and then opened in Illustrator would most likely be in the RGB color mode. An image displayed on a monitor would be RGB, or possibly Indexed Color. A photograph scanned on a high-end drum scanner would most likely be in the CMYK color mode. An image being sent to a 4-color press would be CMYK, too. If you were creating a Illustrator document from scratch, the color mode you choose should represent the eventual output destination of the document, such as on a web page, to an inkjet printer, or a 4-color press.

Switching Between Color Modes

Unfortunately, images do not always arrive in the correct format. For example, you take several photographs with your digital (RGB) camera, but the images are being printed on a 4-color (CMYK) press, or you want to colorize a grayscale image. Changing color modes is a snap, but changing the color mode of an image isn't the problem. The problem is what happens to the digital color information when you change color modes. For example, if you open an RGB image with the intent of sending it out to a 4-color press (CMYK), the smartest course of action is to remain in the RGB color mode through the processing of the image, and then convert the image into the CMYK mode at the end. The reason has to do with how Illustrator moves between those two color spaces. For example, if you move a color-corrected CMYK image into the RGB color mode, and then back to CMYK, the colors shift because Illustrator rounds color values during the change process. On top of that, a CMYK image is 25% larger than an RGB image, and the RGB color mode represents the color space of your monitor, not a printing press. It is impossible to view subtractive CMYK color on an RGB device. If, however, the image originally came to you as a color-corrected CMYK image, then stay in and work inside that color mode.

Changing Color Modes

When you create a new document, you need to select a color mode, either RGB or CMYK, depending on the type of document that you want to produce. For web and other onscreen projects, RGB is the best choice. For commercial printing, CMYK is the best choice. If you want to create documents for both types of projects, you can save a copy of the document and then change the color mode. When you change the color mode, colors will convert to the mode in the document. You will see a shift in color.

Change Color Modes

1. Click the **File** menu, and then click **Save As** to make a copy of the document.

2. Click the **File** menu, and then point to **Document Color Mode**.

3. Click **CMYK Color** or **RGB Color**.

   ◆ If you don't like the change, you can use the Undo command on the Edit menu to reverse the color conversion.

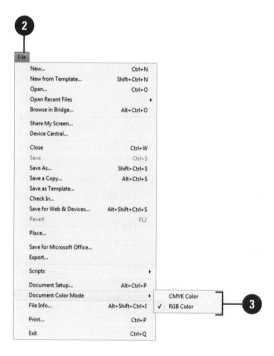

Applying Colors

 IL 3.2

The Tools panel provides color boxes to make it easy for you to apply fill and stroke colors. The color box in the foreground is the Fill box and the outlined box in the background is the Stroke box. When you select an object, fill, or stroke, the color boxes (also known as thumbnails), on the Tools panel display the current colors. To change the fill or stroke color, select an object, fill or stroke, select the Fill or Stroke box, and then select a color from the Color, Swatches, or Color Guide panel.

Apply Colors to an Object, Fill or Stroke

1. Select an object, fill, or stroke using the appropriate selection tool.

2. Click the **Fill** or **Stroke** color box on the Tools panel to choose the color's destination.

3. Click the **Color** button on the Tools panel to apply a color or click **None** to apply no color.

4. Use any of the following methods to change the active fill or stroke colors:

   ◆ Select the **Swatches** panel, and then click a color swatch to change the color.

   ◆ Select the **Color** panel, and then specify a color using the controls.

   ◆ Select the **Color Guide** panel, and then click a color swatch to change the color.

   ◆ Double-click the **Fill** or **Stroke** color box to open the Color Picker dialog box, select a color or enter color values, and then click **OK**.

   ◆ To set default color of black and white, click the **Default Fill and Stroke** icon on the Tools panel.

   ◆ To set switch the current fill and stroke color, click the **Swap Fill and Stroke** icon on the Tools panel.

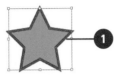

Color panel

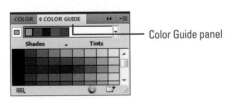

Color Guide panel

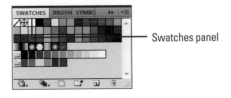

Swatches panel

Working with the Color Panel

IL 3.2

Illustrator not only lets you select virtually any colors you desire, it also lets you store those colors for future use. For example, you create a color scheme for a recurring brochure and you want a way to save those colors, or you're working on an Internet graphic and you need a web-safe color panel. Whatever your color needs, Illustrator stands ready to meet them. The Color panel gives you access to Illustrator's color-generation tools. This single panel lets you create colors using different sliders, spectrum color selectors, a grayscale ramp, and an option that lets you create a color ramp for the current fill and stroke colors. The CMYK spectrum displays a rainbow of colors in the CMYK color gamut. Moving the eyedropper into the spectrum box and clicking lets you select any color and gives you a visual representation of the relationships between various colors. The Grayscale ramp gives you linear access to the 256 available grayscale values.

Work with the Color Panel

1. Select the **Color** panel.

2. Click the **Color Options** menu.

3. Select from the following Color Sliders:

   ◆ **Grayscale.** Creates a single slider going from white (0) to black (100). Converts the lower portion of the Color panel to a grayscale ramp. Clicking anywhere in the ramp changes the active color.

   ◆ **RGB.** Creates three sliders (red, green, and blue). Each slider has a possible value from 0 to 255. Converts the lower portion of the Color panel to the RGB spectrum. Clicking anywhere in the spectrum changes the active color.

   ◆ **HSB.** Creates three additive sliders (hue, saturation, and brightness). Each slider has a possible value from 0 to 255.

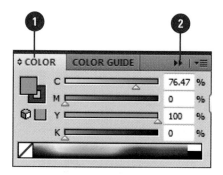

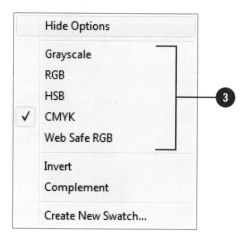

◆ **CMYK.** Creates four subtractive sliders (cyan, magenta, yellow, and black). Each slider has a possible value from 0 to 100. Converts the lower portion of the Color panel to the CMYK spectrum. Clicking anywhere in the spectrum changes the active color.

◆ **Web Safe RGB.** Creates three sliders (red, green, and blue). Each slider has a possible hexadecimal value from 00 to FF. Restricts the color spectrum to only web-safe colors.

4 To change a color, click a color box, use a slider, enter specific color values, or click a color in the spectrum. The box with the red diagonal line is the None color.

5 To change a color using the Adobe Color Picker, double-click a color box, select a color using the color range or color mode options, and then click **OK**.

Cube indicates the color is not web-safe; click to select the closest web color. An alert triangle indicates the color is out of gamut (non-printable).

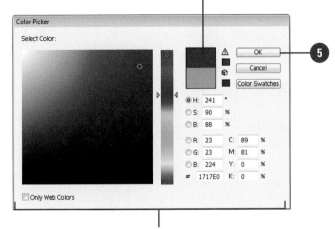

Select options or click the color range to select a color.

Did You Know?

You can identify out of gamut colors. If an out of gamut warning icon (a triangle with an exclamation point) appears below the color boxes on the Color panel, it indicates that the current RGB or HSB color doesn't have a CMYK equivalent, which means you can't use it on a commercial project.

For Your Information

Selecting Colors

In Windows, you can use the Color dialog box, which displays basic and custom color squares and a color matrix with the full range of colors in the color spectrum, to help you select a color. You can enter RGB values for hue, saturation, and luminosity (also known as brightness) to specify a color. **Hue** is a pure color (one without tint or shade); the name of the color (red, green, etc.) is measured by its location on the color wheel. **Saturation** is a measure of how much white is mixed in with the color. A fully saturated color has vivid tones; a less saturated color is more of a washed-out pastel. **Luminosity** is a measure of how much black is mixed with the color. A very bright color contains little or no black. You can also change the hue by moving the pointer in the color matrix box horizontally; you can change the saturation by moving the pointer vertically, and the luminosity by adjusting the slider to the right of the color matrix box. On the Macintosh, you click one of the color modes and select a color, using its controls. You can select RGB values by selecting the color sliders at the top of the dialog box, then choosing RGB Sliders from the pop-up menu, and dragging the Red, Green, and Blue sliders. Or, you can enter values (color numbers) to select a color. You can select hue, saturation, and brightness (or luminosity) values by selecting Color Sliders, choosing HSB Sliders, then dragging the sliders or entering your own values.

Working with the Swatches Panel

 IL 3.2

Illustrator not only lets you select virtually any colors you desire, it also lets you store those colors for future use in a library of color swatches, the Swatches panel. Where the Color panel lets you select virtually any color you need, the Swatches panel lets you save, group, and use specific colors that you use often. In the Swatches panel, you can point to a color box to display a tooltip indicating its color settings. If you want to view more information, you can change the Swatches panel display to make it easier to view and work with colors. To help with color organization, you can also create color groups to keep colors for a specific project together.

Change the Swatches Panel Display

1. Select the **Swatches** panel.

2. Click the **Swatches Options** menu, and then choose from the following options: **Small Thumbnail View, Medium Thumbnail View, Large Thumbnail View, Small List View,** or **Large List View.**

3. To sort the colors in the Swatch panel, click the **Swatches Options** menu, and then click **Sort by Name** or **Sort by Kind** (by solid, gradients, patterns, and groups).

4. To display swatches by type, click the **Show Swatch Kinds Menu** button, and then select an option: **Show All Swatches, Show Color Swatches, Show Gradient Swatches, Show Pattern Swatches,** or **Show Color Groups**.

Did You Know?

You can delete a color or color group from the Swatches panel. Open the Swatches panel, display and select the color or color group you want to delete, and then click the Delete button.

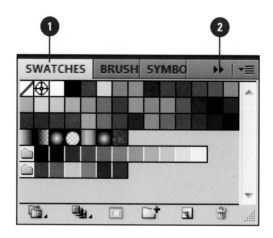

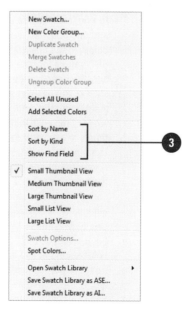

Add, Edit, or Duplicate a Color

1. Select the **Swatches** panel.

2. To edit or duplicate a color, select a swatch color.

   TIMESAVER *Drag a color from the color boxes on the Tools or Control panel to the Swatches panel.*

3. Click the **Swatch Options** button to edit a color or click the **New Swatch** button to add or duplicate a color.

4. For a new or duplicate color, enter a name.

5. For a new or edited color, select a color type, select or deselect the **Global** check box, select a color mode, and then specify the color that you want.

6. Click **OK**.

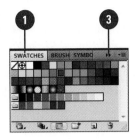

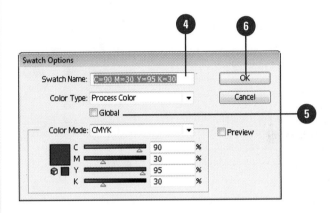

Create a Color Group

1. Select the **Swatches** panel.

2. Select the solid colors that you want in the group.

   Use Shift+click to select contiguous color boxes or Ctrl+click (Win) or Command+click (Mac) to select noncontiguous color boxes.

3. Click the **New Color Group** button.

4. Enter a name.

5. Click **OK**.

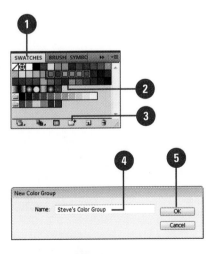

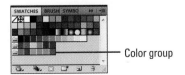

Color group

Working with Swatch Libraries

IL 3.2

In addition to the standard color swatch libraries, such as Basic RGB and Basic CMYK, you can access the Swatch Libraries menu to use colors from all types of color libraries, such as Corporate, Foods, Kids Stuff, Nature, Skintones. After you open a library, you can apply colors to fills and strokes, as well as copy swatches between libraries. After you modify a swatch library, you can save it to create your own user-defined custom swatch library.

Display and Use a Swatch Library

1. Select the **Swatches** panel.

2. Click the **Swatch Libraries** menu, point to a library (if necessary), and then select the swatch library you want.

   ◆ To use default libraries, point to **Default Swatches**, and then click **Basic CMYK**, **Basic RGB**, or one of the other available libraries.

   The Library panel appears displaying the selected Swatch library.

3. To view other related libraries, click the **Load Next Swatch Library** or **Load Previous Swatch Library** button on the Library panel.

4. To copy swatches between libraries, open the libraries, and then drag the color box or color group from one library to another.

   ◆ If a Swatch Conflict dialog box appears, select an option to merge swatches or add a new one.

5. To apply a color to a selected fill or stroke, select the element, click the **Fill** or **Stroke** color box on the Tools or Color panel to choose the color's destination, and then select a color in the Swatch library.

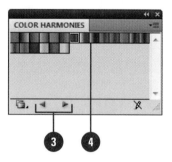

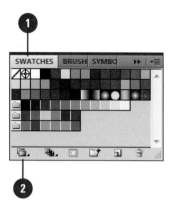

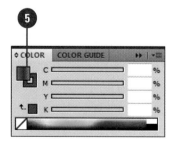

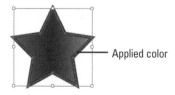

Applied color

Save Customized Swatch Panels

1. Select the **Swatches** panel.

2. Create a customized swatch panel by adding and/or deleting colors from an existing panel.

3. Click the **Swatch Libraries** menu, and then click **Save Swatches**.

4. Enter a name in the Save As box.

5. Click the **Save In** (Win) or **Where** (Mac) list arrow, and then select a location to store the swatch.

6. Click **Save**.

Did You Know?

You can access your customized swatches from the Swatch Libraries menu. When you save swatches in the Color Swatches folder (default location), your customized swatches appear on the User Defined submenu on the Swatch Libraries menu.

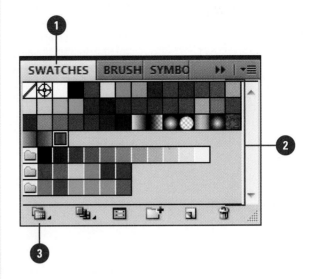

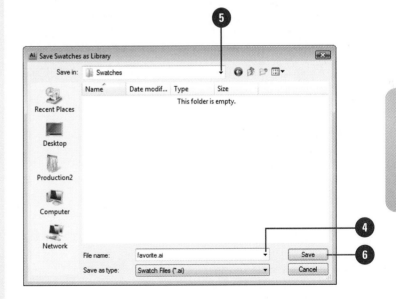

Adding Colors Using the Kuler Panel

IL 3.2

The Kuler panel (**New!**) is an extension to Illustrator that allows you to use groups of color, or themes in your projects. You can use the panel to browse thousands of color themes from the Kuler community. After you find the theme you want, you can add it to the Swatches panel for use in your project. You can access the Kuler panel by using the Extensions submenu on the Window menu. The Kuler panel is also available in the CS4 version of Photoshop, InDesign, Flash, and Fireworks. In many of these programs, you can also create your own theme using complementary harmony rules, share them with others in the Kuler community, and use them in Illustrator.

Browse Themes

1 Click the **Window** menu, point to **Extensions**, and then click **Kuler**.

2 To search for a theme, click in the Search box, enter the name of the theme, a tag, or a creator, and then press Enter (Win) or Return (Mac).

   IMPORTANT *In a search, use only alphanumerical characters (Aa-Zz, 0-9).*

3 To narrow down the browse list, click the popups, and then select the filter options you want. Some include Highest Rated, Most Popular, Newest.

   ◆ To save a search, click the first popup, click **Custom**, enter your search criteria, and then click **Save**.

4 To browse for a theme, click the **View Previous Set of Themes** or **View Next Set of Themes** button.

5 Select a theme in the panel.

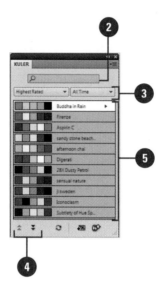

Add Themes to the Swatches Panel

1. Click the **Window** menu, point to **Extensions**, and then click **Kuler**.

2. To narrow down the browse list, click the popups, and then select the filter options you want. Some include Highest Rated, Most Popular, Newest.

   ◆ To save a search, click the first popup, click **Custom**, enter your search criteria, and then click **Save**.

3. To browse for a theme, click the **View Previous Set of Themes** or **View Next Set of Themes** button.

4. Select a theme in the panel.

5. To add the theme to the Swatches panel, click the **Add Selected Theme to Swatches** button.

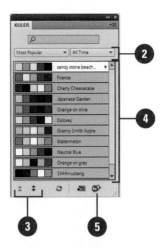

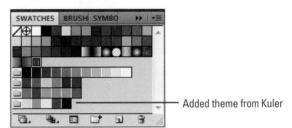

Added theme from Kuler

Replacing Colors

IL 3.2

Illustrator uses global and nonglobal process colors along with spot colors. A global color is one that is updated for all uses, while a non-global color is one that is only updated where it's being used on selected objects. A global process color appears in the Swatches panel with a white corner and no dot, while a nonglobal process color is plain white. A spot color appears with a white corner and a dot. You can change a color back and forth between global and nonglobal by using the Swatch Options dialog box.

Change Global and Nonglobal Colors

- **Switch Between Colors.** To change a color to global or nonglobal, double-click a global or nonglobal process color in the Swatches panel, select or deselect the **Global** check box, and then click **OK**.

- **Edit Colors.** To edit colors, double-click a global or nonglobal process color in the Swatches panel, select the **Preview** check box, drag the sliders to change the color, and then click **OK**.

- **Replace Colors.** To replace a global or spot color (which updates it everywhere it's used), Alt (Win) or Option (Mac) drag the new color over the color that you want to replace.

Spot color   Nonglobal color

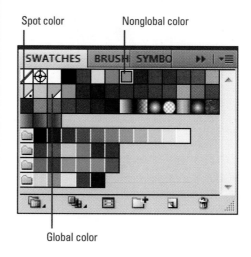

Global color

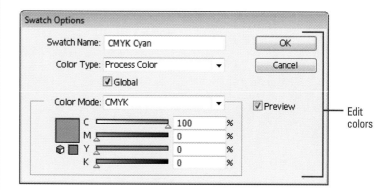

Edit colors

Replace Colors

1. Select an object with the nonglobal process colors that you want to replace.

2. Click the **Select Similar Options** list arrow on the Control panel.

3. Select one of the following options: **All**, **Fill Color**, **Stroke Color**, **Fill & Stroke Color**, or **Stroke Weight**.

4. Click the **Fill** or **Stroke** color box on the Tools or Color panel to choose the color's destination.

5. Select a replacement color from the Swatches or Color Guide panels.

Did You Know?

You can colorize a grayscale image. Select the grayscale image that you want to change, click the Fill box on the Tools or Color panel, and then select a color from the Color, Swatches, or Color Guide panels. Gray areas are recolored with the new color, while a white background remains opaque white.

You can change a color image to grayscale. Select the colored image, click the Edit menu, point to Edit Colors, and then click Convert to Grayscale.

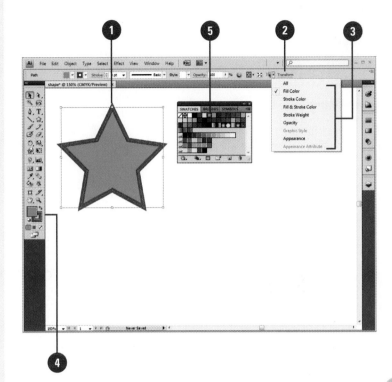

Inverting Colors

Illustrator provides two commands to invert colors, which changes the color to their opposite values on the color scale. The Invert Colors command allows you to invert multiple nonglobal process colors in a selected object, while the Invert command allows you to invert the fill or stroke color (global, nonglobal, or spot).

Invert Nonglobal Colors

1. Select an object with the nonglobal process colors that you want to invert.

2. Click the **Edit** menu, point to **Edit Colors**, and then click **Invert Colors**.

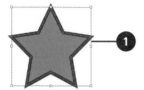
Inverted colors

Invert a Global, Nonglobal, or Spot Color

1. Select an object with the nonglobal process colors that you want to invert.

2. Select the **Color** panel.

3. Click the **Fill** or **Stroke** color box on the Tools or Color panel to choose the color's destination.

4. Click the **Color Options** menu, and then click **Invert**.

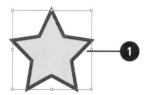

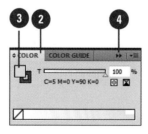

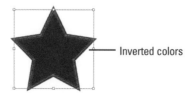
Inverted colors

Using the Color Guide Panel

The Color Guide panel allows you to display and apply variations for a color. Along with the Live Color dialog box, you can edit colors in an object or color group, create new color groups, and apply harmony rules, which are predefined color schemes. Variations appear in the Color Guide panel based on a range of color, left or right from center (the small black triangle). You can change the number of columns that appear as well as the color range.

Select Variation Options

1. Select the **Color Guide** panel.

2. Click the **Color Guide Options** menu, and then click **Color Guide Options**.

3. Set the number of variation steps (columns of color) to display on either side of the center column.

4. Drag the **Variation** slider to set the range of variation.

5. Click **OK**.

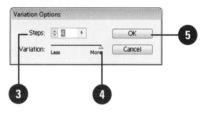

Display Variation Types

1. Select the **Color Guide** panel.

2. Click the **Color Guide Options** menu.

3. Select one of the following variation types:

   ◆ **Show Tints/Shades.** Adds black to the colors on the left and white to the colors on the right of center.

   ◆ **Show Warm/Cool.** Adds red to the colors on the left and blue to the colors on the right of center.

   ◆ **Show Vivid/Muted.** Adds gray to the colors on the left and increases saturation to the colors on the right.

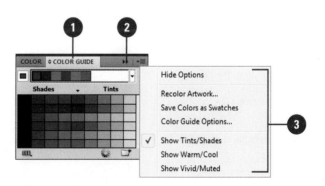

Applying Color with the Color Guide Panel

Apply Colors to an Object, Fill or Stroke

1. Select an object.

2. Click the **Fill** or **Stroke** color box on the Tools or Color panel to choose the color's destination.

3. Select the **Color Guide** panel.

4. Click the **Limit Colors to Swatch Library** button, and then click **None**.

   ◆ If you want to use another swatch for color, you can select it from the menu.

5. Click the **Set Base Color to Current Color** button.

6. Click the **Color Guide Options** menu, and then select a variation type: **Show Tints/Shades**, **Show Warm/Cool**, or **Show Vivid/Muted**.

7. Click the variation color that you want to apply.

   TIMESAVER *Drag a variation color over any unselected object to apply it.*

After you set up the Color Guide panel to display color variations the way you want, you can now start applying colors to objects in your document. You can apply colors to an object based on current colors in the object or use colors from other swatches. Illustrator makes it easy to display and apply variations with Harmony Rules (sets of predefined color schemes), such as Complementary, Analogous, Monochromatic, Shades, or High Contrast. If you want to save a customized set of variations, you can create a color group in the Swatches panel for future use.

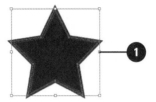

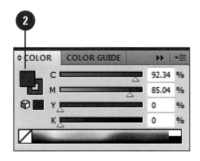

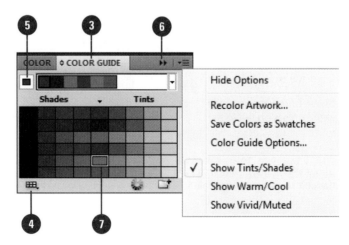

Use Variations Based on Harmony Rules

1. Select an object.

2. Click the **Fill** or **Stroke** color box on the Tools panel to choose the color's destination.

3. Select the **Color Guide** panel.

4. Click the **Limit Colors to Swatch Library** button, and then click **None**.

5. Click the **Set Base Color to Current Color** button.

6. Click the **Harmony Rules** list arrow, and then select a rule.

7. Click the variation color that you want to apply.

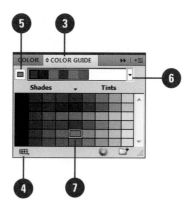

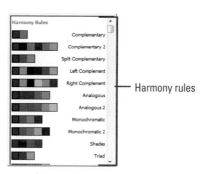

Harmony rules

Create a Color Group

1. Select the **Color Guide** panel.

2. Display the color variations that you want to save as a color group.

3. Click the gray area below the color variations to deselect everything.

4. Click the **Save Color Group to Swatches Panel** button.

Did You Know?

You can copy a single variation to the Swatches panel. Simply drag the color box in the Color Guide panel to the Swatches panel.

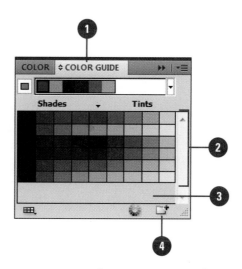

Editing Colors with Live Color

IL 3.4

The Live Color dialog box allows you to change multiple colors in your artwork at the same time by editing and applying color groups. This makes it easy to recolor your artwork. You can apply a color group, such as a harmony rule, to objects, or reassign individual colors within a color group to objects. If you have too many colors within objects, you can also reduce the number of colors used while you reassign them.

Apply Color Groups to an Object with Live Color

1. Select the objects that you want to recolor.

2. Select the **Color Guide** panel.

3. Click the **Edit or Apply Colors** button on the Color Guide panel or click the **Recolor Artwork** button on the Control panel.

4. Click the **Edit** tab.

5. Select the **Recolor Art** check box.

6. Click the **Get Colors from Selected Art** button to create a color group from the selected objects, and then enter a name in the field next to the button for the group.

7. Click the **New Color Group** button to save the color group in the list.

8. To change color groups, select one from the Color Groups list or click the **Harmony Rules** list arrow, and then select a rule.

9. To edit a color, select a color box, and then drag the sliders and the round markers (largest marker is the base color) on the color wheel to display the color you want.

    ◆ Use the buttons below the color boxes to change the wheel display, show saturation or brightness (drag slider to adjust it), add or remove colors, and unlink or link harmony rules.

10. Click **OK**.

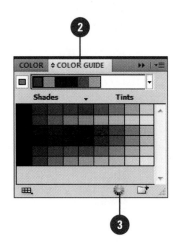

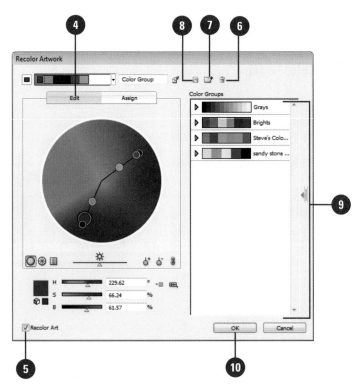

Assign Color Groups to an Object with Live Color

1. Select the objects that you want to recolor.

2. Select the **Color Guide** panel.

3. Click the **Edit or Apply Colors** button on the Color Guide panel or click the **Recolor Artwork** button on the Control panel.

4. Click the **Assign** tab.

5. Select the **Recolor Art** check box.

6. Click the **Get Colors from Selected Art** button to create a color group from the selected objects, and then enter a name in the field next to the button for the group.

7. Click the **New Color Group** button to save the color group in the list.

8. To change color groups, select one from the Color Groups list or click the **Harmony Rules** list arrow, and then select a rule.

9. To reduce the number of colors used in objects, click the **Colors** list arrow and then specify the number of colors you want.

   ◆ Click the **Color Reduction Options** button to specify how you want to recolor the objects.

10. To change a new color, select a color and then use the color sliders.

11. To assign a color, drag a current color to another row.

12. To prevent a color assignment change, click the arrow between the columns (it changes to a line). Click it again to change it back.

13. Click **OK**.

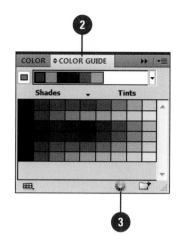

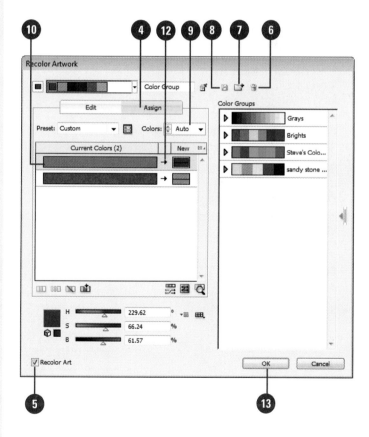

Proofing Colors on the Screen

As you start to use color in your document, it's important to see how your color settings appear. It would be nice to see a printed copy in color to see how colors actually look. However, that is not always possible. Instead you can view a soft proof on your screen to quickly see how your colors will appear. A soft proof simulates the output of your device, such as a printer with a specific type of paper.

Display a Soft Proof

1. Click the **View** menu, and then point to **Proof Setup**.

2. Select from one of the available output devices to simulate, or click **Customize** to setup your own.

3. For a custom soft proof setup, select from the following options:

   ◆ **Device to Simulate.** Select a target device to simulate.

   ◆ **Preserve CMYK Numbers.** Select to use colors as they are and not convert them to the working color space. Deselect to use a rending intent option to display colors.

   ◆ **Rendering Intent.** Select an option to display colors: Perceptual (for continuous-tone images), Saturation (for vivid graphics), Absolute Colorimetric (for color preservation) or Relative Colorimetric (for color accuracy).

   ◆ **Simulate Paper Color.** Select to simulate white paper.

   ◆ **Simulate Black Ink.** Select to simulate dark gray for black.

4. Click **OK**.

5. Click the **View** menu, and then click **Proof Colors**.

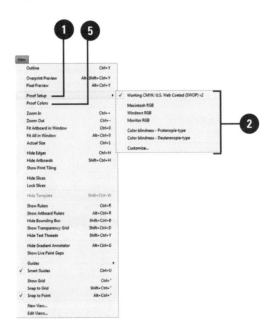

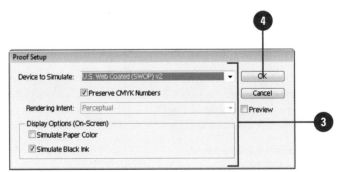

Applying Fills, Strokes, and Gradients

5

Introduction

The Stroke panel makes it easy to change stroke attributes, such as weight (width), position on the path, and its style. The weight of a stroke refers to the thickness of the line. The Eyedropper tool on the Tools panel is another way you can quickly pick up an object's color and stroke attributes and apply them to another object. Instead of using a solid color as an object fill, you can create and use patterns. The process is very simple. In Illustrator, create a pattern using drawing tools, select and drag the object pattern to the Swatches panel, and then give it a name.

A blend uses two or more objects to create a transitional object in between. If you're just getting start with blends, the Make command on the Blend submenu is an easy way to create a blend. All you need to do is select the objects that you want to use, and then choose the command. That's it. If you want a little more control over the way a blend turns out, you can specify options in the Blend Options dialog box. If you want to specify the locations where the blend takes place, you can use the Blend tool. Transparency, or the opacity level of an object, is set in Illustrator by adjusting the Opacity option in the Transparency or Control panels. Along with the Opacity option is the blending mode, which blends colors together for objects in a group as well as all the objects below it.

A gradient is a smooth transition between two or more colors in an object. You can apply one of Illustrator's built-in gradients or create one of your own by using the Gradient panel. There are two types of gradients: Radial (circular) and Linear (horizontal). With the Gradient tool, you can edit gradient colors applied to the object by adding or changing color stops, applying transparency, and changing gradient direction (linear) or angle (radial).

What You'll Do

Apply Fill and Stroke Colors

Change Stroke Attributes

Use the Eyedropper Tool

Use Patterns as Fills

Blend Color Fills

Create Blends Automatically

Apply Blend Options

Create Blends with the Blend Tool

Modify Blended Objects

Set Transparency Options

Control Transparency Effects

Use the Transparency Grid

Apply Gradients

Create Gradients

Edit Gradients

Use the Gradient Tool

Create a Gradient Mesh

Applying Fill and Stroke Colors

IL 3.2, 5.4

The Tools panel provides color boxes to make it easy for you to apply fill and stroke colors. The color box in the foreground is the Fill box and the outlined box in the background is the Stroke box. When you select an object, fill, or stroke, the color boxes (also known as thumbnails), on the Tools panel display the current colors. To change the fill or stroke color, select an object, fill or stroke, select the Fill or Stroke box, and then select a color from the Color, Swatches, or Color Guide panel., or use the Eyedropper to apply a color from the active document.

Apply Colors to an Object, Fill or Stroke

1. Select an object, fill, or stroke using the appropriate selection tool.

2. Click the **Fill** or **Stroke** color box on the Tools or Color panel to choose the color's destination.

3. Click the **Color** button on the Tools panel to apply a color or click **None** to apply no color.

4. Use any of the following methods to change the active fill or stroke colors:

   ◆ Select the **Swatches** panel, and then click a color swatch to change the color.

   ◆ Select the **Color** panel, and then specify a color using the controls.

   ◆ Select the **Color Guide** panel, and then click a color swatch to change the color.

   ◆ Select the **Eyedropper** tool on the Tools panel, and then click anywhere in the active document to change the color.

   ◆ Double-click the **Fill** or **Stroke** color box to open the Color Picker dialog box, select a color or enter color values, and then click **OK**.

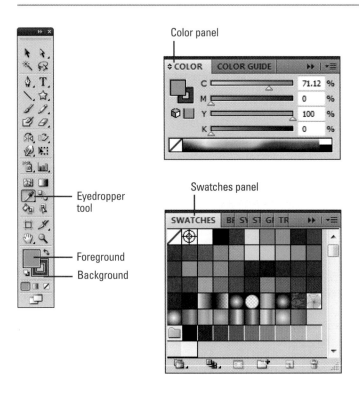

Color panel

Eyedropper tool

Foreground

Background

Swatches panel

Color Picker dialog box

Use Default and Switch the Fill and Stroke Colors

① Click the **Default Colors Fill and Stroke Colors** buttons to revert the fill and stroke colors to their default values of black and white.

② Click the **Switch Fill and Stroke Colors** button to switch current colors.

> **TIMESAVER** *Press D to change the foreground and background colors to their default values of black and white, and press X to switch the current colors.*

Did You Know?

You can add colors from the Color Picker to the Swatches panel. Open the Color Picker dialog box, select the color you want to add to the Swatches panel, click Add To Swatches, type a name for the color, and then click OK.

Changing Stroke Attributes

 IL 2.2

The Stroke panel makes it easy to change stroke attributes, such as weight (width), position on the path, and its style. The weight of a stroke represents the thickness of the line. A weight smaller than .25 may not print and a weight of 0 removes the stroke. In addition to the width of a stroke, you can also specify the position (known as alignment) of the stroke on the path (either center, inside, or outside). Style is what stands out on the page. You can change the stroke style by applying dashes and sharpening or rounding corners and endpoints.

Change the Weight of a Stroke

1. Select one or more objects.

2. Select the **Stroke** panel.

3. Specify or enter a weight in the Stroke or Control panel.

   ◆ Click the up or down arrow, or Shift+click to change the weight by a larger interval.

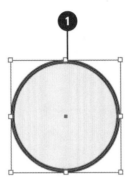

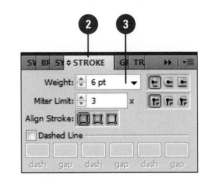

Change the Alignment of a Stroke on the Path

1. Select one or more closed objects.

2. Select the **Stroke** panel.

3. Click one of the following alignment buttons:

   ◆ **Align Stroke to Center.**

   ◆ **Align Stroke to Inside.**

   ◆ **Align Stroke to Outside.**

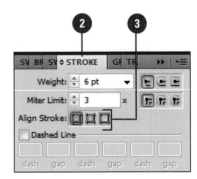

Change Stroke Caps or Joins

1 Select one or more objects.

2 Select the **Stroke** panel.

3 To change the endpoints, click one of the following buttons:

- ◆ **Butt Cap.** Creates a square-edged end.

- ◆ **Round Cap.** Creates a rounded end.

- ◆ **Projecting Cap.** Creates a square-edged end that extends past the endpoint.

4 To change the bends on corner points, click one of the following:

- ◆ **Miter Join.** Creates a pointed join point.

- ◆ **Round Join.** Creates a rounded join point.

- ◆ **Bevel Join.** Creates a beveled (cut off) join point.

Create a Dashed Stroke

1 Select one or more objects.

2 Select the **Stroke** panel.

3 Click one of the Cap buttons.

4 Select the **Dashed Line** check box.

5 Enter a value in the first Dash box.

If you don't enter any more values, the value in the first box is used for the rest of the boxes.

6 Enter a value in the first Gap box.

7 Fill in the remaining boxes.

- ◆ To create a dotted line, click the Round Cap button, enter a dash value of 0, and then enter a gap value greater than or equal to the stroke weight.

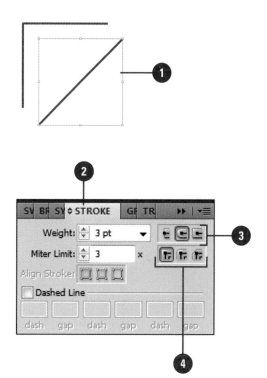

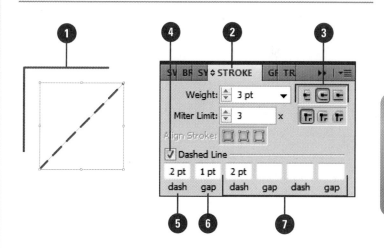

Using the Eyedropper Tool

IL 5.4

The Eyedropper tool on the Tools panel makes it easy to quickly pick up a color from one area of your artwork and apply it to another area. When you click an object with the Eyedropper tool, it picks up the object's color and stroke attributes and displays them in the Tools, Color, and Stroke panels. You can pick up attributes from any type of object, even a graphic image and the object doesn't need to be selected. If an object is selected, the color and stroke attributes are applied to the selected object. The Eyedropper tool also provides options for you to customize the attributes—such as Appearance, Transparency, Focal Fill and Focal Stroke, Character Style and Paragraph Style—that you want to pick up with the tool.

Apply Colors and Attributes with the Eyedropper Tool

1. If you want to apply the pick up color and attributes to one or more objects, then select them.

2. Select the **Eyedropper** tool on the Tools panel.

3. Click an object in any window that contains the color and attributes that you want to pick up and apply.

   - If you want to apply color attributes from the currently selected object and apply them to another object you select, Alt+click (Win) or Option+click (Mac) the objects.

   - To have the Eyedropper tool only pick up an object's color and not other attributes, click the Fill or Stroke box on the Tools or Color panel, and then Shift+click the color to be picked up.

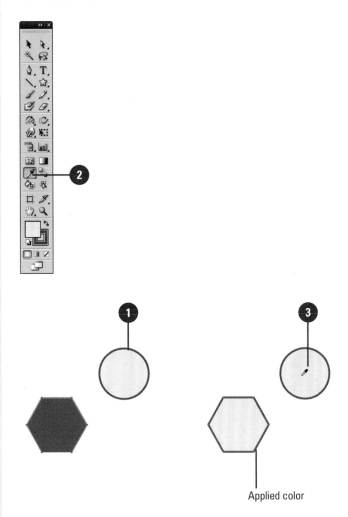

Applied color

Change Eyedropper Options

1. Double-click the **Eyedropper** tool on the Tools panel.

2. In the left column, select the check boxes for the options that you want the Eyedropper to pick up and deselect the ones you don't.

3. In the right column, select the check boxes for the options that you want the Eyedropper to apply and deselect the ones you don't.

4. Click the **Raster Sample Size** list arrow, and then select a sample size for the pick up color and attributes.

5. Click **OK**.

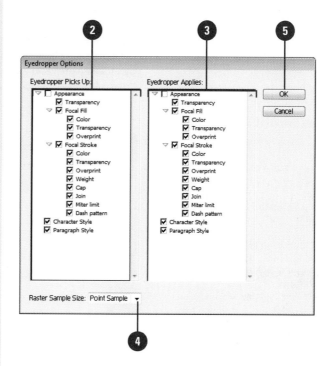

Using Patterns as Fills

IL 2.10

Instead of using solid color or gradients as object fills, you can also create and use patterns. The process is very simple. In Illustrator, create a pattern using tools—such as Rectangle, Ellipse, Polygon, Arc, Spiral, Star, or Flare—on the Tools panel, select and drag it to the Swatches panel, and then give it a name. The pattern consists of a group of objects, which you can also edit using Isolation Mode.

Create a Pattern and Apply it to an Object

1 Draw one or more objects to be used as a pattern.

2 Select the **Selection** tool on the Tools panel.

3 Select all the objects.

4 Click the **Edit** menu, and then click **Define Pattern**.

◆ You can also drag the selection to the Swatches panel, deselect the objects, and then double-click the new swatch.

5 Type a name for the swatch.

6 Click **OK**.

7 To use the pattern as a fill, select an object, select the **Swatches** panel with the pattern, click the **Fill** box on the Tools panel, and then click the pattern in the Swatches panel.

Did You Know?

You can reposition a pattern fill. To reposition the pattern fill or stroke in an object without moving the object, select the Selection tool, hold down ~ (tilde) and drag inside the object.

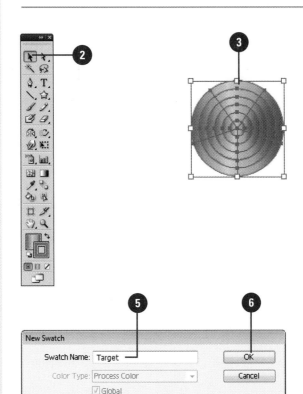

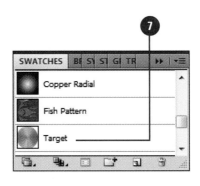

Edit a Pattern

① Select the Swatches panel with the pattern that you want to edit.

② Drag the pattern to an empty area on an artboard.

③ Double-click the object to enter Isolation Mode.

④ With the **Direct Selection** tool, edit individual objects in the pattern, and then click the gray bar to exit Isolation Mode.

⑤ Select the **Selection** tool on the Tools panel.

⑥ Alt+drag (Win) or Option+drag (Mac) the pattern object on the artboard to the original pattern in the Swatches panel to override it.

Did You Know?

You can expand a pattern into individual objects. Select the object with the pattern, click the Object menu, click Expand, select the Fill check box and/or the Stroke check box, and then click OK.

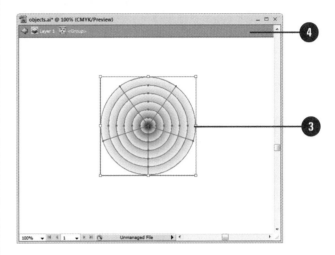

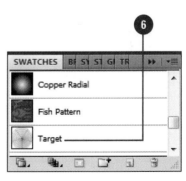

Blending Fill Colors

The Edit Color submenu allows you to blend fill colors for three or more objects. The more objects that you select, the more gradual the color blend. Stroke colors and attributes remain the same. Illustrator takes the objects on the edges (front and back, left and right, and top and bottom) as the starting and ending colors in the blend. All objects in between the starting and ending ones are intermediate blends.

Blend Fill Colors

1. Select three or more objects that contain fill colors.

   ◆ The objects cannot contain global process colors, patterns, or gradients.

2. Click the **Edit** menu, and then point to **Edit Colors**.

3. Select any of the following commands:

   ◆ **Blend Front to Back.** Uses the fill color of the front and back objects in the selection as the starting and ending colors in the blend.

   ◆ **Blend Horizontally.** Uses the fill color of the left side and right side objects as the starting and ending colors in the blend.

   ◆ **Blend Vertically.** Uses the fill color of the top and bottom objects as the starting and ending colors in the blend.

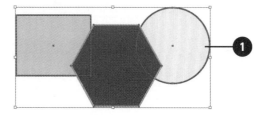

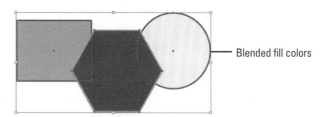

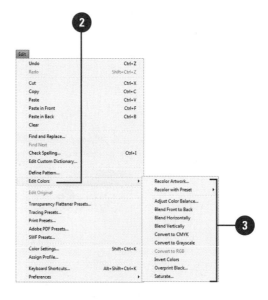

Blended fill colors

Creating Blends Automatically

If you're just getting started with blends, the Make command on the Blend submenu is an easy way to create a blend. All you need to do is select the objects that you want to use in the blend, and then choose the Make command. That's it. Illustrator creates all the transitional objects in between. If you don't like the results, you can undo the blend and try something else. If you no longer want the blend, you can release it, which removes the transitional objects and leaves the original objects and the path.

Make and Release Blend Objects

1. Select two or more objects or groups (with space in between them) that you want to blend.

2. Click the **Object** menu, point to **Blend**, and then click **Make**.

   ◆ To undo the creation of the blend objects, click the **Edit** menu, and then click **Undo**.

3. Select the blend objects.

4. To release the blend objects, click the **Object** menu, point to **Blend**, and then click **Release**.

   The transitional objects between the original objects are removed, while the original objects and path remain intact.

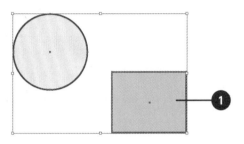

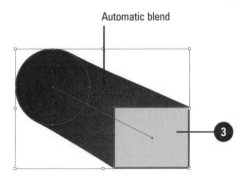

Automatic blend

Applying Blend Options

If you want a little more control over the way a blend turns out, you can specify options in the Blend Options dialog box. The settings automatically apply to any selected objects and future blends. The settings include Smooth Color, Specified Steps (number of transitional steps), Specified Distance, Align to Page, and Align to Path. The Preview option allows you to view your changes on the screen as you make them.

Change and Apply Blend Options

1. Select an existing blend object.

2. Click the **Object** menu, point to **Blend**, and then click **Blend Options**.

3. Select the **Preview** check box to view your changes.

4. Click the **Spacing** list arrow, and then select one of the following:

   - **Smooth Color.** Select to automatically create a smooth color blend based on the number of transitional steps needed.

   - **Specified Steps.** Enter the number of transitional steps (1-1000) that you want.

   - **Specified Distance.** Enter the distance (.1-1000 points) between the transition objects in the blend.

5. Select one of the following orientation buttons:

   - **Align to Page.** Click to align the blend objects perpendicular to the horizontal axes.

   - **Align to Path.** Click to align the blend objects perpendicular to the path.

6. Click **OK**.

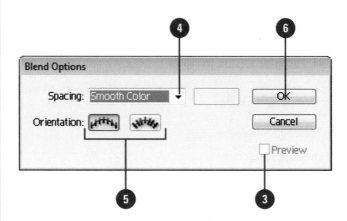

Creating Blends with the Blend Tool

IL 6.3

Create a Blend with the Blend Tool

1 Select two or more objects or groups (with space in between them) that you want to blend.

2 Select the **Blend** tool on the Tools panel.

3 Click the fill of the first object (not the center point) to let Illustrator determine an anchor point to use, or click the anchor point that you want to use.

4 Click the fill or an anchor point on the next object. If the path is open, click an endpoint.

For the best results and smoothest transitions, click anchor points on corresponding locations on the objects.

5 Continue to click corresponding anchor points on the selected objects.

6 To release the blend objects, select the blend, click the **Object** menu, point to **Blend**, and then click **Release**.

If you want to specify the locations where the blend takes place, you can use the Blend tool on the Tools panel. The Blend tool allows you to select the anchor points on the objects to determine the direction of the blend. For the best results and smoothest transitions, click anchor points on corresponding locations on the objects. If you're not sure which anchor points to use, you can also select an object's fill to let Illustrator select the anchor point for you. Experiment with it to determine what works best for you.

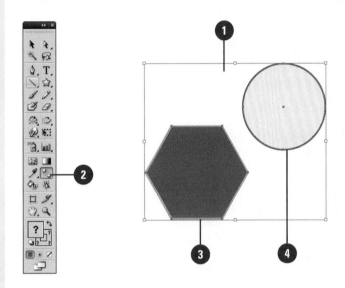

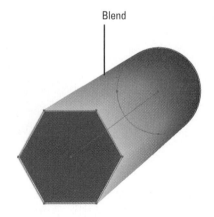

Blend

Modifying Blend Objects

IL 6.3

After you create a blend, you can use commands on the Blend submenu to reverse stacking order, reverse spine location, and replace the spine. These commands allow you to quickly change the look of the blend. If you want to modify a blend, you can change blend objects using other Illustrator features, such as recoloring, reshaping, or transforming. Experiment to determine what works best for you.

Modify Blend Objects

◆ **Reverse Stacking Order.** Changes the stacking order (front to back) without changing the x/y location. Select a blend object, click the **Object** menu, point to **Blend**, and then click **Reverse Front to Back**.

◆ **Reverse Spine.** Changes the x/y location of the blend objects without changing the stacking order. Select a blend object, click the **Object** menu, point to **Blend**, and then click **Reverse Spine**.

◆ **Replace Spine.** Replaces the current spine in a blend with a new path. Create a new path for the spine, select a blend object and the new path, click the **Object** menu, point to **Blend**, and then click **Replace Spine**.

◆ **Recolor.** Select all the objects in the blend that you want to recolor, click the **Recolor Artwork** button on the Control panel, specify the color changes you want, and then click **OK**.

◆ **Transform.** Select all the objects in the blend, and then use the object's bounding box, the **Free Transform** tool, or other transformation tools.

◆ **Reshape Path.** Move one of the original blend objects with the Direct Selection tool or use any of the reshaping path tools.

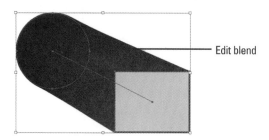
Edit blend

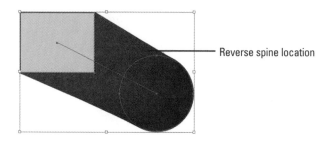
Reverse spine location

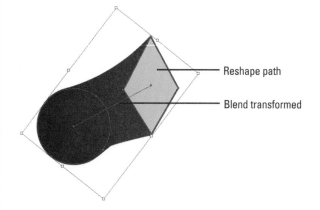
Reshape path

Blend transformed

Setting Transparency Options

 IL 3.3, 5.1

Transparency, or the opacity of an object (to what degree you can see through the object), is set in Illustrator by adjusting the Opacity option in the Transparency, Control, or Appearance panels. The Opacity option allows you to specify a percentage to set the transparency level. Along with opacity, you an also change the blending mode, which controls how object colors blend with other object colors below it. You can apply transparency options to an object, group, or layer. This includes an object's fill or stroke, and type.

Change the Opacity or Blending Mode of an Object

1. Select an object, group, or layer.

   ◆ For a layer, click the target circle on the Layers panel.

   ◆ For type, select individual characters or the entire object.

   ◆ For an object's fill or stroke, click the target circle on the Layers panel, and then click **Fill** or **Stroke** on the Appearance panel.

2. Select the **Transparency** panel.

3. To change opacity, click the **Opacity** list arrow, and then specify a percentage.

4. To change the blending mode, click the **Blending Mode** list arrow, and then select a blending mode.

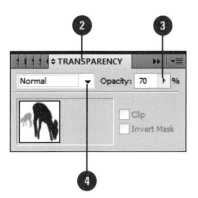

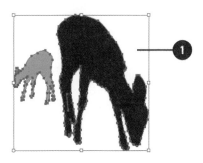

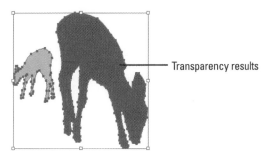

Transparency results

Controlling Transparency Effects

IL 3.3

When you apply a blending mode to a group, the blend is applied to all the objects in the group as well as all the objects below it. If you want to isolate the blend to only the objects nested in the group, you can use the Isolate Blending option in the Transparency panel. You can also use the option on individual objects with overlapping strokes and fills. If objects in a group overlap, you can use the Knockout Group option to control whether objects will show through each other (except for semi-transparent objects) or be knocked out.

Isolate a Blending Mode to Certain Objects

1. Click the target circle for a group or layer on the Layers panel that contains nested objects with a blending mode.

2. Select the **Transparency** panel.

3. Click the **Options** menu, and then click **Page Isolated Blending**.

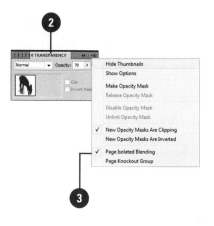

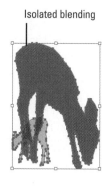

Isolated blending

Use the Knockout Group Option

1. Click the target circle for a group or layer on the Layers panel that contains nested objects.

2. Select the **Transparency** panel.

3. Click the **Options** menu, and then click **Page Knockout Group** to knock out the objects so that you can't see through them. However, you'll still see through any semi-transparent objects. Deselect this option to allow objects to be seen through each other.

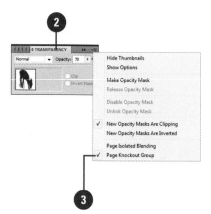

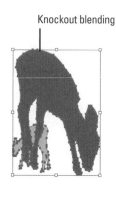

Knockout blending

Using the Transparency Grid

IL 3.3

Select Transparency Grid Preferences

1. Click the **File** menu, and then click **Document Setup**.

2. Click the **Grid Size** list arrow, and then select a size: **Small**, **Medium**, or **Large**.

3. Click the **Grid Colors** list arrow, and then select a color: **Light**, **Medium**, **Dark**, or a specific color.

4. Select the **Simulate Colored Paper** check box to simulate the use of colored paper, which blends with objects.

5. Click the **Preset** list arrow, and then select a resolution.

6. Click **OK**.

Did You Know?

You can show and hide the transparency grid. Click the view menu, and then click Show Transparency Grid or Hide Transparency Grid.

The Transparency grid makes it easier to work with semi-transparent objects. The gray and white checkerboard background allows you to distinguish between different levels of transparencies. You can quickly show or hide the transparency grid by using the Show Transparency Grid command on the View menu. Before you use the command, you can customize the look of the grid in the Document Setup dialog box.

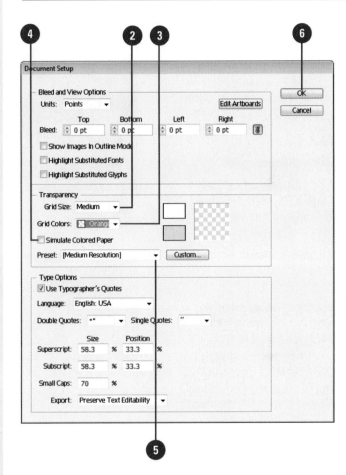

Applying Gradients

IL 3.6

A gradient is a smooth transition between two or more colors in an object. You can apply one of Illustrator's built-in gradients or create one of your own by using the Gradient panel (**New!**). The built-in gradients are available from gradient libraries. After you apply a gradient, you can change the direction or smoothness of the color transition.

Apply a Gradient Fill to an Object

1 Select an object.

◆ For type, convert it to outlines (click the Type menu, and then click Create Outlines), or select the type, and then select Add New Fill from the Appearance panel menu.

2 Select the **Swatches** panel.

3 To open a gradient library, click the **Swatch Libraries** menu, point to **Gradient**, and then select a gradient library.

4 Click a gradient swatch on the Swatches or gradient library panel.

◆ From the **Gradient** panel, you can use the Gradient Fill box list arrow (**New!**) to apply any of the gradients on the Swatches panel.

When you select a swatch from a gradient library, it's automatically added to the Swatches panel.

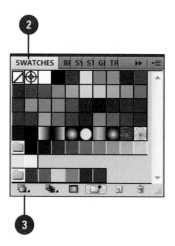

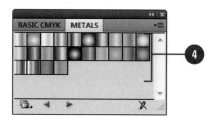

Did You Know?

You can expand a gradient fill to create an effect. Select an object with a gradient fill, click the Object menu, click Expand, click the Specify option in the Expand Gradient To area, and then enter the number of objects that you want to create. For a smooth color transition, enter a large number (100), and then click OK.

Gradient Fill box list arrow

Applied gradient

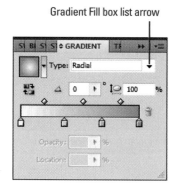

Creating Gradients

IL 3.6

Instead of using one of Illustrator's built-in gradients, you can create your own by using the Gradient panel. It's easy and you can be creative in the process. You can create a gradient with two or more colors and add transparency (**New!**). There are two types of gradients: Radial (circular) and Linear (horizontal). After you create a gradient, you need to save it in the Swatches panel in order to use it again later.

Create a Gradient Fill for an Object

1. Select an object.

2. Select the **Gradient** panel.

3. Click the **Gradient Fill** box on the Gradient panel.

4. Click the left color stop and use the Color panel to create the color you want, or Alt+click (Win) or Option+click (Mac) a color swatch on the Swatches panel.

5. Repeat the previous step for the right color stop.

6. Click the **Type** list arrow, and then select a gradient type: **Radial** or **Linear**.

7. To add color stops, click below the gradient spectrum in a blank area. To remove a color stop, drag it down and away from the gradient spectrum.

8. To adjust the amount of each color in the gradient, drag the diamond above the gradient spectrum.

9. To add transparency, select a color stop, and then specify an **Opacity** value.

10. To save the gradient, drag the Gradient Fill box from the Gradient panel to the Swatches panel.

   ◆ To save and name the gradient, click the **Gradient Fill** box on the Gradient panel, click the **New Swatch** button on the Swatches panel, enter a name, and then click **OK**.

Gradient results

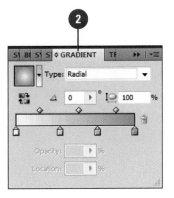

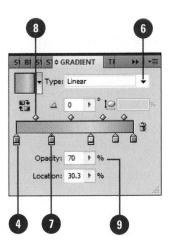

Editing Gradients

After you apply a built-in gradient or use one of your own, you can edit it. You can edit a gradient in an object and keep the gradient in the Swatches panel unchanged or you can edit the gradient in the Swatches panel and keep the gradient in an object unchanged. Editing a gradient is similar to creating one. The techniques are the same. All you need to do is select the element that you want to edit.

Edit a Gradient

1. Select an object with a gradient, or click the gradient swatch on the Swatches panel that you want to edit.

2. Select the **Gradient** panel.

3. Click the **Gradient Fill** box on the Gradient panel, or click the Gradient Fill box list arrow (**New!**), and then select one of the saved gradients (from Swatches panel).

4. To change the gradient type, click the **Type** list arrow, and then select a gradient type: **Radial** or **Linear**.

5. Do any of the following:

   ◆ **Add color stops.** Click below the gradient spectrum in a blank area.

   ◆ **Remove color stops.** Drag it down and away from the gradient spectrum.

   ◆ **Move color stops.** Drag it or enter a **Location** value (**New!**).

   ◆ **Duplicate color stops.** Alt+drag (Win) or Option+drag (Mac) a color stop.

   ◆ **Adjust color amount.** Drag the diamond above the gradient spectrum.

   ◆ **Change Transparency.** Select a color stop, and then specify an **Opacity** value (**New!**).

6. To save the gradient, Alt-drag (Win) or Option-drag (Mac) the Gradient Fill box from the Gradient panel over the old gradient on the Swatches panel.

Edited gradient

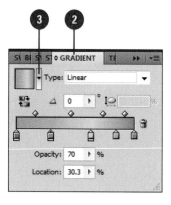

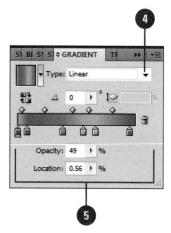

Using the Gradient Tool

 IL 3.6

The Gradient tool on the Tools panel allows you to change how a gradient appears for an object. You can change how gradient colors blend, the angle of a linear gradient, and the location of the center for a radial gradient with a drag of the mouse over the gradient fill. You can also edit gradient colors on the object (**New!**) by adding or changing color stops, applying transparency to color stops, and changing gradient direction (linear) or angle (radial).

Use the Gradient Tool to Change a Gradient

1. Select an object with a gradient that you want to change.

2. Double-click the **Gradient** tool on the Tools panel, which will bring up the Gradient panel.

3. Do any of the following:

   ◆ **Short Color Transitions.** Drag the diamond icon on the object a short distance.

   ◆ **Gradual Color Transitions.** Drag the diamond icon on the object a long distance.

   ◆ **Change Position.** Drag the larger circle on the object.

   ◆ **Reverse Color Direction.** Drag the diamond icon on the object in the opposite direction.

   ◆ **Change Radial Center.** Drag the small circle attached to the larger circle on the object.

   ◆ **Change Linear Angle.** Alt+drag (Win) or Option+drag (Mac) the diamond icon to another angle.

   ◆ **Change Color Stops.** Click below the spectrum line to add, drag to move, and drag away to remove color stops.

   ◆ **Change Transparency.** Double-click a color stop on the object, and then specify an Opacity value in the popup Gradient panel.

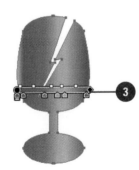

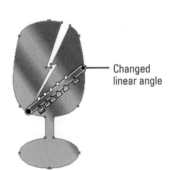

Changed linear angle

Creating a Gradient Mesh

IL 6.2

Create a Gradient Mesh

1 Select an object.

2 Do one of the following:

- ◆ **Irregular Pattern.** Select the **Mesh** tool on the Tools panel, select a fill color for mesh points, click to place the first mesh point, and then continue to click to place other mesh points.

- ◆ **Regular Pattern.** Click the **Object** menu, and then click **Create Gradient Mesh**. Set the number of rows and columns, select the highlight direction, enter a percentage of white highlight (100% = white, 0% = no white), and then click **OK**.

3 To edit a mesh object, select the **Mesh** tool on the Tools panel, and the drag to move a mesh point, Alt-click (Win) or Option-click (Mac) a mesh point to delete it, or select a color, and click to add a mesh point.

Did You Know?

You can convert a gradient to a mesh object. Select an object with a gradient fill, click the Object menu, click Expand, click the Gradient Mesh option, and then click OK.

A mesh object is a multicolored gradient type object that allows colors to flow in different directions and transitions from one point to another. A mesh object uses mesh lines (like a grid) to make it easier for you to modify color flow, transitions, and intensity. The points in the grid are called mesh points (diamonds). Mesh points are like anchor points, except you can assign color to them. The area between four mesh points is a mesh patch, which you can modify the color. You can create two types of mesh objects. One with an irregular pattern of mesh points or one with a regular pattern of mesh points.

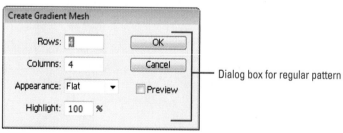

Mesh tool for irregular pattern

Dialog box for regular pattern

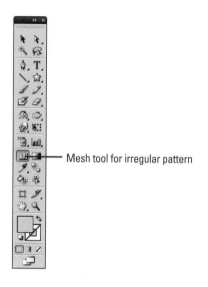

Working with Points and Paths

6

Introduction

When you use Illustrator's vector drawing, or pen tools, Illustrator creates a path to store that information. Paths are defined mathematically using anchor points and segments. Once created, they can be precisely modified to fit any design situation.

Working with the various Pen tools, it's possible to create precise paths, and even create complicated selections around virtually any shape. Once the path is created, it's a simple matter to subtract anchor points, and add new or modify existing anchor points to produce complex paths. It's even possible to convert straight segments (the visible line that connects two anchor points together) into elegantly curved segments, or you can remove the curve from a segment with a single click.

Paths can be used to precisely guide a brush stroke, or the interior of a path can be filled with any color, pattern, or gradient available in Illustrator using Stroke and Fill commands. Paths can even be used to create a clipping mask, which is an object whose shape masks out everything except the contents behind the shape.

What You'll Do

Draw with the Pen Tools

Set Anchor Point Preferences

Move Points and Segments

Convert Points

Add and Delete Anchor Points

Align and Join Anchor Points

Reshape Paths

Split and Divide Paths

Merge Paths

Work with Shape Mode

Work with Pathfinder

Create a Compound Path

Create a Clipping Set

Edit a Clipping Set

Erase to Reshape Paths

Drawing with the Pen Tools

IL 2.1

When you work with Illustrator's Pen tool, you're creating a path. The path consists of curved and straight segments connected by anchor points. When you click with the Pen tool, you create corner points and straight segments. When you drag with the Pen tool, you can create smooth points and curve segments, which have direction handles you can use to change the curved segment. The shape of the curve segment is defined by the length and direction of the direction handles. As you create drawings with the Pen tool, you can turn on Smart Guides to help you align the segments.

Draw a Polygon with the Pen Tool

1. Click the **Fill** box on the Tools panel and then click the **Color** or **None** to specify whether you want to fill the object or not.

2. Select the **Pen** tool on the Tools panel.

3. Click to create the first anchor point.

   ◆ To draw segments constrained to 45 degrees, hold down Shift while you click.

4. Click to create the second anchor point at another location.

   A line segment appears between the two anchor points.

5. Continue to add anchor points.

6. Do any of the following to complete the shape as a:

   ◆ **Open Path.** Click the Pen tool or any other tool on the Tools panel, or Ctrl+click (Win) or ⌘+click (Mac) outside the new shape to deselect it.

   ◆ **Closed Path.** Point to the starting anchor point, and then click it.

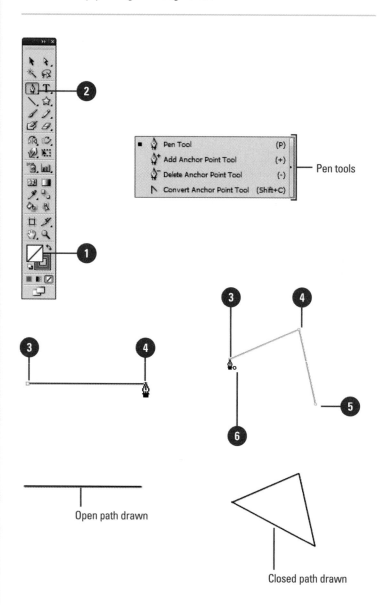

Pen tools

Open path drawn

Closed path drawn

Draw Curves with the Pen Tool

1. Click the **Fill** box on the Tools panel and then click the **Color** or **None** to specify whether you want to fill the object or not.

2. Select the **Pen** tool on the Tools panel.

3. Click and drag to create the first anchor point.

   As you drag, the direction handles move.

4. Release the mouse, and then move to where you want the second point.

5. Click and drag to create the second anchor point.

   A curve segment appears between the two anchor points. As you drag, the direction handles move, which changes the the curve segment.

   The shape of the curve segment is defined by the length and direction of the direction handles.

6. Continue to add anchor points and direction handles.

7. Do any of the following to complete the shape as a:

   ◆ **Open Path.** Click the Pen tool or any other tool on the Tools panel, or Ctrl+click (Win) or ⌘+click (Mac) outside the new shape to deselect it.

   ◆ **Closed Path.** Point to the starting anchor point, and then click it.

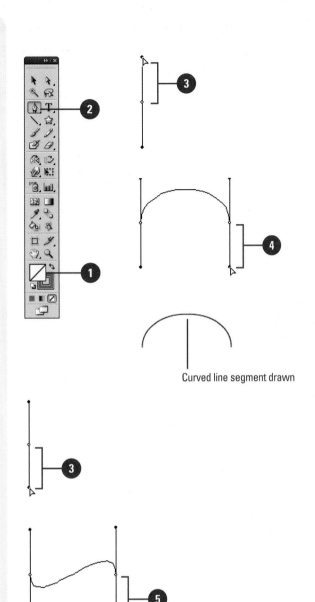

Curved line segment drawn

S-Curve drawn

Setting Anchor Point Preferences

 IL 1.4, 2.1

Illustrator's Selection & Anchor Displays preferences allow you to set selection and anchor options. The Anchor Display options allow you to determine how handles and anchors appear on the screen. As you work with anchor points, it's easier to select them when they appear highlighted on a mouse over, which you can enable in this dialog box.

Move an Anchor Point or Segment

1. Click the **Edit** (Win) or **Illustrator** (Mac) menu, and then point to **Preferences**.

2. Click **Selection & Anchor Display**.

3. Select the Anchor Point and Handle Display options you want to use:

   - **Anchors.** Specify the display of anchor points.

   - **Handles.** Specify the display of handle end points (direction points)

   - **Highlight anchors on mouse over.** Select to highlight the anchor point located directly below the mouse pointer.

   - **Show handles when multiple anchors are selected.** Select to display direction lines on all selected anchor points when you use the Direct Selection or Group Selection tool to select an object.

     Deselect to display direction lines for an anchor point when it is the only anchor point on the path or when the Bezier segment for the direction line is selected and the anchor point is not selected.

4. Click **OK**.

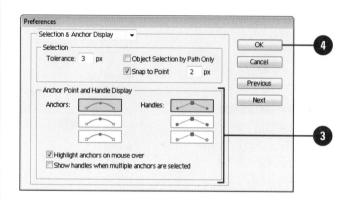

Moving Points and Segments

It's hard to draw a segment right the first time. Moving anchor points and segments is all part of the process of creating artwork. When you move an anchor point, the segments that are connected to it change. When you move a straight segment, the anchor points on the segment move with it. When you move a curve segment, the curve changes, but the connecting anchors remain the same. You can also change a curve segment by adjusting a direction point on the direction handle.

Move an Anchor Point or Segment

1. Select the **Direct Selection** tool on the Tools panel.

2. Click a blank area to deselect all points.

3. Drag an anchor point or drag the middle of a segment.

   ◆ For a smaller move, click the anchor point or segment, and then press an arrow key.

   ◆ To constrain the movement of anchor points or segments to 45 degrees, hold down Shift while dragging.

4. To reshape a curve segment, click an anchor point or a curve segment, and then drag a direction point at the end of the direction handle.

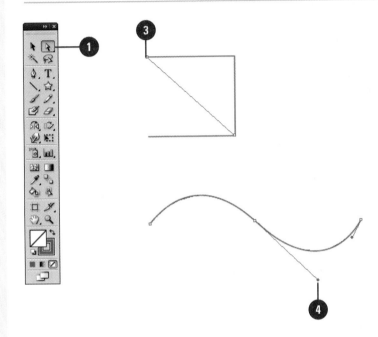

Converting Points

IL 2.1

When you create a curve with the Pen tool, the curve segment after the second anchor point appears on the opposite side as the first curve segment. If you want the second curve segment to appear on the same side as the first, you need to convert the anchor point from a smooth point to a corner point. You can make this conversion as you create the curve segment with the Pen tool or you can do it later with buttons on the Control panel or with the Convert Anchor Point tool.

Convert Points on a Path Using the Control Panel

1. Select the **Direct Selection** tool on the Tools panel.

2. Click the point that you want to convert.

3. Click one of these buttons on the Control panel:

   ◆ Convert to Smooth. Click the **Convert Selected Anchor Points to Smooth** button.

   ◆ Convert to Corner. Click the **Convert Selected Anchor Points to Corner** button.

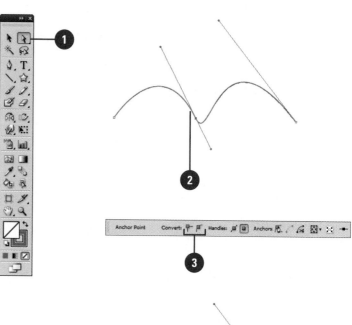

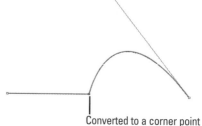

Converted to a corner point

Convert Points on a Path Using the Convert Anchor Tool

1. Select the **Convert Anchor Point** tool on the Tools panel.

   ◆ To turn the Pen tool into a temporary Convert Anchor Point tool, hold down Alt (Win) or Option (Mac).

2. To convert a **corner point to a smooth point**, drag a direction handle from a corner point.

3. To convert a **smooth point to a corner point**, click a smooth point.

   ◆ To convert a smooth point to a corner point with a nonsmooth curve, drag a smooth point so it forms a V shape.

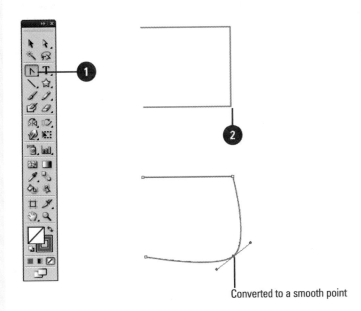

Converted to a smooth point

Adding and Deleting Anchor Points

 IL 2.1

Creating a path is not necessarily the end of the job; in fact, there are many ways you can modify a path once it's been created. For example, you can add, subtract, or delete anchor points on an existing path. You can also modify those points to conform to any desired shape. In addition, existing anchor points can be modified to change the segments connecting the points. Just like anything else in Illustrator, paths are flexible. They can be modified to meet whatever design considerations are needed to make the job successful.

Add Anchor Points

1. Select the **Direct Selection** tool on the Tools panel.

2. Select the object to which you want to add an anchor point.

3. Select the **Add Anchor Point** tool on the Tools panel.

4. Click once on the path to add a new anchor point.

   ◆ If you missed the path, click OK in response to the alert, and then try again.

   When you add an anchor point to a curve segment, a smooth point appears on the path. When you add an anchor point to a straight segment, a corner point appears.

5. Click and drag on the path to add and modify the segment.

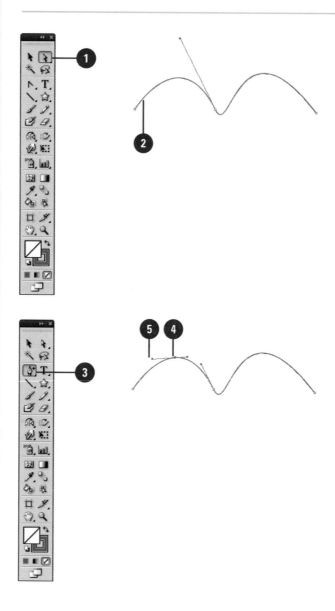

Add Anchor Points to an Open Path

1. Select the **Pen** tool on the Tools panel.

2. Point to the endpoint to which you want to add an anchor point.

   A slash appears next to the Pen pointer.

3. Click the endpoint to make it a corner point or drag it to make a smooth point.

4. Click once on the path to add a new anchor point.

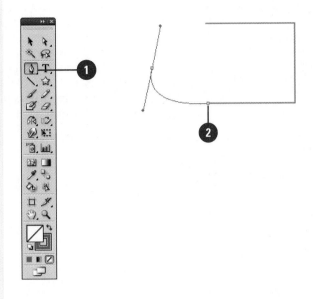

Delete Anchor Points

1. Select the **Direct Selection** tool on the Tools panel.

2. Select the object from which you want to delete an anchor point.

3. Select the **Delete Anchor Point** tool on the Tools panel.

4. Click once on an existing anchor point to remove it from the path.

   The anchor points on either side of the deleted point are now used to define the segment.

   ◆ You can also click a point with the **Direct Selection** tool, and then click the **Remove Selected Anchor Points** button on the Control panel.

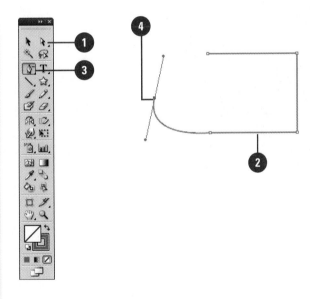

Aligning and Joining Anchor Points

In addition to aligning objects, the Align buttons on the Control panel can also align points on a path along the horizontal and vertical axis. For example, you can use the Vertical Align Center button to align two anchor points to the center point between the two original points along the vertical axis. If you have an open path with two endpoints that you want to connect, you can use the Connect Selected End Points button to connect them with a straight line. You can also join two endpoints into a single point.

Align Anchor Points

1. Select the **Lasso** tool on the Tools panel.

2. Drag to select two or more points on the path.

    ◆ If you want to select points individually, select the **Direct Selection** tool, and then Shift+click the points that you want to select.

3. Click any of the following buttons on the Control panel:

    ◆ Horizontal. Click one of the **Horizontal Align** buttons to move and align the points horizontally.

    ◆ Vertical. Click one of the **Vertical Align** buttons to move and align the points vertically.

    ◆ Overlap. Click a **Horizontal Align** button and then click a **Vertical Align** button (or vice versa) to move and align the points horizontally and vertically.

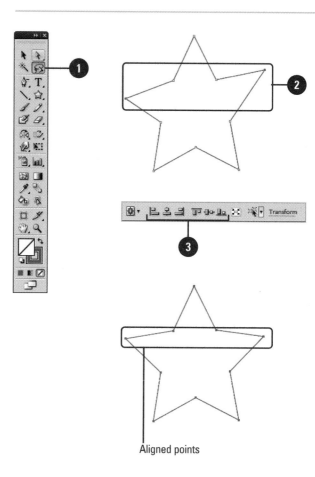

Aligned points

Join Anchor Endpoints with a Straight Line

1. Select the **Direct Selection** tool on the Tools panel.

2. Shift+click the two endpoints that you want to join.

3. Click the **Connect Selected End Points** button on the Control panel.

   A straight line segment connects the two endpoints.

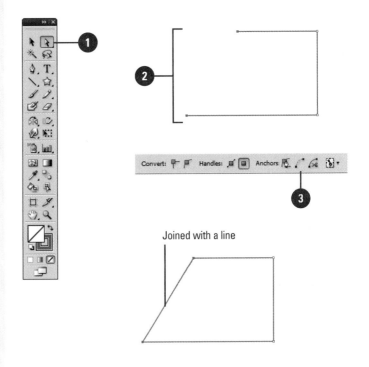

Joined with a line

Join Anchor Endpoints into a Single Point

1. Select the **Direct Selection** tool on the Tools panel.

2. Shift-click the two endpoints that you want to join.

3. Use the **Horizontal Align** and **Vertical Align** buttons on the Control panel to have the endpoints meet in the middle (one on top of the other).

4. Click the **Connect Selected End Points** button on the Control panel.

   The Join dialog box appears.

5. Click the **Corner** or **Smooth** option.

6. Click **OK**.

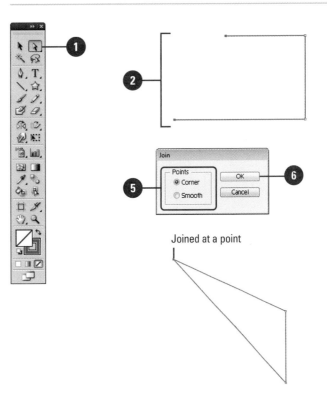

Joined at a point

Reshaping Paths

IL 2.1

The Reshape tool on the Tools panel allows you to move points and segments around to modify paths. This tool is useful for extending the side of an object path. When you select multiple points, you can extend or contract the selected point while leaving the unselected points unchanged. You can also reshape a path with the Pencil or Paintbrush tool.

Use the Reshape Tool

1. Select the **Direct Selection** tool on the Tools panel.

2. Click a blank area to deselect everything, and then click to select an anchor point on a path.

3. Select the **Reshape** tool on the Tools panel.

4. To drag multiple points at the same time, Shift+click or use a selection tool to select the ones that you want.

5. Drag any point or segment.

Did You Know?

You can change the pointer into cross hairs. Press Caps Lock to change the pointer into a Precise Cursor (cross hairs). Press Caps Lock again to change it back.

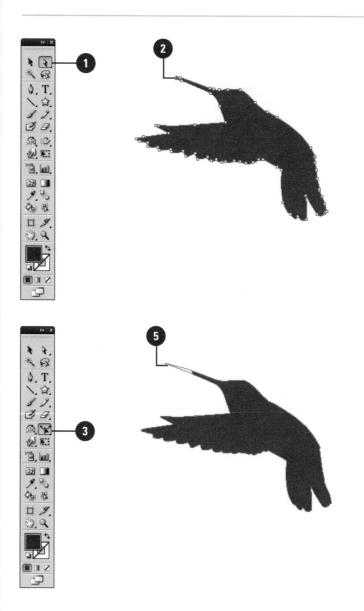

Reshape a Path with the Pencil or Paintbrush Tool

1. Select the **Pencil** tool on the Tools panel to reshape a path that doesn't have a brush stroke, or select the **Paintbrush** tool to reshape a path with a brush stroke.

2. Select the path that you want to reshape. Ctrl+click (Win) or Command+click (Mac) a path.

3. Drag the edge of the path to reshape it.

Did You Know?

You can set Paintbrush options. Double-click the Paintbrush tool on the Tools panel, set the options that you want, including Edit Selected Paths within X pixels, and then click OK.

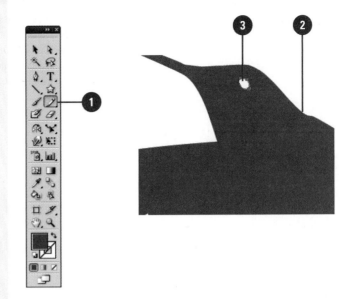

Splitting and Dividing Paths

 IL 2.1

Split a Path

1. Select the **Direct Selection** tool on the Tools panel.

2. Select the object with the path that you want to split.

3. Select the **Scissor** tool on the Tools panel.

4. Click the object's path where you want to split it.

   If you click on a closed path, it turns into an open path. If you click on an open path, it splits it into two paths.

   If you click a line segment, two endpoints appear, one on top of the other.

5. To move the endpoints, select the **Direct Selection** tool, and then drag the selected endpoint to display the endpoint below it.

Did You Know?

You can cut objects with the Knife tool. The Knife tool cuts objects along a freehand path, dividing objects into their compound filled faces. A face is an area undivided by a line segment. Select the Knife tool on the Tools panel, drag the pointer over an object with a curved path, or Alt+drag (Win) or Option+drag (Mac) the artboard with a straight path.

The Scissor tool on the Tools panel allows you to split an open path into two paths or open a closed path. You can split a path at an anchor point or in the middle of a segment. If you want to split a path at an anchor point, you can also use the Cut Path at Selected Anchor Points button on the Control panel. In addition, you can use an object shape to cut out other objects to divide them. Think of it like a cookie cutter.

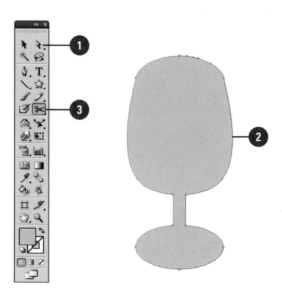

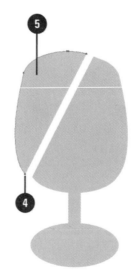

Split a Path Using the Control Panel

1. Select the **Direct Selection** tool on the Tools panel.

2. Select the object with the path, and then click the anchor point that you want to split.

3. Click the **Cut Path at Selected Anchor Point** button on the Control panel.

   A new anchor point appears on top of the selected one.

4. To move the anchor point, drag the selected point to display the other anchor point below it.

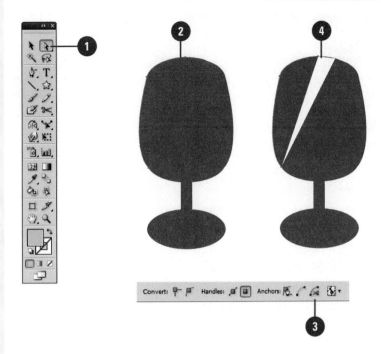

Divide a Path

1. Create or select an object (not a group) that you want to use as the cutting object.

2. Select the **Selection** tool on the Tools panel, and then move the cutting object on top of the objects that you want to divide.

3. Click the **Object** menu, point to **Path**, and then click **Divide Objects Below**.

4. Drag the edge of the path to reshape it.

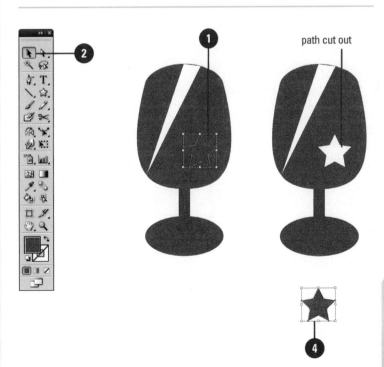

path cut out

Merging Paths

The Blob Brush tool (**New!**) on the Tools panel allows you to merge adjacent paths without strokes. When drawing with the Blob Brush tool, new paths merge with the topmost matching the path that it connects with. This works when the Blob Brush tool is set up to paint with the exact same fill and appearance settings. When you intersect the paths, the Blob Brush tool creates paths with a fill and no stroke.

Create Merged Paths with the Blob Brush Tool

1. Select the **Direct Selection** tool on the Tools panel.

2. Click a blank area to deselect everything, and then click to select an anchor point on a path.

3. Select the **Appearance** panel.

4. Click the **Options** menu, and then deselect the **New Art Has Basic Appearance**.

   When this option is deselected, the Blob Brush tool uses the attributes of the selected artwork.

5. Select the **Blob Brush** tool on the Tools panel.

   Make sure the Blob Brush is set up to have the same fill color, no stroke, and appearance settings as the artwork.

6. Draw paths that intersect with the artwork.

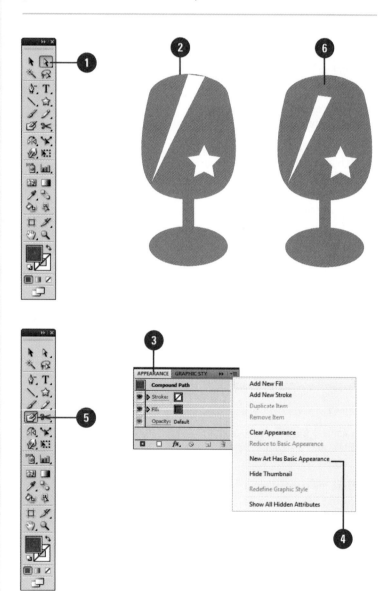

Set Blob Brush Options

1. Double-click the **Blob Brush** tool on the Tools panel.

2. Select from the following options:

   ◆ **Keep Selected.** Select to keep all paths during the merge selected.

   ◆ **Selection Limits Merge.** Select to have the Blob Brush merge only with the selected artwork.

   ◆ **Fidelity.** Specify how far (0.5 to 20 pixels) you need to move to add an anchor point.

   ◆ **Smoothness.** Specify the amount of smoothing applied to the path. The higher the percentage, the smoother the path.

   ◆ **Size.** Specify the size of the brush.

   ◆ **Angle.** Specify the angle of rotation for the brush.

   ◆ **Roundness.** Specify the roundness of the brush.

3. Click **OK**.

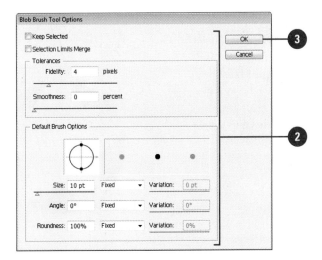

Working with Shape Mode

IL 2.6

If you have overlapping objects, you can use Shape Mode buttons on the Pathfinder panel to create compound shapes, which are editable and releasable (restoring original attributes). You can use Shape Mode buttons (Add to Shape Area, Subtract from Shape Area, Intersect Shape Area, or Exclude Overlapping Shape Areas) on almost any object, except placed or rasterized images, mesh objects, or a single group.

Apply a Shape Mode Command

1. Select two or more overlapping objects.

2. Select the **Pathfinder** panel.

3. Select from the following Shape Mode buttons:

   - **Add to Shape Area.** Use to join the outer edges of selected objects into a compound shape.

   - **Subtract from Shape Area.** Use to remove objects in front of other objects and still preserve paint attributes.

   - **Intersect Shape Area.** Use to preserve object areas that intersect.

   - **Exclude Overlapping Shape Areas.** Use to change overlapping areas to transparency.

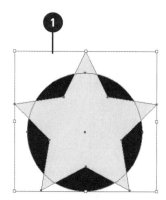

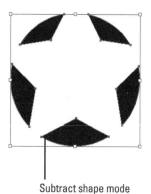

Subtract shape mode

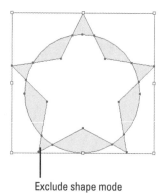

Exclude shape mode

Did You Know?

You can expand a compound shape to create a single path. Select the Selection tool on the Tools panel, select the compound shape, and then click the Expand button on the Pathfinder panel.

You can release a compound shape to restore object attributes. Select the Selection tool on the Tools panel, select the compound shape, and then click the Release Compound Shape on the Options menu on the Pathfinder panel.

Working with Pathfinder

 IL 2.6

The commands in the Pathfinder panel allow you to create a group of separate, non-overlapping closed paths or lines. You start with overlapping objects and you end up with non-overlapping ones. When you use the Pathfinder commands—Divide, Trim, Merge, Crop, Outline, and Minus Back—the original objects can't be restored. You can only undo the operation.

Apply a Pathfinder Command

1 Select two or more overlapping objects.

2 Select the **Pathfinder** panel.

3 Select from the following Shape Mode buttons:

◆ **Divide.** Use to create a separate, non-overlapping object from an overlapping area.

◆ **Trim.** Use to preserve the frontmost object and delete objects behind and overlapping.

◆ **Merge.** Use to merge adjacent or overlapping objects with the same fill attributes.

◆ **Crop.** Use to crop the frontmost object; similar to a clipping mask.

◆ **Outline.** Use to create an outline of the overlapping objects.

◆ **Minus Back.** Use to remove objects in the back, leaving only part of the frontmost object.

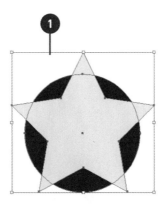

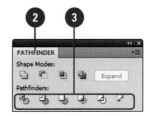

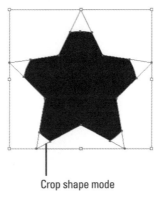

Crop shape mode

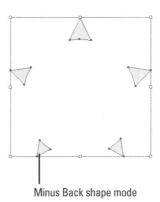

Minus Back shape mode

Did You Know?

You can convert a stroke into a filled object. Select an object with a stroke, click the Object menu, point to Path, and then click Outline Stroke.

Creating a Compound Path

IL 2.6

A compound path is a single object made up from two or more objects. In overlapping areas, a compound path removes the overlapping space displaying the attributes of the backmost object behind it. Think of it like a cookie cutter. After you create a compound path, you can release (restore) it at any time. However, the results are not exact. If you want to add another object to the compound path, you need to arrange the object in front or back of the compound object, select them, and then re-use the Make command for Compound Path.

Create a Compound Path

1. Arrange your objects so that the frontmost object will cut out to reveal the attributes of the backmost object.

2. Select all the objects that you want to include in the compound path.

3. Click the **Object** menu, point to **Compound Path**, and then click **Make**.

4. To add another object to the compound path, arrange the object in front or back of the compound object, select them, and then click the **Object** menu, point to **Compound Path**, and then click **Make**.

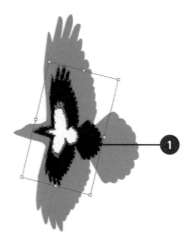

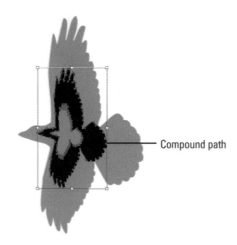

Compound path

Reverse an Object's Fill in a Compound Path

1. Click in a blank area to deselect the compound path.

2. Select the **Direct Selection** tool on the Tools panel.

3. Click the edge of the object for which you want to reverse the fill.

4. Select the **Attributes** panel.

5. Click the **Reverse Path Direction Off** button or **Reverse Path Direction On** button.

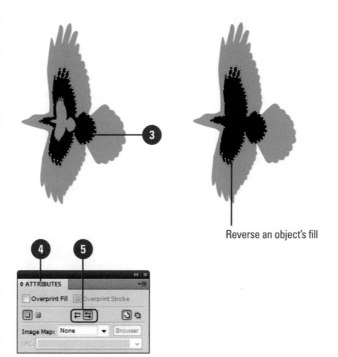

Reverse an object's fill

Release a Compound Path

1. Select the compound path.

2. Click the **Object** menu, point to **Compound Path**, and then click **Release**.

The single object reverts back to individual objects. All the objects are selected and painted with the attributes from the compound path, not their original attributes.

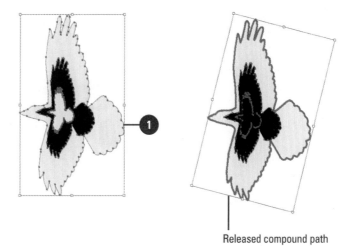

Released compound path

Creating a Clipping Set

IL 2.3, 2.5

A clipping mask, or clipping path, is an object whose shape masks out everything except the contents behind the shape. The clipping mask (vector only) and the masked objects (any artwork) are called a clipping set. You can create a clipping set from a selection of two or more objects or from all objects in a group or layer. The main thing to remember is that the clipping mask object needs to be above the object that you want to mask in the Layers panel or group. When you move or transform a masked object, Illustrator displays only the masked area (**New!**).

Create a Clipping Mask

1. Create or select the clipping mask object that you want to use as the mask.

2. Move the clipping mask object above the object that you want to mask.

3. Select the clipping mask object and the objects you want to mask.

4. Click the **Object** menu, point to **Clipping Mask**, and then click **Make**.

Clipping set

Create a Clipping Mask for a Group or Layer

1. Create or select the clipping mask object that you want to use as the mask.

2. Select the **Layers** panel.

3. Move the clipping mask object and the object that you want to mask into a layer or group.

4. Move the clipping mask object above the object that you want to mask in the Layers panel or group.

5. Select the layer or group.

6. Click the **Make/Release Clipping Mask** button in the Layers panel.

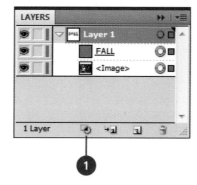

Release Objects from a Clipping Mask

1. Do one of the following to release objects:

   ◆ Select the layer that contains the clipping mask in the Layers panel, click the **Make/Release Clipping Mask** button.

   ◆ Select the group that contains the clipping mask, click the **Object** menu, point to **Clipping Mask**, and then **Release**.

Editing a Clipping Set

IL 2.3, 2.4, 2.5

After you create a clipping set, you can edit the clipping mask or the paths within the clipping set. At the same time you edit a clipping mask, you can add or remove an object from the masked artwork. You can also view and edit the mask independently of all other objects in Isolation Mode (**New!**). When you're editing a clipping set, the main thing to remember is that the clipping mask object needs to be above the object that you want to mask in the Layers panel or group.

Edit a Clipping Set

1. Do one of the following to select the clipping path or set:

    ◆ Select and target the clipping path in the Layers panel.

    ◆ Select the clipping set, click the **Object** menu, point to **Clipping Mask**, and then **Edit Mask**.

2. Do any of the following to edit the clipping mask:

    ◆ Select the **Direct Selection** tool on the Tools panel, and then drag the object's center reference point to move it.

    ◆ Select the **Direct Selection** tool on the Tools panel, and then reshape the clipping path.

    ◆ Apply a fill and stroke to a clipping path.

3. To add or remove an object from the masked artwork, drag the object into or out of the group or layer that contains the clipping path.

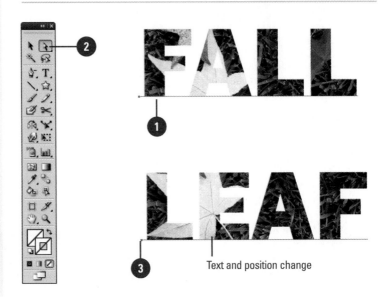

Text and position change

Edit Paths Within a Clipping Set

1. Do one of the following to select the clipping path or set:

   ◆ Select and target the clipping path in the Layers panel.

   ◆ Select the **Direct Selection** tool on the Tools panel, and then point to and click the paths outline.

2. Drag to edit the path.

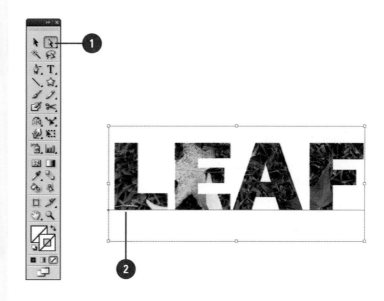

Edit the Masked Object in Isolation Mode

1. Do one of the following to edit the Masked object in Isolation Mode:

   ◆ Select the masked object, and then click the **Isolate Selected Object** button on the Control panel.

   ◆ Select the layer with the masked object in the Layers panel, click the **Layers Option** menu, and then click **Enter Isolation Mode**.

2. Edit the masked object.

3. Click the gray bar or press Esc to exit Isolation Mode.

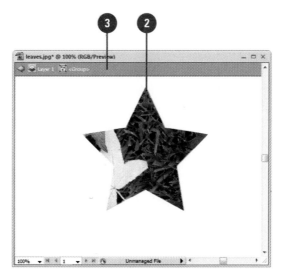

Erasing to Reshape Paths

IL 2.3

When you use the Eraser tool on the Tools panel to remove parts of an object, the remaining parts of the object path are reconnected to reshape and close the path. When you erase inside of a filled object, Illustrator creates a compound path. This is useful when you want to simplify a complex drawing or remove a background. To make it easier to erase, you can also press [or] to decrease or increase the Eraser tool diameter.

Erase Parts of Paths

1 Select the objects that you want to reshape with the Eraser tool.

2 Select the **Eraser** tool on the Tools panel.

3 Drag across the parts of the objects that you want to erase.

◆ Press [or] to decrease or increase the Eraser tool diameter.

The remaining parts of the path reconnect to close the path.

Did You Know?

You can set Eraser tool options.
Double-click the Eraser tool on the Tools panel, and then set the options that you want, including Angle, Roundness, and Diameter, and then click OK.

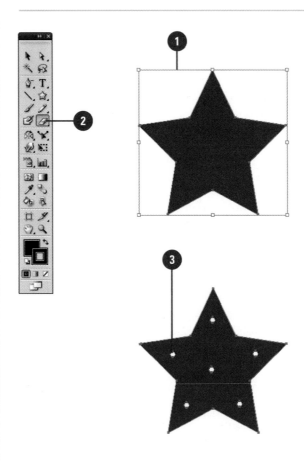

Working with Layers

7

Introduction

To be successful with Adobe Illustrator, you need to be in control. You need to control color, to control elements of the design, and you even need to control the order of design elements. If control is what you crave, then Layers, more than any other feature, helps you achieve that control. Layers give you the ability to separate individual elements of your design, and then control how those elements appear. You can think of Layers as a group of transparent sheets stacked on top of each other. Through the creative use of these electronic sheets, you can blend the elements of two or more layers, and create layers to adjust and control contrast, brightness, and color balance. You can even group layers together to help organize and manage your design.

Layers are a digital designer's canvas, and they are just as real as a stretched canvas is to a natural media designer. The strokes you apply to a real canvas, using a brush, are equivalent to strokes in an Illustrator layer when you use any of the painting tools. The natural artist may use oils or watercolor in the design while the Illustrator artist uses electronic ink. The Layers panel allows you to view the image almost as if you were actually painting or designing with natural media. However, our canvas—the Layers panel—goes far beyond anything possible in the "real" world.

In Illustrator, using multiple layers is the way to control the information within a document. There are times when you will create several layers; each layer will contain a separate aspect of the total design. Having multiple layers allows you to adjust and move each element independently. Eventually, multiple layers may no longer be necessary. However, you might not want to link them together, or even place them within the same folder. Instead, you might want to combine them into a single unit. Once again, Illustrator comes to the rescue by giving you several options for combining layers without flattening the entire document.

What You'll Do

Understand the Layers Panel

Set Layers Panel Options

Create Layers

Select Layers

Delete Layers

Select Objects with Layers

Arrange Layers and Objects

Duplicate Layers and Objects

Lock Layers and Objects

Show and Hide Layers and Objects

Merge Layers and Objects

Move Objects to a Layer

Flatten Artwork

Locate Objects in the Layers Panel

Understanding the Layers Panel

 IL 1.7, 2.8

With the Layers panel, you can control elements of an Illustrator design by assigning separate layers to each individual object. A top-level layer appears at the top of the Layers panel, which indicates the top of the stacking order. You can create layers and sublayers (nested layers) within a top-level layer. The current layer in the Layers panel appears with a black triangle in the upper right corner of the layer. The circle icon on the right is the target, which you can use to apply and edit appearances. A small square next to the target indicates an object selection. The arrowhead next to a layer thumbnail allows you to expand/collapse a layer group. To access the Layers panel, select the Layers panel or, if the Layers panel is not visible, click the Window menu, and then click Layers.

Show/Hide. Click this icon to show and hide the layer, sublayer, group, or object.

Lock/Unlock. Click this icon to lock or unlock the layer, sublayer, group, or object.

Target. Click this icon to apply or edit appearances for an object or group.

Make/Release Clipping Mask. Click the Lock Transparent Pixels, Lock Image Pixels, Lock Position, or Lock All button.

New Sublayer. Click this button to create a new sublayer in the active document.

New Layer Click this button to create a new layer in the active document.

Delete Selection. Click this button to delete the active layer.

Layers Options. Click this button to access a menu of layer-specific commands.

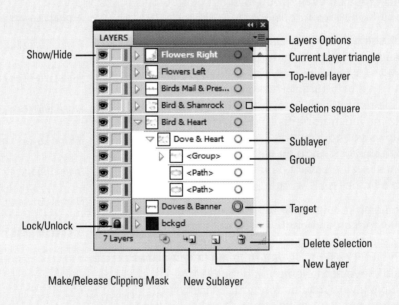

Setting Layers Panel Options

IL 1.7

Illustrator doesn't have a lot of options for controlling the Layers panel itself; in fact, there are only a few—changing the size of the layer row and showing or hiding layers by type. You can choose to view the layer row size in a small (12 pixels), medium (20 pixels), or large (32 pixels) size, or you can select a custom size. You can choose to show or hide thumbnails based on type, including Layers, Top Level Only, Groups, and Objects.

Set Layers Panel Options

1. Select the **Layers** panel.

2. Click the **Layers Options** menu, and then click **Panel Options**.

3. Deselect the **Show Layers Only** check box to show all layers. Select it to show only top-level layers and sublayers.

4. Click an option for Row Size: **Small**, **Medium**, **Large**, or **Other**, and then enter a size (12-100 pixels).

5. Select the check boxes you want for Thumbnails: **Layers**, **Top Level Only**, **Groups**, and **Objects**.

6. Click **OK**.

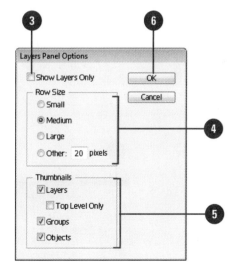

Creating Layers

 IL 1.7

Layers give you control over the design elements of your document, so Illustrator makes sure you have plenty of layers available to you. This flexibility guarantees that you have the creative options to carry your designs to any level you desire. To create a new layer, you must first have an open document. A new document in Illustrator has a single top level layer. If you have more than one document open, make sure the active image is the one to which you want to add a layer. You can quickly create a top level layer or sublayer using a button or add a layer and select options using a dialog box. When you create a new vector object, you also create a sublayer with the name <Path>. Each object that you create or place appears as a new sublayer in the Layers panel.

Create a New Top Level Layer

1. Select the **Layers** panel.

2. Click the top level layer that you want the new layer to appear above.

3. Click the **New Layer** button on the Layers panel.

   A new top level layer appears with the name Layer and the next number in order.

4. To rename the layer, double-click the layer, enter a name, and then click **OK**.

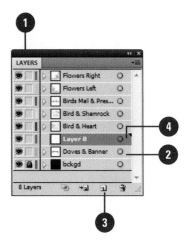

Create a Sublayer

1. Select the **Layers** panel.

2. Click the top level layer or sublayer that you want the new sublayer to appear within.

3. Click the **New Sublayer** button on the Layers panel.

   A new sublayer appears with the name Layer and the next number in order.

4. To rename the layer, double-click the layer, enter a name, and then click **OK**.

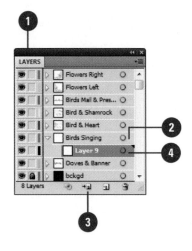

Create a New Top Level Layer or Sublayer with Options

1. Select the **Layers** panel.

2. Click the top level layer that you want the new layer to appear above, or sublayer that you want the new sublayer to appear within.

3. Alt+click (Win) or Option+click (Mac) the **New Layer** or **New Sublayer** button on the Layers panel.

   The Layer Options dialog box appears.

4. Enter a name for the layer or sublayer.

5. Click the **Color** list arrow, and then select a color.

6. Select the check boxes that you want to apply to the layer or sublayer:

   ◆ **Template.** Select to make a template layer uneditable.

   ◆ **Show.** Select to show the layer in the Layers panel.

   ◆ **Preview.** Select to view the layer in Preview view.

   ◆ **Lock.** Select to lock the layer.

   ◆ **Print.** Select to enable printing for the layer. Nonprintable layers appear in italics in the Layers panel.

   ◆ **Dim Images to 50%.** Select to gray out images by the specified percentage.

7. Click **OK**.

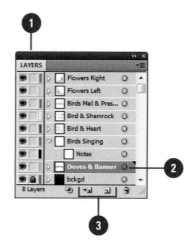

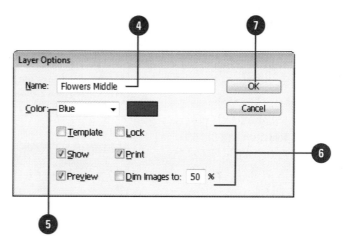

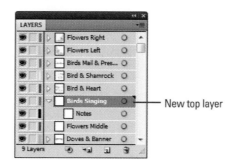

New top layer

Selecting Layers

 IL 1.7

Before you can create a new layer or work on an existing layer, you need to select it first. Simply click the layer name in the Layers panel. A single selected layer appears with the black triangle in the corner and is called the **current layer**. In some cases, such as moving, deleting, or restacking layers, you want to select multiple layers. You can select multiple sublayers or objects at the same nesting level within the same top-level layer. However, you can't select multiple sublayers or objects on different top-level layers.

Select Layers

1. Open a multi-layered document, and then select the **Layers** panel.

2. To select a single layer, click the name in the Layers panel.

3. To select multiple layers in the Layers panel use the following options:

   ◆ **Contiguous Layers.** Click on the first layer, and then Shift+click the last layer to select first, last, and all layers in-between.

   ◆ **Non-Contiguous Layers.** Click on a layer, hold down the Ctrl (Win) or ⌘ (Mac) key, and then click on another layer.

4. To deselect layers in the Layers panel use the following options:

   ◆ **Deselect Individual.** Hold down the Ctrl (Win) or ⌘ (Mac) key, and then click on a layer for a multiple selection.

   ◆ **Deselect All.** Click the **Select** menu, and then click **Deselect Layers**.

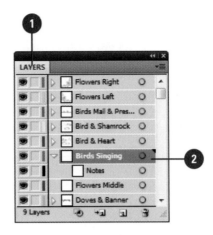

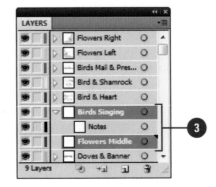

Deleting Layers

IL 1.7

While Illustrator lets you add a lot of layers to a document, it also lets you delete layers. Remember that once you've deleted a layer and saved the document, there is no way to recover the deleted layer. However, while the document is open, you can use the Undo command to recover a deleted layer.

Delete Layers

1. Select the **Layers** panel.

2. Select the layers that you want to delete.

   ◆ Hold down the Ctrl (Win) or ⌘ (Mac) key, and then click to select multiple items.

3. Click the **Delete Layer** button.

4. If prompted, click **Yes** to delete any objects on the layer or sublayer.

Did You Know?

You can delete layers without the prompt. Select the layers that you want to delete, and then drag them onto the Delete Layer button.

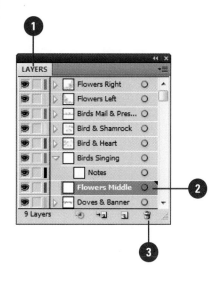

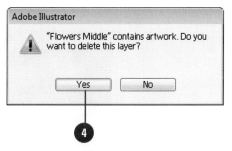

Layer deleted

Selecting Objects with Layers

IL 1.7

In an earlier chapter you learned how to select objects using selection tools on the Tools panel and the Select menu. You can also select objects using the Layers panel. When you click the Selection area to the right of the target circle for a specific layer, all the paths, groups, and objects on the layer become selected. A selection square appears next to that target circle. In addition, the target circle for each path and group becomes selected and ready for editing.

Select and Deselect Objects in a Layer

1. Select the **Layers** panel.

2. To select objects in a layer use the following options:

   ◆ **Top-level.** Click the Selection area for the top-level layer.

   A selection square appears for each sublayer, group, and object on all the layers within it.

   ◆ **Individual Layers.** Expand the top-level layer, and then click the Selection area for the layer that you want to select.

3. To deselect objects in the Layers panel use the following options:

   ◆ **Top-level.** Shift+click the Selection square for the top-level layer.

   ◆ **Individual All.** Expand the top-level layer, and then Shift+click the Selection square.

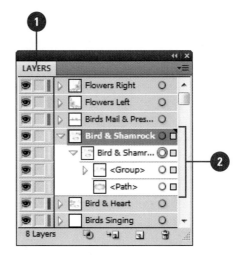

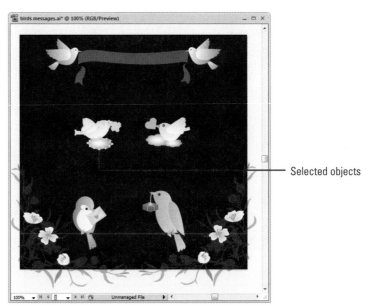

Selected objects

Select Multiple Objects on Different Layers

1. Select the **Layers** panel.

2. Expand the layers with the objects that you want to select in the Layers panel.

3. Click the selection area or target circle for the first object.

4. Shift+click the other individual group or object layers that you want to include in the selection.

   The layers don't need to be adjacent to each other. They can be anywhere in the Layers panel.

5. To deselect a group or object layer, Shift+click the Selection square for the layer.

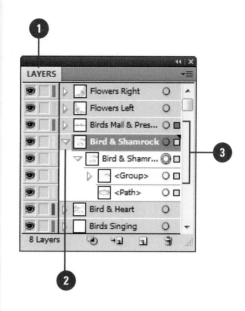

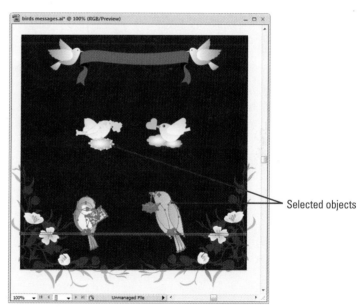

Selected objects

Arranging Layers and Objects

IL 1.7, 2.8

The layers in the Layers panel appear from top to bottom as they appear in the document window. The first layer (top-level layer) at the top of the Layers panel is the topmost layer in the document window. The last layer in the Layers panel is the bottommost layer in the document window. You can change the stacking order of the layers in the Layers panel. When you change the order in the Layers panel, the objects in the document window change too.

Arrange Layers and Objects in the Layers Panel

1. Select the **Layers** panel.

2. Select the layers that you want to move.

3. Drag the selected layers up or down the list in the Layers panel.

   As you drag, the pointer changes to a hand and double black lines or a large black arrow appears.

   The double black lines indicate the new location of the layers within the same indent level when you release the mouse.

   The large black arrow indicates the new location of the layers in a different indent level when you release the mouse.

4. Release the mouse at the location where you want to move the layers.

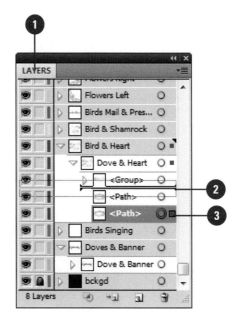

Arrange Objects and Layers Using an Arrange Command

1. Select the **Layers** panel.

2. Select the layers that you want to move.

3. Click the **Object** menu, and then point to **Arrange**.

4. Click one of the following commands:

   ◆ **Send to Current Layer.** Moves the selected layers to the current layer.

   ◆ **Bring to Front.** Moves the selected layers up to the top level.

   ◆ **Bring Forward.** Moves the selected layers up a level.

   ◆ **Send Backward.** Moves the selected layers down a level.

   ◆ **Send to Back.** Moves the selected layers down to the last level.

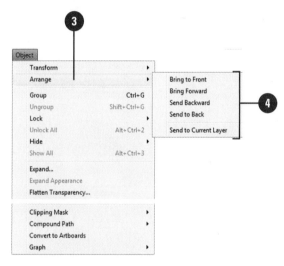

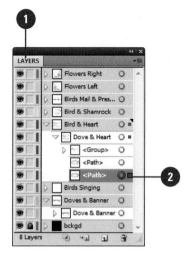

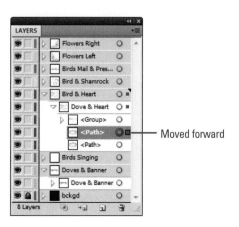

Moved forward

Duplicating Layers and Objects

 IL 1.7

There are times when you will need a copy of a Photoshop layer. Duplicating a layer is a simple process that creates a pixel-to-pixel copy of the selected layer. Once the copied layer is created, it becomes a separate image within the document. You can then begin to make changes to the new layer. Duplicating a layer gives you the ability to control each layer separately and to apply nondestructive effects to your image by making them on a copy of the image instead of the original.

Duplicate Objects and Layers in the Layers Panel

1. Select the **Layers** panel.

2. Select the layers that you want to duplicate.

   ◆ Hold down the Ctrl (Win) or ⌘ (Mac) key, and then click to select multiple items.

3. Click the **Layers Options** menu, and then click **Duplicate "Layer Name."**

Did You Know?

You can duplicate a layer with the New Layer button. Drag the layer over the New Layer button and Illustrator creates an exact copy of the layer and appends the word *copy* at the end of the original layer name.

You can duplicate a layer by dragging a Selection square. Alt+drag (Win) or Option+drag (Mac) the Selection square up or down in the Layers panel to the location where you want to place the duplicate layers.

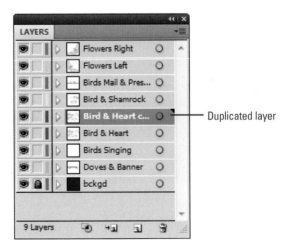

Duplicated layer

Locking Layers and Objects

IL 1.7

When you don't want an object to be moved or modified, you can lock it in the Layers panel. When you lock a layer, the objects remain visible in the document window. When you click the edit (second) column in the Layers, a padlock icon appears indicating the layer is locked. When you lock a layer, all the objects on the layer are locked. To unlock a layer, you simply click the padlock icon to remove it. You can lock/unlock individual layers, multiple layers, and top-level layers.

Lock and Unlock Objects and Layers in the Layers Panel

1. Select the **Layers** panel.

2. Use any of the following:

   ◆ **Lock/Unlock Individual.** Click the edit (second) column for each layer that you want to lock or unlock.

   ◆ **Lock/Unlock Multiple.** Click and drag the edit (second) column.

   ◆ **Lock/Unlock Top-Level.** Click the edit (second) column for the top-level layer.

   All the layers in the top-level are locked/unlocked.

   ◆ **Lock/Unlock Except One.** Alt+click (Win) or Option+click (Mac) the edit (second) column for a top-level layer to lock/unlock all the other top-level layers except the one you clicked.

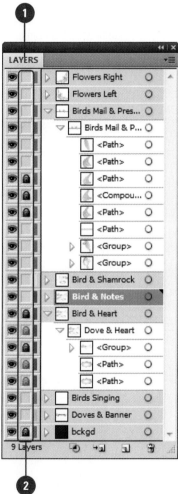

Showing and Hiding Layers and Objects

IL 1.7

When you have a lot of objects in the document window, it can be hard to work with them. In the Layers panel, you hide layers and objects to reduce the clutter and make it easier to work with the layers and objects that you want. When you click the visibility (first) column in the Layers, an eye icon appears indicating the layer is visible. To hide a layer, you simply click the eye icon to remove it. When you hide a top-level layer, all the objects within it are also hidden. The eye icons appear dimmed. You need to make the top-level layer visible to show all the objects within it. Hidden objects don't print and don't appear in the document window in either Preview or Outline views. When you save, close, and reopen your document, any hidden objects remain hidden until you show them.

Show and Hide Objects and Layers in the Layers Panel

1. Select the **Layers** panel.

2. Use any of the following:

   - **Show/Hide Individual.** Click the visibility (first) column for each layer that you want to show or hide.

   - **Show/Hide Multiple.** Click and drag the visibility (first) column.

   - **Show/Hide Top-Level.** Click the visibility (first) column for the top-level layer.

     All the layers in the top-level are shown/hidden.

   - **Show/Hide Except One.** Alt+click (Win) or Option+click (Mac) the visibility (first) column for a top-level layer to show/hide all the other top-level layers except the one you clicked.

Birds hidden

178

Merging Layers and Groups

 IL 1.7

If you have objects on multiple layers and want to consolidate them onto one layer, you can merge them together. You can merge two or more groups, or a combination of groups and sublayers (if they are both in the same top-level layer). However, you can't merge an object with another object. If a layer is locked or hidden, you can still use them in a merge. Before you use the Merge Selected command, it's a good idea to make a copy of your document as a backup to preserve a copy of the separate layers.

Merge Layers and Groups in the Layers Panel

1. Select the **Layers** panel.

2. Select two or more layers, sublayers, or groups that you want to merge.

   ◆ Hold down the Ctrl (Win) or ⌘ (Mac) key, and then click to select multiple items.

3. Click the last layer into which you want to merge the selected layers.

4. Click the **Layers Options** menu, and then click **Merge Selected**.

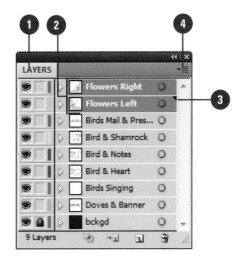

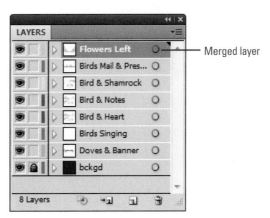

Merged layer

Moving Objects to a Layer

IL 1.7

With the Collect in New Layer command, you can move all the selected layers in the Layer panel into a new layer. You can select top-level layers, sublayers, groups, or objects. With the Release to Layers (Sequence) command, you can move objects or groups that are nested within a top-level layer into separate layers within the same layer. If you want to build an animation, you can use the Release to Layers (Build) command to create a sequence of objects that you can use to create the animation in a program such as Adobe Flash.

Move Objects to a New Layer

1 Select the **Layers** panel.

2 Select the layers that you want to move. The layers must all have the same indent level.

◆ Hold down the Ctrl (Win) or ⌘ (Mac) key, and then click to select multiple items.

3 Click the **Layers Options** menu, and then click **Collect in New Layer**.

Sublayers, groups, or objects are nested in a new sublayer within the same top-level layer.

4 To rename the layer, double-click the layer, enter a name, and then click **OK**.

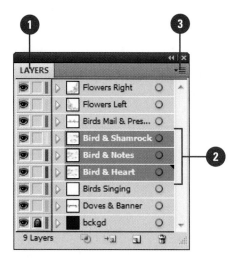

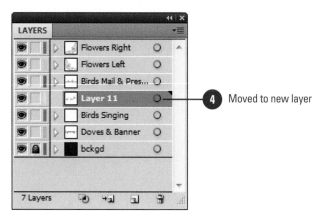

Moved to new layer

Release Objects to New Layers

1. Select the **Layers** panel.

2. Select the top-level layer, sublayer, or group (not an object layer) that you want to use.

3. Click the **Layers Options** menu, and then click **Release to Layers (Sequence)**.

   Sublayers, groups, or objects are nested in a new sublayer within the same top-level layer.

4. To rename the layer, double-click the layer, enter a name, and then click **OK**.

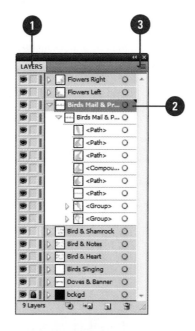

Did You Know?

You can create objects for animation. Select the Layers panel, select the top-level layer, sublayer, or group (not an object layer) that you want to use, click the Layers Options menu, and then click Release to Layers (Build).

After you separate your layers, you can use the Export command on the File menu to export your document layers to a Flash SWF file.

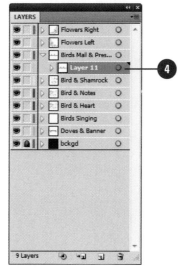

Released to new layer

See Also

See "Export as a Flash Movie" on page 354 for more information on exporting an Illustrator document as a Flash SWF file.

Flattening Layers

IL 1.7

The Flatten Artwork command allows you to flatten an entire document into one top-level layer with sublayers and groups nested within it. After you use the Flatten Artwork command, all objects remain editable and any appearances on layers are applied to all the objects in your document.

Flatten Layers in the Layers Panel

1. Select the **Layers** panel.

2. Select the top-level layer or a layer within it that you want to use as a new main layer for the document.

3. Click the **Layers Options** menu, and then click **Flatten Artwork**.

    If any of the layers are hidden, an alert appears, asking if you want to discard the hidden layers.

4. If prompted, click **Yes** to discard the hidden layers, or click **No** to preserve them.

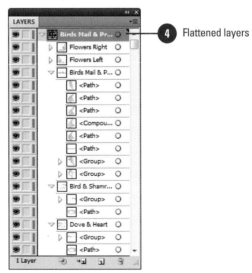

Flattened layers

Locating Objects in the Layers Panel

When the Layers panel contains a lot of layers, groups, and objects, it can be hard to find the one you want to work on, especially if the object is in a collapsed layer. All you need to do is select the object that you want to find in the Layers panel, and then choose the Locate Object command.

Locate an Object in the Layers Panel

1 Select the object that you want to find in the document window.

2 Select the **Layers** panel.

3 Click the **Layers Options** menu, and then click **Locate Object**.

This command changes to Locate Layer if the Show Layers Only panel option is selected.

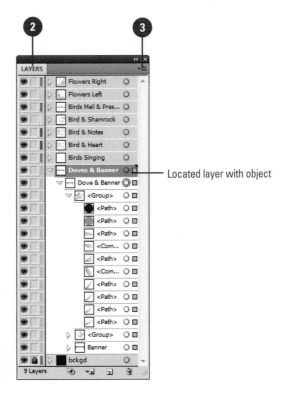

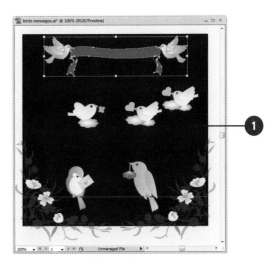

Located layer with object

Working with Type

8

Introduction

Illustrator comes with 6 different type tools: Type, Area Type, Type on a Path, Vertical Type, Vertical Area Type, and Vertical Type on a Path. Three of the tools are used for horizontal type and the other three are used for vertical type. The functionality between the two types is the same; only the direction of the type differs.

Before you can work with type in Illustrator, you need to select it. You can select the entire type object or the characters in the type object. The Selection tool allows you to select both characters and its object, while the Direct Selection tool allows you to select just the characters in the type object or both characters and its object. You can also use the type tools to select only the characters in the type object, not the object itself. If you type, paste, or import more text than a type object can hold, an overflow symbol (a tiny red plus sign in a square) appears on the edge of the type object. You can reshape the type object to display the text or create a thread (link) to another type object. You can thread overflow text from one type object to a new or existing type object.

Illustrator provides two panels to modify characters and paragraphs. With the Character panel, you can change the font family (Arial or Times New Roman) and style (Italic, Bold, or Condensed), as well as change other type attributes, such as size, kerning, scale, tracking, leading, and language. With the Paragraphs panel, you can change type alignment, indenting, and before and after spacing.

When integrating artwork and graphics with your type, you can wrap the text in a type object around another object, such as a graphic. Another type effect, Create Outlines, allows you to convert characters in a type object into a separate object with a path, which you can use as a mask object.

What You'll Do

Use Type Tools

Create Type

Create Area and Path Type

Modify Type on a Path

Import Text

Select Type

Copy or Move Type

Work with Overflow Type

Change Fonts and Font Size

Lead, Kern, and Track Type

Scale and Rotate Type

Align Paragraphs

Indent and Space Paragraphs

Set Tabs

Work with Hyphenation

Work with Type Styles

Use Smart Punctuation

Work with Glyphs

Wrap Type Around an Object

Create Type Outlines

Using Type Tools

 IL 4.1

Use Type Tools

1. Click the Type tool slot on the Tools panel.

   - Click the arrow on the right of the Type tools menu to create a detachable panel.

2. Click one of the following Type tools:

   - **Type.** Creates type that is not associated with a path. You can use it to enter type along the edge of an open path or inside a closed path.

   - **Area Type.** Creates type inside an open or closed path.

   - **Type on a Path.** Creates type along the outer edge of an open or closed path.

   - **Vertical Type.** Creates vertical text and works like the Type tool.

   - **Vertical Area Type.** Creates vertical type inside an open or closed path.

   - **Vertical Type on a Path.** Creates vertical type along the outer edge of an open or closed path.

3. Click a blank area of the artboard, and then type some text.

   - For some Type tools, you can also draw a text box to create the size you want.

Illustrator comes with 6 different type tools: Type, Area Type, Type on a Path, Vertical Type, Vertical Area Type, and Vertical Type on a Path. Three of the tools are used for horizontal type and the other three are used for vertical type. The functionality between the two types is the same; only the direction of the type differs.

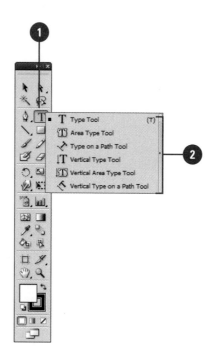

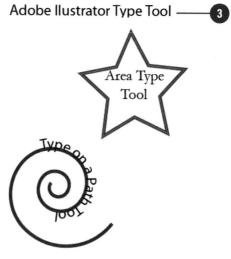

Creating Type

IL 4.1

Illustrator comes with 6 different type tools: Type, Area Type, Type on a Path, Vertical Type, Vertical Area Type, and Vertical Type on a Path. Three of the tools are used for horizontal type and the other three are used for vertical type. The functionality between the two types is the same; only the direction of the type differs. The Type and Type Vertical tools create type known as **point type**, that is not associated with a path. However, you can also use these tools to enter type along the edge of an open path or inside a closed path.

Create Type

1 Select the **Type** or **Vertical Type** tool on the Tools panel.

◆ Click the arrow on the right of the Type tools menu to create a detachable panel.

2 Click a blank area of the artboard to create a type object.

A flashing insertion point appears in the type object.

3 Type some text. Press Enter (Win) or Return (Mac) to start a new line.

◆ To keep the type tool selected so you can create more type objects, hold down Ctrl (Win) or ⌘ (Mac), click outside the current type object, release the key, and then type more text.

4 Select a selection tool or select the type tool again.

Did You Know?

You can create vertical type with the regular Type tool and horizontal type with the Vertical Type tool. Select the type tool you want, hold down the Shift key, click or drag a rectangle, and then type some text.

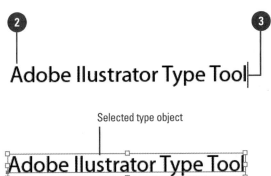

Adobe Ilustrator Type Tool

Selected type object

Adobe Ilustrator Type Tool

Creating Type in a Text Box

Adobe Certified Expert   IL 4.1

With the Type and Vertical Type tools, you can create a rectangle text box any size that you want. When you type text in the type object, it automatically wraps to the size of the box. If you type more text than the box can hold, an overflow symbol (a tiny red plus sign in a square) appears on the edge of the rectangle box. You can reshape the type object to display the text or create a thread (link) to another type object.

Create Type in a Text Box

1. Select the **Type** or **Vertical Type** tool on the Tools panels.

   ◆ Click the arrow on the right of the Type tools menu to create a detachable panel.

2. Drag to create a rectangle text box the size that you want.

   A flashing insertion point appears in the type object.

3. Type some text. The text automatically wraps to the shape of the type object. Press Enter (Win) or Return (Mac) to start a new line.

   ◆ To keep the type tool selected so you can create more type objects, hold down Ctrl (Win) or ⌘ (Mac), click outside the current type object, release the key, and then type more text.

   ◆ If the overflow symbol appears, deselect the type object, select the **Direct Selection** tool on the Tools panel, and then drag a corner to reshape the type object.

4. Select a selection tool or select the type tool again.

Selected type object

Creating Area Type

IL 4.1

With the Area Type and Vertical Area Type Vertical tools, you can add type inside the path of any object or inside an open path. When you add type with these type tools, the object is converted to a type object. So, if you want to preserve the original object, you need to make a copy of it before you add type.

Create Area Type Inside an Object

1. Select the **Area Type** or **Vertical Area Type** tool on the Tools panels.

   ◆ Click the arrow on the right of the Type tools menu to create a detachable panel (optional).

   ◆ If you want to add type to a closed path, you can also use the Type or Vertical Type tools.

2. Click on the edge of the path (closed or open) to which you want to add type.

   A flashing insertion point appears in the type object. Any fill or stroke on the object is removed.

3. Type some text. The text automatically wraps to the shape of the type object. Press Enter (Win) or Return (Mac) to start a new line.

   The type appears inside the object and conforms to its shape.

   ◆ To keep the type tool selected so you can create more type objects, hold down Ctrl (Win) or ⌘ (Mac), click outside the current type object, release the key, and then type more text.

   ◆ If the overflow symbol appears, deselect the type object, select the **Direct Selection** tool on the Tools panel, and then drag a corner to reshape the type object.

4. Select a selection tool or select the type tool again.

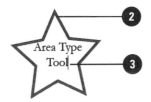

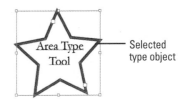

Selected type object

For Your Information

Setting Area Type Options

The Area Type Options dialog box allows you to change the width and height of the type object, add rows and columns, specify text flow in the rows and columns, change the inset spacing between area type and the edge of its type object, and adjust the first line of the type object. Select an area type object, click the Type menu, click Area Type Options, specify the options that you want, and then click OK.

Creating Path Type

IL 4.1

With the Type on a Path and Vertical Type on a Path tools, you can add type along the inner or outer edge of a path. You can place the text on either side of the path, but not on both. If you initially place it on the inner part of the path, you can always move it to the outer part of the path later.

Create Type on a Path

1. Select the **Type on a Path** or **Vertical Type on a Path** tool on the Tools panel.

   ◆ Click the arrow on the right of the Type tools menu to create a detachable panel (optional).

   ◆ If you want to add type to an open path, you can also use the Type or Vertical Type tools.

2. Click on the edge of the path (closed or open) to which you want to add type.

   A flashing insertion point appears in the type object. Any fill or stroke on the object is removed.

3. Type some text. The text automatically wraps to the shape of the type object. Don't press Enter (Win) or Return (Mac).

   The type appears along the edge of the object, conforms to its shape, and removes the fill and stroke.

   ◆ To keep the type tool selected so you can create more type objects, hold down Ctrl (Win) or ⌘ (Mac), click outside the current type object, release the key, and then type more text.

   ◆ If the overflow symbol appears, deselect the type object, select the **Direct Selection** tool on the Tools panel, and then drag a corner to reshape the type object.

4. Select a selection tool or select the type tool again.

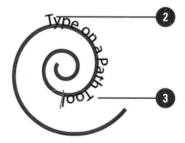

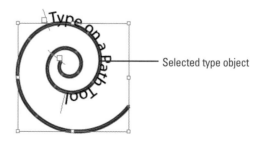

Selected type object

190

Move Type on a Path

1. Select the **Selection** tool or **Direct Selection** tool on the Tools panel.

2. Click on the type.

   Center, left, and right brackets appear around the type.

3. Drag the bracket (not the square) to adjust the position of the type on a path.

   - **Swap Sides.** Drag the Center bracket to the other side to change the inner/outer position of the type along the path.

   - **Left.** Drag to position the left side (or starting point) of the type along the path.

   - **Center.** Drag left or right to position the type along the path.

   - **Right.** Drag to position the right side (or ending point) of the type along the path.

     If the overflow symbol appears, deselect the type object, select the **Direct Selection** tool on the Tools panel, and then drag a corner to reshape the type object.

4. Select a selection tool or select the type tool again.

Did You Know?

You can change type case. To help you format sentences correctly and change capitalization, you can change text case. Select the type that you want to change, click the Type menu, point to Change Case, and then click UPPERCASE, lowercase, Title Case, or Sentence case.

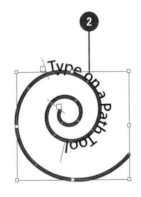

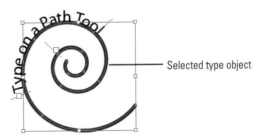

Selected type object

Modifying Type on a Path

After you create type on a path, you can change the alignment, shape, and orientation of the type with the Type on a Path dialog box. You can apply type effects, which include Rainbow, Skew, 3D Ribbon, Stair Step, or Gravity, as well as change alignment and spacing. You can even flip the type on the path. Experiment with the effects and alignment options to create some unique type.

Modify Type on a Path

1 Select the **Selection** tool or **Direct Selection** tool on the Tools panel.

2 Click on the type along the path.

Center, left, and right brackets appear around the type.

3 Click the **Type** menu, point to **Type on a Path**, and then click **Type on a Path Options**.

4 Select the **Preview** check box to view your changes in the document window.

5 Click the **Effect** list arrow, and then select an effect: **Rainbow**, **Skew**, **3D Ribbon**, **Stair Step**, or **Gravity**.

6 Click the **Align to Path** list arrow, and then select an alignment option: **Baseline**, **Ascender**, **Descender**, or **Center**.

7 Specify a spacing value (-36 to 36). The default is Auto.

8 Select or deselect the **Flip** check box to position the type.

9 Click **OK**.

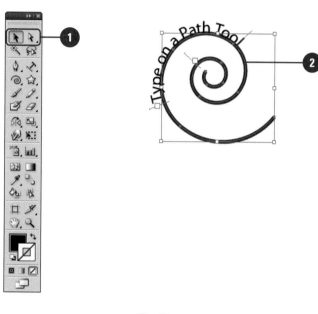

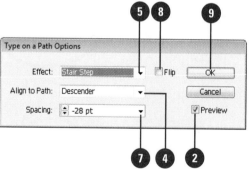

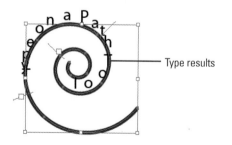

Type results

Importing Text

If you have text in a document that you want to use in your artwork, you can use the Place command to import it into your document. You can import text from the following text formats: plain text (TXT), Rich Text Format (RTF), or Microsoft Word (DOC or DOCX). When you import text using the Place command, Illustrator creates a new type object and places the text in it.

Import Text

1. Click the **File** menu, and then click **Place**.

2. Click the **Files of Type** (Win) or **Enable** (Mac) list arrow, and then click **All Formats** or select a text format:

   - **Text (TXT).** Plain text.

   - **Microsoft Word (DOC).** Microsoft Word 2003 or earlier.

   - **Microsoft Word (DOCX).** Microsoft Word 2007 or later.

   - **Microsoft RTF (RTF).** Rich Text Format.

3. Navigate to the drive or folder location with the text file you want to import.

4. Click the text file you want to place.

5. Click **Place**.

   For some imported files, a dialog box appears, asking for placement options.

6. Select the options you want.

7. Click **OK**.

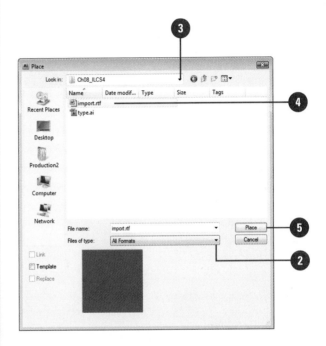

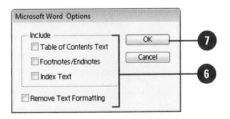

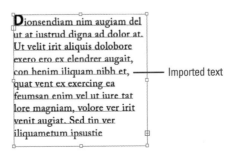

Imported text

Selecting Type

Before you can work with type in Illustrator, you need to select it. You can select the entire type object or the characters in the type object. The Selection tool allows you to select both characters and its object, while the Direct Selection tool allows you to select just the characters in the type object or both characters and its object. You can also use the type tools to select only the characters in the type object, not the object itself.

Select Type and its Object

1. Select the **Selection** tool on the Tools panel.

2. Use the appropriate selection method:

   ◆ **Point Type.** Click on the type.

   ◆ **Path Type.** Click on the path.

   ◆ **Area Type.** Click on the type. For a type object with a fill, click the fill, a character, the baseline, or outer path.

Selected type object

Select a Type Object and Not the Type

1. Select the **Direct Selection** tool on the Tools panel.

2. Click the edge of a path or area type object.

Selected type object

Did You Know?

You can show hidden characters. If it's hard to see spaces and paragraphs, you can show hidden characters to make them easier to see. Click the Type menu, and then click Show Hidden Characters.

Select and Deselect Type and Not its Object

① Select any of the Type tools on the Tools panel.

② Do any of the following to select:

- **Text.** Drag the I-beam cursor to select and highlight a word or line of type.

- **Word.** Double-click a word of type.

- **Paragraph.** Triple-click a paragraph of type.

- **All Text.** Click to place the insertion point, click the **Select** menu, and then click **All**.

   TIMESAVER *Click in a type object, press Ctrl+A (Win) or ⌘+A (Mac) to select all the text.*

③ To deselect the type, Ctrl+click (Win) or Command+click (Mac) outside the type object.

Did You Know?

You can use Smart Guides to help you select text. Click the View menu, and then click Smart Guides to turn the feature on. Click the Edit (Win) or Illustrator (Mac), point to Preferences, click Smart Guides, select the Object Highlighting check box, and then click OK.

① (on toolbar)

Selected word

Selected characters

Selected paragraph

Copying or Moving Type

If you have text in a document that you want to use in your artwork, you can copy and paste it into your Illustrator document. You can place the text into an existing type object or have Illustrator create one for you. In Illustrator, you can copy type in a type object or copy individual characters, and then paste them into another Illustrator artboard or document, or into another program, such as Flash, Photoshop, or a word processing program.

Copy or Move Text from Another Program

① Open the other program, such as Microsoft Word.

② Select the text that you want to copy or move, and then use commands to copy or cut (move) the text.

③ Switch back to Illustrator.

④ To place the text into an existing type object, click in a type object to place the insertion point.

⑤ Click the **Edit** menu, and then click **Paste**.

TIMESAVER *Ctrl+V (Win) or* ⌘*+V (Mac).*

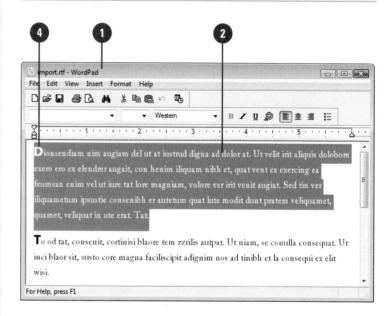

Pasted text

196

Copy Type and its Object

1. Select the **Selection** tool on the Tools panel.

2. Select the type that you want to copy.

3. Click the **Edit** menu, and then click **Copy**.

   TIMESAVER *Ctrl+C (Win) or ⌘+C (Mac).*

4. Click in another Illustrator artboard or document.

   ◆ You can also switch to another program and paste the text.

5. Click the **Edit** menu, and then click **Paste**, **Paste in Front**, or **Paste in Back**.

   TIMESAVER *Ctrl+V (Win) or ⌘+V (Mac).*

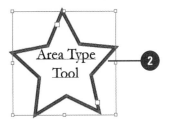

Pasted object

Copy or Move Type from One Object to Another

1. Select the **Type** or **Vertical Type** tool on the Tools panel.

2. Select the type that you want to copy or move.

3. Click the **Edit** menu, and then click **Copy** or **Cut** (move).

   TIMESAVER *Ctrl+C (Win) or ⌘+C (Mac) to copy or Ctrl+X (Win) or ⌘+X (Mac) to cut.*

4. To place the text into an existing type object, click in a type object to place the insertion point.

5. Click the **Edit** menu, and then click **Paste**.

   TIMESAVER *Ctrl+V (Win) or ⌘+V (Mac).*

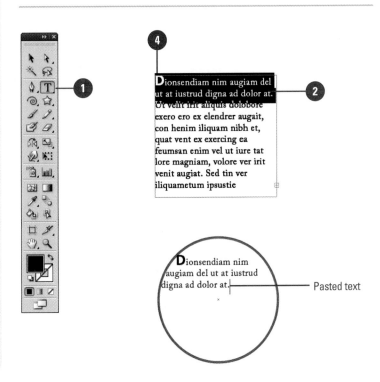

Pasted text

Working with Overflow Type

If you type, paste, or import more text than a type object can hold, an overflow symbol (a tiny red plus sign in a square) appears on the edge of the type object. You can reshape the type object to display the text or create a thread (link) to another type object. You can thread overflow text from one type object to a new or existing type object. After you create a thread between two or more type objects, you can use the Show Text Threads command on the View menu to display the thread connection. If you no longer want to want to thread two or more type objects, you can unthread or disconnect them. When you unthread type objects, the text in the type object remains in the first type object (it may still overflow). When you disconnect type objects, the text in the type objects remains where it is.

Thread Overflow Type to Another Object and Show Text Threads

1. Select the **Selection** tool on the Tools panel.

2. Select the type object with the overflow type.

3. Click the **Out Port** icon on the selected object.

   TIMESAVER *Double-click an Out Port icon with the Selection tool to create a linked copy of the type object.*

   The pointer changes to the Loaded Text pointer.

4. To create a new type object for the overflow text, click a blank area or drag to create a type object.

   To use an existing type object, position the pointer over an existing type object, and then click the object's path. A fill and stroke of None is applied to the path.

   Overflow text from the first type object threads to the second type object.

5. To display a text thread between type objects, select a threaded type object, click the **View** menu, and then click **Show Text Threads**.

Dionsendiam nim augiam del ut at iustrud digna ad dolor at. Ut velit irit aliquis dolobore exero ero ex elendrer augait, con henim iliquam nibh et, quat vent ex exercing ea feumsan enim vel ut iure tat lore magniam, volore ver irit venit augiat. Sed tin ver iliquametum ipsustie

Thread line

conechibh er aufetum quat lute modit dunt pratem veliquamet, quamet, veliquat in ute erat. Tat.

To od tat, consenit, cortinisi blaore tem zzrilis autpat. Ut niam, se conulla consequat. Ut inci blaor sit, susto core magna

Unthread Type Objects

1. Select the **Selection** tool on the Tools panel.

2. Select a threaded type object.

3. Double-click the **In Port** or **Out Port** icon on the selected object.

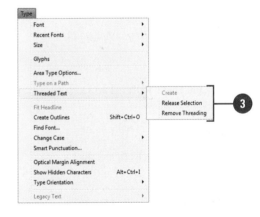

Unthread or Disconnect a Type Object

1. Select the **Selection** tool on the Tools panel.

2. Select a threaded type object that you want to release or disconnect.

3. Do one of the following:

   ◆ **Unthread.** Click the **Type** menu, point to **Threaded Text**, and then click **Remove Threading**.

   ◆ **Disconnect.** Click the **Type** menu, point to **Threaded Text**, and then click **Release Selection**.

Changing Fonts

A **font** is a collection of alphanumeric characters that share the same typeface, or design, and have similar characteristics. With the Character panel, you can change the font family (Arial or Times New Roman) and style (Italic, Bold, or Condensed), as well as change other type attributes, such as size, kerning, scale, tracking, leading, and language. You can also change these and other attributes by using the Type menu and Control panel. You can access the Character panel from the Window menu and the Control panel. After you select the type that you want to change, you can click Character on the Control panel to display the Character panel. As you can see, there are several ways to change font attributes. You can use any one of them. We'll focus on the Character panel. If you want to know which fonts are currently being used in your document or find/change a font in your document, the Find Font dialog box can help you do the job.

Change Font Family and Style

1. Select any type tool, and then select the type that you want to change.

   ◆ You can also select the **Selection** tool, and then click the type object.

2. Select the **Character** panel.

   ◆ Click the **Window** menu, point to **Type**, and then click **Character**.

3. Click the **Font Family** list arrow, and then select a font.

   ◆ To see the font family in the style of the font, click the **Type** menu, point to **Font**, and then select a font.

   TIMESAVER *To reuse a recent font, click the Type menu, point to Recent Font, and then select a font.*

4. Click the **Font Style** list arrow, and then select a font style, such as Italic, Bold, or Condensed.

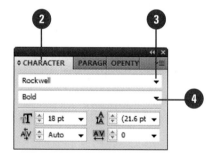

Type results

Adobe Illustrator Type Tool

Find or Change a Font

1. Click the **Type** menu, and then click **Find Font**.

   The fonts in the top list are the ones currently used in your document. The list at the bottom displays fonts in your document or fonts on your computer, depending on your setting.

2. To find a specific font in your document, select it in the top list.

3. Select the check boxes at the bottom to specify the font attributes that you want to find.

4. To replace the font in the top list, select a font in the bottom list. Click the **Replace With Font From** list arrow, and then click System to show all the fonts on your computer.

5. Click **Find** to display the first instance of the font, and then click **Change** to replace it, or click **Change All** to replace all uses of the font in your document.

6. When you're done, click **Done**.

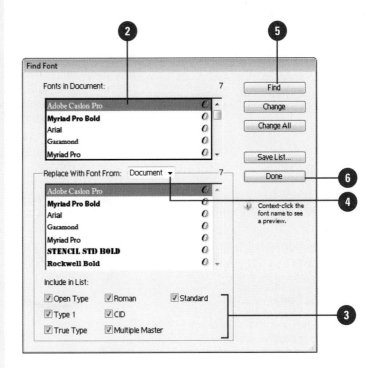

Did You Know?

You can change the type language. Select the Character panel, click the Language list arrow, and then select the language that you want to use. You can also select type using any type tool, and then change the type language to something else.

Changing Font Size

Adobe Certified Expert · IL 4.2

After setting the font family and style, the next attribute to set is the font size. The font size can range from 6 points to 72 points and beyond with the right type of font. Open or TrueType fonts can be scaled to any size and still look and print well.Bitmap (screen fonts), fonts, on the other hand, cannot be scaled and you need to use the available sizes to print well. However, bitmap fonts are the best choice for commercial print jobs. An "O" appears next to an OpenType font, a "TT" appears next to a TrueType font, and an "a" appears next to a bitmap font on the Font submenu.

Change Font Size

1. Select any type tool, and then select the type that you want to change.

   ◆ You can also select the **Selection** tool, and then click the type object.

2. Select the **Character** panel.

3. Enter a font point size, or click the **Font Size** list arrow, and then select a font size. Press Enter (Win) or Return (Mac) to apply the value.

   ◆ You can also hold down Ctrl+Shift (Win) or Command+Shift (Mac), and then press > to increase the point size or press < to decrease the point size.

   The type increases or decreases by the Size/Leading value set in Type preferences.

   Use Ctrl+Alt-Shift (Win) or Command+Option+Shift to change the point size 5 sizes at a time.

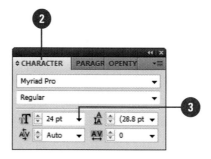

Type results

Did You Know?

What is a point? The size of each font character is measured in points (a point is approximately 1/72 of an inch). You can use any font that is installed on your computer on a document, but the default is 10-point Arial.

Leading Type

IL 4.2

Leading is the distance from the baseline of one line to the baseline of the next line and is measured in points. Each line of type can have a different leading. You can specify a specific setting or use Auto, which is a percentage of the largest type size on each line. Leading is applied to horizontal type. If you want to change vertical spacing in type, you need to adjust horizontal tracking.

Change Type Leading

1. Select any horizontal type tool, and then select the type that you want to change.

    ◆ You can also select the **Selection** tool, and then click the type object.

2. Select the **Character** panel.

    ◆ Click the **Window** menu, point to **Type**, and then click **Character**.

3. Enter a leading point size, or click the **Leading** list arrow, and then select a leading size. Press Enter (Win) or Return (Mac) to apply the value.

    ◆ You can also hold down Alt (Win) or Option (Mac), and then press the **down arrow** to increase the point size or press the **up arrow** to decrease the point size.

    The type increases or decreases by the Size/Leading value set in the Type preferences.

4. To shift characters up or down from the baseline, enter a baseline value, or click the **Baseline** list arrow, and then select a baseline value. A positive size adds space while a negative number removes space. Press Enter (Win) or Return (Mac) to apply the value.

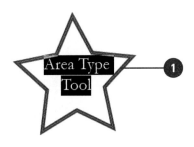

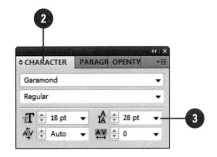

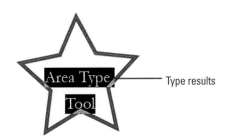

Type results

Kerning Type

Kerning is the amount of space between each individual character that you type. Sometimes the space between two characters is larger than others, which makes the word look uneven. You can use the Character panel to change the kerning setting for selected characters. You can expand or condense character spacing to create a special effect for a title, or realign the position of characters to the bottom edge of the text—this is helpful for positioning copyright or trademark symbols.

Change Type Kerning

1 Select any type tool, and then click between the two characters of type that you want to change the distance between.

◆ You can also select the **Selection** tool, and then click the type object.

2 Select the **Character** panel.

◆ Click the **Window** menu, point to **Type**, and then click **Character**.

3 Enter a kerning size, or click the **Kerning** list arrow, and then select a kerning size. A positive size adds space while a negative number removes space. Press Enter (Win) or Return (Mac) to apply the value.

◆ You can also hold down Alt (Win) or Option (Mac), and then press the **right arrow** to increase the point size or press the **left arrow** to decrease the point size.

The type increases or decreases by the Tracking value set in the Type preferences.

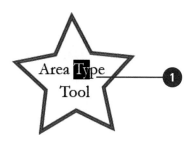

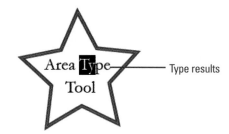
Type results

Did You Know?

You can fit headline type to its object. Select any type tool, select or click in a single-line paragraph of area type, click the Type menu, and then click Fit Headline.

Tracking Type

 IL 4.2

Tracking is the adjustment of space between three or more characters. Typically, you'll track a line of type or a few words depending on the length and design application. This is useful for creating specialize type for a caption or short heading. To adjust space between two characters, kerning is the best choice. To track characters, you need to select them first and then set the Tracking option in the Character panel.

Change Type Tracking

① Select any type tool, and then select the type that you want to change.

◆ You can also select the **Selection** tool, and then click the type object.

② Select the **Character** panel.

◆ Click the **Window** menu, point to **Type**, and then click **Character**.

③ Enter a tracking size, or click the **Tracking** list arrow, and then select a tracking size. A positive size adds space while a negative number removes space. Press Enter (Win) or Return (Mac) to apply the value.

◆ You can also hold down Alt (Win) or Option (Mac), and then press the **right arrow** to increase the point size or press the **left arrow** to decrease the point size.

The type increases or decreases by the Tracking value set in the Type preferences.

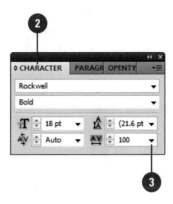

Type results

Scaling Type

IL 4.2

Scaling allows you to make type wider or narrower for horizontal type and taller or shorter for vertical type. You can use the Horizontal Scale and Vertical Scale options in the Character panel to modify type. If the scaling doesn't look quite right, you can always use the Undo command to reverse the command.

Change Type Scaling Horizontally or Vertically

1. Select any type tool, and then select the type that you want to change.

   ◆ You can also select the **Selection** tool, and then click the type object.

2. Select the **Character** panel.

   ◆ Click the **Window** menu, point to **Type**, and then click **Character**.

3. Enter a horizontal or vertical percentage, or click the **Horizontal Scale** or **Vertical Scale** list arrow, and then select a percentage. Press Enter (Win) or Return (Mac) to apply the value. Other ways of scaling text include:

   ◆ To scale a type object, select the object, double-click the Scale tool on the Tools panel, select the **Non-Uniform** option, specify a **Horizontal** and **Vertical** percentage, and then click **OK**.

   ◆ To scale a type object, select the object, select the Free Transform tool on the Tools panel, and then drag a side handle on the bounding box.

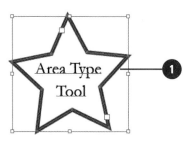

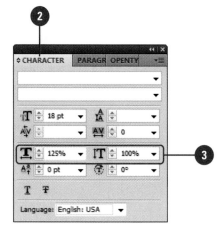

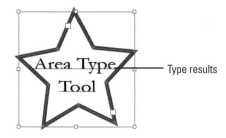

Type results

Rotating Type

 IL 4.2

After you create type, you can rotate text characters or the entire text block to a custom angle. You change the custom angle in the Character panel, which is available on the Type submenu on the Window menu. For text blocks, you can also rotate them horizontally or vertically by using the Horizontal or Vertical command on the Type Orientation submenu on the Type menu.

Rotate Type

1. Select the **Selection** tool or **Direct Selection** tool on the Tools panel.

2. Click the type on the path or select characters in the type.

   Center, left, and right brackets appear around the type.

3. Select the **Character** panel.

   ◆ Click the **Window** menu, point to **Type**, and then click **Character**.

4. Enter a rotation value, or click the **Character Rotation** list arrow, and then select a rotation value. Press Enter (Win) or Return (Mac) to apply the value.

   ◆ Rotate Horizontal or Vertical. Click the **Type** menu, point to **Type Orientation**, and then click **Horizontal** or **Vertical**.

5. Drag the bracket (not the square) to adjust the position of the type on the path.

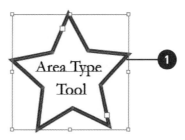

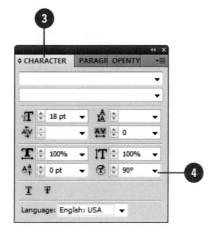

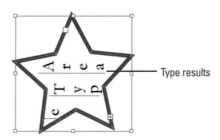

Type results

Aligning Paragraphs

IL 4.2

When you press the Enter (Win) or Return (Mac) in a type object, Illustrator creates a paragraph. You can use the Paragraph panel to align and indent paragraphs in your document. At the top of the Paragraph panel is a set of buttons that you can use to align text in one or more paragraphs. The panel includes the typical options to align: left, center, right and justify. However, it also includes options to justify with only the last line aligned left, center, or right.

Align Paragraphs

1. Select any type tool, and then click in a paragraph or select multiple paragraphs that you want to align.

   ◆ You can also select the **Selection** tool, and then click the paragraph.

2. Select the **Paragraph** panel.

   ◆ Click the **Window** menu, point to **Type**, and then click **Paragraph**.

3. Use any of the following alignment buttons on the panel:

   ◆ **Align Left, Align Center**, or **Align Right.** Click these buttons to align paragraph type left, center, or right.

   ◆ **Justify Left, Center, or Right.** Click these buttons to justify the paragraph text with only the last line aligned left, center, or right.

   ◆ **Justify.** Click to justify all lines.

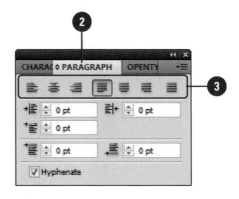

Left aligned

Dionsendiam nim
augiam del ut at
iustrud digna ad
dolor at. Ut velit irit
aliquis dolobore
exero ero ex elendrer
augait, con henim

Dionsendiam nim
augiam del ut at
iustrud digna ad dolor
at. Ut velit irit aliquis
dolobore exero ero ex
elendrer augait, con
henim iliquam nibh et
quat vent ex exercing

Center aligned

Right aligned

Dionsendiam nim
augiam del ut at
iustrud digna ad
dolor at. Ut velit irit
aliquis dolobore
exero ero ex elendrer
augait, con henim

Dionsendiam   nim
augiam del ut at iustrud
digna ad dolor at. Ut
velit   irit   aliquis
dolobore exero ero ex
elendrer augait, con
henim iliquam nibh et
quat vent ex exercing ea

Justified

208

Indenting and Spacing Paragraphs

 IL 4.2

Quickly indent lines of text to precise locations from the left or right margin with the horizontal ruler. Indent the first line of a paragraph (called a **first-line indent**) as books do to distinguish paragraphs. Indent the second and subsequent lines of a paragraph from the left margin (called a **hanging indent**) to create a properly formatted bibliography. Indent the entire paragraph any amount from the left and right margins (called **left indents** and **right indents**) to separate quoted passages. In addition to indenting paragraphs, you can also set the spacing you want before or after a paragraph.

Indent and Space Paragraphs

1. Select any type tool, and then click in a paragraph or select multiple paragraphs that you want to change.

   ◆ You can also select the **Selection** tool, and then click the paragraph.

2. Select the **Paragraph** panel.

   ◆ Click the **Window** menu, point to **Type**, and then click **Paragraph**.

3. Enter a **Left Indent** and/or **Right Indent** value or use the up and down arrows to specify one. Press Enter (Win) or Return (Mac) to apply the value.

4. To create a first-line indent, enter a **First-Line Indent** value or use the up and down arrows to specify one. Press Enter (Win) or Return (Mac) to apply the value.

   ◆ To create a hanging indent, enter a negative value in the First-line Left Indent box.

5. To add spacing between paragraphs, enter a **Space Before Paragraph** and/or **Space After Paragraph** value or use the up and down arrows to specify one. Press Enter (Win) or Return (Mac) to apply the value.

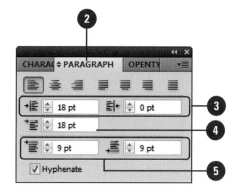

Left Indent

First-Line Indent

Dionsendiam nim augiam del ut at iustrud digna ad dolor at. Ut velit irit aliquis dolobore exero ero ex elendrer augait, con henim iliquam nibh et, quat vent ex exercing ea feumsan enim vel ut iure tat lore magniam, volore ver irit venit augiat. Sed tin ver iliquametum ipsustie consenibh er autetum quat lute modit dunt pratem veliquamet, quamet, veliquat in ute erat. Tat.

To od tat, consenit, cortinisi blaore tem zzrilis autpat. Ut niam, se conulla consequat. Ut inci blaor sit, susto core magna faciliscipit adignim

Right Indent

Setting Tabs

 IL 4.2

In your document, **tabs** set how text or numerical data is aligned in relation to the document margins. A **tab stop** is a predefined stopping point along the document's typing line. Default tab stops are set every half-inch, but you can set multiple tabs per paragraph at any location. Choose from four types of text tab stops: left, right, center, and decimal (for numerical data). In the Tabs panel, you can view a ruler with the current tab setting for the selected type and add, move, or delete tab stops. When you press the Tab key with the insertion point, the text shifts to the next tab stop.

Set Tabs

1. Select any type tool, and then click to place the insertion point in a type object.

2. Select the **Tabs** panel.

   ◆ Click the **Window** menu, point to **Type**, and then click **Tabs**.

   ◆ To use the default tabs, press the tab key to shift the text to the next default tab stop.

3. To move the panel next to the text, click the **Position Panel Above Text** button on the panel.

4. Do any of the following:

   ◆ **Insert.** Click one of the tab stop buttons, and then click in the ruler where you want to place it. You can also enter a number in the X box to insert a tab at an exact position.

   ◆ **Move.** Drag the tab stop left or right or enter an exact position in the X box.

   ◆ **Delete.** Drag a tab stop down off the ruler.

   ◆ **Leader.** Enter a character that repeats in the tabbed space, such as a period.

   ◆ **Align On.** Enter a character that is used with the Decimal tab, such as a decimal point.

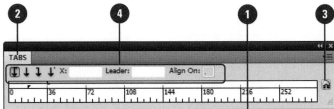

Working with Hyphenation

IL 4.8

When you select the Hyphenate check box in the Paragraph panel, Illustrator automatically add hyphenation as you need it in your document based on the options set in the Hyphenation dialog box. If the Hyphenate check box is not checked, you need to select any existing type to apply hyphenation. The hyphenation options allow you to specify how long a word needs to be before hyphenation takes place, the maximum number of hyphens you can use, and what balance you want between better spacing and fewer hyphens.

Change Hyphenation Options

1. Select any type tool, and then select the type that you want to hyphenate.

2. Select the **Paragraph** panel.

3. To enable hyphenation, select the **Hyphenate** check box.

4. Click the **Paragraph Options** menu, and then click **Hyphenation**.

5. Specify the following options:

    ◆ **Words Longer Than.** Enter the minimum number of characters a word must have before hyphens are added.

    ◆ **After First.** Enter the minimum number of characters that can be inserted before a hyphen.

    ◆ **Before Last.** Enter the minimum number of characters that can be inserted after a hyphen on the next line.

    ◆ **Hyphen Limit.** Enter the maximum number of hyphens in a row (0-25).

    ◆ **Hyphenation Zone.** Drag the slider to adjust the balance of hyphenation between better spacing and fewer hyphens.

    ◆ **Hyphenate Capitalized Words.** Select to hyphenate capitalized words.

6. Click **OK**.

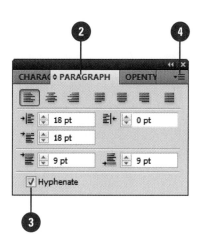

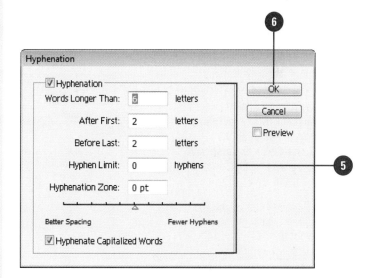

Working with Type Styles

IL 4.3

A **style** is a group of format settings that you can create or modify to get the exact look you want. When you create a new style, you can specify if it applies to paragraphs or characters, and give the style a short name that describes its purpose so you and others know when to use that style. A **paragraph style** is a group of format settings that can be applied only to all of the text within a paragraph (even if it is a one-line paragraph), while a **character style** is a group of format settings that is applied to any block of text at the user's discretion. To modify a style, adjust the formatting settings of an existing style. If you see a style with a plus sign (+) after the name, it means that the type with the applied style also contains other formatting, which you can remove or redefine the style.

Create or Edit Styles

1. Select any type tool, and then select the type that you want to use as the style.

   ◆ You can also select the **Selection** tool, and then click the type object.

2. Select the **Character Styles** or **Paragraph Styles** panel.

   ◆ Click the **Window** menu, point to **Type**, and then click **Character Styles** or **Paragraph Styles**.

3. Use any of the following alignment buttons on the panel:

   ◆ **Create.** Alt+click (Win) or Option+click (Mac) the **Create New Style** button on the Character Styles or Paragraph Styles panel, and then enter a name for the style.

   ◆ **Edit.** Deselect any styles, and then double-click the style that you want to edit.

4. Select a category, such as General, Indents and Spacing, Justification, or Character Color.

5. View the current settings and make any changes that you want.

6. Click **OK**.

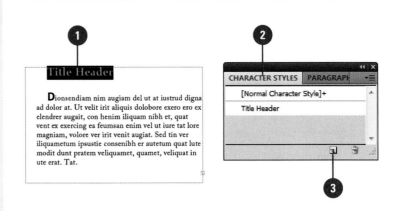

Enter name for a new style

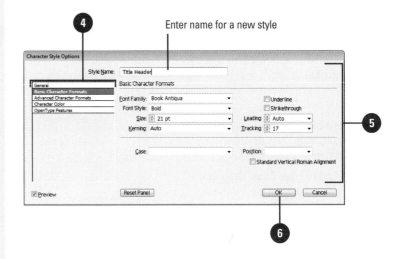

Apply Styles

1. Select any type tool, and then select the type that you want to change.

   For paragraph styling, select a type object or select paragraphs. For character styling, select text, not a type object.

   ◆ You can also select the **Selection** tool, and then click the type object.

2. Select the **Character Styles** or **Paragraph Styles** panel.

3. Click a style name in one of the panels.

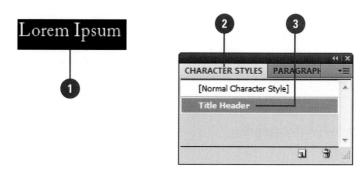

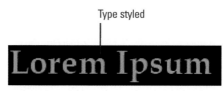

Type styled

Work with Styles

1. Select any type tool, and then select the type with the style that you want to change.

   ◆ You can also select the **Selection** tool, and then click the type object.

2. Select the **Character Styles** or **Paragraph Styles** panel.

3. Do any of the following:

   ◆ Delete a Style. Select a style, and then click the **Delete Selected Styles** button.

   ◆ Remove Overrides. Alt+click (Win) or Option+click (Mac), the style name to remove the plus sign (+).

   ◆ Redefine a Style. Click the appropriate **Options** menu, and then click **Redefine Character Style** or **Redefine Paragraph Style**.

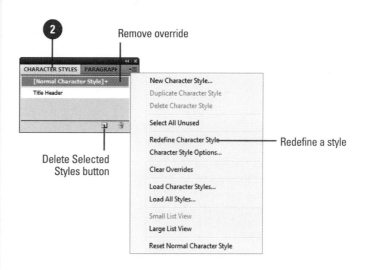

Remove override

Redefine a style

Delete Selected Styles button

Using Smart Punctuation

Smart Punctuation turns your text into professional looking type. Instead of using straight quotes, you can use smart quotes. Instead of using hyphen as dashes, you can use En or Em dashes. You would not want to make these changes manually, but you don't have to. Illustrator can do it for you with the Smart Punctuation command. You can change the entire document all at one time or you can select the type that you want to change.

Use Smart Punctuation

1. Select any type tool, and then select the type that you want to change, or deselect all to convert the entire document.

2. Click the **Type** menu, and then click **Smart Punctuation**.

3. Select the check boxes with the Smart Punctuation options that you want to use.

4. Select the **Selected Text Only** or **Entire Document** option.

5. Select the **Report Results** check box to display a list of your changes on the screen.

6. Click **OK**.

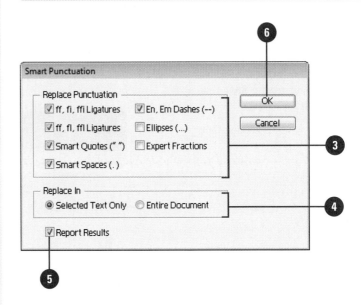

Did You Know?

You can force punctuation marks near the edge to appear outside the type object. Select the type that you want to change, select the Paragraph panel, click the Options menu, and then click Roman Hanging Punctuation.

See Also

See "Setting Up a Document" on page 32 for information on specifying a quotation marks style in the Document Setup dialog box.

Working with Glyphs

 IL 4.4

A glyph is a style variation—such as ligatures, ordinals, swashes, and fractions—for a given character in an OpenType font. OpenType fonts appear with an "O" next to the font name on the Font submenu. OpenType fonts are designed to work well on both Windows and Macintosh operating systems, which reduces font substitution problems when going back and forth between platforms. However, you can always add more character styles to extend the font format. For example, you can change fractions with numerals and slashes to properly formatted fractions. You can automatically insert alternate glyphs with the OpenType panel or insert them manually with the Glyphs panel to extend the font format.

Replace or Insert a Glyph

1. Select any type tool, and then select a character (to replace a glyph) or click in text (to insert a glyph).

2. Select the **Glyphs** panel (from the Type menu).

   ◆ Click the **Window** menu, point to **Type**, and then click **Glyphs**.

3. Select a different font and font style.

4. Click the **Show** list arrow, and then select a glyphs category.

   Alternative for Current Selection or **Entire Font** are common choices.

5. Double-click the glyph that you want to replace or insert.

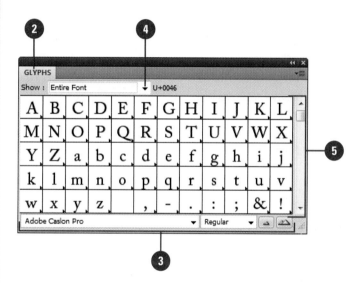

Did You Know?

You can use the OpenType panel to insert glyphs. Select the OpenType panel, select the type that you want to change or deselect all text for the entire document, and then select the buttons with the options for glyphs that you want to apply, such as ligatures, swashes, titling, ordinals, and fractions.

Wrapping Type Around an Object

When integrating artwork and graphics with your type, you can wrap the text around objects to create the results that you want. You can wrap area type around a path, a placed graphic, or another type object. When wrapping type around an object, the important thing is to make sure the wrapped object is in front of the area type object in the same top-level, sublayer, or group.

Wrap and Unwrap Type Around an Object

1. Arrange the object to be wrapped in front of the area type object in the same top-level, sublayer, or group. The objects should be overlapping.

2. Select the object to be wrapped in the Layers panel.

3. Click the **Object** menu, and then point to **Text Wrap Options.**.

    ◆ If prompted, click **OK** to create the text wrap.

4. Click the **Object** menu, point to **Text Wrap**, and then click **Text Warp Options**.

5. Select the **Preview** check box to view your changes as you set options.

6. Enter an **Offset** value to specify the distance between the wrapped object and the type object.

7. Click **OK**.

    You can move the objects to finalize the results. The type will rewrap around the object.

8. To unwrap (release) a text wrap, select the wrapped object (not the type object), click the **Object** menu, point to **Text Wrap**, and then click **Release**.

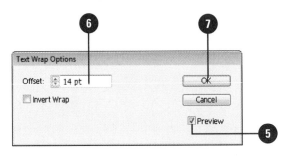

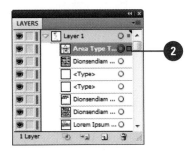

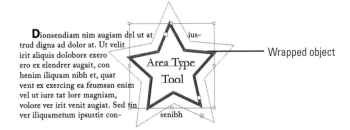

Wrapped object

Creating Type Outlines

The Create Outlines command converts characters in a type object into a separate object with a path. Some characters, such as "A" or "B," that contain an interior shape (known as a counter) are converted into compound objects. After you create an outline, you can reshape the path, use it as a mask object, fill it with a gradient or a mesh, or use it in a compound object. When you create outlines, the fill and stroke attributes and any appearances of the type are applied to the outlines. Before you use the Create Outlines command, it's a good idea to make a copy of the type object or your document as a backup to preserve a copy of the type layers.

Create Type Outlines

1. Select the **Selection** tool on the Tools panel.

2. Select the type object or select characters in the type.

3. Click the **Type** menu, and then click **Create Outlines**.

4. To release a compound object into separate objects, click the **Object** menu, point to **Compound Path**, and then click **Release**.

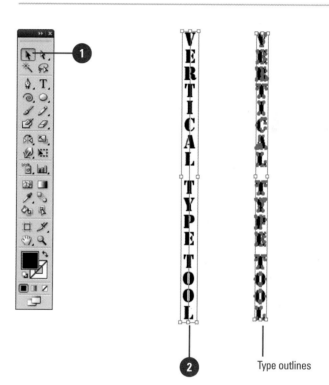

Type outlines

Working with Graphics

9

Introduction

In addition to opening Illustrator documents, you can also open graphic files created in different formats, such as TIFF, JPEG, GIF, and PNG. You open a graphic file the same way you open documents in Illustrator. You can also use Illustrator's Place command to insert artwork. Illustrator lets you place graphic files saved in Photoshop PSD, BMP, JPEG, EPS, and PNG formats, to name a few.

With Illustrator's Place command, you can link or embed an image into your document. Embedding inserts a copy of one document in another. When data is embedded, you can edit it using the menus and toolbars of the program in which it was created. Linking displays information stored in one document into another. After you link or embed a graphic image file into an Illustrator document, you can use the Links panel in Illustrator to manage and work with the files. The Links panel displays a list of all the linked or embedded files in your document.

If you have a raster graphic, such as a JPEG, TIFF, or PSD file in your document, you can use tracing options to convert the graphic into editable vector artwork. You can set options to create a close simulation of the graphic or a more artistic rendering of it and then fine-tune your results.

The Graphic Styles panel allows you to create, save, and apply graphics styles. A graphic style is a collection of attributes that can be applied to a layer, sublayer, group, or object. The Appearance panel allows you to apply and manage multiple attributes of an object. You can apply fills, strokes, opacity, blending mode, effects, and other attributes to objects, layers, groups, or graphic styles. The panel makes it easy to apply, edit, duplicate, restack, or remove attributes.

What You'll Do

Open Graphics

Place Graphics

Place Graphics from Adobe Bridge

Link Graphics

Manage Linked Graphics

Trace Raster Graphics

Convert Tracing to Paths

Apply Graphic Styles

Create Graphic Styles

Edit Graphic Styles

Apply Appearance Attributes

Opening Graphics

IL 7.1

In addition to opening Illustrator documents, you can also open graphic files created in different formats, such as TIFF, JPEG, GIF, and PNG. You open a graphic file the same way you open documents in Illustrator. When you open a graphic file, a tab appears across the top of the Document window, which you can click to display. If you need to manage, organize, or find graphic files, Adobe Bridge is the way to go. With Adobe Bridge, you can search for the graphic files that you want to edit, and then open them in Illustrator.

Open a Graphic Image

1. Click the **File** menu, and then click **Open** to display all file types in the file list of the Open dialog box.

2. Click the **Files of Type** (Win) or **Enable** (Mac) list arrow, and then select a graphic format.

3. Navigate to the drive or folder location with the image you want to open.

4. Click the graphic file you want to open.

   TIMESAVER *Press and hold the Shift key to select multiple contiguous files to open in the Open dialog box.*

5. Click **Open**.

See Also

See "Opening a Document with Adobe Bridge" on page 14-15 or "Placing Graphics from Adobe Bridge" on page 222-223 for more information on finding and opening or placing graphic files from Bridge.

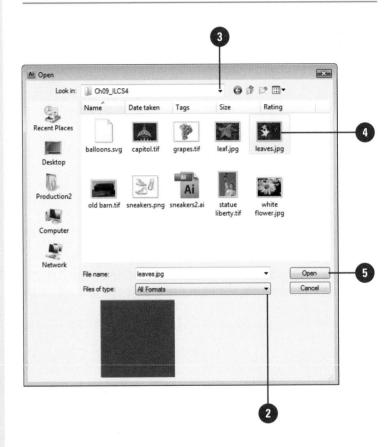

Placing Graphics

IL 7.1

You can use Illustrator's Place command to insert artwork into an open document. To increase your control of the new image information, Illustrator places the new image into a separate layer. Illustrator lets you place graphic files saved in Photoshop PSD, BMP, JPEG, EPS, and PNG formats, to name a few. When you first place a vector-based image into Illustrator, you have the ability to modify the width, height, and rotation while retaining the vector format of the file.

Place a Graphic

1. Open an Illustrator document.

2. Click the **File** menu, and then click **Place**.

3. Navigate to the drive or folder location with the image you want to open.

4. Select the graphic file that you want to place into the active document.

5. Select any of the following options:

   ◆ **Link.** Places a screen version of the graphic and links the document to the graphic file. Deselect to embed a copy of the graphic file image in the document.

   ◆ **Template.** Places a dimmed version of the graphic on a template layer for tracing.

   ◆ **Replace.** Replaces the currently selected image.

6. Click **Place**.

   Illustrator places the image in a new layer, directly above the active layer, and then encloses it within a transformable bounding box.

7. Control the shape by manipulating the corner and side nodes of the freeform bounding box.

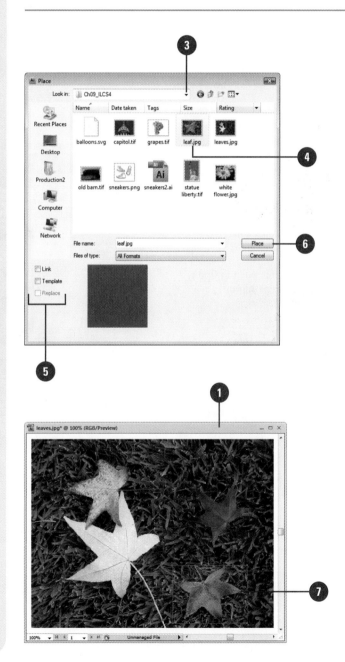

Placing Graphics from Adobe Bridge

Adobe Bridge allows you to search, sort, filter, manage, and process graphic files one at a time or in batches. You can open or place graphics directly into Illustrator by using the Open With (Adobe Illustrator) or Place (In Illustrator) commands in Bridge from the File menu. You can also drag thumbnails from the Bridge into an open Illustrator document window.

Browse and Open Graphics with Adobe Bridge

1 Click the **Go to Bridge** button on the Application bar or click the **File** menu, and then click **Browse in Bridge**.

   Adobe Bridge opens, displaying files and folders on your computer.

2 Navigate to the drive or folder where the file is located.

3 Select the graphic thumbnail representing the file that you want to open in your Illustrator document.

4 Click the **File** menu, point to **Open With**, and then click **Adobe Illustrator CS4**.

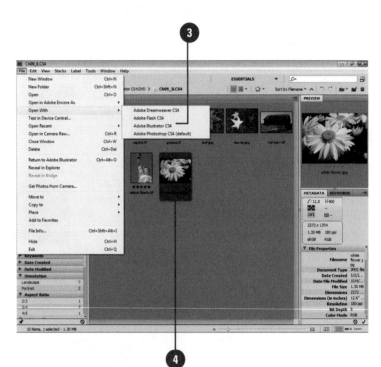

Did You Know?

You can locate a linked graphic in Bridge from Illustrator. In the Links panel, select the graphic name, click the Options menu, and then click Reveal in Bridge.

Place Graphics with Adobe Bridge

1. Click the **Go to Bridge** button on the Application bar or click the **File** menu, and then click **Browse in Bridge**.

    Adobe Bridge opens, displaying files and folders on your computer.

2. Navigate to the drive or folder where the file is located.

3. Select the graphic thumbnail that represents the file you want to place in your Illustrator document.

4. Click the **File** menu, point to **Place**, and then click **In Illustrator**.

Did You Know?

You can drag-and-drop Photoshop elements into Illustrator. In Photoshop, select all or part of an image or a layer, select the Move tool, and then drag the selection or layer into an Illustrator artboard to place an embedded copy of it in your document.

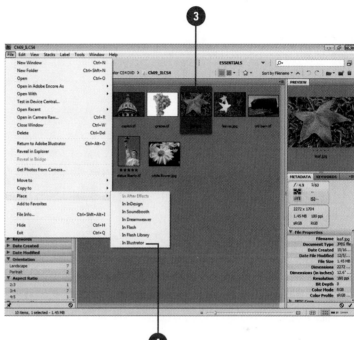

Linking Graphics

 IL 7.2

With Illustrator's Place command, you can link or embed an image into your document. **Embedding** inserts a copy of one document into another. When data is embedded, you can edit it using the menus and toolbars of the program in which it was created (that is, the **source program**). **Linking** displays information stored in one document (the **source file**) into another (the **destination file**). You can edit the linked object from either file, although changes are stored in the source file. If you break the link between a linked object and its source file, the object becomes embedded. As you work with linked or embedded files in the Layers panel, a linked image appears as <Linked File>, while an embedded image appears as an image object

Link to a Graphic

1. Open an Illustrator document.

2. Click the **File** menu, and then click **Place**.

3. Select the graphic file that you want to place into the active document.

4. Select the **Link** check box.

   ◆ To embed a copy of the graphic file image in the document, deselect the **Link** check box.

5. Click **Place**.

   Illustrator places the image in a new layer, directly above the active layer, and then encloses it within a transformable bounding box.

See Also

See "Setting File Handling & Clipboard Preferences" on page 401 for information on setting linking options.

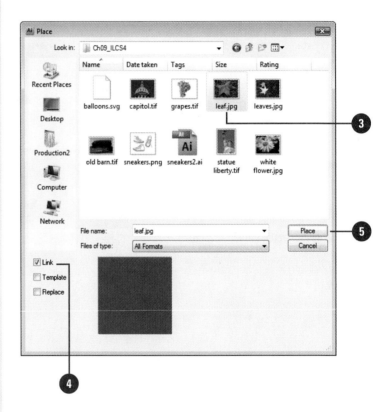

Edit a Linked Graphic in the Source

1. Select the linked graphic.

2. Click **Edit Original** on the Control panel.

   ◆ You can also click the **Edit Original** button on the Links panel.

3. Make the changes that you want in the original program.

4. Return to Illustrator.

5. If prompted, click **Yes** to update your document.

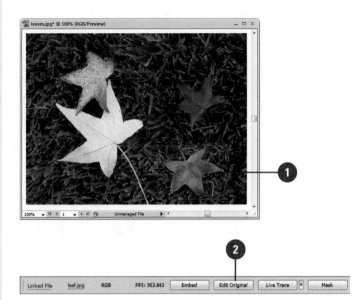

Select Placement Options for Linked Graphics

1. Select the linked graphic.

2. Click **image name** on the Control panel, and then click **Placement Options**.

   ◆ You can also click the **Options** menu in the Links panel, and then click **Placement Options**.

3. Click the **Preserve** list arrow, and then select an option: **Transforms**, **Proportions (Fit)**, **Proportions (Fill)**, **File Dimensions**, or **Bounds**.

4. If available, select an alignment position, and select or deselect the **Clip To Bounding Box** check box.

5. Click **OK**.

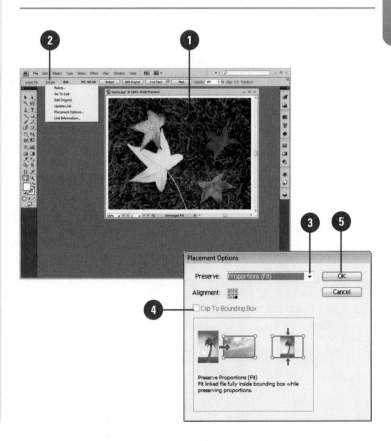

Managing Linked Graphics

Replace a Linked or Embedded Graphic

1. Select the **Links** panel.

2. Select the name of the graphic that you want to replace.

3. Click the **Relink** button on the panel.

   ◆ You can also select the image in the document window, click the **image name** or **Embedded** on the Control panel, and then click **Relink**.

4. Select the graphic file that you want to use as the replacement in the active document.

5. Click **Place**.

   ◆ You can also select the image in the document window, click the **File** menu, click **Place**, select a replacement image, select the **Replace** check box, and then click **Place**.

Did You Know?

You can locate a placed graphic in your document. In the Links panel, select the graphic that you want to find, and then click the Go To Link button on the panel.

After you link or embed a graphic image file into an Illustrator document, you can use the Links panel in Illustrator to manage and work with the files. The Links panel displays a list of all the linked or embedded files in your document. You can use the Links panel to update, replace, or relink a graphic image file. If a linked file is moved from its original location, you need to repair the link the next time you open the document. If a linked file needs to be updated, a warning icon appears in the Links panel to let you know.

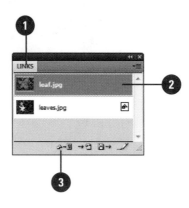

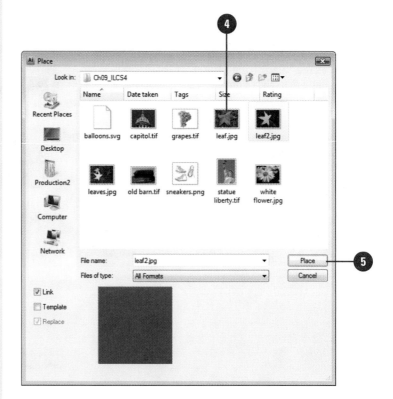

Work with Linked or Embedded Graphics

1 Select the **Links** panel.

2 Select the graphic name that you want to change.

3 Do any of the following:

◆ Update a Link. Click the **Update Link** button on the panel.

◆ Go to Link. Click the **Go To Link** button on the panel.

◆ Edit Original. Click the **Edit Original** button on the panel to open the program that created the file and edit it..

◆ View Information. Double-click the graphic name, view the information, and then click **OK**.

◆ Change from Linked to Embedded. Click the **Options** menu, and then click **Embed Image**.

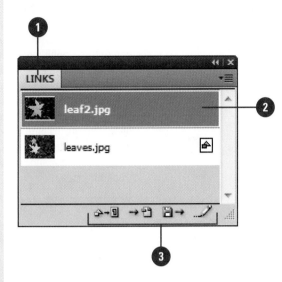

Did You Know?

You can change the display of the Links panel. In the Links panel, click the Options menu, and then select a display option, such as Show All, Show Missing, Show Modified, Show Embedded, Sort by Name, Sort by Kind, or Sort by Status.

See Also

See "Setting File Handling & Clipboard Preferences" on page 401 for information on setting linking options.

Tracing Raster Graphics

IL 7.3

If you have a raster graphic, such as a JPEG, TIFF, or PSD file, in your document, you can use tracing options to convert the graphic into editable vector artwork. You can set options to create a close simulation of the graphic or a more artistic rendering of it and then fine-tune your results. The Live Trace command detects and traces the color and shading in a raster graphic to create an editable vector object. You can use tracing presets (recommended for first time users), such as Simple Trace, Hand Drawn Sketch, or Inked Drawing, or set your own tracing options in the Tracing Options dialog box. Tracing options are live, which means that you can apply these options before or after using the Live Trace command. When applied, a traced object is known as a live trace object.

Trace a Raster Graphic

① Open or place a raster graphic in a document.

② Select the graphic that you want to trace.

   ◆ You can also select a live trace object to change it.

③ Use one of the following:

   ◆ **Preset.** Click the **Tracing Presets and Options** list arrow on the Control panel, and then select a tracing preset.

   ◆ **Last Used.** Click the **Live Trace** button on the Control panel. If prompted, click **OK**.

   ◆ **Set Options.** Click the **Tracing Presets and Options** list arrow on the Control panel, and then click **Tracing Options**.

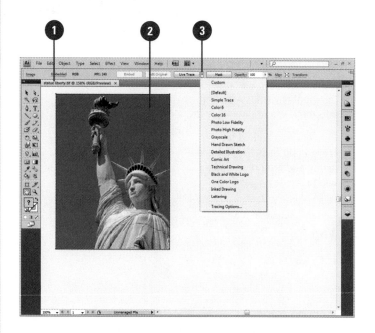

Tracing options available on the Control panel.

Did You Know?

You can create, edit, or delete tracing presets. Click the Edit menu, and then click Tracing Presets. Click New to create a new preset. Select an existing one, and then click Edit or Delete. You can also import and export tracing presets.

Select Tracing Options

1 To apply tracing options to an existing live trace object, select it.

2 Click the **Object** menu, point to **Live Trace**, and then click, and then click **Tracing Options**.

 ◆ You can also click the **Tracing Presets and Options** list arrow on the Control panel, and then **Tracing Options**.

3 Click the **Preset** list arrow, and then select a preset as the basis of your own settings.

4 Select the **Preview** check box to view your changes as you set options.

5 Specify options in the following areas:

 ◆ Adjustment. Select a color mode, and then set other related settings. Specify a **Blur** value to reduce noise and other marks. Select **Resample** to change the resolution for the graphic.

 ◆ Trace Settings. Select the **Fill** and/or **Strokes** check boxes, and then specify related options.

 ◆ View. Select a **Raster** option to show a view of the graphic, and then select a **Vector** option to show a view of the tracing object.

6 Click **Set Default**.

Did You Know?

You can restore a traced graphic back to its original state. Select the traced object, click the Object menu, point to Live Trace, and then click Release.

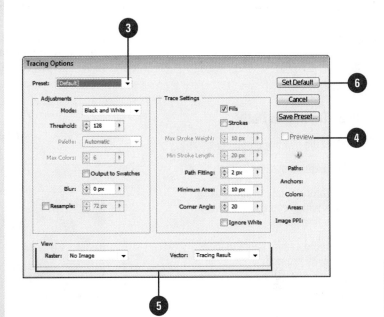

Converting Tracing to Paths

IL 7.3

Convert Tracing to Paths

1. Select the live trace object.

2. Click **Expand** on the Control panel.

   Illustrator creates a multitude of paths, which you can view using the Layers panel.

3. Select the **Layers** panel to view the newly created paths.

Did You Know?

You can convert a traced object to a live paint group. This is useful when you want to paint a traced object. Select the traced object, and then click Live Paint on the Control panel.

After you finish creating a live trace object, you can convert (expand) it to a path. When you expand a live trace object, it no longer remains a live trace object. It becomes a standard path, which you can reshape and recolor. The Expand button on the Control panel converts a live trace object into paths, which you can view and change on the Layers panel.

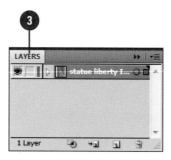

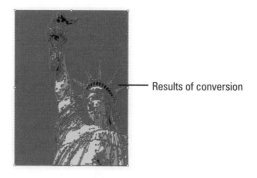

Results of conversion

Applying Graphic Styles

The Graphic Styles panel allows you to create, save, and apply graphic styles. A graphic style is a collection of attributes that can be applied to a layer, sublayer, group, or object. Graphic styles are similar in nature to character or paragraph styles. From the Graphic Styles panel, you have access to a host of graphic style libraries from which to choose a style. You can view styles for graphics and text (**New!**). Not sure how a style will look? Now you can preview a thumbnail (**New!**) before you apply it. If you still don't like it after you apply it, you can remove it without affecting the underlying path. When you apply a graphic style to a layer or group, the style is applied to all objects on it.

Apply a Graphic Style

1. Select an object with the **Selection** tool or click the target circle for a layer, sublayer, group, or object in the **Layers** panel.

2. Select the **Graphic Styles** panel.

3. Click the **Graphic Styles Libraries** menu, and then select a library.

4. Click a graphic style thumbnail in the graphic styles library.

   The graphic style is added to the Graphic Styles panel.

5. To preview and view styles, use any of the following:

   ◆ **Preview.** Right+click (Win) or Option+click (Mac) a graphic style thumbnail to display a preview of the style (**New!**).

   ◆ **View.** Click the **Options** menu, and then click **Use Square for Preview** or **Use Text for Preview** (**New!**). Select a view size: **Thumbnail View**, **Small List View**, or **Large List View**.

6. Click a graphic style thumbnail in the Graphic Styles panel to apply it to the selected object.

7. To remove all the graphic styles, click the **Default Graphic Style** thumbnail in the upper left corner of the Graphic Styles panel.

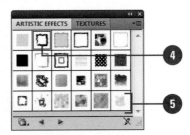

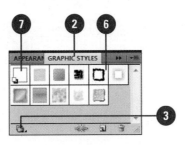

Graphic styles result

Creating Graphic Styles

 IL 5.2

You can create a graphic style from an existing object or duplicate an existing graphic style and then change it. I think the best way is to apply the attributes you want to an object, and then use the object to create a graphic style. Although, if you see a graphic style from one of the libraries that is close to what you want, you can quickly duplicate the graphic style, and then make changes to it.

Create a Graphic Style from an Object

1. Select an object with the **Selection** tool or click the target circle for a layer, sublayer, group, or object in the **Layers** panel.

2. Select the **Graphic Styles** panel.

3. Alt+click (Win) or Option+click (Mac) the **New Graphic Style** button on the panel.

4. Enter a name for the graphic style.

5. Click **OK**.

Did You Know?

You can create a graphic style from attributes in the Appearance panel. Drag the thumbnail from the Appearance panel onto the Graphic Styles panel. Double-click the graphic style, enter a name, and then click OK.

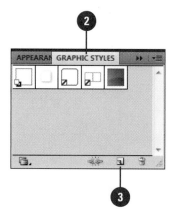

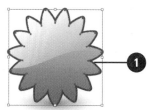

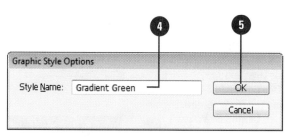

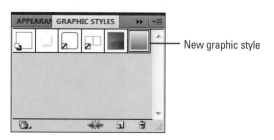

New graphic style

Duplicate a Graphic Style

① Select the **Graphic Styles** panel.

② Select the graphic style that you want to duplicate.

③ Click the **New Graphic Style** button on the panel.

The duplicate graphic style is added to the Graphic Styles panel.

④ Double-click the duplicate graphic style.

⑤ Rename the graphic style.

⑥ Click **OK**.

Did You Know?

You can view graphic style attributes. Select the Graphic Styles and Appearance panels, click the graphic style in the Graphic Styles panel, and then view its attributes in the Appearance panel.

You can save a graphic styles library. Select the Graphic Styles panel, display only the styles that you want to save in a library (delete the ones that you don't want), click the Options menu, click Save Graphic Styles, enter a name, and then click Save. When you save the library in the default location, the new library appears on the User Defined submenu on the Graphic Styles Libraries menu on the panel.

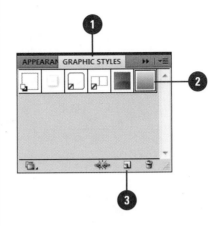

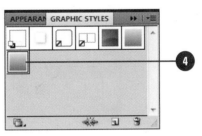

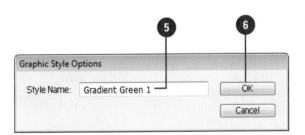

Editing Graphic Styles

After you create a graphic style, you can make changes to it. However, when you make changes to the graphic, your changes are applied to any object that uses the graphic style. If you want this to happen, then you are good to go. If not, you can make a duplicate of the graphic style and then make changes to it. If you no longer need or want a graphic style, you can delete it. When you delete a graphic style, any attributes that are linked to an object remain with the object, but any updates will not be applied.

Edit a Graphic Style

1 Select an object with the **Selection** tool or click the target circle for a layer, sublayer, group, or object in the **Layers** panel.

2 Select the **Graphic Styles** panel.

3 Apply the graphic style that you want to edit to the selected object.

4 Select the **Appearance** panel.

5 Modify the appearance of the style in the Appearance panel.

6 Click the **Options** menu, and then click **Redefine Graphic Style**.

◆ You can also Alt-drag (Win) or Option-drag (Mac) the edited style from the Appearance panel onto the original style in the Graphic Styles panel.

Did You Know?

You can merge graphic styles. Select the Graphic Styles panel, Ctrl+click (Win) or ⌘+click (Mac) the graphics styles you want to combine, click the Options menu, click Merge Graphic Styles, enter a name, and then click OK.

You can merge a style with an object's attributes. (**New!**) Alt+drag (Win) or Option+drag (Mac) the style from the Graphic Styles panel to the object. To preserve the color of type when applying a graphic style, click the Options menu, and then click Override Character Color to deselect it.

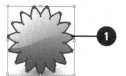

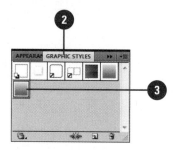

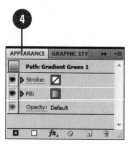

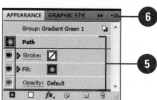

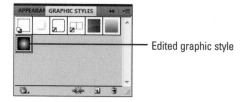

Edited graphic style

Delete a Graphic Style

1. Select the **Graphic Styles** panel.

2. Select the graphic style that you want to delete.

3. Click the **Delete Graphic Style** button on the panel.

4. Click **Yes** to confirm the deletion.

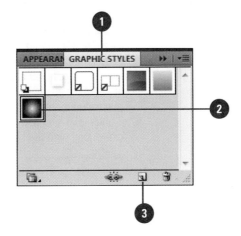

Break the Link to a Graphic Style

1. Select an object with the **Selection** tool or click the target circle for a layer, sublayer, group, or object in the **Layers** panel.

2. Select the **Graphic Styles** panel.

3. Click the **Break Link to Graphic Style** button on the panel.

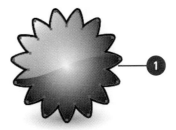

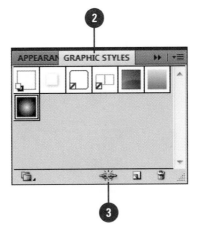

Applying Appearance Attributes

IL 5.1

The Appearance panel allows you to apply and manage multiple attributes to an object. You can apply fills, strokes, opacity, blending mode, effects, and other attributes to objects, layers, groups, or graphic styles. The panel makes it easy to apply, edit, duplicate, restack, or remove attributes. You can click links to open panels and option dialog boxes for effects, strokes, and fills (**New!**). When you have a lot of attributes for an object, it can be hard to work with them. In the Appearance panel, you can hide attributes (**New!**) to reduce the clutter and make it easier to work with the attributes that you want, much like working with the Layers panel.

Apply and Change Appearance Attributes

1. Select an object with the **Selection** tool or click the target circle for a layer, sublayer, group, or object in the **Layers** panel.

2. Select the **Appearance** panel.

   The currently targeted layer appears in bold with a type name at the top.

3. Click **Fill**, **Stroke**, **Opacity**, or other available attributes to display a panel with options.

4. Specify the options and values that you want to set for the attribute.

5. To apply multiple fill or stroke attributes, click the **Add New Fill** or **Add New Stroke** button on the panel.

6. To show or hide attributes, click the visibility column for each attribute that you want to show or hide.

Did You Know?

You can copy appearance attributes. In the Layers panel, Alt+drag (Win) or Option+drag (Mac) the target circle for the item that you want to copy onto the target circle for another layer, group, or object.

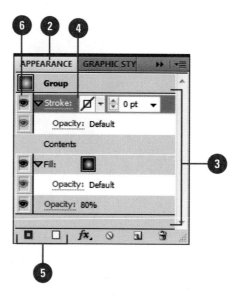

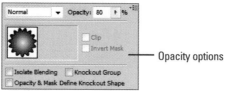

Opacity options

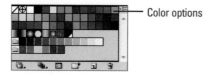

Color options

Remove Appearance Attributes

1. Select an object with the **Selection** tool or click the target circle for a layer, sublayer, group, or object in the **Layers** panel.

2. Select the **Appearance** panel.

3. Select the attribute that you want to delete.

4. Do one of the following:

   ◆ **Delete.** Removes an appearance attribute, except for stroke and fill. Click the **Delete Selected Item** button on the panel.

   ◆ **Clear Except Stroke and Fill.** Removes all the appearance attributes, except the stroke and fill. Click the **Options** menu, and then click **Reduce to Basic Appearance**.

   ◆ **Clear.** Removes all the appearance attributes and changes the stroke and fill to None. Click the **Clear Appearance** button on the panel.

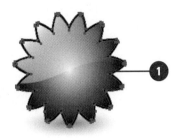

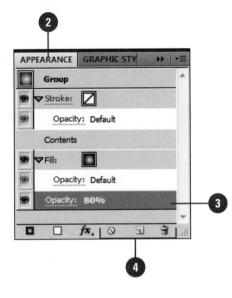

Did You Know?

You can expand an object's appearance attributes. Select the object with the appearance attributes that you want to expand, click the Object menu, and then click Expand Appearance. The paths used to create the attributes are changed to separate objects within a group, which can then be edited.

Manipulating Artwork
with Effects

10

Introduction

Adobe Illustrator effects are a designer's dream come true. With effects you can turn an image into an oil painting or a watercolor; you can even change night into day. Illustrator's Effect menu includes over 100 highly creative effects from Illustrator and Photoshop, which can be applied once, reapplied, or combined with other filters to create any effect your imagination can dream up.

The potential combination of effects and images literally runs into the millions. This means that effects are truly an undiscovered territory. As a matter of fact, the Photoshop Effect Gallery lets you view the effects of one or more filters on the active document. This level of power gives you unbelievable creative control over your images.

Take a moment to view some of the various effects that Illustrator offers. Because there are over 100 effects available, we can't show you all of them, but we think you'll enjoy viewing the selection at the end of the chapter.

What You'll Do

Apply Illustrator Effects

Apply the Convert to Shape Effect

Apply the Scribble Effect

Apply the Inner or Outer Glow Effect

Apply the Drop Shadow Effect

Apply 3D Effects

Change Raster Effect Settings

Work with the Effect Gallery

Use the Gaussian Blur Effect

Use the Unsharp Mask Effect

Apply Multiple Effects

Control Effects Using Selections

View Various Effects

Applying Illustrator Effects

IL 5.1, 5.2, 5.3

Illustrator effects change the appearance of an object, not its underlying path, and are fully editable. The effects can be edited or removed without permanently affecting the object. So, you can experiment with an effect and then undo it if you don't like it. The Illustrator effects appear at the top of the Effect menu. Most of the Illustrator effects are vector-based for the display and upon output, so they can be modified without affecting the object. However, some of the effects—Drop Shadow, Inner Glow, Outer Glow, and Feather—are rasterized (converted from vector to raster) upon output, which doesn't allow for non-destructive modification without affecting the object. After you apply an effect, it appears on the Appearance panel, where you can make changes. If you apply an effect to a targeted layer, sublayer, or group, it automatically is applied to all current and future objects on the target. If you use graphic styles, you can also apply effects to them.

Apply an Illustrator Effect

1. Select the **Layers** panel, and then select the target circle for a layer, sublayer, group or object.

   ◆ To apply an effect to a part of an object, click the **Stroke** or **Fill** on the Appearance panel.

2. Click the **Effect** menu, point to a submenu under Illustrator Effects (if needed), and then select an effect.

3. To preview an effect in your document, select the **Preview** check box (if available).

4. Select the options you want for the selected effect; options vary depending on the effect.

5. Click **OK**.

Did You Know?

You can edit an applied effect. Select the layer, object or object's stroke or fill, open the Appearance panel, double-click the effect, make changes, and then click OK.

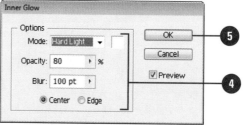

Apply an Illustrator Effect in Graphic Styles

1. Select a style name or swatch on the Graphic Styles panel or select an object that uses a graphic style.

   The style name appears in the Appearance panel.

2. Click the **Effect** menu, point to a submenu under Illustrator Effects (if needed), and then select an effect.

3. To preview an effect in your document, select the **Preview** check box (if available).

4. Select the options you want for the selected effect; options vary depending on the effect.

   If you enter a value in a box, press Tab to update the preview.

5. Click **OK**.

6. Click the **Options** button on the Appearance panel, and then click **Redefine Graphic Style** to update the style.

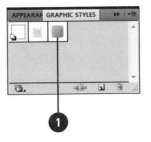

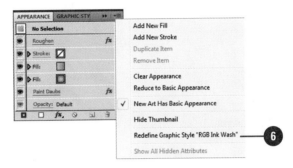

Did You Know?

You can remove an effect from a layer, object, or graphic style. Select the layer, object, or graphic style, open the Appearance panel, select the effect name, and then click the Delete Selected Item button. If you're removing an effect from a style, click the Options button on the Appearance panel, and then click Redefine Graphic Style to update the style.

Applying the Convert to Shape Effect

With the Illustrator Convert to Shape effect, you can change an object's outline to a rectangle, rounded rectangle, or ellipse without changing the actual underlying path. In the Shape Options dialog box, you can specify the width and height of the converted shape. The size can be set to an absolute value or a relative one based on the original object.

Apply the Convert to Shape Effect

1. Select the **Layers** panel, and then select the target circle for a layer, sublayer, group or object.

2. Click the **Effect** menu, point to **Convert to Shape**, and then click **Rectangle**, **Rounded Rectangle**, or **Ellipse**.

3. To preview an effect in your document, select the **Preview** check box (if available).

4. Click the **Absolute** or **Relative** option, and then enter values for width and height.

   For the Relative option, if you want the shape to be larger or smaller than the actual path, enter a positive or negative value.

5. For a Rounded Rectangle shape, enter a **Corner Radius** value.

6. Click **OK**.

Selection

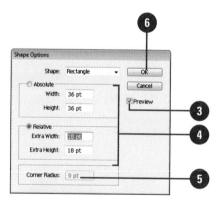

Did You Know?

You can round off sharp corners without converting the shape. Select the shape, click the Effect menu, point to Stylize, and then click Round Corners.

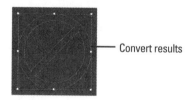

Convert results

Applying the Scribble Effect

IL 5.1, 5.3

If you want to make an object's fill look as though it was drawn with a pen or pencil, the Illustrator Scribble effect is the one for you. In the Scribble Options dialog box, you can use one of the many presets to create the look you want. It make the job easy. The presets include Childlike, Dense, Loose, Sharp, Sketch, Swash, Tight, and Zig-zag. After you select a preset (even if it's just the Default), you can adjust individual settings to customize the Scribble effect. As you make changes, you can preview the results in your document.

Apply the Scribble Effect

1. Select the **Layers** panel, and then select the target circle for a layer, sublayer, group or object.

2. Click the **Effect** menu, point to **Stylize**, and then click **Scribble**.

3. To preview an effect in your document, select the **Preview** check box (if available).

4. Select from the following options:

   ◆ **Settings.** Click the **Settings** popup to select a preset for the Scribble effect.

   ◆ **Angle.** Enter an **Angle** value or rotate the dial to change the angle of the sketch lines.

   ◆ **Path Overlap.** Drag the **Path Overlap** slider toward Outside to have the sketch lines extend beyond the edge of the path, or toward Inside to have the sketch lines stay inside the path along with the degree of random variation.

   ◆ **Line Options.** Change the **Stroke Width** for the lines, the **Curviness** for the lines (angle sharply or loosely) along with the degree of random variation, and the **Spacing** for the lines (tight or loose) along with the degree of random variation.

5. Click **OK**.

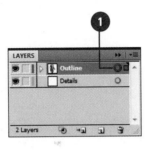

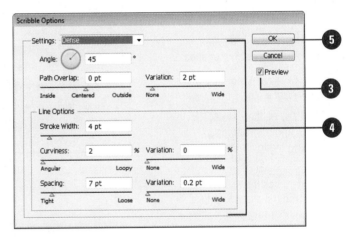

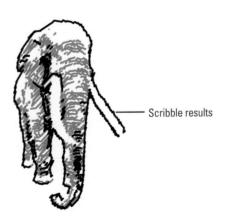

Scribble results

Applying the Inner or Outer Glow Effect

With the Illustrator Inner Glow or Outer Glow effect, you can apply a color special effect to an object. The inner glow effect spreads a color from the edge of an object inward, while the outer glow effect spreads a color from the edge of an object outward. You can also apply both effects to the same object. As you make changes, you can preview the results in your document. It's important to remember that the Inner Glow and Outer Glow effects are rasterized (converted from vector to raster) upon output.

Apply the Inner Glow or Outer Glow Effect

1. Select the **Layers** panel, and then select the target circle for a layer, sublayer, group or object.

2. Click the **Effect** menu, point to **Stylize**, and then click **Inner Glow** or **Outer Glow**.

3. To preview an effect in your document, select the **Preview** check box (if available).

4. Select from the following options:

   ◆ **Color.** Click the **Color** box, and then select a glow color.

   ◆ **Blend Mode.** Click the **Mode** popup, and then select a blending mode for the glow color.

   ◆ **Opacity.** Click the arrow, and then drag the slider to adjust the transparency of the glow.

   ◆ **Blur.** Click the arrow, and then drag the slider to adjust how far the glow extends inward or outward.

   ◆ **Center or Edge.** For the Inner Glow effect, click **Center** to have the glow spread outward from the center of the object, or click **Edge** to have the glow spread inward from the edge of the object toward the center.

5. Click **OK**.

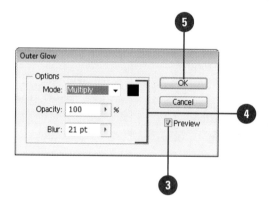

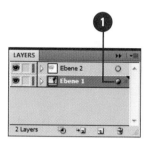

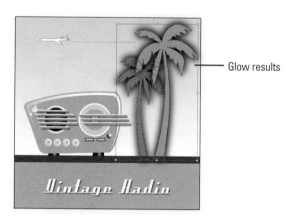

Glow results

Applying the Drop Shadow Effect

IL 5.1, 5.3

The Illustrator Drop Shadow effect allows you to apply soft, natural shadows to an object. With the Drop Shadow effect, you can specify a color blend, opacity (degree of transparency), offset, blur, and shadow color. As you make changes, you can preview the results in your document. You can apply the Drop Shadow effect to images and editable text. It's important to remember that the Drop Shadow effect is rasterized (converted from vector to raster) upon output.

Apply the Drop Shadow Effect

1. Select the **Layers** panel, and then select the target circle for a layer, sublayer, group or object.

2. Click the **Effect** menu, point to **Stylize**, and then click **Drop Shadow**.

3. To preview an effect in your document, select the **Preview** check box (if available).

4. Select from the following options:

   ◆ **Blend Mode.** Click the **Mode** list arrow, and then select a blending mode for the shadow color.

   ◆ **Opacity.** Click the arrow, and then drag the slider to adjust to see thoroughness of the shadow.

   ◆ **X and Y Offset.** Enter the distance of the shadow.

   ◆ **Blur.** Click the arrow, and then drag the slider to adjust how far the shadow extends inward or outward.

   ◆ **Color.** Click the **Color** option, and then select a color or click the **Darkness** option and specify a percentage.

5. Click **OK**.

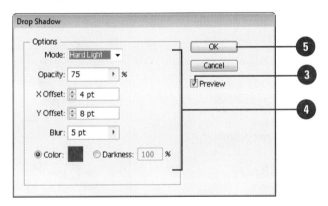

Shadow results

Applying 3D Effects

IL 5.1, 5.3

With the Illustrator 3D Effects, you can create 3D objects from 2D objects. The 3D Effects include Extrude & Bevel, Revolve, and Rotate. You can specify multiple appearance options including: position, rotation, surface, lighting, shading. Every 3D object is composed of multiple surfaces, such as a front, back, and sides. You can map 2D artwork (as a symbol) from the Symbols panel to each surface on a 3D object to create the look that you want.

Create a 3D Object

1. Select the object that you want to change.

2. Click the **Effect** menu, point to **3D**, and then click **Extrude & Bevel**.

   ◆ Click **More Options** to display all available options in the dialog box.

3. To preview an effect in your document, select the **Preview** check box (if available).

4. Select from the following options:

   ◆ **Position.** Specifies object perspective and rotation angle.

   ◆ **Extrude & Bevel.** Specifies the extent of object depth and bevel.

   ◆ **Surface.** Specifies the surface of the 3D object.

   ◆ **Lighting.** Adds one or more light sources, varies the light intensity, changes shading color, and changes the light source direction.

   ◆ **Map Art.** Click to map 2D artwork (as a symbol) onto the surface of a 3D object.

5. Click **OK**.

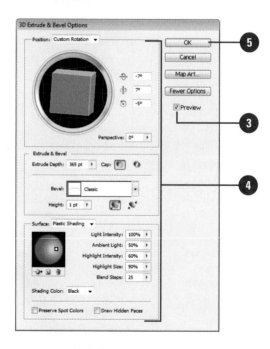

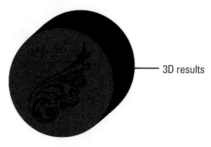

3D results

Create a 3D Revolving Object

1. Select the object that you want to change.

2. Click the **Effect** menu, point to **3D**, and then click **Revolve**.

   ◆ Click **More Options** to display all available options in the dialog box.

3. To preview an effect in your document, select the **Preview** check box (if available).

4. Select from the following options:

   ◆ **Position.** Specifies object perspective and rotation angle.

   ◆ **Revolve.** Specifies how to sweep the path around the object to create a 3D object.

   ◆ **Surface.** Specifies the surface of the 3D object.

   ◆ **Lighting.** Adds one or more light sources, varies the light intensity, changes shading color, and changes the light source direction.

   ◆ **Map Art.** Click to map 2D artwork (symbol) onto the surface of a 3D object.

5. Click **OK**.

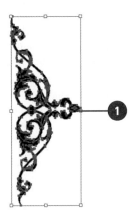

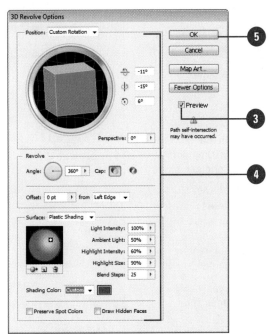

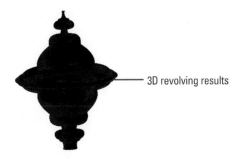

3D revolving results

Changing Raster Effects Settings

Some of the Illustrator effects—Drop Shadow, Inner Glow, Outer Glow, and Feather—and all of the Photoshop effects, are rasterized upon output. You can control how a raster effect looks in your document and how it will output from Illustrator by using the Document Raster Effects Settings dialog box. The available options allow you to specify a color model, resolution, background type (white or transparent), as well as apply anti-alias, create a clipping mask, and preserve spot colors. These options are globally applied to all raster effects. The raster settings convert a vector object to a bitmap image. If you want to apply raster settings to an individual object, you can specify many of the same options in the Rasterize dialog box.

Change Raster Effects Settings

1. Click the **Effect** menu, and then click **Document Raster Effects Settings**.

2. Select from the following options:

   ◆ **Color Mode.** Select a color mode: **CMYK**, **RGB**, **Grayscale**, or **Bitmap**.

   ◆ **Resolution.** Select a screen size in points per inch (ppi). Use **Screen** for web or video output, **Medium** for desktop printers, or **High** for commercial printing.

   ◆ **Background.** Use **White** to make any transparent areas white or **Transparent** to make the background transparent by creating an alpha channel.

   ◆ **Anti-alias.** Select to apply anti-alias to soften the edges of a rasterized object.

   ◆ **Create Clipping Mask.** Select to create a clipping path around the image and specify a size to extend the effect. If you selected the Transparent option, you don't need to select this option.

   ◆ **Preserve Spot Colors.** Select to preserve spot colors.

3. Click **OK**.

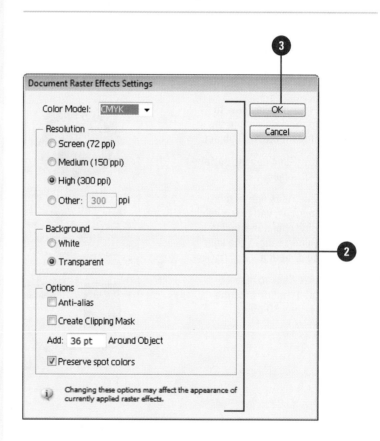

Convert Vector Objects to Bitmap Images

1. Select the **Layers** panel, and then select the target circle for a layer, sublayer, group or object.

2. Click the **Object** menu, and then click **Rasterize**.

3. Select from the following options:

   ◆ **Color Mode.** Select a color mode: **CMYK**, **RGB**, **Grayscale**, or **Bitmap**.

   ◆ **Resolution.** Select a screen size in points per inch (ppi). Use **Screen** for web or video output, **Medium** for desktop printers, **High** for commercial printing, or **Use Document Raster Effects Resolution** to apply the global resolution.

   ◆ **Background.** Use **White** to make any transparent areas white or **Transparent** to make the background transparent by creating an alpha channel.

   ◆ **Anti-alias.** Use **Art Optimized (Supersampling)** to soften shape edges. Use **Type Optimized (Hinted)** to soften type edges. Use **None** to keep edges jagged.

   ◆ **Create Clipping Mask.** Select to create a clipping path around the image and specify a size to extend the effect. If you selected the Transparent option, you don't need to select this option.

   ◆ **Preserve Spot Colors.** Select to preserve spot colors.

4. Click **OK**.

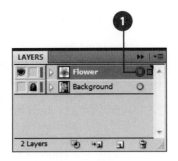

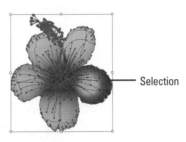

Selection

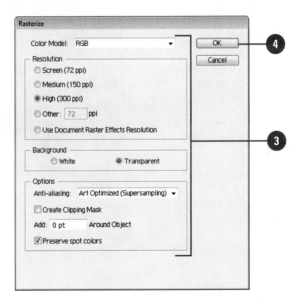

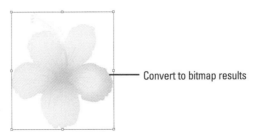

Convert to bitmap results

Working with the Effect Gallery

The Effect Gallery enables you to maintain complete and total control over Photoshop effects. In essence, the Effect Gallery gives you access to all of Photoshop's effects and lets you apply the effects to any image, while viewing a large preview of the results. The Effect Gallery dialog box is composed of three sections—Image Preview, Effect Selection, and Effect Controls. When you use the Effect Gallery to modify the image, you see exactly how the image will look; there is no guesswork involved. When you apply an effect to an image, you are physically remapping the pixel information within the image. Illustrator provides over 50 Photoshop effects and the combinations of those effects are astronomical. That means there are a lot of different combinations available for you to try…have fun.

Work with the Photoshop Effect Gallery

1. Select the **Layers** panel, and then select the layer you want to modify with an effect.

2. Click the **Effect** menu, and then click **Effect Gallery**.

3. Change the image preview by clicking the plus or minus zoom buttons, or by clicking the black triangle and selecting from the preset zoom sizes.

4. If necessary, drag the lower right corner in or out to resize the Effect Gallery dialog box.

5. Click the **expand triangle**, located to the left of the individual categories, to expand an effect category. Effect categories include:

   ◆ Artistic
   ◆ Blur
   ◆ Brush Strokes
   ◆ Distort
   ◆ Pixelate
   ◆ Sharpen
   ◆ Sketch

- ◆ Stylize
- ◆ Texture
- ◆ Video

⑥ Click an effect from the expanded list to view its default effects on the image.

⑦ Modify the results of the effect using the effect controls.

⑧ To temporarily hide the Effect Selections, click the **Show/Hide Effect Thumbnails** button, located to the left of the OK button.

⑨ Click **OK**.

Did You Know?

You can reapply a specific effect using a shortcut. Press Shift+Ctrl+E (Win) or Shift+⌘+F (Mac) to reapply the last effect to the image.

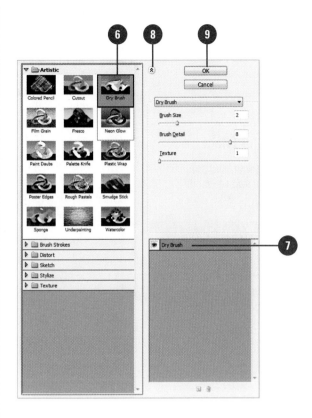

Using the Gaussian Blur Effect

You can also apply the Photoshop Gaussian Blur effect that blurs an image or a selection by a controllable amount. The Gaussian Blur effect can be used to add a sense of depth to the image. For example, you could select and blur the background of an image while leaving the foreground in focus. The outcome of the effect is to create a hazy, out-of-focus effect on the image or selection.

Use the Gaussian Blur Effect

1. Select the **Layers** panel, and then select the layer you want to modify with an effect.

2. Click the **Effect** menu, point to **Blur**, and then click **Gaussian Blur**.

3. Drag the **Radius** slider or enter a pixel value to increase or decrease the amount of Gaussian blur applied to the image.

4. Click **OK**.

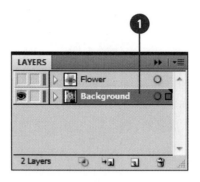

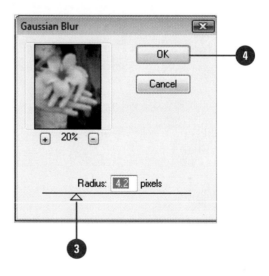

Using the Unsharp Mask Effect

The Photoshop Unsharp Mask effect creates a visually sharper image by locating pixels that differ in value from surrounding pixels. When the effect is applied to the image, the bordering pixels specified by the threshold option get lighter and the darker pixels get darker. It's important to understand that the Unsharp Mask does not actually sharpen the image; it only attempts to create the illusion of sharpness. Be careful; an over-application of this effect creates harsh images with ragged edges and shadows. Also, the effects of the Unsharp Mask effect appear more severe when viewed with the low resolution of a computer than when the document is output to a printer.

Use the Unsharp Mask Effect

1. Select the **Layers** panel, and then select the layer you want to modify with an effect.

2. Click the **Effect** menu, point to **Sharpen**, and then click **Unsharp Mask**.

3. Select from the following options:

   ◆ **Amount.** Drag the slider or enter a value to determine how much to increase the contrast of pixels.

   ◆ **Radius.** Drag the slider or enter a value to determine the number of pixels surrounding the edge pixels that affect the sharpening.

   ◆ **Threshold.** Drag the slider or enter a value to determine how different the sharpened pixels must be from the surrounding area before they are considered edge pixels and sharpened by the effect.

4. Click **OK**.

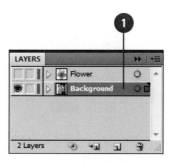

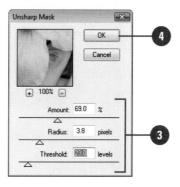

The Unsharp Mask filter applied to the image.

Applying Multiple Effects

Not only does Photoshop's Effect Gallery let you apply and view an effect, it lets you view the multiple effects of two or more filters. The Effect Gallery has its own Layers panel, and you can have multiple effect layers. The order of the effects influences their impact on the image, so when you use more than one effect, try dragging the layer up or down in the stack to see the different possibilities. Experiment with different stacking orders to create unique, eye-popping special effects.

Apply Multiple Effects

1. Select the **Layers** panel, and then select the layer you want to modify with an effect.

2. Click the **Effect** menu, and then click **Effect Gallery**.

3. Select the effect you want.

4. Adjust the effect as necessary.

5. Click the **New Layer Effect** button, located at the bottom of the Effect Adjustments section. You can add as many effects layers as needed.

6. Select and adjust a second effect (repeat steps 3 and 4).

7. Adjust each individual effect by clicking on the effect layer you want to change.

8. To change the effect's influence on the image, drag an effect layer to another position in the stack.

9. To temporarily show or hide the effect on the image, click the **Show/Hide** button.

10. To delete a selected effect layer, click the **Delete** button.

11. Click **OK**.

IMPORTANT *Once you click the OK button, the effects are permanently applied to the active image, unless it's a Smart Object.*

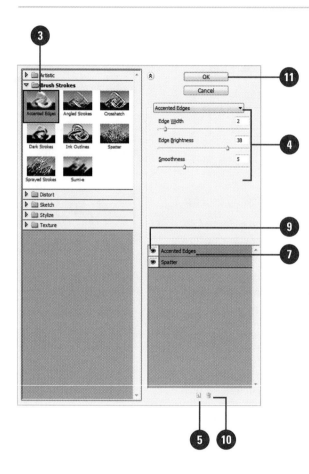

Controlling Effects Using Selections

When you apply an effect, Illustrator applies the effect equally to the entire image. Unfortunately, that might not be what you had in mind. For example, you might want to apply the Gaussian Blur effect to a portion of the image. In that case, Illustrator's selection tools come to the rescue. The primary purpose of making a selection is to define a work area, and when you select an area before applying an effect, the only area impacted by the effect will be the selected area.

Control Effects Using Selections

1. Select the **Layers** panel, and then select the layer to which you want to apply an effect.

2. Select the **Direct Selection** tool on the Tools panel, and then make a selection in the document window.

3. Click the **Effect** menu, and then click **Effect Gallery**.

4. Select any Photoshop effects.

5. Adjust the effect options until you see the effect you want.

6. Click **OK**.

   The effect is only applied to the selected areas of the image.

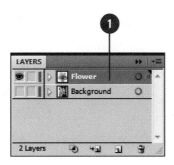

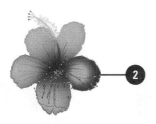

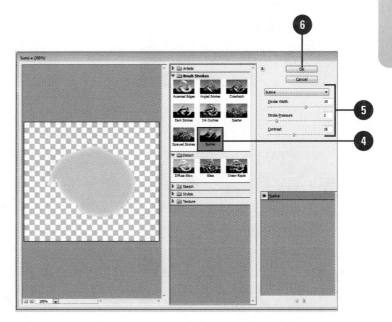

Viewing Various Effects

Illustrator and Photoshop provide a bountiful selection of over 100 effects.. Take a moment to view some of the various effects you can use. The original image is shown to the right, and we've displayed some common effects on the following pages. A good thing to think about when using effects is your original image. Look at the background colors, and see if they will look good with some of the effects. The best thing to do is open an image that has a lot of varied details, and then apply some effects to see what looks good to you.

Various Effects

Cutout

Dry Brush

Fresco

Panel Knife

Accented Edges

Glass

Diffuse Glow

Note Paper

Stamp

Glowing Edges

Grain

Spatter

Mosaic Tiles

Stained Glass

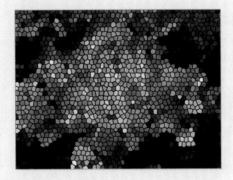

Graphic Pen

Plastic Wrap

Drawing and Painting

11

Introduction

After you create a path using the Pencil tool or other drawing tool, you can use the Live Paint command or the Live Paint Bucket tool to convert the paths into a Live Paint Group that you can paint. Before you start using the Live Paint Bucket tool, it's important to select the painting options that you want to use beforehand.

With the Live Paint Bucket tool, you can recolor a Live Paint Group. When you click an area formed by intersecting lines in a Live Paint Group, the Live Paint Bucket tool applies fill and stroke paint attributes. When you apply fill or stroke attributes, you're actually recoloring faces (fills) and edges (strokes) and not the path itself. With the Live Paint Selection tool, you can select faces (fills) and edges (strokes) in a Live Paint Group. Before you start using the Live Paint Selection tool, it's important to choose the selection options that you want to use beforehand. If you create a gap in a closed path in a Live Paint Group, the face (fill) of the object disappears. With the Gap Options dialog box, you can specify gap detection options to avoid this problem.

The Brushes panel allows you to draw with different brush tips, creating free style lines, shapes, patterns, and textures. There are four main categories of brushes: Scatter, Calligraphic, Art, and Pattern. You can use brushes that come built-in with Illustrator in Brush libraries or you can create your own. Illustrator's paintbrush tool was designed to reproduce the visual effect of applying paint to an artboard. When you use a stylus and a pressure sensitive drawing tablet, the Paintbrush tool is pressure-sensitive too. You select brushes from the Brushes panel or other Brush libraries to use with the Paintbrush tool.

What You'll Do

Use the Pencil Tool

Create Live Paint Groups

Set Live Paint Bucket Tool Options

Use the Live Paint Bucket Tool

Use the Live Paint Selection Tool

Modify Live Paint Groups

Set Gap Options

Use the Brushes Panel

Use the Paintbrush Tool

Create and Edit Scatter Brushes

Create and Edit Calligraphic Brushes

Create and Edit Art Brushes

Create and Edit Pattern Brushes

Work with Brushes

Work with Liquify Tools

Using the Pencil Tool

IL 2.6

The Pencil tool is exactly what its name implies...a pencil. If you like to draw freehand or sketch objects, especially with a drawing tablet, the Pencil tool is right for you. You can use the Pencil tool in several ways. You can draw new line segments to create a path, reshape a path, or add to a path. You can customize the way the Pencil tool works by setting preferences in the Pencil Tool Preferences dialog box.

Use the Pencil Tool

1. Select the **Pencil** tool on the Tools panel.

2. Select a stroke color and weight and a fill of **None** on the Tools and Stroke panels.

3. Click the **View** menu, and then click **Pixel View** to view the drawing with attributes or click **Outline View** to view the drawing as lines (wireframe).

4. Use any of the following methods:

   ◆ **New Path.** Drag in a blank area to create an open or closed path. To create a closed path, hold down Alt (Win) or Option (Mac) while you finish drawing.

   ◆ **Reshape Path.** Drag along the edge of a selected open or closed path.

   ◆ **Add to Path.** Drag from an endpoint of an open path.

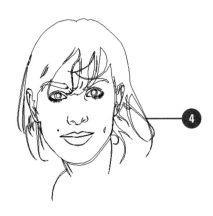

Did You Know?

You can erase all or part of a path with the Path Eraser tool. Select the Path Eraser tool (same slot at the Pencil tool), and then drag along the path that you want to erase.

Set Pencil Tool Options

1. Double-click the **Pencil** tool on the Tools panel.

2. Drag the slider or enter a **Fidelity** value (.5-20). Fidelity determines how far the mouse (or stylus) must move before an anchor point is added. A higher value creates fewer anchor points and a smoother path while a lower value creates more anchor points and a rougher path.

3. Drag the slider or enter a **Smoothness** value (0-100). A high value creates a smoother curve, while a low value creates more bends.

4. Select or deselect any of the following check boxes:

   ◆ **Fill New Pencil Strokes.** Select to fill new paths with the current fill color.

   ◆ **Keep Selected.** Select to keep pencil paths selected after you draw them.

   ◆ **Edit Selected Paths.** Select to enable Reshaping for the Pencil tool within the specified pixel range (2-20).

5. To revert settings back to the defaults, click **Reset**.

6. Click **OK**.

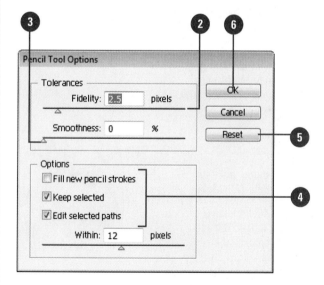

Creating Live Paint Groups

Live Paint allows you to fill open or closed paths by creating Live Paint Groups. After you create a path using the Pencil tool or other drawing tool, you can use the Live Paint command or the Live Paint Bucket tool to convert the paths into a Live Paint Group that you can paint. You can also convert a traced object from a raster graphic into a Live Paint Group, and then paint it. The Live Paint Bucket tool allows you to click an area formed by intersecting lines to apply fill (known as face) and stroke (known as edges) attributes. As you reshape the Live Paint objects, the paint attributes also change.

Create Live Paint Groups

1. Create a drawing using any of the drawing tools or use the Live Trace command to create a path from a raster graphic.

   For the best results, use a drawing with multiple intersecting lines that you can fill.

   ◆ To create a Live Paint Group from type, click the **Type** menu, and then click **Create Outlines** to create path outlines.

   ◆ To create a Live Paint Group from a symbol or blend, click the **Object** menu, and then click **Expand** to create paths.

2. Select all the paths using selection tools on the Tools panel.

3. Click the **Object** menu, point to **Live Paint**, and then click **Make**.

   ◆ You can also click the **Live Paint Bucket** tool on the Tools panel, and then click the selected paths.

   The paths are nested together into a Live Paint Group, which appears in the Layers panel.

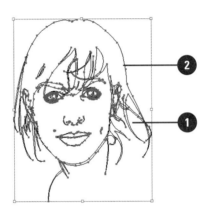

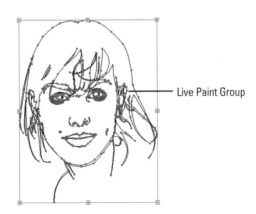

Live Paint Group

Convert a Traced Object to a Live Paint Group

1 Open or place a raster graphic in an Illustrator document.

2 Select the graphic that you want to trace.

◆ You can also select a Live Trace object to change it.

3 Click the **Live Trace** button on the Control panel. If prompted, click **OK**.

4 Select all the paths using selection tools on the Tools panel.

5 Click the **Live Paint** button on the Control panel.

◆ You can also click the **Object** menu, point to **Live Paint**, and then click **Make**.

◆ You can also click the **Live Paint Bucket** tool on the Tools panel, and then click the selected paths.

The paths are nested together into a Live Paint Group, which appears in the Layers panel.

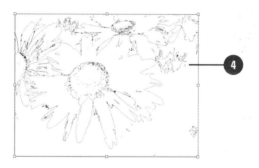

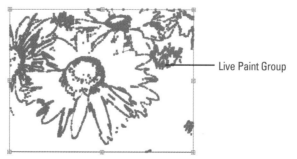

Live Paint Group

Setting Live Paint Bucket Tool Options

With the Live Paint Bucket tool on the Tools panel, you can recolor fills and strokes in a Live Paint Group. Before you start using the Live Paint Bucket tool, it's important to select the painting options that you want to use beforehand. You can quickly set Live Paint Bucket tool options by double-clicking the tool on the Tools panel. In the Live Paint Bucket Options dialog box, you set options to paint fills and/or paint strokes in a Live Paint Group. To make it easier to paint fills and strokes, you can also select the Cursor Swatch Preview option to display a color strip above the Live Paint Bucket pointer with the current or last color used along with two adjacent colors. In addition, you can specify a highlight color to make it easier to identify fill and stroke areas.

Select Options for Paint Fills or Strokes with the Live Paint Bucket Tool

1. Double-click the **Live Paint Bucket** tool on the Tools panel.

2. Select the **Paint Fills** check box to paint fills with the Live Paint Bucket tool.

3. Select the **Paint Strokes** check box to paint strokes with the Live Paint Bucket tool.

4. Click **OK**.

   ◆ If only **Paint Fills** or **Paint Strokes** is selected, you can Shift-click with the Live Paint Bucket tool to switch between painting fills and applying stroke colors and weight.

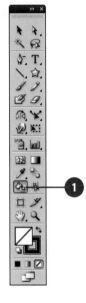

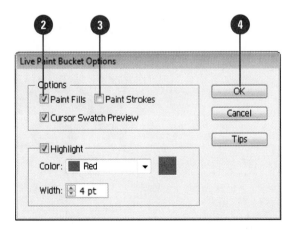

Set Live Paint Bucket Tool Preferences

1. Double-click the **Live Paint Bucket** tool on the Tools panel.

2. Select the **Cursor Swatch Preview** check box to display a color strip above the Live Paint Bucket pointer with the current or last color used, along with two adjacent colors.

3. Select the **Highlight** check box to change the highlight color, and then select a color and specify a width.

4. To get helpful tips, click **Tips**.

5. Click **OK**.

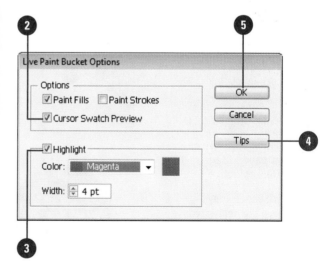

Using the Live Paint Bucket Tool

 IL 6.6

With the Live Paint Bucket tool on the Tools panel, you can recolor a Live Paint Group. When you click an area formed by intersecting lines in a Live Paint Group, the Live Paint Bucket tool applies fill and stroke paint attributes. When you apply fill or stroke attributes, you're actually recoloring faces (fills) and edges (strokes) and not the path itself. Each edge can have a different color (even None) and weight. You can customize the way the Live Paint Bucket tool works by setting preferences in the Live Paint Bucket Options dialog box.

Fill Faces with the Live Paint Bucket Tool

1. Select the **Live Paint Bucket** tool on the Tools panel.

   ◆ Make sure the **Paint Fills** option is set in the Live Paint Bucket Options dialog box. Double-click the **Live Paint Bucket** tool.

   ◆ If only Paint Fills or Paint Strokes is selected in Options, you can Shift-click with the **Live Paint Bucket** tool to switch between painting fills and applying stroke colors and weight.

2. Display a Live Paint Group object.

3. Select a fill color on the Swatches, Tools, or Control panels to use with the Live Paint Bucket tool.

   ◆ If the Cursor Swatch Preview appears above the pointer, you can press the left or right arrow keys to select or display the next or previous color from the Swatches panel.

4. Point to the face that you want to fill. The face becomes highlighted.

5. Click an individual face or drag multiple faces.

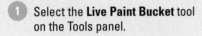

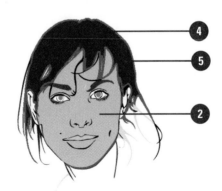

Change Stroke Edges with the Live Paint Bucket Tool

1. Select the **Live Paint Bucket** tool on the Tools panel.

   ◆ Make sure the **Paint Strokes** option is set in the Live Paint Bucket Options dialog box. Double-click the Live Paint Bucket tool.

   ◆ If only Paint Fills or Paint Strokes is selected in Options, you can Shift-click with the Live Paint Bucket tool to switch between painting fills and applying stroke colors and weight.

2. Display a Live Paint Group object.

3. Select a stroke color, weight, or other attributes on the Strokes, Tools, or Control panels to use with the Live Paint Bucket tool.

   ◆ To remove colors from stroke edges, select **None**.

4. Point to the edge that you want to change. The edge becomes highlighted.

5. Click an individual edge or drag multiple edges.

   ◆ Double-click an edge to apply the current stroke attributes to all contiguous edges that have the same color and weight.

   ◆ Triple-click an edge to apply the current stroke color and attributes to all edges that have the same attributes.

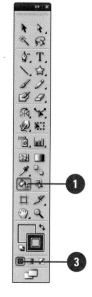

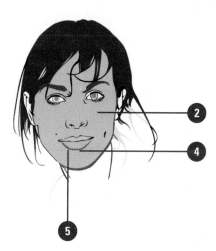

Using the Live Paint Selection Tool

 IL 6.6

With the Live Paint Selection tool on the Tools panel, you can select faces (fills) and edges (strokes) in a Live Paint Group. Before you start using the Live Paint Selection tool, it's important to choose the selection options that you want to use beforehand. You can quickly set Live Paint Selection tool options by double-clicking the tool on the Tools panel. In the Live Paint Selection Options dialog box, you set options to select fills and/or to select strokes in a Live Paint Group. In addition, you can specify a highlight color for the selection. It's a good idea to select a different color than the Live Paint Bucket tool; they are initially set to the same color.

Set Live Paint Selection Tool Options

1. Double-click the **Live Paint Selection** tool on the Tools panel.

2. Select the **Select Fills** check box to paint fills with the Live Paint Selection tool.

3. Select the **Select Strokes** check box to paint strokes with the Live Paint Selection tool.

4. Select the **Highlight** check box to change the highlight color, and then select a color and specify a width.

5. Click **OK**.

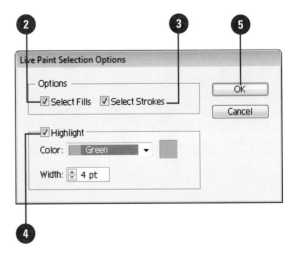

Use the Live Paint Selection Tool

① Select the **Live Paint Selection** tool on the Tools panel.

② Display a Live Paint Group object.

③ Click a face or edge.

④ Shift-click to select or deselect additional faces or edges.

⑤ Do any of the following:

◆ **Fills.** Select a fill color, gradient, or pattern.

◆ **Strokes.** Select a stroke color, weight, or other attributes. Select None to hide stroke edges.

◆ **Delete.** Press Backspace or Delete to remove the selected faces or strokes.

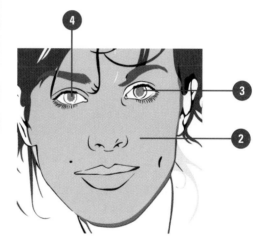

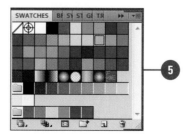

Modifying Live Paint Groups

After you create a Live Paint Group, you can use Isolation Mode to reshape, move, and add to the group. To make your group easier to select and modify, you can show a bounding box with star-filled selection handles around the path. If you no longer want a selected path, you can remove it using the Delete key. When you modify a path in a Live Paint Group, colors automatically refill and line segments reshape.

Reshape or Move Paths in a Live Paint Group

1. Select the **Selection** tool on the Tools panel.

2. Click the **View** menu, and then click **Bounding Box**.

3. Select a path or area in a group.

4. Click the **Isolate Selected Object** button on the Control panel.

    TIMESAVER *Double-click the Live Paint Group to isolate it.*

5. Do any of the following:

    ◆ Select the **Selection** tool, and then drag a handle to modify it or drag the path to move it.

    ◆ Select the **Direct Selection** tool, click an anchor point, and then drag to modify the segment.

6. Click the gray bar above the document to exit Isolation Mode.

Add Paths to a Live Paint Group

1. Select the **Selection** tool on the Tools panel.

2. Click the **View** menu, and then click **Bounding Box**.

3. Select a path or area in a group.

4. Click the **Isolate Selected Object** button on the Control panel.

   TIMESAVER *Double-click the Live Paint Group to isolate it.*

5. Draw the path that you want to add to the group using drawing tools on the Tools panel.

6. Click the gray bar above the document to exit Isolation Mode.

   ◆ You can also draw a path on a layer, select the new path and the Live Paint Group, and then click **Merge Live Paint** on the Control panel.

Did You Know?

You can expand a Live Paint Group. Select the Live Paint Group, and then click Expand on the Control panel. Now, you can edit individual components of the Live Path Group path.

You can release a Live Paint Group. Select the Live Paint Group, click the Object menu, point to Live Paint, and then click Release. Now, you can edit individual components of the Live Path Group path.

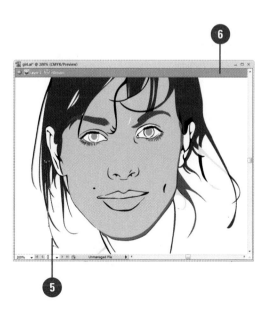

Setting Gap Options

IL 6.6

If you create a gap in a closed path in a Live Paint Group, the face (fill) of the object disappears. With the Gap Options dialog box, you can specify gap detection options to avoid this problem. You can select a predefined gap size or enter one of your own along with a gap preview color.

Set Gap Options

1. Select the **Direct Selection** tool on the Tools panel.

2. Select a Live Paint Group.

3. Click the **Gap Options** button on the Control panel.

4. Select the **Preview** check box to view your changes as you set options.

5. Select the **Gap Detection** check box to enable the feature.

6. Click the **Paint Stops At** list arrow, and then select a gap option.

   ◆ Select the **Custom** check box to specify a custom size.

7. Click the **Gap Preview Color** list arrow, and then select a color.

8. Click the **Close gaps with paths** button to apply these settings to the document.

9. Click **OK**.

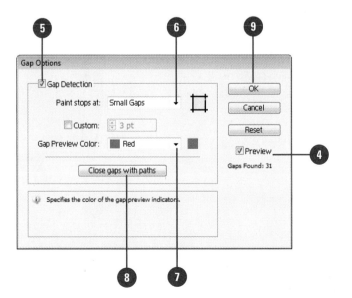

Using the Brushes Panel

Use and Apply Brushes to a Path with the Brushes Panel

1. Select the **Brushes** panel.

2. Select a path with any of the selection tools.

3. To change the Brushes panel view, click the **Options** menu, and then select any of the following view available options:

   ◆ **Show Calligraphic Brushes**, **Show Scatter Brushes**, **Show Art Brushes**, or **Show Pattern Brushes**

   ◆ **Thumbnail View**

   ◆ **List View**

4. Click the **Brush Libraries Menu** button on the panel, point to a brush category, and then select a brush library.

5. Click a brush in the library panel to add it to the Brushes panel.

   ◆ You can also drag a brush from any brushes panel onto a path to apply it.

6. Click a brush on the Brushes panel to apply it to the selected path.

The Brushes panel allows you to draw with different brush tips, to create free style lines, shapes, patterns, and textures. There are four main categories of brushes: Scatter, Calligraphic, Art, and Pattern. You can use built-in brushes that come with Illustrator (stored in Brush libraries) or you can create your own. Sometimes it's hard to find a brush. To make it easier, you can use the Options menu to change the panel views. Brushes are live, which means that any previous use of a brush can be updated when you change the brush.

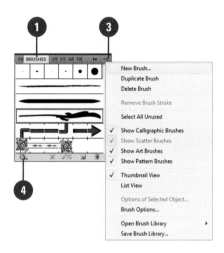

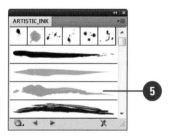

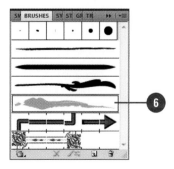

Using the Paintbrush Tool

Illustrator's paintbrush tool was designed to reproduce the visual effect of applying paint to an artboard. When you use a stylus and a pressure-sensitive drawing tablet, the Paintbrush tool is pressure-sensitive too. You select brushes from the Brushes panel or other Brush libraries to use with the Paintbrush tool. You can customize the way the Paintbrush tool works by setting preferences in the Paintbrush Tool Preferences dialog box.

Set Paintbrush Tool Options

1. Double-click the **Paintbrush** tool on the Tools panel.

2. Drag the slider or enter a **Fidelity** value (.5-20). Fidelity determines how far the mouse (or stylus) must move before an anchor point is added. A higher value creates fewer anchor points and a smoother path while a lower value creates more anchor points and a rougher path.

3. Drag the slider or enter a **Smoothness** value (0-100). A high value creates a smoother curve, while a low value creates more bends.

4. Select or deselect any of the following check boxes:

   ◆ **Fill New Brush Strokes.** Select to fill new paths with the current fill color.

   ◆ **Keep Selected.** Select to keep brush paths selected after you draw them.

   ◆ **Edit Selected Paths.** Select to enable changing an existing path with the Paintbrush tool within the specified pixel range (2-20).

5. To revert settings back to the defaults, click **Reset**.

6. Click **OK**.

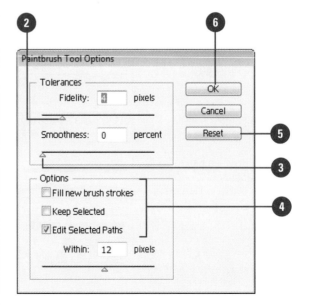

Use the Paintbrush Tool

1. Select the **Paintbrush** tool on the Tools panel.

2. Select **None** for the fill color.

3. Select the **Brushes** panel.

4. Select a brush on the panel.

   ◆ You can also click the **Brush** list arrow on the Control panel, and then select a brush.

5. Do any of the following:

   ◆ **Open Path.** Drag to draw a path that doesn't connect.

   ◆ **Closed Path.** Drag to draw a path, and then Alt+drag (Win) or Option+drag (Mac) to close it.

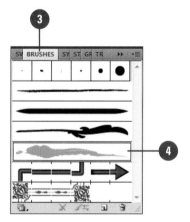

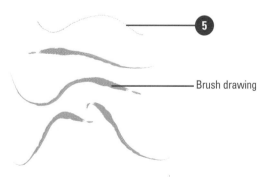

Brush drawing

Creating and Editing Scatter Brushes

 IL 6.4

Scatter brushes disperse copies of an object along a path. You create a scatter brush from a path, compound path, type character, or type outline. When you use a scatter brush, the brush is applied using a fixed or random method along a path. You use a similar method to create and edit a Scatter brush. You use the Scatter Brush Options dialog box to set the options that you want.

Create or Edit a Scatter Brush

1. Select the **Brushes** panel.

2. Do one of the following:

   ◆ **Create.** Select one or more objects, click the **New Brush** button on the panel, click the **New Scatter Brush** option, and then click **OK**. Enter a name for the brush.

   ◆ **Edit.** Deselect any brushes, and then double-click a Scatter brush.

3. For the **Size, Spacing, Scatter**, and **Rotation** options, click the list arrow, and then select one of the following options:

   ◆ **Fixed.** Enter a single fixed value.

   ◆ **Random.** Drag sliders or enter a range for variable value.

   ◆ **Pressure, Stylus Wheel, Tilt, Bearing, or Rotation.** Drag sliders or enter values when using a drawing tablet.

4. Specify the following options:

   ◆ **Size.** Determines the size of the scatter objects.

   ◆ **Spacing.** Determines the spacing between the scatter objects.

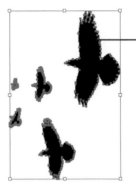

Selection for creating a brush

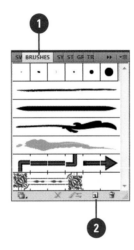

Creates a new brush

- ◆ **Scatter.** Determines the distance between the path and the objects.

- ◆ **Rotation.** Specifies the rotation range relative to the page or path.

⑤ Click the **Method** list arrow, and then select an option:

- ◆ **None.** Retains colors from the Brushes panel.

- ◆ **Tints.** Changes black areas in the brush stroke to the current stroke color.

- ◆ **Tints and Shades.** Changes colors in the brush stroke to tints of the current stroke color.

- ◆ **Hue Shift.** Change the current stroke color to the Key color and change other colors to hue colors. Select the Key color that you want.

⑥ Click **OK**.

If the brush is being used, an alert appears.

⑦ Click **Apply to Strokes** to apply the modified brush option to existing strokes or **Leave Strokes** to apply the modified brush only to new strokes.

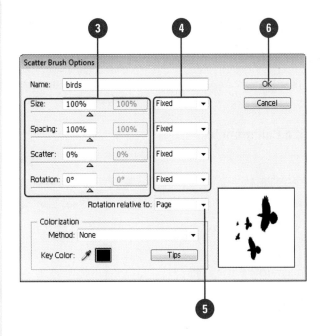

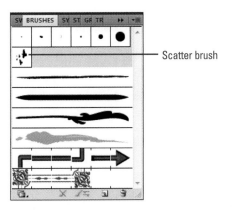

Scatter brush

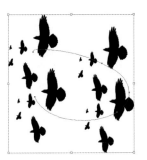

Creating and Editing Calligraphic Brushes

IL 6.4

Calligraphic brushes resemble strokes you create with a Calligraphy pen. When you use a calligraphic brush, it applies the brush to the center of the path. You use a similar method to create and edit a Calligraphic brush. You use the Calligraphic Brush Options dialog box to set the options that you want. The options include Angle, Roundness, and Diameter.

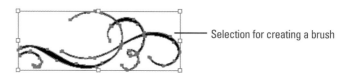

Selection for creating a brush

Create or Edit a Calligraphic Brush

1. Select the **Brushes** panel.

2. Do one of the following:

   ◆ **Create.** Select one or more objects, click the **New Brush** button on the panel, click the **New Calligraphic Brush** option, and then click **OK**. Enter a name for the brush.

   ◆ **Edit.** Deselect any brushes, and then double-click a calligraphic brush.

3. For the **Angle**, **Roundness**, and **Diameter** options, click the list arrow, and then select one of the following options:

   ◆ **Fixed.** Enter a single fixed value.

   ◆ **Random.** Drag sliders or enter a range for a variable value.

   ◆ **Pressure, Stylus Wheel, Tilt, Bearing, or Rotation.** Drag sliders or enter values if using a drawing tablet.

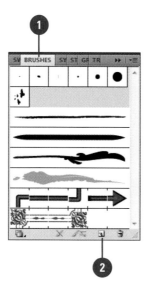

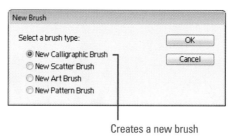

Creates a new brush

278

④ Specify the following options:

◆ **Angle.** Enter a value (-180 to 180) to specify the angle of rotation for the brush.

◆ **Roundness.** Enter a value (0-100%) to specify the roundness of the brush. Drag a black dot in the preview away from or towards the center.

◆ **Diameter.** Drag a slider or enter a value (0-1296 points) to specify the diameter of the brush.

⑤ Click **OK**.

If the brush is being used, an alert appears.

⑥ Click **Apply to Strokes** to apply the modified brush option to existing strokes or **Leave Strokes** to apply the modified brush only to new strokes.

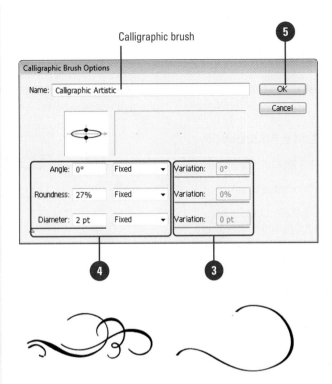

Calligraphic brush

Creating and Editing Art Brushes

 IL 6.4

Art brushes create artistic strokes when painting. When you use an Art brush, it stretches a brush shape or object shape evenly along the center of a path. You use a similar method to create and edit an Art brush. You can use the Art Brush Options dialog box to set the options that you want. The options include: Direction, Size, and Flip Along or Flip Across.

Create or Edit a Art Brush

① Select the **Brushes** panel.

② Do one of the following:

◆ **Create.** Select one or more objects, click the **New Brush** button on the panel, click the **New Art Brush** option, and then click **OK**. Enter a name for the brush.

◆ **Edit.** Deselect any brushes, and then double-click an art brush.

③ Specify the following options:

◆ **Direction.** Select an icon to specify the direction of the artwork in relation to the line.

◆ **Size.** Enter a width relative to the original width. Select the Proportional check box to keep the artwork scaled.

◆ **Flip Along or Flip Across.** Select to change the orientation of the artwork in relation to the line.

Selection for creating a brush

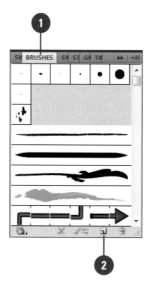

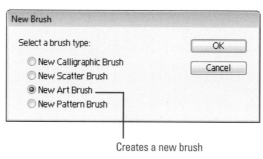

Creates a new brush

4 Click the **Method** list arrow, and then select an option:

- ◆ **None.** Retains colors from the Brushes panel.

- ◆ **Tints.** Changes black areas in the brush stroke to the current stroke color.

- ◆ **Tints and Shades.** Changes colors in the brush stroke to tints of the current stroke color.

- ◆ **Hue Shift.** Changes the current stroke color to the Key color and changes other colors to hue colors. Select the Key color that you want.

5 Click **OK**.

If the brush is being used, an alert appears.

6 Click **Apply to Strokes** to apply the modified brush option to existing strokes or **Leave Strokes** to apply the modified brush only to new strokes.

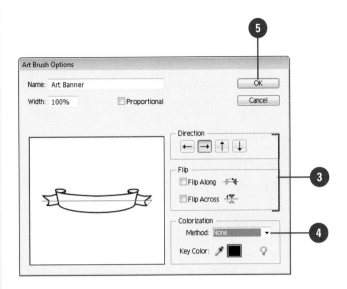

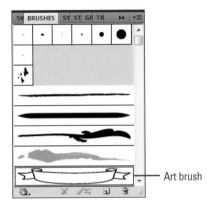

Art brush

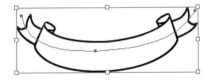

Creating and Editing Pattern Brushes

 IL 6.4

Pattern brushes paint with a pattern. Pattern brushes work the same way as Scatter brushes; however, they follow the path exactly, while Scatter brushes don't. You use a similar method to create and edit a Pattern brush. You use the Pattern Brush Options dialog box to set the options that you want. The options include Scale, Spacing, Tile Buttons, Flip Along or Flip Across, and Fit.

Create or Edit a Pattern Brush

① Select the **Brushes** panel.

② Do one of the following:

◆ **Create.** Select one or more objects, click the **New Brush** button on the panel, click the **New Pattern Brush** option, and then click **OK**. Enter a name for the brush.

◆ **Edit.** Deselect any brushes, and then double-click a pattern brush.

③ Specify the following options:

◆ **Scale.** Enter a value to adjust the size of tiles relative to the original size.

◆ **Spacing.** Enter a value to adjust the spacing between tiles.

◆ **Tile Buttons.** Select to apply different patterns to different parts of a path.

◆ **Flip Along or Flip Across.** Select to change the orientation of the artwork in relation to the line.

◆ **Fit.** Select an option to adjust the size of the tile.

Selection for creating a brush

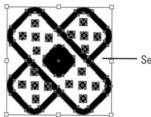

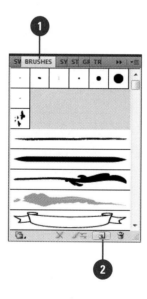

Creates a new brush

④ Click the **Method** list arrow, and then select an option:

- ◆ **None.** Retains colors from the Brushes panel.

- ◆ **Tints.** Changes black areas in the brush stroke to the current stroke color.

- ◆ **Tints and Shades.** Changes colors in the brush stroke to tints and shades of the current stroke color.

- ◆ **Hue Shift.** Changes the current stroke color to the Key color and changes other colors to hue colors. Select the Key color that you want.

⑤ Click **OK**.

If the brush is being used, an alert appears.

⑥ Click **Apply to Strokes** to apply the modified brush option to existing strokes or **Leave Strokes** to apply the modified brush only to new strokes.

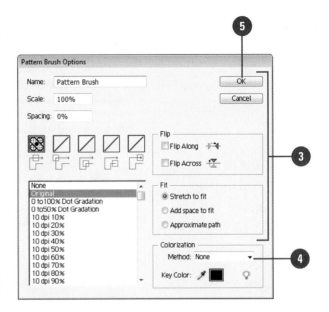

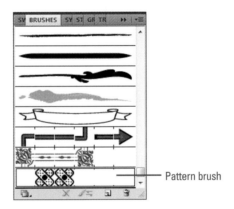

Pattern brush

Working with Brushes

As you create and edit brushes in the Brushes panel or add them into the Brushes panel from other brush libraries, it's important to save them in a brush library if you want to use them again in the future. You can create your own brush libraries by using the Save Brushes command on the Options menu. The Save Brushes command saves all the brushes currently in the Brushes panel, so you need to delete the ones that you don't want in the library. In addition to deleting brushes in the Brushes panel, you can also remove brush strokes from objects.

Remove Brush Strokes and Delete Brushes

1. Select the **Brushes** panel.

2. Do any of the following:

   ◆ **Delete from Object.** Select the objects with brushes that you want to remove, and then click the **Remove Brush Stroke** button on the panel.

   ◆ **Delete from Brushes Panel.** Deselect all objects, select the brush you want to delete, and then click the **Delete Brush** button on the panel. Click **Yes** to confirm the deletion.

   If the brush is currently being used in objects, click **Expand Strokes** to convert the brush to paths or click **Remove Strokes** to remove them from the objects.

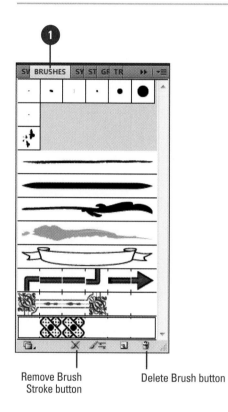

Remove Brush Stroke button

Delete Brush button

Did You Know?

You can convert brush strokes into outlined paths. Select the brushed path, click the Object menu, and then click Expand Appearance. Now, you can edit individual components of the brushed path.

Save a Brush Library

1. Select the **Brushes** panel.

2. Display the brushes that you want to save in the Brushes panel. Remove the ones that you don't want.

3. Click the **Brushes Libraries Menu** button, and then click **Save Brushes**.

4. Enter a name for the brushes library.

5. Click **Save**.

6. To open the brush library, click the **Brush Libraries Menu** button, point to **User Defined**, and then select the saved library.

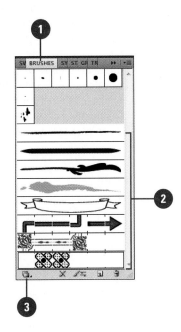

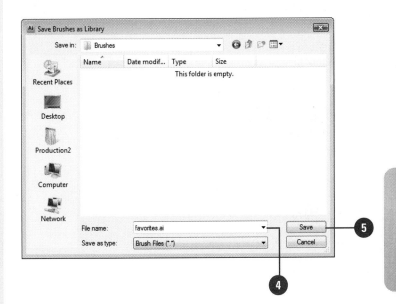

Working with Liquify Tools

Illustrator provides Liquify tools on the Tools panel that allow you to distort a path quickly and easily with the click of a mouse. The Liquify tools include Warp, Twirl, Pucker, Bloat, Scallop, Crystallize, and Wrinkle. All the tools are grouped together in the same slot on the Tools panel. The tools work the same way, they each apply a different distortion effect. You can change the way each tool works by selecting options in the tool's Options dialog box, which you can open by double-clicking the tool on the Tools panel. Some of the common options you can change include brush dimensions.

Use a Liquify Tool

1. Select the liquify tool (**Warp**, **Twirl**, **Pucker**, **Bloat**, **Scallop**, **Crystallize**, or **Wrinkle**) that you want to use on the Tools panel.

2. To change tool options, double-click the tool on the Tools panel, specify the options that you want, and then click **OK**.

   The options vary depending on the liquify tool

3. Position the cursor (which changes to a circle with a crosshair in the middle) over the path that you want to change.

4. Click and/or drag to apply the distortion to the path.

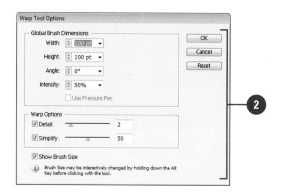

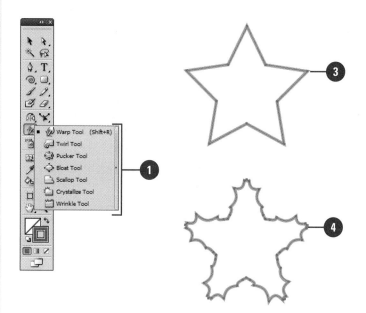

Using Symbols

12

Introduction

If you use the same object in multiple places in a document, you can use the Symbols panel to store and use it as an instance. A symbol is stored once and used multiple times as an instance, which speeds up printing and reduces the size of your document. Each instance is linked to the original symbol. When you break the link between a symbol and an instance, the instance is converted back to a normal object.

You can place instances one at a time or create a collection of instances with the Symbol Sprayer tool, known as a symbol set. This allows you to quickly create artistic designs without a lot of experience.

With the Symbols panel, you can create, edit, rename, duplicate, and delete symbols. You can create your own symbol from a selected object or you can use the ones provided by Illustrator. Illustrator gives you access to more than 30 different symbol libraries, which include Arrows, Artistic Texture, Flowers, Fashion, Maps, and Nature to name a few.

The Symbol Sprayer allows you to create a symbol set. After you create a symbol set, you can use one of 7 other symbolism tools to modify it. The symbolism tools include: Symbol Shifter (to shift direction and bring forward or send backward), Symbol Scruncher (to move instances closer or farther apart), Symbol Sizer (to increase or decrease size), Symbol Spinner (to change the orientation), Symbol Stainer (to increase or decrease the transparency), Symbol Screener (to recolor with tints), and Symbol Styler (to apply a graphic style). With the Expand command, you can break the link between an instance and the original symbol or break apart a symbol set.

What You'll Do

Use the Symbols Panel

Use Symbol Libraries

Work with Symbols

Duplicate and Edit Symbols

Break Symbol Links

Use the Sprayer Tool

Set Symbolism Tool Options

Use the Symbol Shifter Tool

Use the Symbol Scruncher Tool

Use the Symbol Sizer Tool

Use the Symbol Spinner Tool

Use the Symbol Stainer Tool

Use the Symbol Screener Tool

Use the Symbol Styler Tool

Expand Symbol Instances

Using the Symbols Panel

 IL 6.5

If you use the same object in multiple places in a document, you should store it in the Symbols panel and use it as an instance. A symbol is stored once in the Symbols panel and used multiple times as an instance, which speeds up printing and reduces the size of your document. Each instance is linked to the original symbol. When you select an instance on the artboard, the symbol is selected in the Symbols panel. You can place instances one at a time or create a collection of instances with the Symbol Sprayer tool, known as a **symbol set**. This allows you to quickly create artistic designs without a lot of experience. With the Symbols panel you can create, edit, rename, duplicate, and delete symbols.

Create Instances with the Symbols Panel

1. Select the **Symbols** panel.

2. To change the Symbols panel view, click the **Options** menu, and then select any of the following view available options:

   ◆ **Thumbnail View**

   ◆ **Small List View**

   ◆ **Large List View**

   ◆ **Sort by Name**

3. Select a symbol on the panel.

4. Click the **Place Symbol Instance** button on the panel.

   ◆ You can also drag a symbol from the Symbols panel onto an artboard.

Did You Know?

You can duplicate an instance on the artboard. Alt+drag (Win) or Option+drag (Mac) the instance on the artboard.

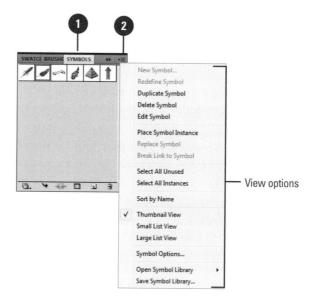

View options

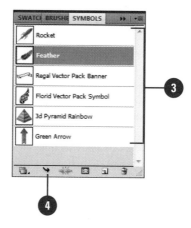

288

Using Symbol Libraries

 IL 6.5

Instead of creating your own symbols, you can use the ones provided by Illustrator. Illustrator gives you access to more than 30 different symbol libraries, which include Arrows, Artistic Textures, Flowers, Fashion, Maps, and Nature, to name a few. When you open a symbol library from the Symbols panel, a new panel appears, displaying the library symbols. Instead of opening each library separately, you can use the Load Previous Symbol Library or Load Next Symbol Library buttons on the panel to quickly view libraries to find the symbols you want. When you click a library symbol, it's added to the Symbols panel.

Use Symbol Libraries

1. Select the **Symbols** panel.

2. Select a path with any of the selection tools.

3. Click the **Symbol Libraries Menu** button on the panel, and then select a symbol library.

4. Click the **Load Previous Symbol Library** or **Load Next Symbol Library** button to view other libraries.

5. Click a symbol in the library panel to add it to the Symbols panel.

6. Select a symbol on the Symbols panel.

7. Click the **Place Symbol Instance** button on the panel.

   ◆ You can also drag a symbol from the Symbols panel or any symbols library onto an artboard.

Did You Know?

You can arrange symbols on the Symbols panel. In the Symbols panel, you can drag a symbol to a new spot.

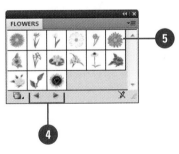

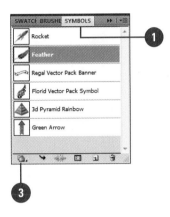

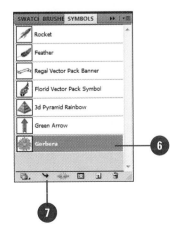

Working with Symbols

IL 6.5

With the Symbols panel you can create, edit, rename, duplicate, and delete symbols. You can use any object (path, type, and graphics to name a few) in Illustrator to create a symbol. There are two types of symbols: Graphic and Movie Clip (used for Flash, more later). As you create symbols in the Symbols panel or add them into the Symbols panel from other symbol libraries, it's important to save them in a symbol library if you want to use them again in the future. The Save Symbols command saves all the symbols currently in the Symbols panel, so you need to delete the ones that you don't want in the library.

Create a Symbol from an Object

1. Create the object that you want to use, and then select it using the **Selection** tool on the Tools panel.

2. Select the **Symbols** panel.

3. Click the **New Symbol** button on the panel.

    ◆ You can also drag the object directly to a blank area on the Symbols panel from an artboard.

4. Type a name for the symbol.

5. Click the **Graphic** option.

6. Click **OK**.

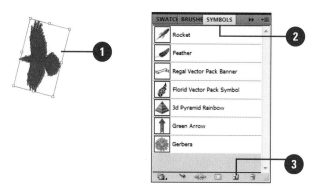

Did You Know?

You can create a symbol with the dialog box. Select the object, and then Alt+drag (Win) or Option+drag (Mac) the object onto the New Symbol button on the panel.

You can change symbols options. Select the symbol in the Symbols panel, click the Symbol Options button on the panel, change the options that you want, and then click OK.

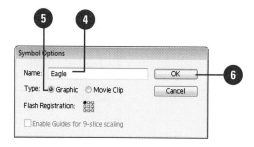

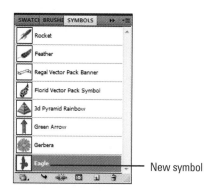

New symbol

Delete Symbols

① Select the **Symbols** panel.

② Select the symbols that you want to delete.

③ Click the **Delete Symbol** button on the panel.

◆ You can also drag a symbol over the Delete Symbol button to delete it.

④ If there are no instances of the deleted symbol, click **Yes** to confirm the deletion. If there are instances, click **Expand Instances** to convert the instance to paths or click **Delete Instances** to remove them.

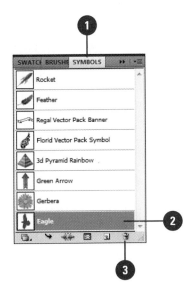

Save and Create a Symbols Library

① Select the **Symbols** panel.

② Display the symbols that you want to save in the Symbols panel. Remove the ones that you don't want.

③ Click the **Symbol Libraries Menu** button, and then click **Save Symbols**.

④ Enter a name for the symbols library.

⑤ Click **Save**.

⑥ To open the symbol library, click the **Symbol Libraries Menu** button, point to **User Defined**, and then select the saved library.

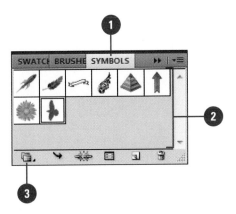

Duplicating and Editing Symbols

IL 6.5, 8.2

Instead of creating your own symbols, you can duplicate an existing symbol (from a symbol library) that is close to what you want and then edit it. It's faster than creating one from scratch. When you edit a symbol, Illustrator creates a temporary instance in Isolation Mode, where you can make your changes. When you exit Isolation Mode, your changes are applied to all linked instances in your document.

Duplicate a Symbol

1. Select the **Symbols** panel.

2. Select the symbol that you want to duplicate.

3. Drag the symbol onto the **New Symbol** button on the panel.

   ◆ You can also select an instance on the artboard, and then click **Duplicate** on the Control panel.

4. Click the **Symbol Options** button on the panel.

5. Type a name for the symbol.

6. Click **OK**.

   The two symbols are the same and linked to the same instances on the artboard.

   ◆ To make them different, click the **Break Link to Symbol** button on the panel, and then edit it.

Did You Know?

You can assign names to instances for export to Flash. Select the instance on the artboard, enter a name in the Instance Name field on the Control panel. This is helpful when you export the instances to Adobe Flash for use in movies.

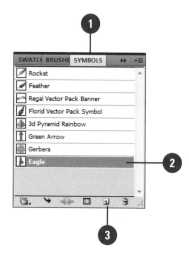

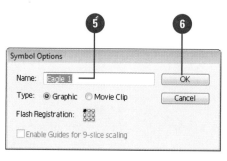

Edit a Symbol

1. Select the **Symbols** panel.

2. Double-click the symbol that you want to edit.

   ◆ You can also select the symbol, click the **Options** menu, and then click **Edit Symbol**.

   ◆ If you're working with an instance, select it, and then click **Edit Symbol** on the Control panel.

   A temporary instance of the symbol appears in isolation mode.

3. Make the changes that you want to the symbol.

4. Click the gray bar above the document to exit Isolation Mode.

   The symbol updates in the Symbols panel and all instances of the symbol are updated as well.

Did You Know?

You can replace the symbols in a symbol set. Select a symbol set on an artboard using the Selection tool, click a replacement symbol on the Symbols panel, click the Options menu, and then click Replace Symbol.

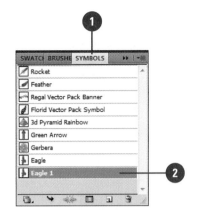

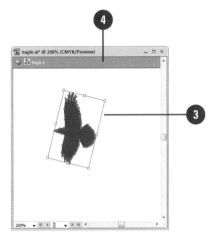

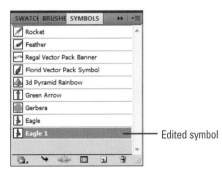

Edited symbol

Breaking Symbol Links

IL 6.5

When you create an instance of a symbol, the instance is linked to the symbol, which speeds up printing and reduces the size of your document. When you break the link between a symbol and an instance, the instance converts to a normal object. If you don't want an instance to be updated when you edit a symbol, you can break the link between the symbol and the instance (which creates a normal object), and then create a new symbol with the normal object.

Break a Link Between a Symbol and an Instance

1. Select the instance on the artboard in which you want to break the symbol link.

2. Select the **Symbols** panel.

3. Click the **Break Link to Symbol** button on the panel.

   ◆ You can also click the **Break Link** button on the Control panel.

Break a Link and Create a New Symbol

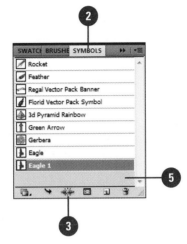

1. Select the instance on the artboard in which you want to break a symbol link.

2. Select the **Symbols** panel.

3. Click the **Break Link to Symbol** button on the panel.

   ◆ You can also click the **Break Link** button on the Control panel.

4. Make the changes that you want to the object (no longer an instance) on the artboard.

5. Drag the object to a blank area on the Symbols panel from an artboard to create a new symbol.

6. Type a name for the symbol.

7. Click the **Graphic** option.

8. Click **OK**.

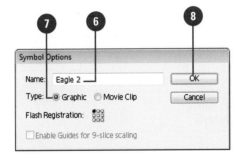

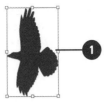

New symbol

Using the Symbol Sprayer Tool

IL 6.5

The Symbol Sprayer tool allows you to spray multiple instances of a symbol to create a symbol set. The symbol set appears on the artboard containing all the instances within a bounding box. After you create a new symbol set, you can add or delete instances or quickly create another set. You can customize the way the Symbol Sprayer tool works by setting options in the Symbolism Tools Options dialog box.

Use the Symbol Sprayer Tool

1 Select the **Symbol Sprayer** tool on the Tools panel.

2 Select the **Symbols** panel.

3 Select the symbol that you want to use.

4 Click once to create a single instance or click and hold or drag to create multiple instances.

The symbol set of instances appears in a bounding box.

5 Do any of the following:

◆ **Create New Symbol Set.** Ctrl+click (Win) or Command+click (Mac) in a blank area outside the bounding box, and then click again, click and hold, or drag.

◆ **Add Instances to Symbol Set.** Select the symbol set, click a symbol on the Symbols panel, and use the **Symbol Sprayer** tool.

◆ **Delete Instances from a Symbol Set.** Select the symbol set, select the **Symbol Sprayer** tool, Alt+click (Win) or Option+click the instances in the symbol set that you want to delete.

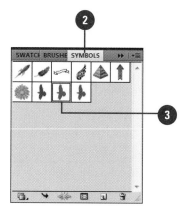

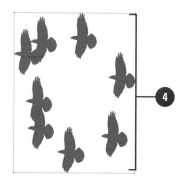

Setting Symbolism Tools Options

 IL 6.5

Illustrator comes with 8 symbolism tools: Symbol **Sprayer**, Symbol **Shifter**, Symbol **Scruncher**, Symbol **Sizer**, Symbol **Spinner**, Symbol **Stainer**, Symbol **Screener**, and Symbol **Styler**. While each tool does a different job, you can set common and specific options for any of them in one place: the Symbolism Tools Options dialog box. The common options are Diameter, Intensity, and Symbol Set Density.

Set Symbolism Tools Options

1. Double-click any symbolism tool on the Tools panel.

2. Enter a **Diameter** value (1-999 points) to specify a default size for the symbols.

3. Enter an **Intensity** value (1-10) that designates the rate at which the tools create symbols or changes. The lower the value, the slower the action.

4. Enter a **Symbol Set Density** value (1-10) to specify the distance between instances. The higher the value, the closer the instances.

5. Select the **Show Brush Size and Intensity** check box to have the current diameter setting display as a ring around the tool pointer.

6. Click a symbolism button to specify or display options for the tool.

   ◆ **Symbol Sprayer.** For the available options, select **Average** to add instances based on an average sampling of adjacent instances or **User Defined** to set a value.

7. Click **OK**.

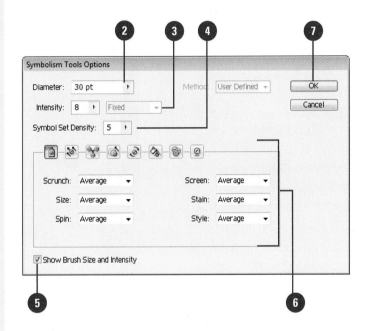

Using the Symbol Shifter Tool

The Symbol Shifter tool allows you to modify the attributes of an existing symbol set. You can shift the direction of instances or change the stacking order (bring forward or send backward) of instances. You can set either of these with a click of the mouse. You can customize the way the Symbol Shifter tool works by setting options in the Symbolism Tools Options dialog box.

Use the Symbol Shifter Tool

1. Select the symbol set that you want to use.

2. Select the **Symbol Shifter** tool on the Tools panel.

3. Drag in the symbol set to shift the instances in the direction you want.

4. Do any of the following to shift the position of an instance:

   ◆ **Bring Forward.** Shift+click an instance.

   ◆ **Send Backward.** Alt+Shift+click (Win) or Option+Shift+click (Mac) an instance.

Did You Know?

You can set Symbol Shifter options.
Double-click the Symbol Shifter tool on the Tools panel, specify the options you want (see page 297 for details), and then click OK.

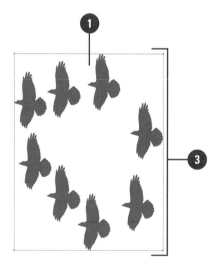

Using the Symbol Scruncher Tool

IL 6.5

The Symbol Scruncher tool allows you to move instances in an existing symbol set closer together (scrunched) or farther apart. It's easy to do. Simply click and hold or drag inside the symbol set to scrunch instances. Press an additional key to move instances farther away. You can customize the way the Symbol Scruncher tool works by setting options in the Symbolism Tools Options dialog box.

Use the Symbol Scruncher Tool

1. Select the symbol set that you want to use.

2. Select the **Symbol Scruncher** tool on the Tools panel.

3. Do any of the following to move instances closer for farther apart:

   ◆ **Move Closer.** Click and hold an instance or drag across instances inside the symbol set.

   ◆ **Move Away.** Alt+click (Win) or Option+click (Mac) an instance or drag across instances inside the symbol set.

Did You Know?

You can set Symbol Scruncher options. Double-click the Symbol Scruncher tool on the Tools panel, specify the options you want (see page 297 for details), and then click OK.

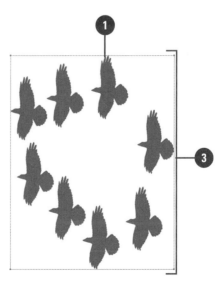

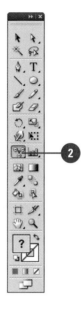

Using the Symbol Sizer Tool

The Symbol Sizer tool allows you to resize individual instances in the symbol set. It's easy to do. Simply, click and hold or drag inside the symbol set to enlarge instances. Press an additional key to reduce instances. This way, you can get the visual look you want. You can customize the way the Symbol Sizer tool works by setting options in the Symbolism Tools Options dialog box.

Use the Symbol Sizer Tool

1. Select the symbol set that you want to use.

2. Select the **Symbol Sizer** tool on the Tools panel.

3. Do any of the following to resize instances:

   ◆ Larger. Click and hold an instance or drag across instances inside the symbol set.

   ◆ Smaller. Alt+click (Win) or Option+click (Mac) an instance or drag across instances inside the symbol set.

Did You Know?

You can set Symbol Sizer options. Double-click the Symbol Sizer tool on the Tools panel, specify the options you want (see page 297 for details), and then click OK.

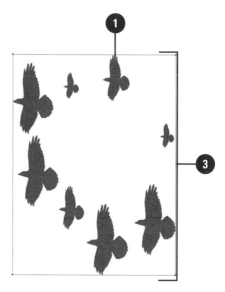

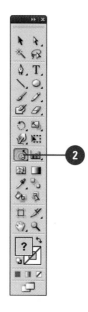

Using the Symbol Spinner Tool

IL 6.5

The Symbol Spinner allows you to change the orientation of individual instances in the symbol set. Unlike other symbolism tools, click and hold doesn't do anything. With this tool, you drag inside the symbol set in the direction you want to rotate the instance. A rotation icon appears as you drag to specify the current direction. You can customize the way the Symbol Spinner tool works by setting options in the Symbolism Tools Options dialog box.

Use the Symbol Spinner Tool

1. Select the symbol set that you want to use.

2. Select the **Symbol Spinner** tool on the Tools panel.

3. Drag an instance in the symbol set in the direction you want it rotated.

   A rotation icon appears as you drag to indicate the current direction.

Did You Know?

You can set Symbol Spinner options. Double-click the Symbol Spinner tool on the Tools panel, specify the options you want (see page 297 for details), and then click OK.

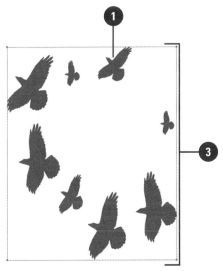

Using the Symbol Stainer Tool

IL 2.10, 3.6, 6.5

The Symbol Stainer allows you to recolor instances in an existing symbol set. You can recolor solid fills, patterns, and gradients with different tints (shades) of the current fill color for individual instances in the symbol set. This is useful for adding variation to instances. You can customize the way the Symbol Stainer tool works by setting options in the Symbolism Tools Options dialog box.

Use the Symbol Stainer Tool

1. Select the symbol set that you want to use.

2. Select the **Symbol Stainer** tool on the Tools panel.

3. Select the fill color that you want to use.

4. Do any of the following to recolor the tint of instances:

   ◆ **Increase Tint.** Click and hold an instance or drag across instances inside the symbol set.

   ◆ **Decrease Tint.** Alt+click (Win) or Option+click (Mac) an instance or drag across instances inside the symbol set.

Did You Know?

You can set Symbol Stainer options. Double-click the Symbol Stainer tool on the Tools panel, specify the options you want (see page 297 for details), and then click OK.

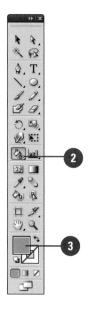

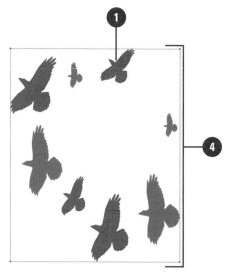

Using the Symbol Screener Tool

IL 3.3, 6.5

The Symbol Screener tool allows you to make instances in an existing symbol set more transparent. You can increase or decrease the opacity for individual instances in the symbol set. This is useful for creating a faded look to instances. You can customize the way the Symbol Screener tool works by setting options in the Symbolism Tools Options dialog box.

Use the Symbol Screener Tool

1. Select the symbol set that you want to use.

2. Select the **Symbol Screener** tool on the Tools panel.

3. Do any of the following to increase or decrease instance opacity (transparency):

   ◆ **Increase.** Click and hold an instance or drag across instances inside the symbol set.

   ◆ **Decrease.** Alt+click (Win) or Option+click (Mac) an instance or drag across instances inside the symbol set.

Did You Know?

You can set Symbol Screener options. Double-click the Symbol Screener tool on the Tools panel, specify the options you want (see page 297 for details), and then click OK.

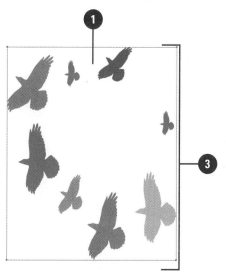

Using the Symbol Styler Tool

The Symbol Styler tool allows you to apply the currently selected graphic style on the Graphic Styles panel to instances in an existing symbol set. It's easy to do. Simply click and hold or drag instances inside the symbol set to apply the graphic style. The longer you hold down the mouse, the greater the intensity of the applied style. You can customize the way the Symbol Styler tool works by setting options in the Symbolism Tools Options dialog box.

Use the Symbol Styler Tool

1. Select the symbol set that you want to use.

2. Select the **Symbol Styler** tool on the Tools panel.

3. Select the **Graphic Styles** panel.

4. Select the graphic style that you want to apply to instances in the selected symbol set.

5. Do any of the following to apply or remove a graphic style:

   ◆ **Apply Style.** Click and hold an instance or drag across instances inside the symbol set.

   The longer you hold down the mouse, the greater the intensity of the applied style.

   ◆ **Decrease Style Intensity.** Alt+click (Win) or Option+click (Mac) an instance or drag across instances inside the symbol set.

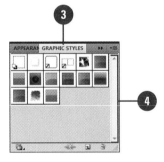

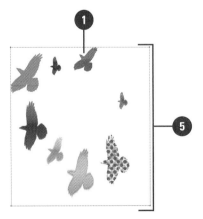

Did You Know?

You can set Symbol Styler options. Double-click the Symbol Styler tool on the Tools panel, specify the options you want (see page 297 for details), and then click OK.

Expanding Symbol Instances

With the Expand command, you can break the link between an instance and the original symbol or break apart a symbol set. When you break the link between an instance and a symbol, the individual paths become nested in a group. When you break apart a symbol set, the individual instances are nested in a group, but the links to the original symbol are maintained.

Expand an Instance or a Symbol Set

1 Select the the instances or symbol set that you want to expand.

2 Click the **Object** menu, and then click **Expand** or **Expand Appearance** (if the instance contains an effect).

3 Select the **Object** and **Fill** check boxes.

4 Click **OK**.

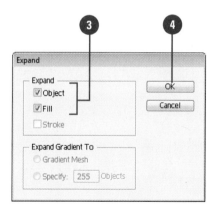

Automating the Way You Work

13

Introduction

Actions are similar to recording information on a tape; they record Illustrator commands and, like a tape recorder, can be played back at any time. Actions can be applied to any number of images. You can modify existing actions, and save them into a user-defined set. It's even possible to save them and send them to another Illustrator user. This chapter is dedicated to all the Illustrator users who are tired of doing something over and over again. If you have ever considered using actions as a part of your design workflow, then you're in for a wonderful journey of discovery.

A script is a series of commands that instructs Illustrator to perform a set of specified actions. These actions can be simple, affecting only a single object, or more complex, affecting many objects. Scripts are useful for repetitive tasks and can be used as a creative tool to streamline tasks that are time consuming and boring. You can use one of Illustrator's built-in scripts, such as ExportDocsAsFlash or Live Trace, or create one of your own.

What You'll Do

Examine the Actions Panel

Build a New Action

Record an Action

Control the Playback of a Command

Add a Stop to an Action

Insert Non-Recordable Command into an Action

Add a Command to an Action

Delete a Command from an Action

Work with Batch File Processing

Open and Use Scripts

Create and Edit Data Variables

Create a Data Graph

Examining the Actions Panel

The Actions panel is where you create, save, modify, and store all of your actions. The analogy of a tape recorder is often used in describing the Actions panel, and it's actually a good way to think of actions. The action itself is a recording, and the Actions panel is the tape recorder. When you begin an action, the panel records each step in the process, saves them, and then lets you play them back on another image. In order to record and play actions, you need to understand how to use the Actions panel.

Examine the Actions Panel

① Select the **Actions** panel.

② Check the toggle box to toggle an action on or off.

③ Click the dialog box to toggle the dialog function on or off.

④ Click the **expand triangle** to expand or contract an action or set.

⑤ Click the **Options** menu to access all of the Actions panel options.

Did You Know?

You can convert your Actions into single-click buttons. Click the Actions Options button, and then click Button Mode. When the Actions panel is in Button Mode, you cannot access or edit the steps in the individual actions. To access the standard Actions panel, click the Actions Options button, and then click Button Mode to uncheck the option.

6 The following buttons are accessible at the bottom of the Actions panel, from left to right:

- ◆ **Stop.** Click to stop recording and save an action.

- ◆ **Record.** Click to begin recording an action.

- ◆ **Play.** Click to begin execution of the selected action.

- ◆ **Create New Set.** Creates a new action set.

  Sets are like file folders; they store individual actions.

- ◆ **Create New Action.** Starts the process of creating a new action.

- ◆ **Delete.** Click to delete the selected action or set.

6

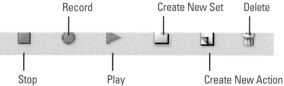

Record   Create New Set   Delete

Stop   Play   Create New Action

Did You Know?

You can save actions into sets. Action sets are like file folders; they hold groups of actions. Select the Actions panel, click the Create New Set button, enter a name for the set, and then click OK.

You can save action sets as files. Select the Actions panel, click the set you want to save, click the Options menu, click Save Actions, enter a name for the file, specify a location, and then click Save.

You can restore actions to the default set. Select the Actions panel, click the Options menu, click Reset Actions, and then click OK to replace or Append to combine with the current set.

Building a New Action

 IL 2.11

Building an action is almost as simple as clicking the record button on a tape recorder. Actions are simply a series of program instructions. When you build an action, you're instructing Illustrator what to name the action, where to store it, and what shortcut keys, if any, will be used to activate the action. Since an action is simply a record of the work performed on an image, it's a good idea to plan out what you intend to do, and then build the action. Remember, actions are designed for tasks you plan to do repeatedly. It wouldn't make sense to create an action for a one-time use.

Build a New Action

1. Open a document, and then select the **Actions** panel.

2. Click the **Create New Action** button.

3. Enter a name for the action in the Name box.

4. Click the **Set** list arrow, and then select in which set to save the Action.

5. Click the **Function Key** list arrow, and then click F1 - F12 to assign your new action to a function key.

6. Select the **Shift** or **Control** (Win) or **Command** (Mac) check boxes to require the pressing of the Shift key, or the Ctrl (Win) or ⌘ (Mac) key in conjunction with the function key.

   For example, F1, or Shift+F1, or Ctrl+F1, or Shift+Ctrl+F1.

7. Click the **Color** list arrow, and then select from the available colors.

   IMPORTANT *If you choose a color for the action, it will only be visible if the actions are viewed in Button Mode.*

8. Click **Record** to begin creating the action.

9. Click the **Stop** button on the Actions panel.

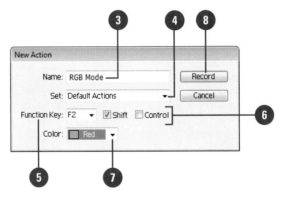

Controlling the Playback of a Command

Control the Playback of a Command

1. Open a document, and then select the **Actions** panel.

2. Click the **expand triangle** of the action you want to modify.

3. Select the action that you want to play.

4. To remove commands from playback, uncheck the command or commands you do not want to execute.

5. Make a selection if necessary for use with the action.

6. Click the **Play** button on the Actions panel to run the action without executing the unchecked command(s).

7. Recheck the command(s) to return them to executable status.

Did You Know?

You can specify the playback speed. Select the Actions panel, click the Options menu, click Playback Options, specify a speed (Accelerated, Step By Step or Pause For), and then click OK.

You can copy an action. Select the Actions panel, drag the action over the Create New Action button on the panel or select the action, click the Options menu, and then click Duplicate.

Not all actions are created perfectly. Sooner or later, you'll work through the process of action building only to find out (after the action is saved), that you forgot a step, or you need to remove or modify an existing step. Fortunately, Illustrator doesn't make you recreate the action; all you have to do is modify it. When you create an action, all of the commands execute in the order they appear in the list of action steps. However, it's possible you might occasionally want to skip one of the steps in the list, without permanently deleting it. To play an action, simply select it and then click the Play button.

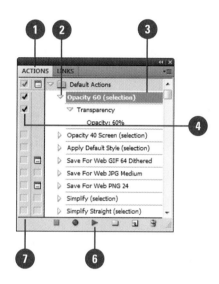

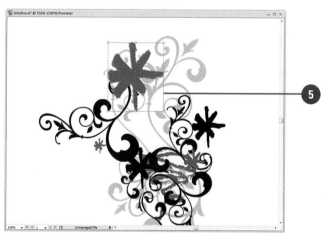

Adding a Stop to an Action

 IL 2.11

There are times when you want to make changes to individual files during the playback of an action. For example, you create an action to balance the contrast in an image, and one of the commands you use is a Levels adjustment. Although none of the other commands need user modification during playback, an optimum Levels adjustment is specific to individual images. What you want is the action to perform (automatically) all of the steps, except Levels. When the action reaches the point where the Levels adjustment would be applied, you want the action to stop and let you make changes that are appropriate for that particular image and then move on to complete the rest of the steps when you've finalized the Levels adjustment by clicking OK.

Add a Stop to an Action

1. Open a document, and then select the **Actions** panel.

2. Click the **expand triangle** of the action you want to modify.

3. Click the command directly above where you want to place the action.

4. Click the **Actions Options** menu, and then click **Insert Stop**.

5. Enter a message associated with the purpose of the stop action.

6. Select the **Allow Continue** check box to add a Continue button to the stop alert box.

7. Click **OK**.

8. Click the **Play** button on the Actions panel to run the action.

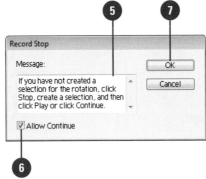

Did You Know?

You can run an action inside an action. Select the Actions panel, click the command directly above where you want to insert the run step for another action, click the Record button, click the action to be added, click the Play button to record the second action into the first action, and then click Stop.

Inserting a Non-Recordable Command into an Action

IL 2.11

When you create an action, not all commands and tools can be recorded, such as Selection, Pen, Paintbrush, Pencil, Pencil, Gradient, Mesh, Eyedropper, Live Paint Bucket, and Scissors tools or Effects and View menu commands. However, you can insert many non-recordable commands into an action by using an Insert Menu Item command. The Insert Menu Item command can be used when recording an action or after it has been recorded. Inserted commands do not execute until the action is played, so the file remains unchanged when the command is inserted. This gives you the ability to experiment with different non-recordable commands without the risk of damaging a valuable image.

Insert a Non-Recordable Command into an Action

1 Open a document, and then select the **Actions** panel.

2 Click an action, and then click the **expand triangle**.

3 Click the name of the action to insert the item at the end of the action, or click a specific action step to insert the item after the selected step.

4 Click the **Actions Options** button, and then click **Insert Menu Item**.

5 Select a command from the available options (the command is selected by clicking and selecting an item from Illustrator's drop-down menu system).

6 Click **OK**.

The non-recordable command is added to the action steps.

IMPORTANT *When you use the Insert Menu Item command for a command that opens a dialog box, you cannot disable the modal control in the Actions panel.*

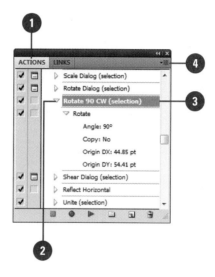

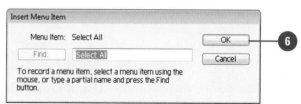

Adding a Command to an Action

IL 2.11

Actions are very versatile; in fact, almost anything that can be done to an image can be placed into an action. You might find that as you perform an action, you need to add an additional command. You can do this with ease; that's why actions are so great to work with. For example, you might create an action to convert an image from the RGB to the CMYK mode, and after you save the action, you decide it would be great to include an effect. You don't have to throw away the previous action and start all over; all you have to do is select where the command will be inserted, restart the action, and perform the new step. The Actions panel is a powerful time-saving tool, and if you forget a step, it's also a breeze to modify.

Add a Command to an Action

1. Open a document, and then select the **Actions** panel.

2. Click the **expand triangle** of the action to which you want to add the command.

3. Click the command directly above where you want to insert the new command.

4. Click the **Actions Options** menu, and then click **Start Recording**.

5. Add the additional command by selecting an Illustrator option.

6. When you're finished adding commands, click the **Stop** button on the Actions panel.

   The next time the action is run, the additional command will be performed.

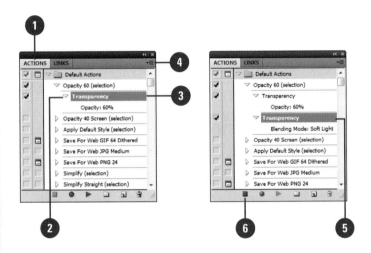

Did You Know?

You can change the order of commands in an action. Select the Actions panel, drag the command you want to change up or down in the actions stack. Release the mouse when you see a dark line underneath the command where you want the action.

For Your Information

Using Modal Controls with an Action

Modal controls are pauses in an action that allow you to modify a command before proceeding. Modal controls are available for every command that utilizes a dialog box, or any command that requires the pressing of the Enter/Return key to process the effect. Select the Actions panel, click the second column to activate or deactivate the Modal Control button.

Deleting a Command from an Action

IL 2.11

Occasionally, you may want to permanently delete a command from an existing action. If that's the case, Illustrator makes the process quick and easy. An action consists of a group of steps. As the action executes, each step is completed in the order in which it appears within the action list. No one step is dependent upon another, so if you want to remove a step, it's a simple process of deletion. Once the command is removed, the action will perform as if the deleted command never existed.

Delete a Command from an Action

1. Open a document, and then select the **Actions** panel.

2. Click the **expand triangle** of the action from which you want to delete the command.

   IMPORTANT *You cannot delete a command from a running action.*

3. Click the command you want to delete.

4. Select from three deletion methods:

   ◆ Drag the command over the **Delete** button.

   ◆ Click the command, click the **Delete** button, and then click **Yes** in the Delete the Selection alert box.

   ◆ Click the command, and then hold down the Alt (Win) or Option (Mac) key, and then click the **Delete** button to delete the command without the alert box message.

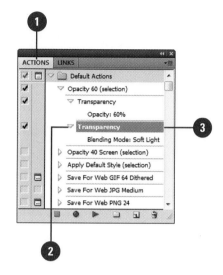

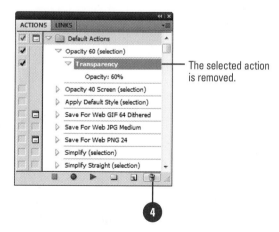

The selected action is removed.

Working with Batch File Processing

There is nothing more exciting than working on a new creative project, and watching your designs come to life. Conversely, there is nothing more tiresome than having to apply a new creative concept or correction individually to many additional images. For example, you just spent three hours coming up with a procedure to apply color and blending modifications to one of the company's logos. The photo logo looks great; however, you now have apply color and blending modifications to one of the company's logos. You could create an action, but you would still have to open each image and apply the action 50 times. The solution is to batch process the images after you have created the action. Batch file processing lets you apply an action to an entire folder of images, and all you have to do is click a button. Now, what could be simpler than that?

Work with Batch File Processing

1. Create a new folder, and then move all the images into the folder.

   IMPORTANT *These files must be Illustrator files. There should not be any other files, such as text files, inside this folder.*

2. Create a second folder to hold the modified images (optional).

3. Select the **Actions** panel.

4. Click the **Actions Options** menu, and then click **Batch**.

5. Select from the following Play options:

   ◆ Click the **Set** list arrow, and then select the Set containing the Action you want to apply to the images.

   ◆ Click the **Action** list arrow, and then select the correct Action.

6. Click the **Source** list arrow, and then select an image source from the following: Folder, or Data Sets.

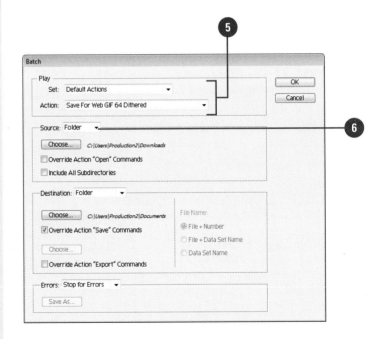

7 Click **Choose** (available if Folder is selected as the source), and then select the location of the image folder.

8 Select the check boxes for any options you want:

◆ **Override Action "Open" Commands.** Select to use an open command embedded into the Action.

◆ **Include All Subfolders.** Select to batch process any images located in folders embedded in the main image folder.

9 Click the **Destination** list arrow, and then click **None**, **Save and Close**, or **Folder**.

10 Specify options for the **Save** or **Export** commands:

◆ Click **Choose** (available if Folder is selected as the source), and then select the destination of the modified images.

◆ Select the **Override Action "Save" Commands** or **Override Action "Export" Commands** check box to use a save or export command embedded into the Action.

◆ Select File Name options to create sequential files name in a batch sequence.

11 Click the **Errors** list arrow, select an errors option, and then click **Save As** to save your error information, if necessary.

12 Click **OK**.

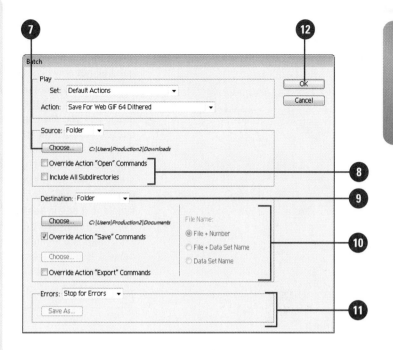

Opening and Using Scripts

A **script** is a series of commands that instructs Illustrator to perform a set of specified actions. These actions can be simple, affecting only a single object, or more complex, affecting many objects. The actions can call not only Illustrator, but also invoke other applications. Scripts are useful for repetitive tasks and can be used as a creative tool to streamline tasks that are time consuming and boring. A scripting language lets you ask a question (an event), and use the answer to that question to perform any commands (an action) that are available in Illustrator. You can use one of Illustrator's built-in scripts, such as Export Docs As Flash or Live Trace, or create one of your own. To create your own scripts you need a working knowledge of a scripting language like JavaScript, and either a script-editing application or a simple text editor, such as Notepad (Win), TextEdit (Mac) BBEdit or even Microsoft Word. The languages you can use to perform scripting are varied and include Visual Basic, AppleScript, and JavaScript, to name a few. As a matter of fact, the Scripts Events Manager lets you set JavaScript and Illustrator Actions to run automatically when a specified Illustrator event occurs.

Use Built-in Scripts

1. Click the **File** menu, and then point to **Scripts**.

2. Select one of the following built-in scripts:

   - **ExportDocsAsFlash.**

   - **Flex Skins.** Then select **Create Flex 3 Skin** or **Export Flex 3 Skin.**

   - **LiveTrace.**

   - **SaveDocsAsPDF.**

   - **SaveDocsAsSVG.**

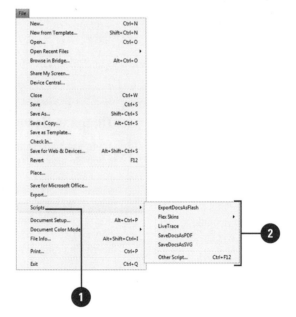

Open and Use Enhanced Scripting

1 Open a text editor, and then create a script using any approved scripting language.

2 Save the document with the correct extension, for example, ActiveLayer.js for JavaScript.

3 To access the script in Illustrator, click the **File** menu, point to **Scripts**, and then click **Other Script**.

4 Navigate to the folder or drive where your script file is located.

5 Click the script that you want to run.

6 Click **Open** to run the script.

Your script appears in a browser window.

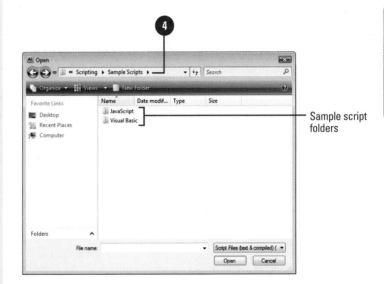

Sample script folders

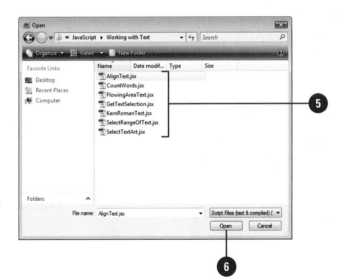

Defining and Editing Data Variables

 IL 6.9

When you work with objects in Illustrator, you can define variables to drive them in a template document. Data-driven objects make it possible to create multiple versions of an object quickly and precisely. For example, you need to produce several web banners using the same template. Instead of creating each banner, one at a time, you can use data-driven graphics to generate web banners using variables and data sets. Any artwork can be converted into a template for data-driven graphics by defining variables for objects in the image. A **data set** is a collection of variables and associated data. You can switch between data sets to upload different data into your template. You can work with variables and data sets in the Variables panel. The left column displays the variables name and the right column displays the bound object name as shown in the Layers panel. There are four types of variables: Visibility, Text String, Linked File, and Graph Data.

Create Data Variables

1 Select the **Variables** panel.

2 Select from the available options:

◆ Visibility. Select the object that you want to show or hide, and then click the **Make Visibility Dynamic** button.

◆ Text String. Select the text object, and then click the **Make Object Dynamic** button.

◆ Linked File. Select the linked file, and then click the **Make Object Dynamic** button.

◆ Graph Data. Select the graph object, and then click the **Make Object Dynamic** button.

◆ Variable. Click the **New Variable** button. To bind it to an object, select the object and variable, and then click the **Make Object Dynamic** or **Make Visibility Dynamic** button.

3 To delete a variable, select it, click the **Delete Variable** button, and then click **Yes** or **No** for all occurrences.

Text Variable

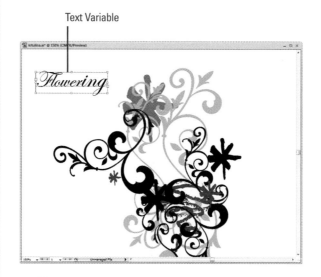

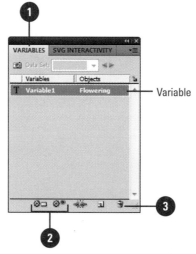

Variable

Create a Data Set

1. Select the **Variables** panel.

2. Display the variables that you want in the data set.

3. Click the **Capture Data Set** button on the panel to create a data set.

4. Edit the objects associated with the variables on the artboard.

   Image visibility, the text in a type layer, or exchanging one image for another, can now be controlled through changing variables.

5. Click the **Capture Data Set** button on the panel to create another data set.

6. Repeat Steps 4 and 5 for each variable in the template.

7. To switch between data sets, click the **Data Set** list arrow, and then select a data set.

8. To apply the data on the artboard to the current data set, click the **Options** menu, and then click **Update Data Set**.

Did You Know?

You can delete a data set. Select the Variables panel, click the Data Set list arrow, select the data set that you want to delete, click the Options menu, and then click Delete Data Set.

You can rename a data set. Select the Variables panel, click the Data Set list arrow, select the data set that you want to rename, select the name in the Data Set box, type a name, and then press Enter (Win) or Return (Mac).

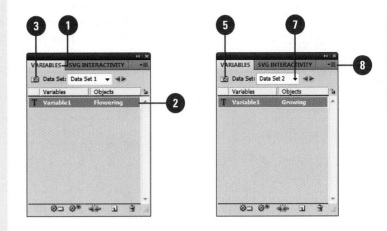

Text variable changes

Creating a Data Graph

A graph allows you to display data in a visual way. With Illustrator, you can create nine different graphs: Column, Stacked Column, Bar, Stacked Bar, Line, Area, Scatter, Pie, and Radar. After you select the type of graph you want to create, you draw the size of the graph you want, and then enter data in the Graph Data window. To edit and modify a graph, select the graph object, and use commands on the Graph submenu on the Object menu.

Create a Data Graph

1. Select a graph tool on the Tools panel.

2. Drag to create a data graphic the size that you want. Alt+drag (Win) or Option+drag (Mac) to draw from the center.

3. Enter data labels in the first row and column for the graph in the Graph Data window. Press Enter (Win) or Return (Mac) to add the text.

4. Enter data for the graph in the Graph Data window. Press Enter (Win) or Return (Mac) to add the data.

5. Click the **Apply** button to display your data changes in the graph on the artboard.

6. When you're done, click the **Close** button in the Graph Data window.

7. To edit and modify graphs, select the graph object, click the **Object** menu, point to **Graph**, and then select a graph command: **Type**, **Data**, **Design**, **Column**, or **Marker**.

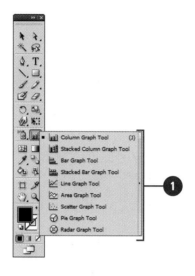

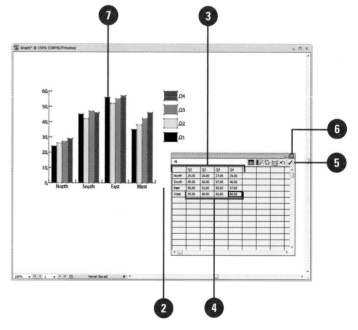

Proofing and Printing Documents

14

Introduction

The Print command is probably the most used of all Illustrator's print options. The Print command is a portal to other menus that let you control specific printing functions, such as crop marks and bleeds, output ink, graphics, and color management. Color separations divide artwork into four plates by color, known as process colors. Each plate represents a CMYK (Cyan, Magenta, Yellow, and Black) color. The Separations Preview panel allows you to preview color separations on your screen. You can preview spot color objects and check for rich black areas and overprinting. If you frequently use custom settings to send an Illustrator document to a local printer or commercial printer for printing, you can save time by creating a preset. Before you print your document, it's important to check the Summary category in the Print dialog box. The summary information is good to have if you're having problems printing your job at commercial printer.

When you save a document, you have the ability to save more than just Illustrator information. You can save copyright, camera, and even image category information. This data is saved with the file as metadata in the XMP format (Extensible Metadata Platform) in Illustrator files, and can be recognized and accessed by any application, such as Adobe Bridge, that reads XMP metadata. The Document Info panel allows you to view information about a selected object or the entire document. You can display information about graphic styles, brushes, spot colors, patterns, gradients, fonts, linked images, and embedded images by using the Options menu.

What You'll Do

Use Spell Check

Use the Custom Dictionary

Find and Replace Text and Elements

Find and Change Fonts

Print a Document

Print with Presets

Set General Print Options

Set Marks and Bleed Options

Set Graphics Options

Preview Color Separations

Set Output Options

Set Advanced Options

Set Color Management Options

Check for Print Problems

Insert File Information

Use the Document Info Panel

Using Spell Check

There's nothing more embarrassing than creating a document that contains misspelled words. Although you wouldn't use Illustrator if all you needed to do was create a text document, Illustrator includes a fully functional spell checking system, which at least lets you make sure all of your words are spelled correctly.

Use Spell Check

1. Open a document that contains one or more Type objects.

2. Click the **Edit** menu, and then click **Check Spelling**.

3. Click **Start**.

4. When Illustrator encounters a word not in its dictionary, it displays that word in the Word Not Found box, and allows you to choose one of the following options:

   ◆ **Ignore.** Ignore this word one time.

   ◆ **Ignore All.** Ignore all instances of this word.

   ◆ **Change.** Change the word, based on the selected suggestion.

   ◆ **Change All.** Change all occurrences of the word, based on the selected suggestion.

   ◆ **Add.** Add the word to Illustrator's dictionary.

   Illustrator continues to highlight misspelled words until the document is completely scanned.

5. To specify additional find and ignore options, click the **Options** button.

6. When you're finished, click **Done**.

The highlighted word has been identified by spell checker.

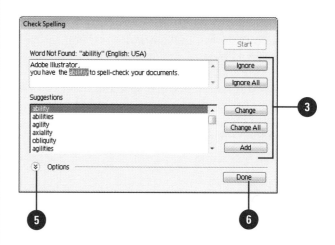

Using Custom Dictionaries

 IL 4.7

Use a Custom Dictionary

1. Click the **Edit** menu, and then click **Edit Custom Dictionary**.

2. Do any of the following:

   ◆ **Add an Entry.** Enter an entry, and then click **Add**.

   ◆ **Delete an Entry.** Select an entry, and then click **Delete**.

   ◆ **Change an Entry.** Select an entry, edit it, and then click **Change**.

3. When you're finished, click **Done**.

Illustrator comes with a custom dictionary for the spell checker. If you need to manage dictionary content, you can use the Edit Custom Dictionary dialog box to add, delete, or edit words. The ability to edit the dictionary becomes useful when you accidentally enter a word that you don't want in the dictionary, or you have some specialty words that you want to enter in all at once.

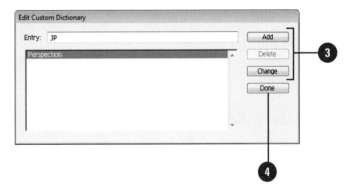

Finding and Replacing Text and Elements

In the editing process, it is sometimes helpful to find and replace a particular word or phrase because the text needs to be changed, either in one spot or globally throughout the document. The Find and Replace command makes it easy to locate and replace specific text in a document. In addition to text, you can also find and replace other elements, such as a bullet character, tab character, Em Space, and quotation marks.

Use Find and Replace

① Click the **Edit** menu, and then click **Find and Replace**.

② Enter the text to locate in the Find box.

③ Select from the following **Find and Replace** options:

◆ **Match Case.** Select to search for the word in the same case as typed in the Find box.

◆ **Find Whole Word.** Select to search for whole words as typed in the Find box.

◆ **Check Hidden Layers.** Select to search hidden layers.

◆ **Check Locked Layers.** Select to search locked layers.

◆ **Search Backwards.** Select to search in the reverse direction.

④ Enter the replacement text in the Replace With box.

⑤ Click **Find** to locate the next occurrence of the word:

◆ Click **Replace** to change the word.

◆ Click **Replace & Find** to automatically change the word and locate the next occurrence.

◆ Click **Replace All** to change all occurrences of the word.

⑥ When you're finished, click **Done**.

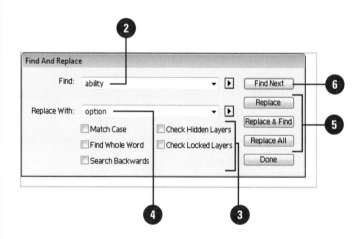

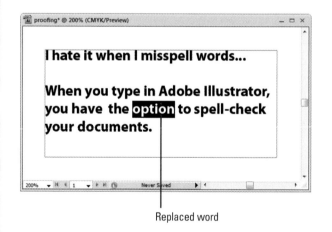

Replaced word

Use Find and Replace Elements

1. Click the **Edit** menu, and then click **Find and Replace**.

2. Click the **Arrow** button next to the Find box, and then select the element type that you want to find.

   The special characters are added to the Find box. You can also add text too.

3. Select from the following **Find and Replace** options:

   ◆ **Match Case.** Select to search for the word in the same case as typed in the Find box.

   ◆ **Find Whole Word.** Select to search for whole words as typed in the Find box.

   ◆ **Check Hidden Layers.** Select to search hidden layers.

   ◆ **Check Locked Layers.** Select to search locked layers.

   ◆ **Search Backwards.** Select to search in the reverse direction.

4. Click the **Arrow** button next to the Replace With box, and then select the element type that you want to use for replacement.

   The special characters are added to the Replace With box. You can also add text.

5. Click **Find** to locate the next occurrence of the word:

   ◆ Click **Replace** to change the word.

   ◆ Click **Replace & Find** to automatically change the word and locate the next occurrence.

   ◆ Click **Replace All** to change all occurrences of the word.

6. When you're finished, click **Done**.

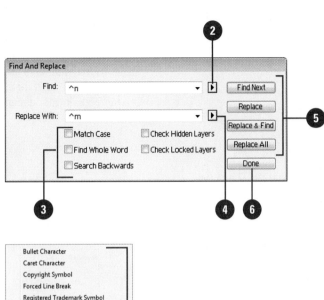

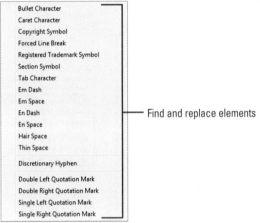

Find and replace elements

Finding and Changing Fonts

Say you create some artwork using a certain font. After the customer or client reviews, they ask you to change it. Instead of manually changing each use of the font, you can use the Find Font command to quickly find and change every instance of the font in your document. If you're not sure what fonts are used in your document, the Find Font dialog box gives you a list. If there are paragraphs with inconsistent use of capitalization in your document, you can also use change case options to fix them.

Find or Change a Font

1. Click the **Type** menu, and then click **Find Font**.

   The fonts in the top list are the ones currently used in your document. The list at the bottom displays fonts in your document or on your computer, depending on your setting.

2. To find a specific font, select it in the top list.

3. Select the check boxes at the bottom to specify the font attributes that you want to find.

4. To replace the font in the top list, select a font in the bottom list. Click the **Replace With Font From** list arrow, and then click System to show all the fonts on your computer.

5. Click **Find** to display the first instance of the font, and then click **Change** to replace it, or click **Change All** to replace all uses of the font in your document.

6. When you're done, click **Done**.

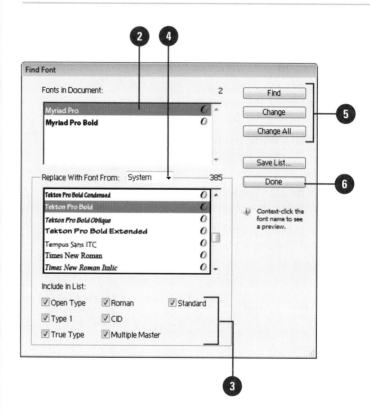

Change Case

① Select the type for which you want to change case.

② Click the **Type** menu, and then point to **Change Case**.

③ Select one of the following:

◆ **UPPERCASE.**

◆ **lowercase.**

◆ **Title Case.**

◆ **Sentence case.**

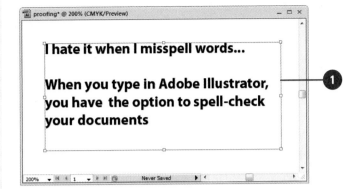

I hate it when I misspell words...

When you type in Adobe Illustrator, you have the option to spell-check your documents

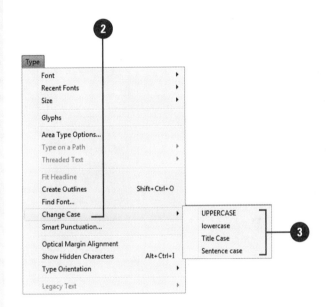

Type

Font	▶
Recent Fonts	▶
Size	▶
Glyphs	
Area Type Options...	
Type on a Path	▶
Threaded Text	▶
Fit Headline	
Create Outlines	Shift+Ctrl+O
Find Font...	
Change Case	▶
Smart Punctuation...	
Optical Margin Alignment	
Show Hidden Characters	Alt+Ctrl+I
Type Orientation	▶
Legacy Text	▶

UPPERCASE
lowercase
Title Case
Sentence case

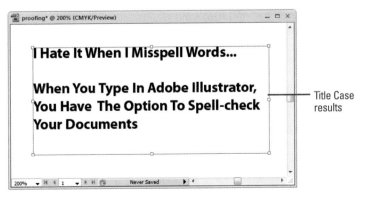

I Hate It When I Misspell Words...

When You Type In Adobe Illustrator, You Have The Option To Spell-check Your Documents

Title Case results

Printing a Document

 IL 9.5

The Print command is probably the most used of all Illustrator's print options. The Print command is a portal to other menus that let you control specific printing functions, such as crop marks and bleeds, output ink, graphics, and color management. Understand that the options available for the Print command will be partially determined by your default printer. For example, if your default printer uses more than one paper tray, you will see options for selecting a specific tray for the current print job. In spite of the differences, there are some universal options for all print jobs, and these are covered here.

Print a Document

1. Click the **File** menu, point to **Document Color Mode**, and then click **CMYK Color** or **RGB Color**.

   ◆ Check your printer for the best color mode setting.

2. Click the **File** menu, and then click **Print**.

3. Click the **Print Preset** list arrow, and then select a preset.

4. Click the **Printer** list arrow, and then select an available printer.

5. Click the **PPD** list arrow, and then select a PPD (if available).

   ◆ A PPD (PostScript Printer Description) is a printer driver, a specific file used by commercial and specialty printers to define an output device.

6. Select a print category (**General**, **Marks and Bleed**, **Output**, **Graphics**, **Color Management**, **Advanced**) with your desired settings.

7. Select the options that you want; see other pages in this chapter for option specifics.

8. Use the navigation buttons to view preview pages. Drag artwork in the preview to move it around.

9. When you're finished, click **Print**.

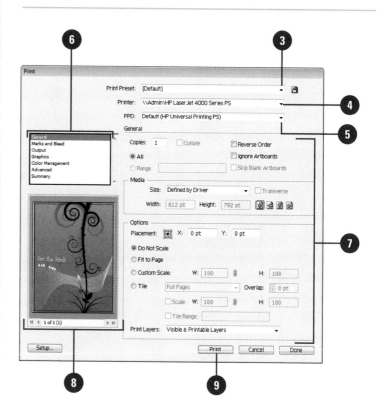

Printing with Presets

 IL 9.5

If you frequently use custom settings to send an Illustrator document to a local printer or commercial printer for printing, you can save time by creating a preset. Adobe Creative Suite programs, including Illustrator, InDesign, Photoshop, and Acrobat, provides built-in presets that you can use in any of the programs. When you create your own preset, you can also use it in other CS programs.

Create a Preset for Printing

1. Click the **Edit** menu, and then click **Print Presets**.

2. Perform any of the following:

    ◆ New. Click **New**, specify the options that you want, and then click **OK**.

    ◆ Edit. Select a custom preset (not a predefined one), click **Edit**, change the options, and then click **OK**.

    ◆ Delete. Select a custom preset (not a predefined one), and then click **Delete**.

    ◆ Import. Click **Import**, navigate to the preset file, select it, and then click **Open**.

    ◆ Export. Select a preset, click **Export**, specify a location and name, and then click **Save**.

3. Click **OK**.

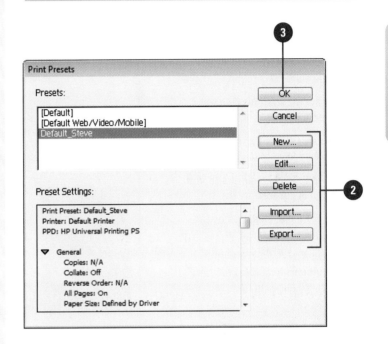

Setting General Print Options

 IL 9.5

Set General Print Options

1 Click the **File** menu, and then click **Print**.

2 Click the **General** category.

3 Select from the various General and Media options:

- ◆ **Copies.** Enter the number of copies you want to print.

- ◆ **Collate.** Select to print artboard pages in collated order.

- ◆ **All or Range.** Select an option to print all or a range of artboard pages.

- ◆ **Reverse Order.** Select to print artboard pages in reverse order.

- ◆ **Ignore Artboards.** Select to print artwork from all artboards on a single page.

- ◆ **Skip Blank Artboards.** Select to not print blank artboard pages.

- ◆ **Size.** Select a page size.

- ◆ **Transverse.** Select to rotate the printed artwork 90 degrees.

  This option is only available when your PPD supports it.

- ◆ **Width and Height.** For a custom page size, specify a width and height.

- ◆ **Orientation.** Click an icon to select a page orientation.

The General category in the Print dialog box allows you to set the page size and orientation (Portrait Up, Portrait Down, Landscape Left, Landscape Right), number of artboards to print, and artboard scale and tiling options. You can also ignore and skip blank artboards for printing. In addition, you can specify which layers you want to print: Visible & Printable Layers, Visible Layers, or All Layers.

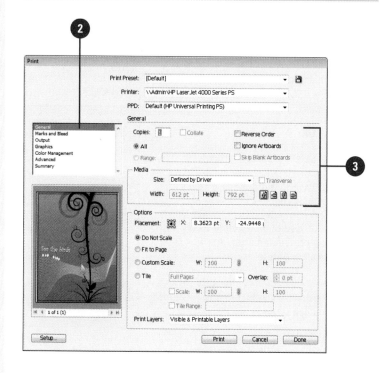

4 Select from the various options:

◆ **Placement.** Click a square on the Placement icon to select an origin for aligning artwork to the page.

◆ **Do Not Scale.** Select to not scale artboards during printing.

◆ **Fit to Page.** Select to scale artboards to the page during printing.

◆ **Custom Scale.** Select to specify a custom width and height for artboards during printing.

◆ **Tile.** Select to tile artwork on multiple pages.

◆ **Print Layers.** Select an option to print layers: Visible & Printable Layers, Visible Layers, or All Layers.

5 When you're finished, click **Done**.

Did You Know?

You can show and hide print tiling in the document window to preview pages. Click the View menu, and then click Show Print Tiling or Hide Print Tiling.

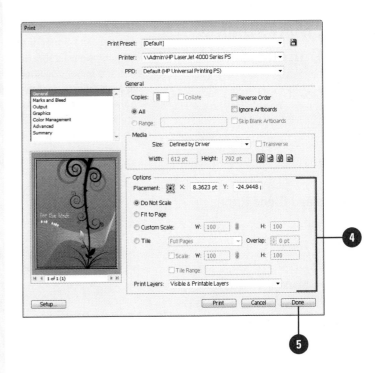

Setting Marks and Bleed Options

IL 9.5

The Marks and Bleed category in the Print dialog box allows you to select printer's marks and create a bleed. Printer marks appear at the edge of the printable page. Commercial printers use printer marks to trim the paper, registration marks to align printing plates, and color bars to print colors properly. Bleed is the amount of artwork that appears outside of the printing area, which includes the bounding box and trim marks. Bleed is useful as a margin of error. It makes sure that ink is printed to the edge of the page so that there are no gaps between the artwork and the edge of the trimmed document page. Your commercial printer can advise you on bleed settings based on your print job.

Set Marks and Bleed Print Options

1. Click the **File** menu, and then click **Print**.

2. Click the **Marks and Bleed** category.

3. Select from the various Marks options:

   - **All Printer's Marks.** Select to enable the following check boxes: Trim Marks, Registration Marks, Color Bars, and Page Information.

   - **Trim Marks.** Select to add trim lines for cutting the page.

   - **Registration Marks.** Select to add small targets for aligning color separations.

   - **Color Bars.** Select to add small color squares with color information for the printer.

   - **Page Information.** Select to add labels with document information: name, artboard number, time and date, plate color, and screen angle.

   - **Printer Mark Type.** Select a type: Roman or Japanese.

   - **Trim Mark Weight.** Specify a thickness for the trim marks.

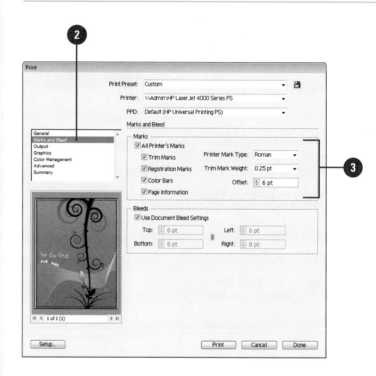

- **Offset.** Specify an offset value (0-72 points) for the distance between trim marks and the bounding box.

  Enter an offset value to make sure that any printer's marks will not be overlapped by the bleed.

4 Select from the various Bleeds options:

- **Use Document Bleed Settings.** Select to use bleed settings defined in the New Document dialog box.

- **Top, Left, Bottom, and Right.** Enter values to define the bleed area.

  Your commercial printer can advise you on bleed settings based on your print job.

5 When you're finished, click **Done**.

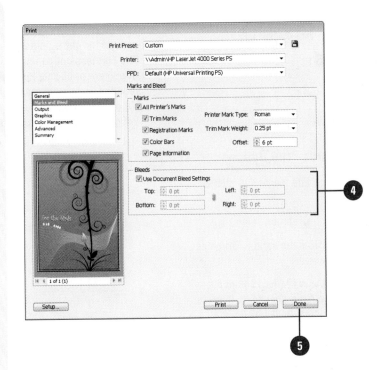

Setting Graphics Options

IL 9.5

The Graphics category in the Print dialog box allows you to set printing options for paths, fonts, PostScript files, gradients, meshes, and blends. The Flatness option (under Paths) controls how well objects in your document print on a PostScript printer. The Automatic setting is recommended. If a document has problems printing, adjust the Flatness level. When you include type in your document, the printer that you use in your document need to be downloaded to your printer.

Set Graphics Print Options

1. Click the **File** menu, and then click **Print**.

2. Click the **Graphics** category.

3. Select from the various Graphics options:

   ◆ **Flatness (Paths).** Select the Automatic check box to use a setting supplied by Illustrator.

   If you have problems printing a document, adjust the Flatness level, and then reprint it.

   ◆ **Download (Fonts).** Select a download option: None, Subset (only characters, or glyphs, used), or Complete (all fonts used).

   ◆ **PostScript (Options).** Choose from Language Level 2 or LanguageLevel 3. Level 3 delivers the best speed and quality if you are printing to a PostScript 3 device.

   ◆ **Data Format (Options).** Choose ASCII or Binary to determine how the data is sent to the printer.

   ◆ **Compatible Gradient and Gradient Mesh Printing.** Select only if you're having problems printing gradients or gradient meshes.

4. When you're finished, click **Done**.

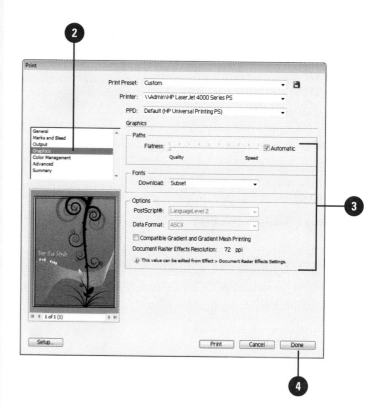

Previewing Color Separations

IL 9.3, 9.4

Color separations divides artwork into four plates by color, known as process colors. Each plate represents a CMYK (Cyan, Magenta, Yellow, and Black) color. The Separations Preview panel (**New!**) allows you to preview color separations on your screen. You can preview spot color objects and check for rich black areas and overprinting. Rich black is process black ink mixed with color inks for increased opacity and richer color instead of a normal black, while overprinting prevents the knockout of overlapping areas and makes those areas transparent. This is used to avoid the need for trapping and avoid gaps between touching colors. Use it when your artwork doesn't share common ink color. In the Separations Preview panel, you can use the Visibility column to show and hide different separation color inks to preview your artwork on the artboard.

Preview Color Separations with the Separations Preview Panel

1. Open a document that contains the artwork that you want to preview.

2. Select the **Separations Preview** panel.

3. Select the **Overprint Preview** check box.

4. Do any of the following:

   ◆ **Hide Separation Ink.** Click the eye icon for each ink you want to hide. Click the eye icon again to make the effects of the ink visible.

   ◆ **Hide All Separation Inks Except One.** Alt+click (Win) or Option+click (Mac) the eye icon to show just one ink color. Click the eye icon again to make all the inks visible.

   ◆ **View All Inks.** Click the CMYK eye icon.

5. Deselect the **Overprint Preview** check box to return to normal view.

Setting Output Options

The Output category in the Print dialog box allows you to create and print color separations. When you choose to create color separations, you also have the option of selecting which color plates that you want to print. Since options vary from job to job, check with your commercial printer for help with specific values for your print job. Some of the options include Mode (composite or separation), Emulsion, Image, and Resolution.

Set Output Print Options

1. Click the **File** menu, and then click **Print**.

2. Click the **Output** category.

   Check with your commercial printer for help with specific values for your print job.

3. Select from the various Output options:

   ◆ **Mode.** Select an output mode: Composite, Separations (Host-Based), or In-RIP Separations.

   Use Composite to print a general print job (not separations); use Separations (Host-Based) to have Illustrator create the separations; or use In-RIP Separations to have Illustrator create a PostScript file that creates the separations.

   ◆ **Emulsion.** Select an option: Up (Right Reading) or Down (Right Reading).

   ◆ **Image.** Select an option: Positive or Negative.

   ◆ **Resolution.** Select a printer resolution. The first number represents the halftone screen ruling (LPI) and the second number represents the device resolution (DPI).

   Check with your commercial printer for these settings.

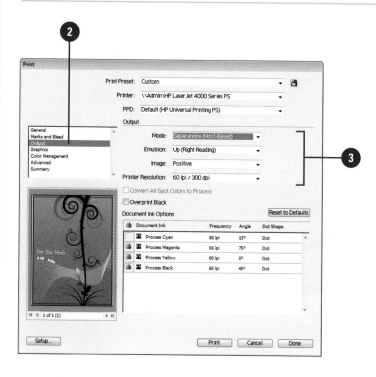

④ If you selected a Separation option from the Mode menu, select from the various Document Ink options:

- ◆ **Document Inks.** For each process or spot color that you don't want to print, click the printer icon.

- ◆ **Convert All Spot Colors to Process.** Select to convert all spot colors in the artwork to process colors.

- ◆ **Overprint Black.** Select to allow black fills and strokes to overprint color underneath.

⑤ When you're finished, click **Done**.

Setting Advanced Options

The Advanced category in the Print dialog box allows you to set options for the overprinting and transparency flattening of vector artwork when you print. You can set overprint options for fills and strokes for color composite or separations printing. You can use the Flattener Preview panel to highlight the areas affected by flattening artwork. If you have problems printing vector objects to a non-PostScript printer, select the Print as Bitmap option to convert vector objects to bitmap raster images for print purposes.

Set Advanced Print Options

1. Click the **File** menu, and then click **Print**.

2. Click the **Advanced** category.

3. Select from the various Advanced options:

   ◆ **Print as Bitmap.** Select if you have problems printing vector objects to a non-PostScript printer.

   ◆ **Overprints.** Select an overprint option:

   Preserve. Use to keep the file's overprint settings.

   Discard. Use to discard the file's overprint settings.

   Simulate. Use to simulate overprinting for proofing purposes.

   ◆ **Preset.** Select a resolution option:

   High Resolution. Use for high-quality color separations.

   Medium Resolution. Use for desktop PostScript printing.

   Low Resolution. Use for black and white printing.

   Custom. Click to select custom settings.

4. When you're finished, click **Done**.

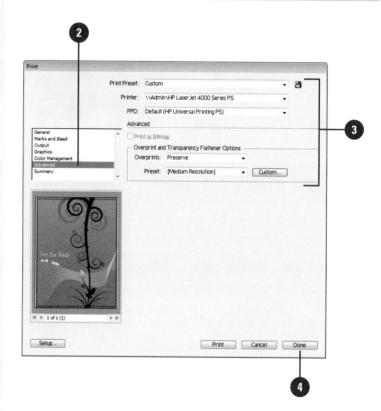

Preview Flattened Artwork

1. Click the **Window** menu, and then click **Flattener Preview**.

2. Click the **Highlight** list arrow, and then select a highlight option.

   Options vary depending on the content of the artwork.

3. To display a fresh preview based on your current settings, click **Refresh**.

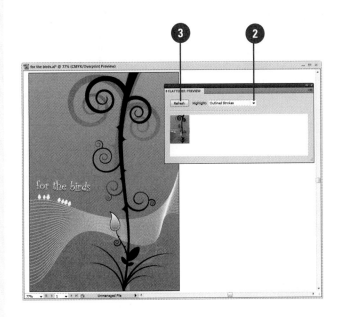

Create a Preset for Transparency Flattener

1. Click the **Edit** menu, and then click **Transparency Flattener Presets**.

2. Perform any of the following:

   ◆ New. Click **New**, specify the options that you want, and then click **OK**.

   ◆ Edit. Select a custom preset (not a predefined one), click **Edit**, change the options, and then click **OK**.

   ◆ Delete. Select a custom preset (not a predefined one), and then click **Delete**.

   ◆ Import. Click **Import**, navigate to the preset file, select it, and then click **Open**.

   ◆ Export. Select a preset, click **Export**, specify a location and name, and then click **Save**.

3. Click **OK**.

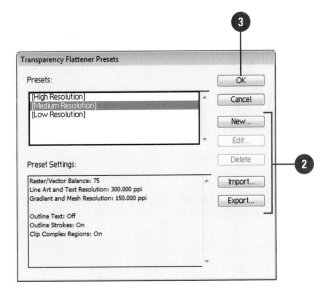

Setting Color Management Options

 IL 3.1

The Color Management category in the Print dialog box allows you to select a printer profile and rendering intent for printing. Rendering intent specifies how the program converts colors to the destination color space. In most cases, it's best to use the default options for Color Management unless you've been give specific instructions from a printer to change them.

Set Color Management Print Options

1. Click the **File** menu, and then click **Print**.

2. Click the **Color Management** category.

3. Select from the various Color Management options:

   ◆ **Color Handling.** Select a color option: Let Illustrator determine colors or Let PostScript printer determine colors.

   ◆ **Printer Profile.** Select the profile for your output device.

   ◆ **Rendering Intent.** Select an option to specify how the program converts colors to the destination color space.

   ◆ **Preserve Color Numbers.** Select to preserve the color mode when a color profile is not available. Deselect to have Illustrator convert colors for use on the output device.

4. When you're finished, click **Done**.

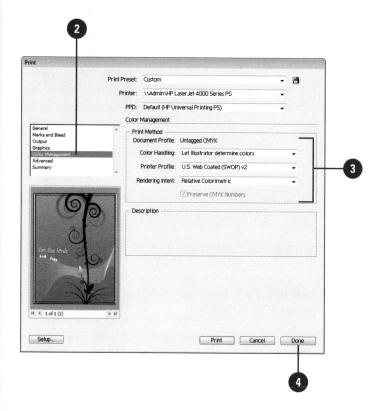

Checking for Print Problems

IL 9.5

Before you print your document, it's important to check the Summary category in the Print dialog box. The summary information is good to have if you're having problems printing your job at a commercial printer. You can save the information and send it to the printer to help diagnose the problem. The important area is the Warnings box, which displays warning about printing problems with your document. Check to make sure your print job is clear of all warnings before you send it to a printer.

View Summary Print Options

1. Click the **File** menu, and then click **Print**.

2. Click the **Summary** category.

3. Scroll through the print summary to review your print settings.

4. Check the Warnings box for problems or warning that you should fix before you print.

5. To print the summary information to a file, click **Save Summary**, enter a name, specify a location, and then click **Save**.

6. When you're finished, click **Done**.

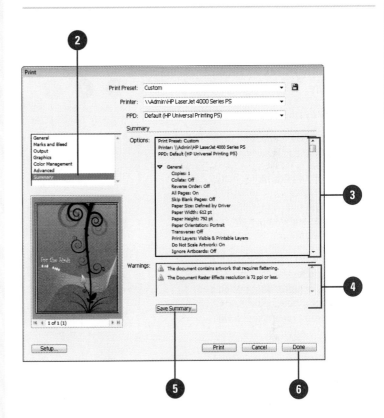

Inserting File Information

 IL 1.13

When you save a document, you have the ability to save more than just Illustrator information. You can save copyright, camera, and even image category information. This data is saved with the file as metadata in the XMP format (Extensible Metadata Platform) in Illustrator files, and can be recognized and accessed by any application, such as Adobe Bridge, that reads XMP metadata. In addition, if an image is a photograph, you can save data specifying the type of image, where it was shot, or the camera used. You can even get information on shutter speed and fstop. You can do the same with video and audio data too. That information will not only protect your intellectual property, but will supply you with vital statistics on exactly how you created that one-of-a-kind artwork.

Insert File Information into a Document

1. Open a document.

2. Click the **File** menu, and then click **File Info**.

3. Click the **Description** tab, and then enter information concerning the document title, description of file, author and any copyright information.

4. Click the **IPTC** tab to enter information concerning the image's creator, description and keywords, location where photograph was taken, date created, copyright, and usage terms.

5. Click the **Camera Data** tab, which reveals information about the camera that took the image.

6. Click the **Video Data** tab or **Audio Data** tab to reveal information about video and audio data, and then enter your video and audio data.

7. Click the **Mobile SWF** tab, and then enter the file information for a mobile SWF document.

8. Click the **Categories** tab, and then enter category keywords for search purposes.

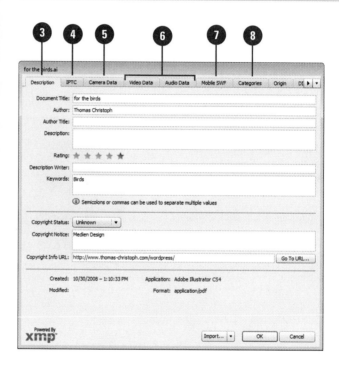

9 Click the **Origin** tab, and then enter data pertaining to the origin of the image.

10 Click the **DICOM** tab, and then enter data pertaining to the Digital Imaging and Communications in Medicine options (patient name, ID, etc.).

11 Click the **History** tab to view historical information about the active document, such as dates last opened and saved, and a list of image adjustments.

12 Click the **Illustrator** tab, and then select an Illustrator document profile.

13 Click the **Advanced** tab to view additional information on the active document, such as EXIF, and PDF document properties.

14 Click the **Raw Data** tab to view raw RDF/XML information.

15 Click **OK**.

Did You Know?

You can add metadata to files saved in the PSD, PDF, EPS, PNG, GIF, JPEG, and TIFF formats. The information is embedded in the file using XMP (Extensible Metadata Platform). This allows metadata to be exchanged between Adobe applications and across operating systems.

You can use the XMP Software Development Kit to customize the creation, processing, and interchange of metadata. You can also use the XMP kit to add fields to the File Info dialog box. For information on XMP and the XMP SDK, check the Adobe Solutions Network.

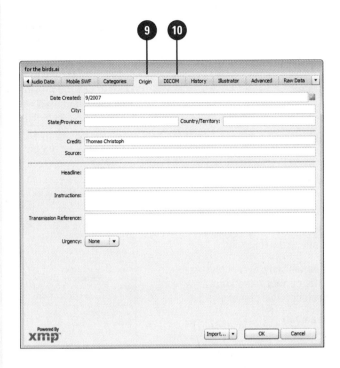

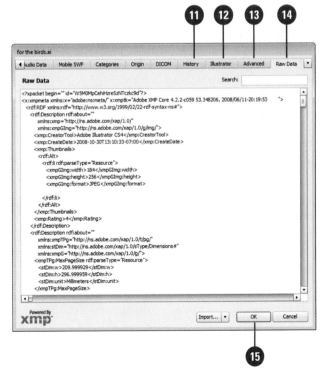

Using the Document Info Panel

The Document Info panel allows you to view information about a selected object or the entire document. You can display information about graphic styles, brushes, spot colors, patterns, gradients, fonts, linked images, and embedded images by using the Options menu. If you want to use the provided information in another document, you can also save the data as a text file.

Use the Document Info Panel

1. Select the object that you want to review information about.

2. Select the **Document Info** panel.

3. Click the **Options** menu, and then select any of the following:

   ◆ **Selection Only.** Select for info on the current selection. Deselect for all objects.

   ◆ **Document.**

   ◆ **Objects.**

   ◆ **Graphic Styles.**

   ◆ **Brushes.**

   ◆ **Spot Color Objects.**

   ◆ **Pattern Objects.**

   ◆ **Gradient Objects.**

   ◆ **Fonts.**

   ◆ **Linked Images.**

   ◆ **Embedded Images.**

   ◆ **Font Details.**

4. To save the information to a text file, click the **Options** menu, click **Save**, enter a name for the file, specify a location, and then click **Save**.

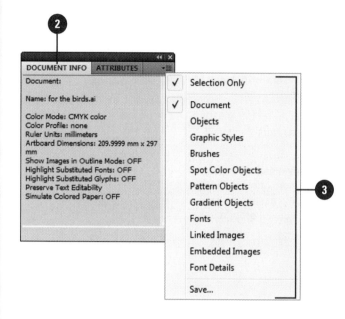

Exporting a Document

15

Introduction

After you finish creating your document in Illustrator, you can save or export your artwork in another file format for use in other programs. There are five file formats to which you can save your artwork, which include AI (Adobe Illustrator), Adobe PDF (Portable Document Format), EPS (Encapsulated PostScript), FXG (Adobe Flex), and SVG (Scalable Vector Graphics). These file format are native to Illustrator, which means they preserve Illustrator content, including multiple artboards, when you re-open them.

If you want to save your artwork in another file format, you need to export it. Illustrator allows you to export your artwork in 13 different file formats, including Flash, Photoshop, Bitmap, JPEG, and PNG. When you export from Illustrator, your content is altered using the Options dialog box for the specific file format. If you want to use an Illustrator document in a Microsoft Office program, you need to save the document as a PNG (Portable Network Graphics) image with the Save for Microsoft Office command.

If you frequently create the same kind of document, then you should create a template. A template is a special document that makes it easier to reuse frequently used material in order to create a new document. An Illustrator Template file uses the (AIT) file format instead of the normal (AI) document file format.

What You'll Do

Export a Document

Understanding Export File Formats

Export as a Bitmap

Export as a TIFF

Export to Photoshop

Export with Presets

Export as a Flash Movie

Save as Adobe PDF

Save as an EPS

Save as Adobe Flex

Save for Microsoft Office

Save as a Template

Exporting a Document

After you finish creating your document in Illustrator, you can export it for use in other programs. If you have a document with text, you can export it to a text document, which you can open in a word processing program. If you have a document with artwork, you can export it as a PSD file (for use in Photoshop) or a JPEG file (for use on the web). See the list on the next page for more information about all the file formats. If you have multiple artboards in a document, many file formats preserve them or create multiple page documents during export (**New!**).

Export a Document

1. Click the **File** menu, and then click **Export**.

2. Enter a name for the file in the File Name (Win) or Save As (Mac) box.

3. Click the **Format** popup (Mac) or **Save as Type** list arrow (Win), and then select a file format.

   See the list on the next page for more information about all the file formats.

4. Navigate to the drive or folder location where you want to save the document.

5. To preserve artboards, select the **Use Artboards** check box (if available), and then select the **All** or **Range** option. If you selected the Range option, enter a range.

6. Click **Save**.

   For some formats, an Options dialog box appears, prompting you for additional settings.

7. If prompted, specify the options that you want, and then click **OK**.

   ◆ For help, point to an option to display a description at the bottom of the Options dialog box.

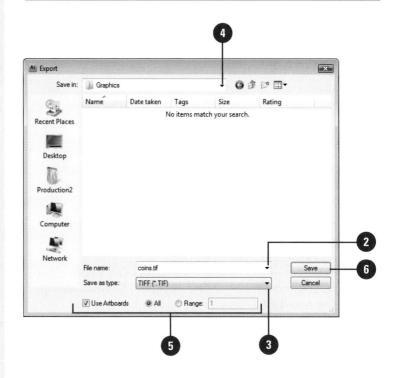

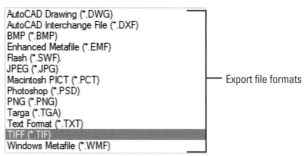

Export file formats

AutoCAD Drawing (*.DWG)
AutoCAD Interchange File (*.DXF)
BMP (*.BMP)
Enhanced Metafile (*.EMF)
Flash (*.SWF)
JPEG (*.JPG)
Macintosh PICT (*.PCT)
Photoshop (*.PSD)
PNG (*.PNG)
Targa (*.TGA)
Text Format (*.TXT)
TIFF (*.TIF)
Windows Metafile (*.WMF)

Understanding Export File Formats

Export File Formats

Format	Usage
BMP	Uses the BMP (Bitmap) format. This is the standard image format on the Windows platform.
Targa	Uses the Targa format for high-end image editing on the Windows platform.
PNG	Uses the PNG (Portable Network Graphics) format. This format is used for saving images to the Web; it supports up to 16 million colors and 256 levels of transparency.
AutoCAD Drawing	Uses the DWG format. This format creates a file used for 2 and 3 dimensional design data.
AutoCAD Interchange File	Uses the DXF (Drawing Interchange Format, or Drawing Exchange Format) format. This format create a CAD (Computer Aided-Design) data file.
Enhanced Metafile	Uses the EMF format. This drawing format (32-bit) uses metafile commands to create simple artwork.
Flash	Uses the SWF movie format. This format creates a movie for use on the Web using the Flash player.
JPEG	Uses the JPG or JPEG (Joint Photographic Experts Group) format. This format uses a compression method to reduce the size of image files primarily for the Web.
Macintosh PICT	Uses the PICT or PICT Resource format. This is the standard image format on the Macintosh platform.
Photoshop	Uses the PSD (Photoshop) format (the default), which saves layers, channels, notes, and color profiles.
TIFF	Uses the TIFF (Tagged-Image File Format) format. These files can be opened by almost any image-editing or layout program. TIFF is a common format for printing and saving flattened images without losing quality.
Text Format	Uses the TXT format. This format creates a plain text document.
Windows Metafile	Uses the WMF format. This drawing format (16-bit) uses metafile commands to create simple artwork.

Exporting as a Bitmap

A bitmap document (BMP) is a raster image, which means it's made up of individual pixels. Since an Illustrator document is made up of vector data, the artwork in the document is converted from mathematical calculations to individual pixels. During the export process, you can specify a color mode for the pixels, resolution size (the number of pixels per inch), and whether you want to smooth out the edges with Anti-Alias.

Export a Document as a Bitmap

1. Click the **File** menu, and then click **Export**.

2. Enter a name for the file in the File Name (Win) or Save As (Mac) box.

3. Click the **Format** popup (Mac) or **Save as Type** list arrow (Win), and then click **BMP (*.BMP)**.

4. Navigate to the drive or folder location where you want to save the document.

5. Click **Save**.

6. Click the **Color Mode** list arrow, and then select a color mode: **RGB**, **Grayscale**, or **Bitmap**.

7. Select one of the resolution options.

8. Select the **Anti-Alias** check box to smooth out the edges of the image.

9. Click **OK**.

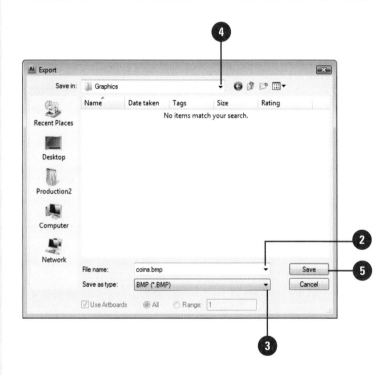

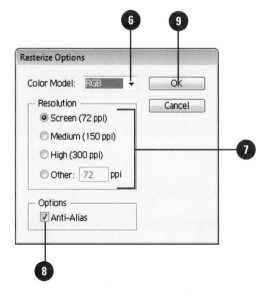

Exporting as a TIFF

TIFF (Tagged-Image File Format) files can be opened by almost any image-editing or layout program. TIFF is a common format for printing and saving flattened images without losing quality. During the export process, you can specify a color mode for the pixels, resolution size (the number of pixels per inch), and whether you want to smooth out the edges with the Anti-Alias option, compress the image with the LZW compression method, and embed the color profile in the image. If you have multiple artboards in a document, these are preserved (**New!**).

Export a Document as a TIFF

1. Click the **File** menu, and then click **Export**.

2. Enter a name for the file in the File Name (Win) or Save As (Mac) box.

3. Click the **Format** popup (Mac) or **Save as Type** list arrow (Win), and then click **TIFF (*.TIF)**.

4. Navigate to the drive or folder location where you want to save the document.

5. To preserve artboards, select the **Use Artboards** check box (if available), and then select the **All** or **Range** option. If you selected the Range option, enter a range.

6. Click **Save**.

7. Click the **Color Mode** list arrow, and then select a color mode: **RGB**, **CMYK, or Grayscale.**.

8. Select one of the resolution options.

9. Specify the following options:

   ◆ **Anti-Alias.** Select to smooth out the edges of the image.

   ◆ **LZW Compression.** Select to compress the image.

   ◆ **Byte Order.** Select a destination operating system for the image.

   ◆ **Embed ICC Profile.** Select to attach the color profile of the document to the image.

10. Click **OK**.

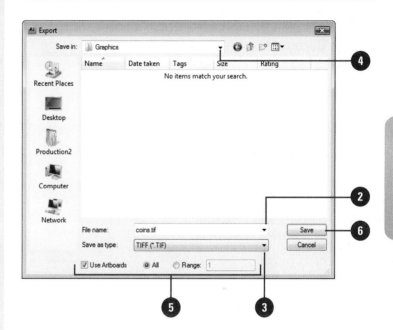

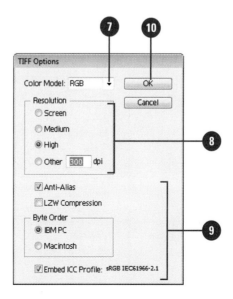

Exporting to Photoshop

Adobe Photoshop is a graphics and image editing program. When you export artwork to Photoshop, Illustrator converts objects into pixels and preserves layers and transparency. Other conversions include removing strokes and effects from text and changing opacity masks to layer masks. During the export process, you can specify a color mode for the pixels, resolution size (the number of pixels per inch), and whether you want to flatten or preserve layers, smooth out the edges with the Anti-Alias option, and embed the color profile in the image. In addition to exporting, you can also copy and paste objects into Photoshop, which automatically creates Smart Objects that you can re-edit in Illustrator.

Export a Document as a Photoshop File

1. Click the **File** menu, and then click **Export**.

2. Enter a name for the file in the File Name (Win) or Save As (Mac) box.

3. Click the **Format** popup (Mac) or **Save as Type** list arrow (Win), and then click **Photoshop (*.PSD)**.

4. Navigate to the drive or folder location where you want to save the document.

5. Click **Save**.

6. Click the **Color Mode** list arrow, and then select a color mode: **RGB**, **CMYK or Grayscale**.

7. Select one of the resolution options.

8. Specify the following options:

   ◆ **Flat Image.** Select to flatten image as one layer.

   ◆ **Write Layers.** Select to preserve layers and maximum editability for objects and text.

   ◆ **Anti-Alias.** Select to smooth out the edges of the image.

   ◆ **Embed ICC Profile.** Select to attach the color profile of the document to the image.

9. Click **OK**.

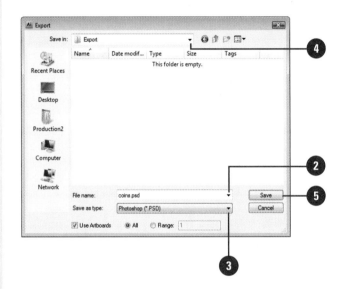

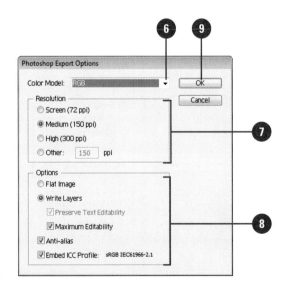

Exporting with Presets

If you frequently use custom settings to export an Illustrator document to an Adobe PDF or Flash SWF file, you can save time by creating a preset. Adobe Creative Suite programs, including Illustrator, InDesign, Photoshop, and Acrobat, provide built-in presets that you can use in any of the programs. When you create your own preset, you can also use it in other CS programs. The process for creating a preset for an Adobe PDF or Flash SWF is similar; just the settings are different.

Create a Preset for Adobe PDF or Flash SWF

1. Click the **Edit** menu, and then click **Adobe PDF Presets** or **SWF Presets**.

2. Perform any of the following:

   - **New.** Click **New**, specify the options that you want, and then click **OK**.

   - **Edit.** Select a custom preset (not a predefined one), click **Edit**, change the options, and then click **OK**.

   - **Delete.** Select a custom preset (not a predefined one), and then click **Delete**.

   - **Import.** Click **Import**, navigate to the preset file, select it, and then click **Open**.

   - **Export.** Select a preset, click **Export**, specify a location and name, and then click **Save**.

   For PDF files, the preset is saved with the *.joboptions* extension.

3. Click **OK**.

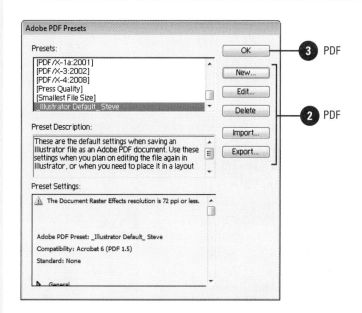

PDF ③

PDF ②

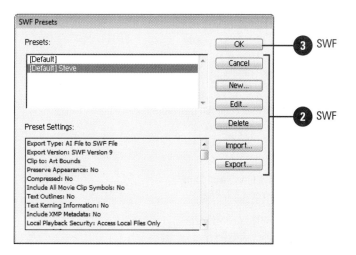

SWF ③

SWF ②

Exporting as a Flash Movie

 IL 8.3

Adobe Flash is a vector-based animation and interactivity program. If you want to use individual Illustrator objects in Flash, you can simply copy and paste them directly into a Flash movie document (FLA). However, if you want to create a Flash movie (SWF) that you can use on a web page and display using Flash Player, you should use the Export command. The Export command gives you options to specify how you want to create a SWF movie. If you have multiple artboards in a document, these are preserved in the SWF file format (**New!**).

Export a Document as a Flash Movie

1 Click the **File** menu, and then click **Export**.

2 Enter a name for the file in the File Name (Win) or Save As (Mac) box.

3 Click the **Format** popup (Mac) or **Save as Type** list arrow (Win), and then click **Flash (*.SWF)**.

4 Navigate to the drive or folder location where you want to save the document.

5 To preserve artboards, select the **Use Artboards** check box, and then select the **All** or **Range** option. If you selected the Range option, enter a range.

6 Click **Save**.

7 Click the **Preset** list arrow, and then select a preset option, or specify your own options to create a custom preset.

◆ To create a preset that you can use later, set your options, click **Save Preset**, enter a name, and then click **OK**.

8 Click the **Export As** list arrow, and then select an export method.

9 Click the **Version** list arrow, and then select a target Flash Player version.

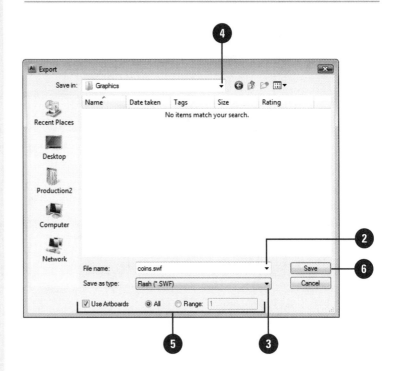

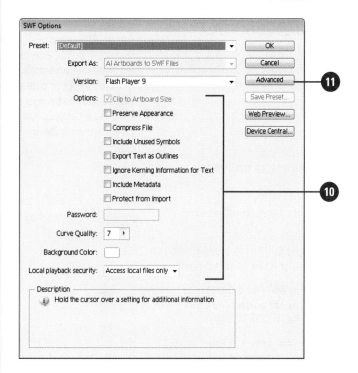

10 Specify the following options:

- ◆ **Clip to Artboard Size.** Select to export only objects within an artboard.

- ◆ **Preserve Appearance.** Select to flatten artwork to a single layer.

- ◆ **Compress File.** Select to compress the SWF file.

- ◆ **Include Unused Symbols.** Select to export all defined symbols.

- ◆ **Export Text as Outlines.** Select to convert type to vector paths.

- ◆ **Ignore Kerning Information for Text.** Select to export text without kerning.

- ◆ **Include Metadata.** Select to export metadata with the file.

- ◆ **Protect from Import.** Select to prevent changes to the SWF.

- ◆ **Password.** Select to protect the file with a password.

- ◆ **Curve Quality.** Select a number for Bezier curve accuracy. The higher the number, the more accurate.

- ◆ **Background.** Specify a background color for the file.

- ◆ **Local Playback Security.** Specify whether you want to access only local file or network files.

11 To set image compression and quality or animation frame rates and layer order options, click **Advanced**.

12 Click **OK**.

Saving as Adobe PDF

If a co-worker or client doesn't have Illustrator, you can create an Adobe PDF of a document for them to review your work. Adobe PDF (Portable Document Format) is a useful file format for document sharing, viewing, and proofing with Adobe Acrobat Reader, which is free for download on the web at *www.adobe.com*. If recipients of the file have Adobe Acrobat, they can add comments to an Adobe PDF. If you have multiple artboards in a document, these are preserved in the Adobe PDF file format (**New !**).

Save a Document as an Adobe PDF

1. Click the **File** menu, and then click **Save As**.

2. Enter a name for the file in the File Name (Win) or Save As (Mac) box.

3. Click the **Format** popup (Mac) or **Save as Type** list arrow (Win), and then click **Adobe PDF (*.PDF)**.

4. Navigate to the drive or folder location where you want to save the document.

5. Select the **All** or **Range** option to create individual pages for each artboard. If you selected the Range option, enter a range.

6. Click **Save**.

7. Click the **Adobe PDF Preset** list arrow, and then select a preset option, or specify your own options to create a custom preset.

   ◆ To create a preset that you can use later, set your options, click **Save Preset**, enter a name, and then click **OK**.

8. Select a category (General, Compression, etc.) from the list to display options.

9. Specify the options for the category that you want.

   ◆ To reset options to defaults, hold down Alt (Win) or Option (Mac), and then click **Reset**.

10. Click **Save PDF**.

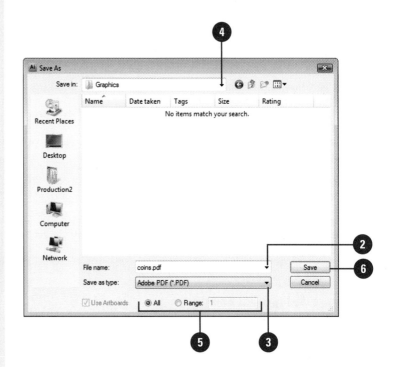

Use Adobe PDF Preset Options

1 Follow steps 1 through 6 on the previous page.

2 Click the **Adobe PDF Preset** list arrow, and then select one of the following presets:

- **Illustrator Default.** Creates PDFs that preserve all Illustrator content, which can be reopened in Illustrator, InDesign, or QuarkXPress.

- **High Quality Print.** Creates PDFs for quality printing on desktop printers and proofing devices.

- **PDF/X-1a: 2001/2003.** Creates PDFs that meet printing standards for Acrobat Reader 4.0 or later. Useful for a CMYK workflow.

- **PDF/X-3: 2002/2003.** Creates PDFs that meet printing standards for Acrobat Reader 7.0 or later. Useful for a color-managed workflow.

- **PDF/X-4.** Creates PDFs that meet printing standards for Acrobat Reader 7.0 or later. Useful for a color-managed workflow with added support for preserving transparency.

- **Press Quality.** Creates PDFs for high quality print production (digital printing or separations).

- **Smallest File Size.** Creates compressed PDFs for use on the Web or e-mail distribution.

3 Click **OK**.

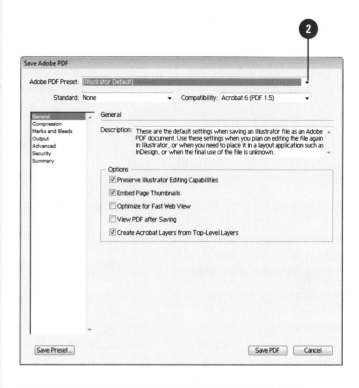

Adobe PDF Presets

Saving as an EPS

EPS (Encapsulated PostScript) is a commonly used file format that you can import into graphics, word processing, and page layout programs. An EPS file can contain vector and bitmap graphics, so it makes the format more versatile for use in other programs. EPS does a good job of preserving graphic objects in an Illustrator document. If you have multiple artboards in a document, these are preserved in the EPS file format (**New!**).

Save a Document as an EPS File

1. Click the **File** menu, and then click **Save As**.

2. Enter a name for the file in the File Name (Win) or Save As (Mac) box.

3. Click the **Format** popup (Mac) or **Save as Type** list arrow (Win), and then click **Illustrator EPS (*.EPS)**.

4. Navigate to the drive or folder location where you want to save the document.

5. To preserve artboards, select the **Use Artboards** check box, and then select the **All** or **Range** option. If you selected the Range option, enter a range.

6. Click **Save**.

7. Click the **Version** list arrow, and then select an Illustrator EPS version.

8. To create an image preview for Open dialog boxes, click the **Format** list arrow, select a format, and then select the **Transparent** or **Opaque** option.

9. If the artwork contains transparent objects and overprints, specify the options you want.

10. Select the **Embed Fonts (for other applications)** check box to attach fonts used in the document to the image file, so they will be available in other programs.

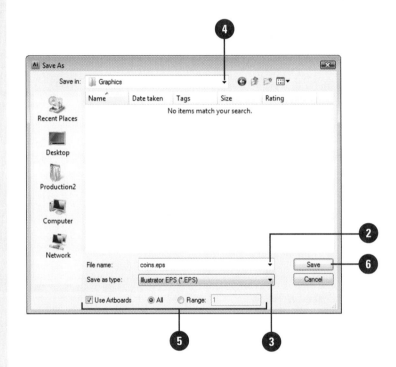

358

11 Specify the following options:

◆ **Include Linked Files.** Select to embed linked files in artwork.

◆ **Include Document Thumbnails.** Select to create a thumbnail image of the artwork.

◆ **Include CMYK PostScript in RGB Files.** Select to allow the use of RGB output when it's not supported in a program.

◆ **Compatible Gradient and Gradient Mesh Printing.** Select to allow older printers and PostScript devices to print gradients and gradient meshes by converting them to JPEG.

◆ **Use Printer's Default Screen.** Select to use a printer's default settings.

◆ **Adobe PostScript.** Select a PostScript level to save with the image. PostScript Language Level 2 is widely used. If you want to work with mesh objects, use Level 3.

12 Click **OK**.

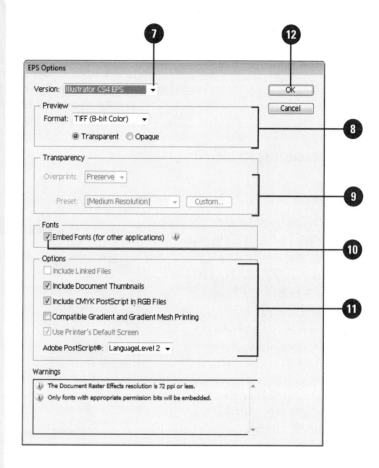

Saving as Adobe Flex

FXG (Flash XML Graphics) is a file format based on a subset of MXML, the XML-based programming language used by Adobe Flex, which you can use to build rich Internet applications. Illustrator allows you to save your artwork in the FXG file format (**New!**). When you save a document for use in Adobe Flex, the FXG Options dialog box appears, where you can specify the save options you want. If you have multiple artboards in a document, these are preserved in the FXG file format (**New!**).

Save a Document as Adobe Flex File

1. Click the **File** menu, and then click **Save As**.

2. Enter a name for the file in the File Name (Win) or Save As (Mac) box.

3. Click the **Format** popup (Mac) or **Save as Type** list arrow (Win), and then click **FXG (*.FXG)**.

4. Navigate to the drive or folder location where you want to save the document.

5. To preserve artboards, select the **Use Artboards** check box, and then select the **All** or **Range** option. If you selected the Range option, enter a range.

6. Click **Save**.

7. Specify the options that you want.

   ◆ For help, point to an option to display a description at the bottom of the Options dialog box.

8. Click **Show Preview** to see a preview of your artwork in FXG.

9. Click **Show Code** to see the resulting code for your artwork in your browser.

10. Click **OK**.

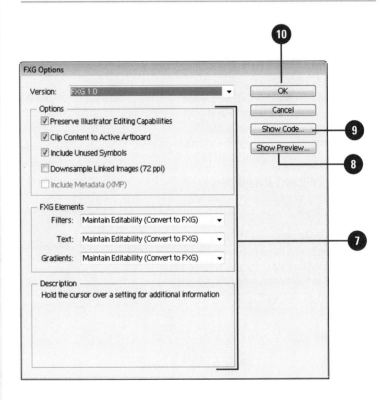

Saving a Document for Microsoft Office

The Illustrator format (AI) is not compatible with Microsoft Office programs. If you want to use an Illustrator document in a Microsoft Office program, you need to save the document as a PNG (Portable Network Graphics) image. This format makes transparent areas opaque. In a Microsoft Office program, you can insert the PNG image file by using the Insert Picture command. To save a document as a PNG image, you use the Save for Microsoft Office command on the File menu.

Save a Document for Microsoft Office

1. Click the **File** menu, and then click **Save for Microsoft Office**.

   The Save for Microsoft Office dialog box appears with the PNG file format.

2. Enter a name for the file in the File Name (Win) or Save As (Mac) box.

3. Navigate to the drive or folder location where you want to save the document.

4. Click **Save**.

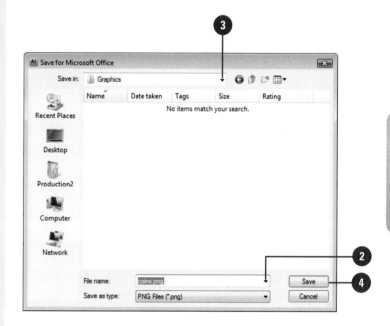

Saving as a Template

IL 1.2

If you find yourself frequently creating the same kind of document, then you should create a template. A template is a special document that makes it easier to reuse frequently used material in order. An Illustrator Template file uses the (AIT) file format instead of the normal (AI) document file format. When you create a new document from a template, a new document appears with the filename "Untitled", so you don't mistakenly make and save changes over the template file.

Save a Document as a Template

1. Open a new or existing document.

2. Create a custom document.

3. Click the **File** menu, and then click **Save As Template**.

   The Templates folder appears, displaying different types of templates available for Illustrator.

4. Type a name for the new template.

5. Click the **Files of Type** (Win) or **Enable** (Mac) list arrow, and then click **Illustrator Template (*.AIT)**, if necessary.

6. Navigate to a different location if you want to save your custom templates in a folder other than the Illustrator Templates folder.

7. Click **Save**.

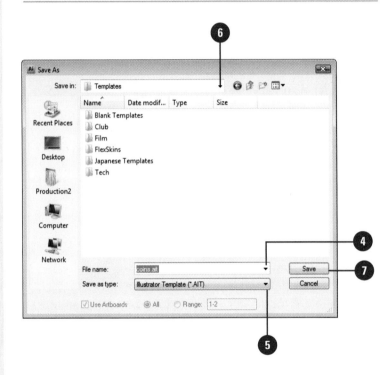

Designing for the Web and Devices

16

Introduction

If you need to manipulate a photographic image to place it on the Web, there's not a better program on the market than Adobe Illustrator that will do the job for you. Illustrator uses various document formats such as JPEG, GIF, PNG, SWF (Flash movie), SVG, and WBMP (Wireless BMP), to save images for the Web. For example, the JPEG format is used primarily for compressing photographic images, while the GIF format is used for compressing clip art and text. Each format is designed to serve a purpose, and knowing when to use a specific format will help you design fast-loading, dynamic web documents.

However, saving files in a specific file format is not the only way Illustrator helps you create web-friendly images; you can also slice images. When you slice an image, you're cutting the image into several pieces. Since the Internet handles smaller packets of information more efficiently than one large piece, slicing an image makes the whole graphic load faster, and Illustrator helps you slice images with ease.

What You'll Do

Save for the Web

Work with Save For Web Options

Optimize an Image to File Size

Work with Web File Formats

Optimize a JPEG Document

Optimize a GIF Document

Optimize a PNG-8 Document

Optimize a PNG-24 Document

Optimize a WBMP Document

Slice Images the Easy Way

Work with Slices

Arrange Slices

Save a Slice Image for the Web

Add HTML Text or an URL to a Slice

Optimize SWF or SVG for the Web

Saving for the Web

Illustrator's Save For Web & Devices command is a dream come true for preparing images for the Internet, or even for saving images in a quick-loading format for Microsoft PowerPoint slide presentations, and you don't even have to leave Illustrator. The Save For Web & Devices command lets you open any Illustrator document, and convert it into a web-friendly format using the GIF, JPEG, PNG, SWF, SVG, or WBMP formats. You can even try different optimization settings or compare different optimizations using the 2-Up or 4-Up panes. In addition, the dialog area below each image provides optimization information on the size and download time of the file.

Save for the Web

1. Open a document.

2. Click the **File** menu, and then click **Save For Web & Devices**.

3. Click the **Original**, **Optimized**, **2-Up**, or **4-Up** tabs to view the document using different layouts.

4. Click one of the sample images to change its default format.

   IMPORTANT *If you're viewing the document using 2-Up or 4-Up, the first image is the original. You can't change the original; you can only edit one of the sample images.*

5. Click the **Preset** list arrow, and then select a new format from the available options.

6. Click the **Optimized File Format** list arrow, and then select from the following options:

   ◆ **GIF.** The Graphics Interchange Format is useful for clip art, text, or images that contain a large amount of solid color. GIF uses lossless compression.

   ◆ **JPEG.** The Joint Photographic Experts Group format is useful for images that contain a lot of continuous tones, like photographs. JPEG uses lossy compression.

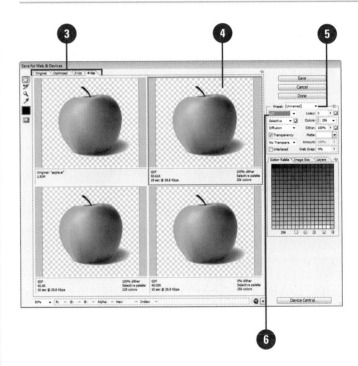

- ◆ **PNG-8.** The Portable Network Graphics 8-bit format functions like the GIF format. PNG uses lossless compression.

- ◆ **PNG-24.** The Portable Network Graphics 24-bit format functions like the JPEG format. PNG-24 uses lossless compression.

- ◆ **SWF.** The Adobe Flash movie format.

- ◆ **SVG.** The Scalable Vector Graphics image file format.

- ◆ **WBMP.** The Wireless Bitmap format converts an image into black and white dots, for use on output devices like cell phones and PDAs.

7   Select from the various options that will change based on your File Format selection.

8   Click the **Color Table** palette (available for the GIF and PNG-8 formats), and add, subtract, or edit colors in the selected document.

9   To change the selected image's width and height, select the **Image Size** palette, and then make adjustments.

10   To move the selected image directly into the Device Central application, click the **Device Central** button.

11   Click **Save**.

12   Enter a name, and then select a location in which to save the image file.

13   Click **OK**.

Illustrator saves the modified file and returns you to the original image.

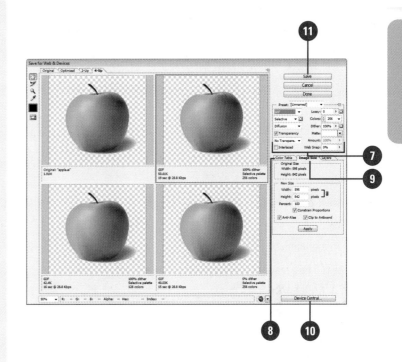

For Your Information

Working with Matte and Transparency

The Matte option, when available, specifies the background color used to fill anti-aliased edges that lie adjacent to transparent areas of the image. When the Transparency option is selected, the matte is applied to edge areas to help blend the edges with a web background of the same color. When the Transparency option is not selected, the matte is applied to transparent areas. Choosing the None option for the matte creates hard edges if Transparency is selected; otherwise, all transparent areas are filled with 100% white. The image must have transparency for the Matte options to be available.

Working with Save For Web Options

IL 8.1

When you choose Save For Web & Devices, you are able to save your image in one of six web formats: GIF, JPEG, PNG, or SWF, SVG, WBMP. The Save For Web & Devices dialog box comes with options that will help you through the process. For example, if you choose the JPEG format, you can select the amount of compression applied to the image or, if you select the GIF format, you can choose how many colors are preserved with the image. The PNG format lets you save images in an 8-bit (256 colors) or a 24-bit (millions of colors) format. The options available with Save For Web & Devices give you the control you need to produce small image files with high quality.

Work with Save For Web Options

1. Open a document.

2. Click the **File** menu, and then click **Save For Web & Devices**.

3. Select from the various Save For Web & Devices tools:

   ◆ **Hand Tool.** Drag inside the image to change the view of a document.

   ◆ **Slice Select Tool**. Select a predefined image slice.

   ◆ **Zoom Tool.** Click on the image to expand the view size.

   ◆ **Eyedropper Tool**. Drag within the image to perform a live sampling of the colors.

4. Click the **Select Download Speed** button, and then select bandwidth options for the selected document.

5. Click the **Zoom** list arrow, and then select a view size for the sample images.

6. Click the **Toggle Slice Visibility** button to show or hide the image slices.

7. Click the **Preview in Default Browser** list arrow, and then select the image.

8. Click **Save**.

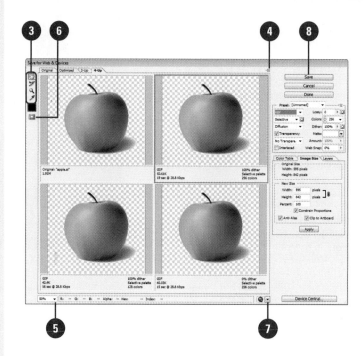

Optimizing an Image to File Size

 IL 8.1

The Save For Web & Devices dialog box has many options to help you create the exact image you need—including helping you compress an image down to a specific file size. For example, you've just created an image you want to display on the Web, but the maximum file size you can use is 35 KB. You could experiment with compression options in the Save For Web & Devices settings, or you could use the Optimize to File Size option.

Optimize an Image to File Size

1. Open a document.

2. Click the **File** menu, and then click **Save For Web & Devices**.

3. Click the **2-Up** tab, and then select the sample image to the right.

4. Click the **Optimize Menu** button, and then click **Optimize To File Size**.

5. Enter a file size in the Desired File Size data box.

6. Click the **Current Settings** option or the **Auto Select GIF/JPEG** option to let Illustrator choose between the JPEG or GIF format.

7. Click the following Use options:

   ◆ **Current Slice**

   ◆ **Each Slice**

   ◆ **Total of All Slices**

8. Click **OK**.

   Illustrator compresses the selected sample.

9. Click **Save** to save the compressed image.

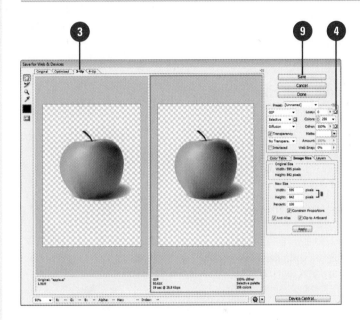

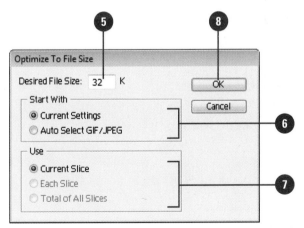

Working with Web File Formats

If you design web documents, you know that the size of your images is very important. Illustrator gives you the option of compressing images in one of six formats appropriate for use on the Web: GIF, JPEG, PNG, SWF, SVG, and WBMP. The GIF format compresses images that contain solid colors with sharp, definable edges, such as clip art and text. The JPEG format reduces the size of image files that contain a lot of soft transitional colors, such as photographs. The PNG format is a hybrid format designed to take the place of the GIF and JPEG format. Finally, the WBMP format was created to display images on low-resolution devices like cell phones and PDAs by converting the image into dots of black and white. Illustrator will help you transform your images into whatever format you need in order to create stunning web images.

Work with Web File Formats

1. Open a document.

2. Click the **File** menu, and then click **Save For Web & Devices**.

3. Click the **Original**, **Optimized**, **2-Up**, or **4-Up** tabs to view the document using different layouts.

4. Select one of the samples.

5. Click the **Optimized File Format** list arrow, and then select a format from the available options.

6. Select the options you want to use to change image compression, and then specify your desired color options.

7. Click **Save**.

   The Save Optimized As dialog box appears.

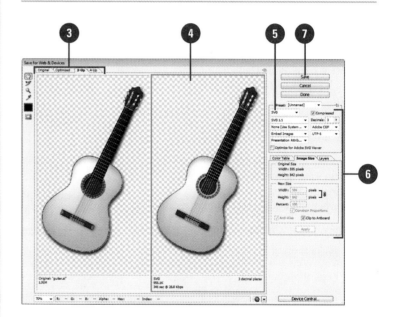

8　Enter a file name in the Save As box.

9　Click the **Save as Type** (Win) or **Format** (Mac) list arrow, and then select to save the image in HTML and Images, Images Only, or HTML Only.

10　Click the **Save In** (Win) or **Where** (Mac) list arrow, and then select the location in which to save the file.

11　Click the **Settings** and **Slices** list arrows to further define the output files (if you save a single image without slices, you can leave these settings at their default values).

12　Click **Save**.

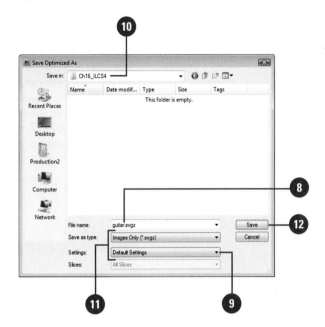

For Your Information

Creating an HTML File for an Image

When you save an optimized file using the Save Optimized As command, you can choose to generate an HTML file for the image. This file contains all the necessary information to display your image in a web browser.

Optimizing a JPEG Document

Illustrator comes complete with everything you will need to properly compress any JPEG Document. The Internet can generally be slow to navigate, and your visitors typically do not have much patience. When you compress a JPEG image, you're essentially removing information from the image to reduce its file size and speed up the loading time. The unfortunate result of that reduction is loss of image quality. Internet graphics are not always the best quality; however, reducing file size is a necessary evil to keep visitors from clicking off your site and moving to another. To keep visitors happy, your JPEG images must load fast, and Illustrator is just the application to help you accomplish that goal.

Optimize a JPEG Document

1. Open a document.

2. Click the **File** menu, and then click **Save For Web & Devices**.

3. Click the **Original**, **Optimized**, **2-Up**, or **4-Up** tabs to view the document using different layouts.

4. Click one of the sample images to change its default format.

5. Click the **Optimized File Format** list arrow, and then click **JPEG**.

6. Select from the following Quality options:

   ◆ **Compression Quality.** Click the list arrow, and then select a preset JPEG quality from Low (poor quality) to Maximum (best quality).

   ◆ **Quality Amount.** Enter a JPEG quality compression value (0 to 100). The lower the value, the more information (color) is sacrificed for image size.

   ◆ **Blur.** JPEG images compress better when the image has soft edges. Apply the Blur option to increase the softness of the image (at a sacrifice of image quality).

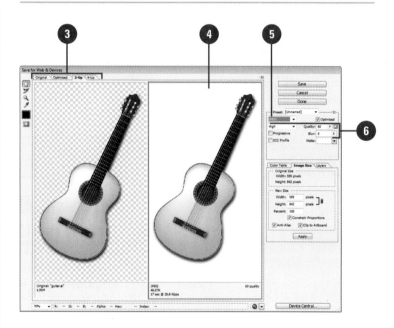

7 Click the **Matte** list arrow, and then select from the available options.

JPEG images do not support transparency. If your image contains transparent areas, use the Matte option to fill them in using a specific color.

8 Select the **Optimized** check box to further compress the image. This is not supported by all browsers.

9 Select from the following options:

◆ **Progressive.** Select the check box to load a JPEG in three progressive scans. Not supported by all browsers.

◆ **ICC Profile.** Select the check box to embed an ICC color profile into the JPEG image. This increases file size but helps maintain color consistency between monitors and operating systems.

10 Click **Save** to save the current image using the Save Optimized As dialog box.

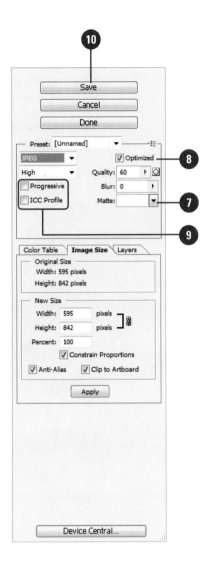

Optimizing a GIF Document

 IL 8.1

The GIF file format is used primarily for images that contain solid colors with sharp edges, such as clip art, text, line art, and logos. Since the Internet can generally be slow to navigate, using the GIF format for images significantly reduces their file size, and will create fast-loading graphics. The GIF format supports 8-bit color, and creates a document with a maximum of 256 colors (the fewer colors, the smaller the file size). The GIF format has been around long enough for it to be considered a "native" Internet format. A **native format** is one that does not require a specific plug-in for the browser to display the file.

Optimize a GIF Document

1. Open a document.

2. Click the **File** menu, and then click **Save For Web & Devices**.

3. Click the **Original**, **Optimized**, **2-Up**, or **4-Up** tabs to view the document using different layouts.

4. Click one of the sample images to change its default format.

5. Click the **Optimized File Format** list arrow, and then click **GIF**.

6. Select from the following options:

   Color Options:

   ◆ **Reduction.** Click to select a visual reduction method for the image's colors.

   ◆ **Colors.** Enter or select a value from 2 to 256 maximum colors.

   ◆ **Web Snap.** Enter or select a value from 0% to 100% to instruct the GIF compression utility how many of the image colors should be web-safe.

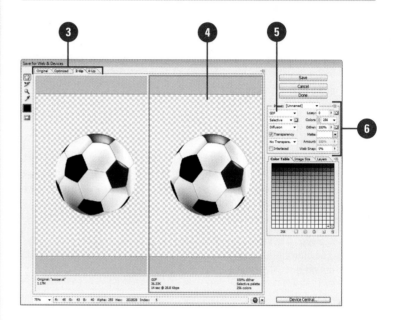

Dither Options:

◆ **Method.** Click the list arrow, and then select from the available dithering schemes. Dithering refers to how the GIF format mixes the available colors in the image.

◆ **Amount.** Enter or select a value from 0% to 100% to instruct the GIF compression utility how many of the image's colors should be dithered.

Transparency Options:

◆ **Transparency.** Check to keep the transparent areas of a GIF image transparent.

◆ **Matte.** Click to fill the transparent areas of a GIF image.

◆ **Dither.** Click to select a dithering scheme and enter an amount for the mixing of the matte color.

Other Options:

◆ **Interlaced.** Check to have the GIF image load in three scans.

◆ **Lossy.** Enter or select a value from 0 to 100 to instruct the GIF compression utility how much image loss is allowed.

7 Click **Save** to save the current image using the Save Optimized As dialog box.

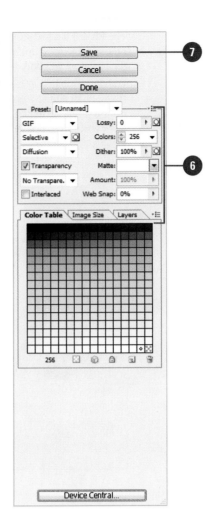

Optimizing a PNG-8 Document

 IL 8.1

The PNG-8 file format is used primarily for images that contain solid colors with sharp edges—clip art, text, line art, and logos—and was designed as an alternative to the GIF file format. Since the PNG-8 format generates an image with a maximum of 256 colors, it significantly reduces an image's file size. While similar to the GIF file format, the PNG-8 format is not completely supported by older browsers. However, it is considered a native format for the creation of Flash animation movies.

Optimize a PNG-8 Document

1. Open a document.

2. Click the **File** menu, and then click **Save For Web & Devices**.

3. Click the **Original**, **Optimized**, **2-Up**, or **4-Up** tabs to view the document using different layouts.

4. Click one of the sample images to change its default format.

5. Click the **Optimized File Format** list arrow, and then click **PNG-8**.

6. Select from the following options:

   Color Options:

   ◆ **Reduction.** Click to select a visual reduction method for the colors in the image.

   ◆ **Colors.** Enter or select a value from 2 to 256 maximum colors.

   ◆ **Web Snap.** Enter or select a value from 0% to 100% to instruct the PNG-8 compression utility how many of the image's colors should be web-safe.

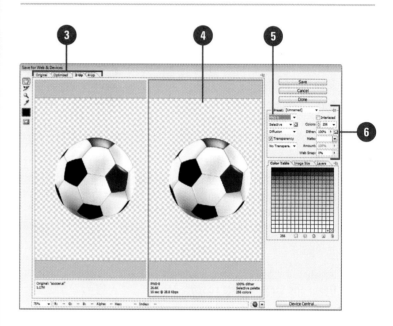

Dither Options:

◆ **Method.** Click the list arrow, and then select from the available dithering schemes. Dithering is how the PNG-8 format mixes the available image's colors.

◆ **Amount.** Enter or select a value from 0% to 100% to instruct the PNG-8 compression utility how many of the image's colors should be dithered.

Transparency Options:

◆ **Transparency.** Check to keep the transparent areas of a PNG-8 image transparent.

◆ **Matte.** Click to fill the transparent areas of a PNG-8 image.

◆ **Dither.** Click to select a dithering scheme and enter an amount for the mixing of the matte color.

Other Options:

◆ **Interlaced.** Check to have the PNG image load in three scans.

7 Click **Save** to save the current image using the Save Optimized As dialog box.

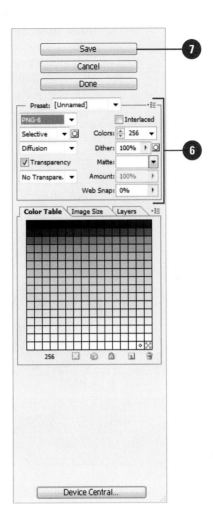

Optimizing a PNG-24 Document

 IL 8.1

The PNG-24 file format is used primarily for images that contain lots of colors with soft transitional edges, such as photographs, and was designed as an alternative to the JPEG file format. The PNG-24 format generates an image with millions of colors, and still manages to reduce the size of a file. While similar to the JPEG file format, the PNG-24 uses lossless compression, and does not compress files as small as the JPEG format. So for the time being, most designers are still using the JPEG format for creating faster-loading web graphics.

Optimize a PNG-24 Document

1. Open a document.

2. Click the **File** menu, and then click **Save For Web & Devices**.

3. Click the **Original**, **Optimized**, **2-Up**, or **4-Up** tabs to view the document using different layouts.

4. Click one of the sample images to change its default format.

5. Click the **Optimized File Format** list arrow, and then click **PNG-24**.

6. Select from the following options:

   Transparency Options:

   ◆ **Transparency.** Check to keep the transparent areas of a PNG-24 image transparent.

   ◆ **Matte.** Click to fill the transparent areas of a PNG-24 image.

   Other Options:

   ◆ **Interlaced.** Check to have the PNG-24 image load in three scans.

7. Click **Save** to save the current image using the Save Optimized As dialog box.

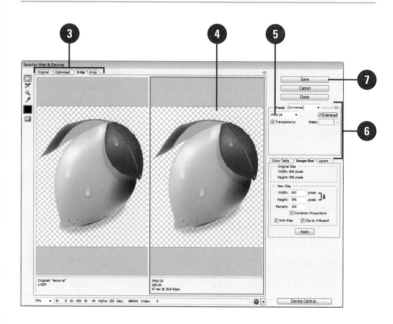

376

Optimizing a WBMP Document

IL 8.1

The WBMP file format is used for images that are displayed on small hand-held devices such as PDAs and cell phones. The WBMP format generates an image with only 2 pixel colors (black and white), which significantly reduces the file size of the image. The WBMP format is new to the world of wireless devices, and while it creates small images, using only black and white pixels results in very low-quality images.

Optimize a WBMP Document

1. Open a document.

2. Click the **File** menu, and then click **Save For Web & Devices**.

3. Click the **Original**, **Optimized**, **2-Up**, or **4-Up** tabs to view the document using different layouts.

4. Click one of the sample images to change its default format.

5. Click the **Optimized File Format** list arrow, and then click **WBMP**.

6. Select from the following options:

   ◆ **Method.** Click the list arrow, and then select from the available dithering schemes. Dithering is how the WBMP format mixes the available colors in the image.

   ◆ **Amount.** Enter or select a value from 0% to 100% to instruct the WBMP compression utility how many of the image's colors should be dithered.

7. Click **Save** to save the current image using the Save Optimized As dialog box.

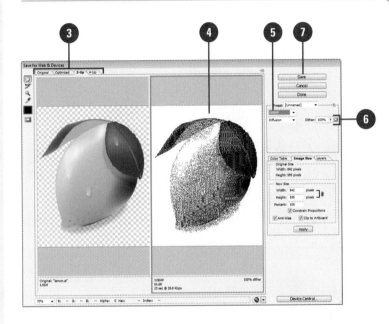

Slicing Images the Easy Way

Illustrator allows you to slice a document into smaller pieces. You might want to slice an image to create interactive links; however, the best reason is speed. You gain speed by compressing individual slices to reduce the image size. You can draw directly on an image to create a user-defined slice using the Slice tool. When you create a slice, Illustrator also creates **auto slices**, which fill the space in the image that is not defined by user defined slices. There are two types of automatic slices: auto slices and subslices. Subslices show overlapping user-defined slices. User-defined slices are identified by a solid blue line, while auto slices are identified by dotted red lines. The slices also are numbered from left to right and top to bottom. If you want to make changes to the slice, you need to select it first. When you edit or move the layer contents, the slice automatically changes.

Create a User Slice with the Slice Tool

1. Open a document.

2. Select the **Slice** tool on the Tools panel.

   IMPORTANT *To make slicing a little easier, drag a few guides from the Ruler bar to help guide your slicing tool.*

3. Drag and release the slice tool in the document to create a rectangular or square slice.

   ◆ To constrain the slice to a square, hold down Shift as you drag.

4. Continue to drag and release until you have the image correctly sliced.

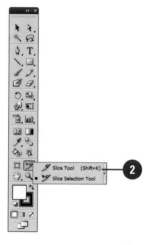

User slice

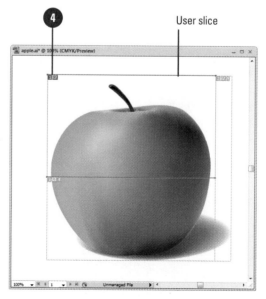

Create a User Slice from a Selected Object

1. Open a document.

2. Select the object that you want to use to create a slice.

3. Click the **Object** menu, point to Slice and then click **Make** or **Create from Selection**.

Working with Slices

IL 8.1

After you create slices within an image, you can use the Options bar or the Save For Web & Devices dialog box to work with slices. You can select options to show or hide slices, select one or more slices, delete or duplicate slices, and view or change slice settings. If you have an image with more than one slice, you need to optimize the slices in the Save For Web & Devices dialog box. You can use the Optimize menu to link multiple slices together. For linked slices in the GIF and PNG-8 format, Illustrator uses the same color palette and a dithering pattern to hide the seams between slices.

Work with Slices in the Illustrator Window

1. Open a document with slices.

2. Use any of the following:

   ◆ **Show or Hide Slices.** Click the **View** menu, and then click **Show Slices** or **Hide Slices**.

   ◆ **Select Slices.** Click the **Slice Selection** tool, and then click the slice you want. Use Shift+click or drag to select multiple slices.

   ◆ **Delete Slices.** Select the slices, and then press Delete.

   ◆ **Duplicate Slices.** Select the slices, and then Alt (Win) or Option (Mac) and drag the selection.

   ◆ **View Slice Options.** Click the **Slice Selection** tool, select the slice you want, click the **Object** menu, point to **Slice**, and then click **Slice Options**.

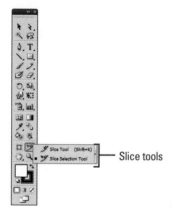

Slice tools

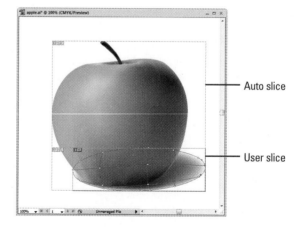

Auto slice

User slice

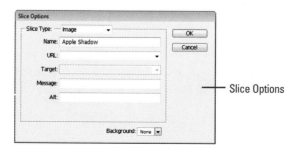

Slice Options

Work with Slices in the Save For Web & Devices Dialog Box

1. Open a document with slices.

2. Click the **File** menu, and then click **Save For Web & Devices**.

3. Select the file type you want, select any options, and then make any adjustments you want.

   ◆ **Show or Hide Slices.** Click the **Toggle Slices Visibility** button.

   ◆ **Show or Hide Auto Slices.** Click the **Preview** menu, and then click **Hide Auto Slices**.

   ◆ **Select Slices.** Click the **Slice Select** tool, and then click the slice you want. Use Shift+click or drag to select multiple slices.

   ◆ **View Slice Options.** Click the **Slice Select** tool, and then double-click the slice you want.

   ◆ **Link Slices.** Select the slices you want to link, click the Optimize menu double-arrow (Win) or arrow (Mac) button, and then click Link Slices.

   A link icon appears on the slices.

   ◆ **Unlink Slices.** Select the slice, click the **Optimize** menu double-arrow (Win) or arrow (Mac) button, and then click **Unlink Slice** or **Unlink All Slices**.

4. When you're done, click **Save** to save the image or click **Done** to save your settings.

   TIMESAVER *Hold down Ctrl (Win) or Command (Mac) to switch between the Slice tool and the Slice Select tool.*

Toggle Slices Visibility button

Preview menu

4

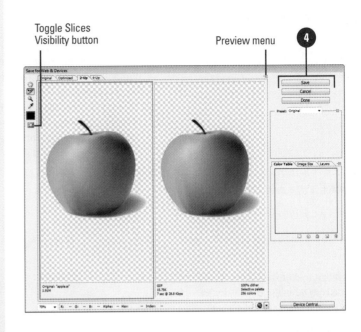

Slice Select button   Auto slice hidden

Optimize menu

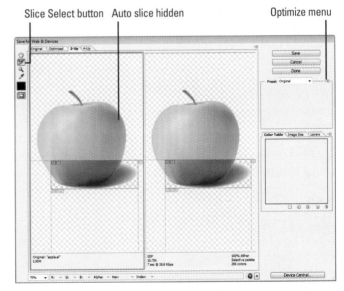

Arranging Slices

IL 8.1

Moving and resizing objects in Illustrator is a common task. You can move or resize slices in the same basic way you do other objects. In addition to moving slices, you can also align them along an edge or to the middle, and evenly distribute them horizontally or vertically. When you align and distribute slices, you can reduce the amount of unnecessary auto slices, thereby creating smaller files and faster load times. When you have slices overlapping each other, you can change the stacking order to move them up or down in the order. For example, if you have one slice behind another, you can bring the slice forward one level at a time or to the top (front).

Move or Resize Slices

① Open a document with slices.

② Select the slices you want to move or resize.

③ To move a slice selection, drag the slice to a new location. You can press Shift to constrain movement up, down, or diagonally.

④ To resize a slice, drag the side or corner handle of the slice. When you select adjacent slices with common edges, the slices resize together.

◆ You can also set exact slice position or size on the Control panel.

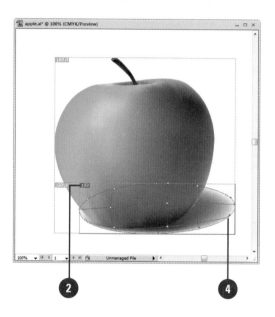

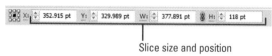

Slice size and position

Did You Know?

You can copy and paste a slice. You can copy and paste a slice like any other object using the Copy and Paste commands. If you copy a slice to Dreamweaver, it retains information from the original file in Illustrator.

You can snap slices to a guide, user slice, or other object. Click the View menu, and then click Snap to Grid or Snap to Point. When you move a slice toward an element, the slice snaps to the elements within 4 pixels.

Align, Distribute, or Stack Slices

1. Open a document with slices.

2. Select the slices you want to arrange.

3. To align slices, select the alignment button on the Control panel you want: **Horizontal Align** Left, Center, or Right, and **Vertical Align** Top, Center, or Bottom.

4. To evenly distribute slices, select the distribute button on the Control panel you want: **Vertical Distribute** Top, Center, or Bottom, and **Horizontal Distribute** Left, Center, or Right.

5. To change the slice stacking order, click the **Object** menu, point to **Arrange**, and then select the command you want: **Bring To Front**, **Bring Forward**, **Send Backward**, or **Send To Back**.

Did You Know?

You can combine user and auto slices. Click the Object menu, point to Slice, and then click Combine Slices.

You can divide user and auto slices. Select the slice using the Slice Select tool, click the Object menu, choose Slice, and then click Divide Slices. In the Divide Slice dialog box, select options to divide the slice horizontally or vertically, down or across in equal parts, or enter an exact size in pixels, and then click OK.

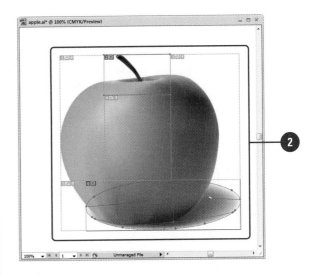

Saving a Sliced Image for the Web

 IL 8.1

After you create slices within an image, you can export and optimize each slice using the Save For Web & Devices command, which saves each slice as a separate file and creates the code to display them on a web page. After you click Save in the Save For Web & Devices dialog box, the Save Optimized As dialog box appears. You can use this dialog box to access the Output Settings dialog box and set output options to control the format of HTML files, the names of files and slices, and the way Illustrator saves background images.

Save a Slice for the Web

1. Open a document with the slice you want to save.

2. Click the **File** menu, and then click **Save For Web & Devices**.

3. Select the file type you want, select any options, and then make any adjustments you want.

4. Click **Save**.

5. Click the **Save as Type** (Win) or **Format** (Mac) list arrow, and then select whether to save the images in **HTML and Images**, **Images Only**, or **HTML Only**.

6. Click the **Settings** list arrow, and then select the output settings you want. Default Settings is recommended for normal use.

   See the next page for details about selecting output settings.

7. Click the **Slices** list arrow, and click **All Slices**, **All User Slices**, or **Selected Slices**.

8. Click **Save**.

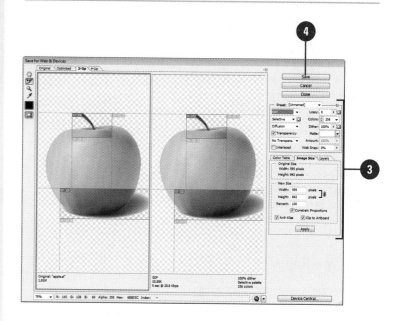

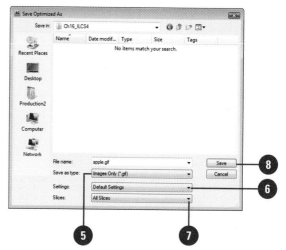

Set Output Options for Slices

1. Open a document with the slice you want to save.

2. Click the **File** menu, and then click **Save For Web & Devices**.

3. Click **Save**.

4. Click the **Save as Type** (Win) or **Format** list arrow, and then select the format you want.

5. Click the **Settings** list arrow, and then click **Other**.

6. Click the **Output Type** list arrow, and then click **Slices**.

7. Select the following options:

   ◆ **Generate Table.** Uses an HTML table to display slices.

   ◆ **Empty Cells.** Specifies the way to convert empty slices to table cells.

   ◆ **TD W&H.** Specifies whether to include width and height for table data.

   ◆ **Spacer Cells.** Specifies when to add empty spacer cells.

   ◆ **Generate CSS.** Creates a Cascading Style Sheet (CSS) to display the slices.

   ◆ **Referenced.** Specifies how to reference slice positions using CSS.

   ◆ **Default Slice Naming.** From the list menus, select the options to specify a slice naming scheme.

8. Click **OK**.

9. Click the **Slices** list arrow, and then select the slices option you want.

10. Click **Save**.

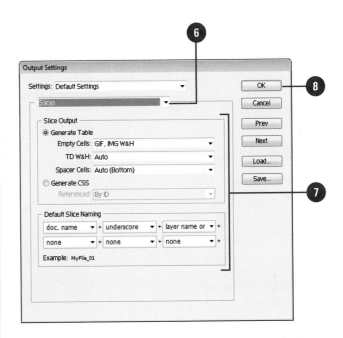

Adding HTML Text or an URL Link to a Slice

 IL 8.1

If you want to include text within a slice for use on the Web, you can enter plain or formatted text with standard HTML tags directly on a slice with the type **No Image**. The text doesn't show up in Illustrator; you need to use a web browser to see it. Don't enter too much text as it might affect the exported layout. You can add text using the Slice Select tool on the tools panel, or in the Save For Web & Devices dialog box. If you want to create a hyperlink out of a slice for use on the Web, you can add an URL to a slice with the type **Image**.

Add HTML Text to a Slice

1 Open a document with the slice.

2 Open the Slice dialog box to add text using one of the following:

   ◆ **Tools Panel.** Select the **Slice Selection** tool on the Tools panel, select the slice you want to add HTML text, click the **Object** menu, point to **Slice**, and then click **Slice Options**.

   ◆ **Save For Web & Devices dialog box.** Click the **File** menu, click **Save For Web & Devices**, and then double-click the slice to which you want to add HTML text.

3 Click the **Slice Type** list arrow, and then click **No Image**.

4 Enter the text you want.

5 Click the **Background** list arrow, and then select a background: **None**, **Matte**, **Eyedropper Color**, **White**, **Black**, or **Other**.

6 Select the **Text is HTML** check box to include HTML formatted tags.

7 Select the horizontal and vertical cell alignment options you want.

   ◆ To line up text in cells in the same row, set a common baseline for all cells in the row.

8 Click **OK**.

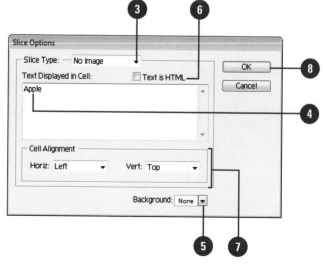

Add an URL Link to a Slice

1 Open a document.

2 Select the **Slice Selection** tool on the Tools panel.

3 Double-click the slice to which you want to add an URL link.

4 Click the **Slice Type** list arrow, and then click **Image**.

5 Enter an URL address or select a previously created one from the list. Be sure to use the complete URL address, such as *http://www.perspection.com*.

6 If you want to enter a target frame:

♦ **_blank**. Displays the linked file in a new window.

♦ **_self**. Displays the linked file in the same frame as the original file.

♦ **_parent**. Displays the linked file in its own original parent frameset.

♦ **_top**. Replaces the entire browser window with the linked file, removing all current frames.

7 Click **OK**.

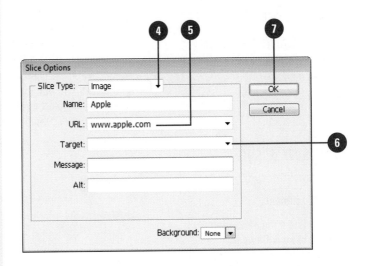

Optimizing SWF or SVG for the Web

 IL 8.1, 8.2

If you're creating elements for use on the web, the SWF and SVG file formats can do the job. The SWF (Shockwave Flash) file format is used for creating movies and animations using vector graphics and displayed with the Flash Player, typically on the web. The SVG (Scalable Vector Graphics) file format is used for creating high-quality graphics on the web, in print, and on resource-limited handheld devices. SVG is made up of an XML markup language for describing two-dimensional vector graphics, which also supports animation.

Optimize a SWF or SVG Document

1. Open a document.

2. Click the **File** menu, and then click **Save For Web & Devices**.

3. Click the **Original**, **Optimized**, **2-Up**, or **4-Up** tabs to view the document using different layouts.

4. Click one of the sample images to change its default format.

5. Click the **Optimized File Format** list arrow, and then click **SWF** or **SVG**.

6. Select options for the following formats:

   ◆ **SWF.** Specify options for the Flash Player version, type of export, curve quality, frame rate, compression, protect file, text as outline, loop and preserve (appearance or editability).

   ◆ **SVG.** Specify options for the DTD version, glyphs, embed or link images, CSS properties, compression, decimals, font type, encoding, and Adobe SVG Viewer optimization.

7. Click **Save** to save the current image using the Save Optimized As dialog box.

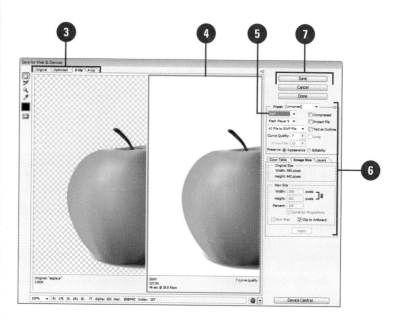

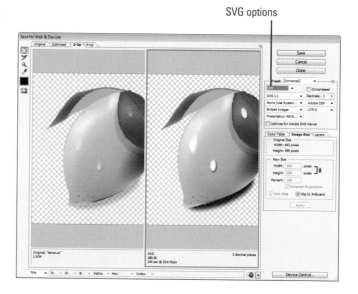

SVG options

Customizing the Way You Work

17

Introduction

No description of Adobe Illustrator would be complete without that well-known, but little utilized area called Preferences. Illustrator preferences serve several purposes. They help customize the program to your particular designing style, and they help you utilize available computer resources to increase the overall performance of the program.

As you use Illustrator, you'll come to realize the importance of working with units and rulers. Precision is the name of the game when you are working with images. What about the color of your guides, grids, and slices? No big deal, you say. Well, if you've ever tried viewing a blue guide against predominantly blue artwork, you know exactly why guide color is important. By working through preferences, such as Display Performance and Scratch Disks, speed increases of up to 20% can be achieved.

In addition, customizing the program helps make you more comfortable, and studies show that the more comfortable you are as a designer, the better your designs. Plus, being comfortable allows you to work faster, and that means you'll accomplish more in the same amount of time. What does setting up preferences do for you? They make Illustrator run faster, you work more efficiently, and your designs are better. That's a pretty good combination. Illustrator doesn't give you Preferences to confuse you, but to give you choices, and those choices give you control.

What You'll Do

Set General Preferences

Change Selection & Anchor Preferences

Set Type Preferences

Change Units & Display Performance Preferences

Set Slices and Hyphenation Preferences

Select Plug-Ins

Select Scratch Disks

Set User Interface Preferences

Set File Handling & Clipboard Preferences

Work with Appearance of Black Preferences

Define Shortcut Keys

Use Drawing Tablets

Setting General Preferences

IL 1.4

Illustrator's General preferences help you configure some of the more common features of the program. Some of the options include keyboard increment choices to move selected objects with arrow keys, anti-aliased artwork to smooth out edges, showing tooltips to display onscreen help tags, and scaling stroke & effects to scale an object's stroke weight and appearance when you it. You can also click the Reset All Warning Dialogs to allow warnings for which you previously selected the Don't Show Again check box.

Set General Preferences

1 Click the **Edit** (Win) or **Illustrator** (Mac) menu, and then point to **Preferences**.

2 Click **General**.

3 Select the various options you want to use:

◆ **Keyboard Increment.** Enter a distance value (0-1296 points) that a selected object moves when an arrow key is pressed.

◆ **Constrain Angle.** Enter the angle (-360 to 360) for the x and y axes. Many tool operations and other measurements are calculated relative to this angle.

◆ **Corner Radius.** Enter a value (0-1296 points) to specify the curvature in the corners of objects drawn with the Rounded Rectangle tool.

◆ **Disable Auto Add/Delete.** Select to disable the behavior of the Pen tool to change to the Add Anchor Point or Delete Anchor Point tool when you point to an anchor.

◆ **Use Precise Cursors.** Select to use crosshairs instead of the tool icon for drawing and editing tools.

◆ **Anti-aliased Artwork.** Select to display smoother edges of vector objects.

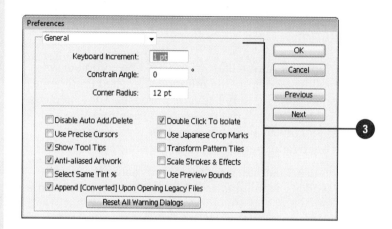

- ◆ **Show Tool Tips.** Select to display a popup tag with a name or short description when you point to a program item, such as a button or tool.

- ◆ **Select Same Tint %.** Select to select only objects with the same spot color and tint percentage as the currently selected object when you use the Fill Color and Stroke Color commands.

- ◆ **Append [Converted] Upon Opening Legacy Files.** Select to append "[Converted]" to Illustrator 11 or earlier files when you open them.

- ◆ **Double Click To Isolate.** Select to place a double-clicked group in Isolation Mode.

- ◆ **Use Japanese Crop Marks.** Select to use Japanese-style crop marks when you print separations.

- ◆ **Transform Pattern Tiles.** Select to transform a pattern when you use a transformation tool on an object that contains a pattern.

- ◆ **Scale Strokes & Effects.** Select to scale an object's stroke weight and appearance when you scale an object by using its bounding box, the Scale tool or the Free Transform tool.

- ◆ **Use Preview Bounds.** Select to include an object's stroke weight and any effects when calculating its dimensions.

- ◆ **Reset All Warning Dialogs.** Click to allow warnings for which you previously selected the Don't Show Again check box.

④ Click **OK**.

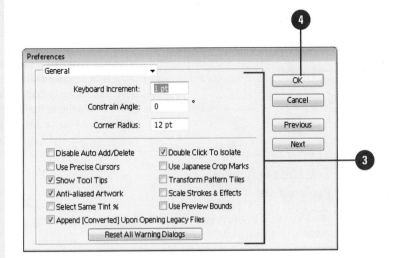

Changing Selection & Anchor Display Preferences

 IL 1.4

Illustrator's Selection & Anchor Displays preferences allow you to set selection and anchor relation options. The Selection options include Tolerance, which specifies a value within which an anchor point becomes selected when you click near it; Object Selection by Path Only, which selects an object when you click a path segment or anchor point; and Snap to Point, which snaps objects to an anchor point or guide within the specified value. The Anchor Display main options include Anchors and Handles, which allow you to select the display of anchor points and handle end points.

Change Selection & Anchor Display Preferences

1. Click the **Edit** (Win) or **Illustrator** (Mac) menu, and then point to **Preferences**.

2. Click **Selection & Anchor Display**.

3. Select the Selection Options you want to use:

   ◆ **Tolerance.** Enter a value (in pixels) within which an anchor point becomes selected when you click near it with the Direct Selection tool.

   ◆ **Object Selection by Path Only.** Choose to select an object with the Selection or Direct Selection tool when you click a path segment or anchor point.

      Deselect to select a filled object in Preview view with a selection tool when you click the filled area.

   ◆ **Snap to Point.** Select to snap objects to an anchor point or guide within the specified value (in pixels).

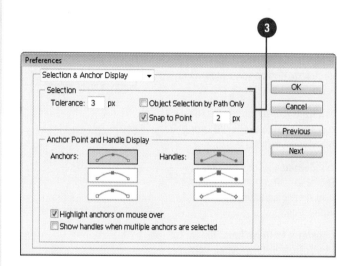

④ Select the Anchor Point and Handle Display options you want to use:

◆ **Anchors.** Specify the display of anchor points.

◆ **Handles.** Specify the display of handle end points (direction points)

◆ **Highlight anchors on mouse over.** Select to highlight the anchor point located directly below the mouse pointer.

◆ **Show handles when multiple anchors are selected.** Select to display direction lines on all selected anchor points when you use the Direct Selection or Group Selection tool to select an object.

   Deselect to display direction lines for an anchor point when it is the only anchor point on the path or when the Bezier segment for the direction line is selected and the anchor point is not selected.

⑤ Click **OK**.

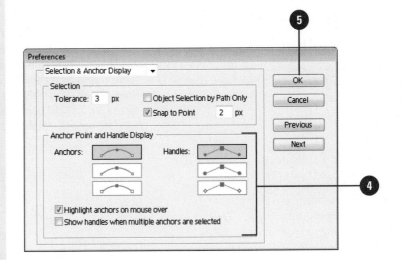

Setting Type Preferences

 IL 1.4

Although Illustrator is not by definition a typesetting application, such as Adobe InDesign, it does have some very powerful type features. For example, Adobe Illustrator allows you to set options to customize the way you select text. In addition, Illustrator's type menu lets you see fonts exactly as they will print or display. For designers who use a lot of fonts, this WYSIWYG (What You See Is What You Get) font menu is a timesaver. You can use Type preferences to help you select the type and font options you want to use.

Set Type Preferences

1 Click the **Edit** (Win) or **Illustrator** (Mac) menu, and then point to **Preferences**.

2 Click **Type**.

3 Specify values for Size/Leading, Tracking, and Baseline Shift to increment selected text each time you press a keyboard shortcut for the command.

4 Select from the following Type options you want to use:

◆ **Type Object Selection by Path Only.** Choose to select text when you click on a type path.

Deselect to select text when you click with a selection tool on or near the type.

◆ **Show Asian Options.** Select to display Japanese, Chinese, and Korean type options in the Character and Paragraph panels.

◆ **Show Font Names In English.** Select to display non-roman fonts using their roman names.

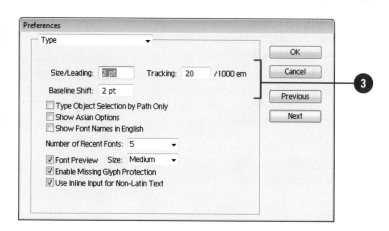

- ◆ **Font Preview Size.** Select to display fonts on the menu in small, medium, or large size.

- ◆ **Enable Missing Glyph Protection.** Select to automatically select incorrect, unreadable characters between roman and non-roman (Japanese or Cyrillic) fonts.

- ◆ **Use Inline Input for Non-Latin Text.** Select to type non-Roman characters directly into Illustrator instead of using a separate dialog box.

5 Click **OK**.

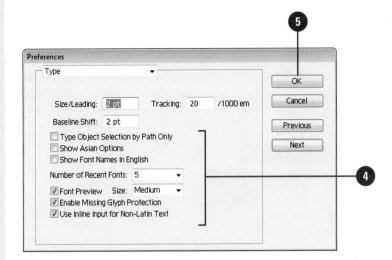

Changing Units & Display Performance Preferences

 IL 1.4

While changing the measurable units and rulers do not affect output quality, they do help to measure information in a document consistent with the specific output device. In Units & Performance preferences, you can set units of measure for general, stroke, and type related features. The General option (Units) sets a unit of measure for rulers, dialog boxes, and Transform, Control, and Info panels. To maximize preformance in Illustrator, you can drag the Hand Tool slider to specify a balanced performance setting between Full Quality and Faster Updates.

Change Units & Display Performance Preferences

1 Click the **Edit** (Win) or **Illustrator** (Mac) menu, and then point to **Preferences**.

2 Click **Units & Display Performance**.

3 Select from the following Units options you want to use:

   ◆ **General.** Select a unit of measure for rulers, dialog boxes, and Transform, Control, and Info panels.

   ◆ **Stroke.** Select a unit of measure for the Strokes panel and Stroke Weight field on the Control panel.

   ◆ **Type.** Select a unit of measure for the Character and Paragraph panels.

   ◆ **Asian Type.** Select a unit of measure for Asian type.

   ◆ **Numbers Without Unit Are Points.** Select to not convert points to picas when Picas is set as the General unit.

   ◆ **Identify Objects By.** For dynamic objects, select an option to assign variables to the Object Name or an XML ID.

4 Drag the Hand Tool slider to specify a performance setting.

5 Click **OK**.

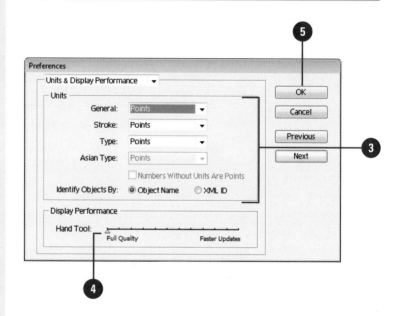

Setting Slices and Hyphenation Preferences

Set Slices and Hyphenation Preferences

1. Click the **Edit** (Win) or **Illustrator** (Mac) menu, and then point to **Preferences**.

2. Click **Slices**.

3. Select from the following Slice options you want to use:

   ◆ **Show Slice Numbers.** Select to show slice numbers.

   ◆ **Line Color.** Click the list arrow, and then select a line color for slices.

4. Click the list arrow, and then click **Hyphenation**.

5. Select from the following Hyphenation options you want to use:

   ◆ **Default Language.** Select a default language for use with Hyphenation.

   ◆ **Exceptions.** Enter words in the New Entry box that you want hyphenated a certain way (include the hyphen), and then click Add. To delete an entry, select it from the list, and then click Delete.

6. Click **OK**.

Illustrator allows you to slice a document into smaller pieces. You might want to slice an image to create interactive links; however, the best reason is speed. You gain speed by compressing individual slices to reduce the image size. In Slices preferences, you can set options to show a slice number on the screen for easier management and select a line color for slices. In Hyphenation preferences, you can set options to specify a default language, and enter words in the New Entry box that you want hyphenated a certain way.

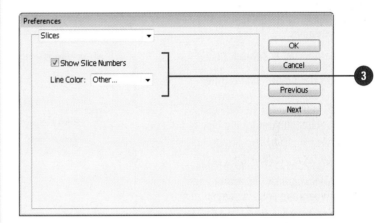

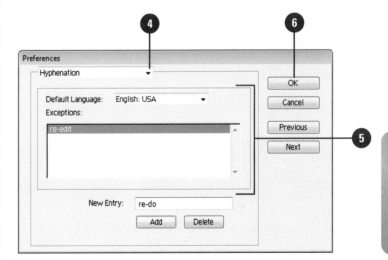

Selecting Plug-Ins

 IL 1.4

The Plug-ins preferences give you the ability to organize your plug-ins by saving them in one or more folders. These additional folders are typically used to hold third-party plug-ins. When selected, plug-ins contained within the folder will be available in Illustrator. Organizing your plug-ins into folders helps keep your projects focused and reduces the clutter of plug-ins when you want to select them.

Select Plug-Ins Preferences

① Click the **Edit** (Win) or **Illustrator** (Mac) menu, and then point to **Preferences**.

② Click **Plug-Ins & Scratch Disks**.

③ Select the **Additional Plug-Ins Folder** check box if you have additional plug-ins stored outside the default Illustrator plug-ins folder.

   IMPORTANT *The first time you select this option, Illustrator asks you where the plug-ins are stored.*

④ If you change the location of your additional plug-ins folder, you can always click Choose and navigate to it.

⑤ Click **OK**.

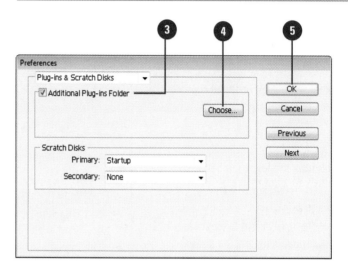

Selecting Scratch Disks

 IL 1.4

The Scratch Disk preferences are available to help you get the best performance out of your computer by letting you choose one or more hard drives for scratch operations. When your computer doesn't have enough RAM to perform an operation, Illustrator uses free space on any available drive, known as a Scratch Disk. Illustrator runs faster when you divide the Scratch Disk workload. Scratch operations are performed on your hard drive and take place when Illustrator is using one of its many filters and adjustments. Illustrator detects and displays all available disks in Plug-ins & Scratch Disks preferences, where you can select the disks you want to use. By assigning additional hard drives to the task, you speed up Illustrator's overall performance. Scratch Disk changes take effect the next time you start Illustrator.

Select Scratch Disks Options

1 Click the **Edit** (Win) or **Illustrator** (Mac) menu, and then point to **Preferences**.

2 Click **Plug-ins & Scratch Disk**.

3 Click the **Primary** list arrow, and then select a location for use as a virtual memory location for processing.

4 Click the **Secondary** list arrow, and then select a location for use as a secondary virtual memory location for processing when needed.

   IMPORTANT *Illustrator holds scratch disk space as long as the application is open. To delete scratch disk space you must close Illustrator.*

5 Click **OK**.

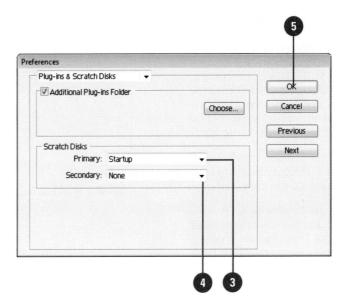

Setting User Interface Preferences

 IL 1.4

User Interface preferences give you control over some user interface features. If you prefer to use individual windows for your documents, you can turn off the Open Documents As Tabs option; otherwise it's on by default. You can use the Brightness control to specify different shades of gray for display panels. In addition, you can also set options to automatically collapse icon panels when you click away from them, and allow you to open documents as tabs instead of individual document windows.

Set User Interface Preferences

1. Click the **Edit** (Win) or **Illustrator** (Mac) menu, and then point to **Preferences**.

2. Click **User Interface**.

3. Select from the following Interface options:

   ◆ **Brightness.** Drag the slider to specify a gray value from Dark to Light for the background of all panels.

   ◆ **Auto-Collapse Icon Panels.** Automatically collapses icon panels when you click away.

   ◆ **Open Documents As Tabs.** Select to open documents as tabs instead of individual document windows.

4. Click **OK**.

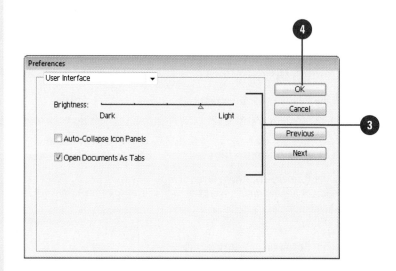

Setting File Handling & Clipboard Preferences

IL 1.4, 9.3

In File Handling & Clipboard preferences, you can set file linking and copying to the Clipboard options. You can set file linking options to display linked images as low-resolution to increase performance and specify how to update the links. In addition, you can set options to specify what format you want to use to copy content to the Clipboard. The available options include PDF and AICB (a PostScript format). For the AICB option, you can also select an option to copy the selection as a set of detailed paths or preserve the selection's appearance and any overprinting.

Work with File Handling & Clipboard Preferences

1 Click the **Edit** (Win) or **Illustrator** (Mac) menu, and then point to **Preferences**.

2 Click **File Handling & Clipboard**.

3 Select from the following Files options:

  ◆ **Use Low Resolution Proxy for Linked EPS.** Select to display linked images as low-resolution to increase performance.

  ◆ **Update Links.** Specify how to update linked images: Automatically (no dialog box), Manually (update in the Links panel), or Ask When Modified (use dialog box).

4 Select from the following Clipboard on Quit options:

  ◆ **Copy As PDF.** Select to copy a selection to the Clipboard in the PDF file format, which preserves transparency.

  ◆ **Copy As AICB.** Select to copy a selection to the Clipboard in the AICB file format (a PostScript format). Select an option to copy the selection as a set of detailed paths or to preserve the selection's appearance and any overprinting.

5 Click **OK**.

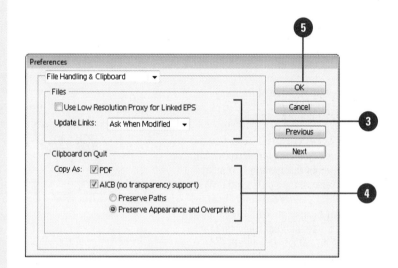

Working with Appearance of Black Preferences

 IL 1.4

Work with Appearance of Black Preferences

1. Click the **Edit** (Win) or **Illustrator** (Mac) menu, and then point to **Preferences**.

2. Click **Appearance of Black**.

3. Select from the following Appearance of Black options:

   ◆ On Screen. Select **Display All Blacks Accurately** to display blacks based on actual CMYK color values or select **Display All Blacks as Rich Black** to display all blacks as rich blacks (a mix of CMYK values).

   ◆ Printing / Exporting. Select **Output All Blacks Accurately** to print blacks using actual CMYK color values on RGB and grayscale devices, or select **Output All Blacks as Rich Black** to print blacks as rich blacks (a mix of CMYK values) on RGB devices.

4. Click **OK**.

If a printer uses a combination of CMYK inks instead of the actual 100K black tone to create a rich black look, you can set options in the Appearance of Black preferences to specify how you want to create the appearance of black in your documents. There are two available options to determine the appearance of black in your document: one for On Screen and another one for Printing/Exporting. Each of the options allows you to specify how you want to work with the appearance of black (true black or rich black) in your documents.

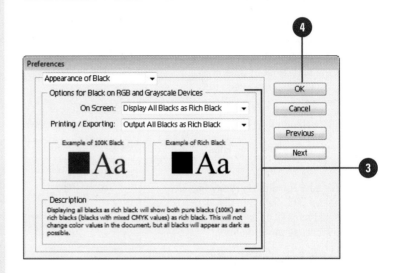

Defining Shortcut Keys

 IL 1.9

A wise man once wrote "time is money," and Illustrator is a program that can consume a lot of time. That's why the Illustrator application uses keyboard shortcuts. **Keyboard Shortcuts**, as their name implies, let you perform tasks in a shorter period of time. For example, if you want to open a new document in Illustrator, you can click the File menu, and then click New, or you can abandon the mouse and press Ctrl+N (Win) or ⌘+N (Mac) to use shortcut keys. Using shortcut keys reduces the use of the mouse and speeds up operations. In fact, a recent study in the American Medical Journal suggested that the use of shortcut keys significantly cuts down on repetitive stress, and reduces instances of carpal tunnel syndrome. Illustrator raises the bar by not only giving you hundreds of possible shortcut keys, but also actually allowing you to define your own shortcuts.

Create a Keyboard Shortcut

1. Click the **Edit** menu, and then click **Keyboard Shortcuts**.

2. Click an arrow (left column) to expand the menu that contains the command for which you want to create a shortcut.

3. Select an item from the Commands list.

4. Use the keyboard to create the new shortcut. For example, press Ctrl+N (Win) or ⌘+N (Mac).

5. Click **OK**.

6. Click **OK**.

For Your Information

Working with Shortcuts

In addition to adding shortcuts, you can delete any of them you don't want and even print out a summary of shortcuts defined in Illustrator. Shortcuts can be used for the Application and Panel menus, as well as for your tools in the Tools panel. Click the Edit menu, click Keyboard Shortcuts, and then use the appropriate buttons, such as Save (Shortcut Set), Delete (Shortcut Set), Clear (remove shortcut), or (Shortcut Set), Clear (remove shortcut), to perform the tasks you want.

Using Drawing Tablets

When you design on a computer, you're leaving the natural world of oil, watercolor, and canvas, for the electronic world of computer monitors and pixels (don't worry, it's a relatively painless transition). Without a doubt, there are many differences between traditional and digital design; however, it's not necessary to abandon all aspects of the natural media world. For example, the computer mouse has always been a problem with designers who miss the feel and control of a brush in their hands. Fortunately, technology came to the rescue several years ago, with the invention of the drawing tablet. Drawing tablets combine a drawing surface and a brush-like drawing tool in the form of a pen. A designer picks up the pen and moves it across the drawing tablet surface. In turn, the drawing tablet interprets those movements as brush strokes. Not only does Illustrator

fully support drawing tablet technology, it also interprets the particular drawing style of the designer. For example, pushing harder with the brush against the drawing tablet instructs Illustrator to create a wider stroke, or to apply more color. Drawing tablets have helped to translate the control of working with real art brushes on canvas, into the world of the digital designer. Of all the manufacturers, Wacom stands out as the leader in drawing tablet technology. Wacom returns the feel of designing with a brush to the digital designer's world, and the software required to power the tablet works seamlessly with Illustrator and the Windows or Macintosh operating systems. To check out which tablet might be right for your needs, point your browser to *www.wacom.com* and check out the available options.

Wacom tablet

Drawing pen

Working Together with Adobe Programs

18

Introduction

Adobe programs are designed to work together so you can focus on what you need to do, rather than on how to do it. In fact, the Adobe programs share tools and features for your most common tasks so you can work uninterrupted and move seamlessly from one program to another. Adobe Creative Suite is an integrated collection of programs that work together to help you create designs in print, on the Web, or on mobile devices. When you install Adobe Creative Suite or a stand-alone Adobe program, you also get additional Adobe programs—Bridge, Version Cue, Drive, ConnectNow, Device Central, and Extension Manager—to help you perform specific jobs, such as locating, downloading, and modifying images for projects, managing files and program extensions and testing files for different mobile devices.

Adobe Bridge is a program that lets you view, open, modify, and manage images located on your computer from any Adobe Creative Suite program. Adobe Bridge is literally the glue that binds Adobe Creative Suite programs together into one cohesive unit with shared tools. Bridge allows you to search, sort, filter, manage, and process image files one at a time or in batches. You can also use Bridge to do the following: create new folders; rename, move, delete and group files; edit metadata; rotate images; create web galleries and contact sheets; and run batch commands. You can also import files from your digital camera and view file information and metadata.

What You'll Do

Explore Adobe Programs

Explore Adobe Bridge

Get Started with Adobe Bridge

Get Photos from a Digital Camera

Work with Raw Images from a Digital Camera

Work with Images Using Adobe Bridge

Set Preferences in Adobe Bridge

Apply Image Adjustments

Create a Web Photo Gallery

Automate Tasks in Adobe Bridge

Share My Screen

Manage Files Using Adobe Version Cue

Work with Adobe Drive

Explore Adobe Device Central

Check Content Using Adobe Device Central

Use Adobe Extension Manager

Exploring Adobe Programs

Adobe Creative Suite 4

Adobe Creative Suite 4 is an integrated collection of programs that work together to help you create designs in print, on the Web, or on mobile devices. Adobe's Creative Suite 4 comes in different editions with different combinations of Adobe programs. The main programs for print design include InDesign and Acrobat Professional; for graphic design the programs include Photoshop, Illustrator, and Fireworks; for video and sound design the programs include Premiere, After Effects Professional, Encore, and Soundbooth; and for web design the programs include Flash Professional, Dreamweaver, Fireworks, and Contribute.

Working Together with Adobe Programs

When you install Adobe Creative Suite 4 or a stand-alone Adobe program, you also get additional Adobe programs—Bridge, Version Cue, Drive, ConnectNow, Device Central, and Extension Manager—to help you perform specific jobs such as managing files and program extensions and testing files for mobile devices.

Adobe Bridge

Adobe Bridge CS4 is a file management/batching program that manages and processes images while you work in your other Adobe programs. To use Bridge, click Browse in Bridge on the File menu within an Adobe product, such as Flash, or from the desktop use the Start menu (Win) or go to the Applications folder (Mac).

Adobe Version Cue

Adobe Version Cue is a file tracking management program you can use to keep track of changes to a file as you work on it or if you work collaboratively on the same files with colleagues. You use Adobe Bridge as a central location from which to use Version Cue. You can track Adobe and non-Adobe program files.

Adobe Drive

Adobe Drive (**New!**) allows you to connect to and use Version Cue servers as if they were a local hard drive or mapped network drive. After you set up a connection, you can work with Version Cue files by using the Open, Import, Export, Place, Save, or Save As dialog boxes, and Explorer (Win) or Finder (Mac).

Adobe ConnectNow

The Share My Screen command (**New!**) on the File menu allows you to connect to Adobe ConnectNow, which is a secure Web site where you can start an online meeting. You can share and annotate your computer screen or take control of an attendee's computer. During the meeting, you can communicate by sending chat messages, using live audio, or broadcasting live video.

Adobe Device Central

Adobe Device Central CS4 allows you to test your content to see how it would look on a variety of mobile devices. You can interact with the emulated device in a way that allows you to test your content in real-world situations. Device Central provides a library of devices and each device includes a profile with information about the device, including media and content support types.

Adobe Extension Manager

Adobe Extension Manager CS4 allows you to install and delete added program functionality, known as extensions, to many Adobe programs.

Exploring Adobe Bridge

Inspector panel
Displays or hides
Version Cue panels.

Folders panel
Displays the folders
on your computer in
a tree structure.

Workspaces (New!)
Choose from common
workspaces.

Quick Search (New!)
Search for file names,
keywords, folder names.

Preview panel
Displays a preview of
the selected image.

**File path
(New!)**
To trace file
back to its
folder.

Favorites panel
Displays links
to common
features and
favorite places.

Filter panel
Displays files
based on filter
criteria.

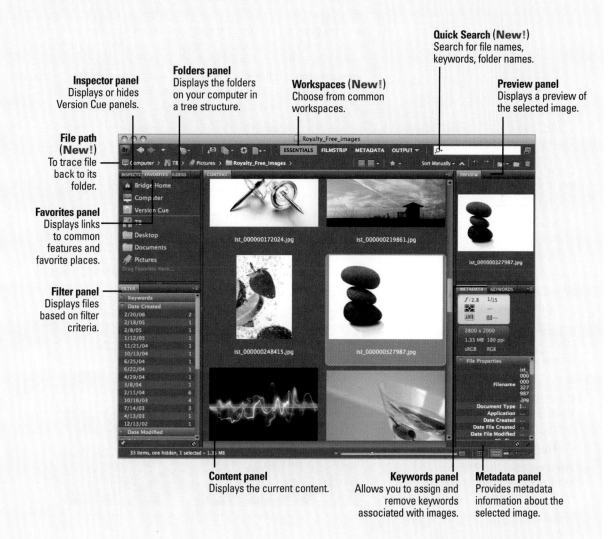

Content panel
Displays the current content.

Keywords panel
Allows you to assign and
remove keywords
associated with images.

Metadata panel
Provides metadata
information about the
selected image.

Getting Started with Adobe Bridge

Adobe Bridge CS4 is a stand-alone program that lets you view, open, and manage images located on your computer from any Adobe Creative Suite 4 program. Adobe Bridge is literally the glue that binds Adobe Creative Suite 4 programs and shared tools together into one cohesive unit. Adobe Bridge integrates with shared tools including Adobe Version Cue, a file tracking project management program. The Bridge program provides a set of panels that make it easy to find, view, and manage the files on your computer or network. As you work with Bridge, you'll open, close, and move (dock and undock) the panels to meet your individual needs. After you customize the workspace, you can save the location of the panels as a custom workspace, which you can display using the Workspace command on the Window menu. Bridge also provides some predefined workspaces.

Get Started with Adobe Bridge

1. Launch your Adobe product, click the **File** menu, and then click **Browse in Bridge**.

   ◆ You can also start Adobe Bridge CS4 from the Start menu (Win) or the Applications folder (Mac).

2. To open and close a panel, click the **Window** menu, and then click the panel name you want.

3. To move a panel, drag the panel tab you want to another location in the Bridge window.

4. To save a workspace, click the **Window** menu, point to **Workspace**, click **New Workspace**, type a name, and then click **OK**.

5. To display a workspace, click the **Window** menu, point to **Workspace**, and then click the workspace you want.

6. When you're done, click the **Close** button in the Bridge window.

The Launch Bridge button on the Application bar

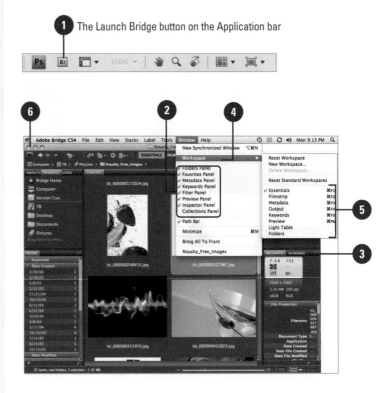

408

Getting Photos from a Digital Camera

If you have raw or other images from your digital camera, you can use the Get Photos from Camera command in Adobe Bridge to retrieve and copy them to your computer. This allows you to specify where you want to store the files, rename them if you want, preserve metadata, or convert them to the DNG format. When you convert raw files to the DNG format, you specify preview size, compression, and whether to preserve the raw image data or embed the original raw file.

Import Raw and Other Files from a Camera

1. In Adobe Bridge, click the **File** menu, and then click **Get Photos from Camera** or click the camera icon on the Application bar. (**New!**)

2. Click the **Get Photos From** popup, and then select the source camera or memory card.

3. Create a new subfolder to store the images (optional).

4. To rename the files, select a method, and then enter file name text.

5. Select the options you want:

   ◆ **Preserve Current Filename in XMP.** Select to save the current filename as image metadata.

   ◆ **Open Adobe Bridge.** Select to open and display the files in Adobe Bridge.

   ◆ **Convert To DNG.** Select to convert Camera Raw files to DNG. Click Settings to set DNG conversion options.

   ◆ **Delete Original Files. (New!)** Select to delete original files from camera or memory card.

   ◆ **Save Copies To.** Select to save copies to another folder for backup.

6. To apply metadata to the files, click **Advanced Dialog**.

7. Click **Get Photos**.

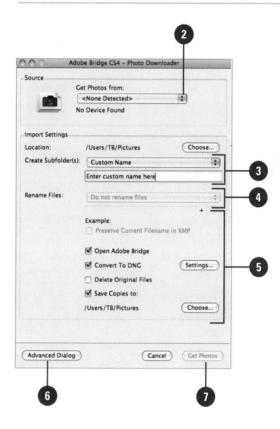

Working with Raw Images from a Digital Camera

Raw image file formats are created by most mid- to high-end digital cameras and contain information about how the image was taken. The raw format turns off all camera adjustments, and simply saves the image information. Using the raw format is as close to using traditional film as a digital camera can get. Raw images are larger; however, the increase in file size gives you more information that can be used by Camera Raw to adjust the image. From Adobe Bridge, you can use Camera Raw to open raw files, JPEG, and TIFF files to make image enhancements. If you're not sure what to do, you can click Auto to have Camera Raw do it or drag color sliders to adjust options manually. Raw images can be converted into 16-bit images. When you use a 16-bit image, you have more control over adjustments such as tonal and color corrections. Once processed, raw images can be saved in the DNG, TIFF, PSD, PSB, or JPEG formats. After you make Camera Raw adjustments, you can save the settings so you can use them later.

Set Camera Raw Preferences

1. In Adobe Bridge, click the **Edit** (Win) or **Adobe Bridge** (Mac) menu, and then click **Camera Raw Preferences**.

2. Select the preferences you want:

   ◆ **General.** Specify where Camera Raw file settings are stored. Use Sidecar XMP files to store settings separately, or Camera Raw Database to store settings in a searchable database.

   ◆ **Default Image Settings.** Select options to automatically apply settings or set defaults.

   ◆ **Camera Raw Cache.** Set a cache size to shorten loading time for thumbnails and previews.

   ◆ **DNG File Handling.** Select options to ignore XMP files or update embedded content.

   ◆ **JPEG and TIFF Handling.** (**New!**) Automatically open JPEGs and/or TIFFs in Camera Raw.

3. Click **OK**.

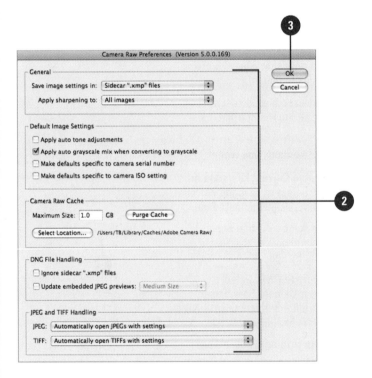

Modify a File in Camera Raw

1. Right-click the image, and then click **Open in Camera Raw**.

2. Use the **Zoom**, **Hand**, **Rotate**, **Crop**, and **Straighten** tools to change the size, orientation, and position of the image, or use the **White Balance** tool to set the white balance or the **Color Sampler** tool to sample a color, or use the **Retouch** and **Red Eye Removal** tools to correct the image. Use the **Adjustment Brush** and **Graduated Filter** for local adjustments.(**New!**)

3. Select from the available image view options:

   - **Image Preview.** Displays the active image.

   - **Zoom Level.** Changes the view of the active image.

   - **Histogram.** Displays information on the colors and brightness levels in the active image.

4. Click the **Basic**, **Tone Curve**, **Detail**, **Lens**, **HSL/ Grayscale**, **Split Toning**, **Lens Corrections**, or **Camera Calibration** tabs, and then click **Auto** (Basic tab) or drag sliders to modify the color and tonal values of the image.

5. Click **Save Image** to specify a folder destination, file name, and format for the processed images.

6. Select the images you want to synchronize (apply settings) in the Filmstrip (if desired, click Select All), and then click **Synchronize**.

7. Click the **Camera Raw Menu** button to **Load**, **Save**, or **Delete** a specific set of Raw settings, or to modify dialog box settings.

8. Click **Done** to process the file, but not open it, or click **Open Image** to process and open it in Photoshop. Hold Alt (Win) or Option (Mac) to use **Open Copy** or **Reset**.

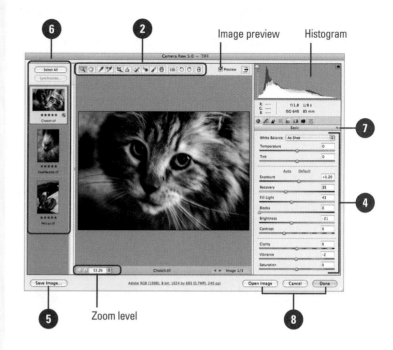

Image preview   Histogram

Zoom level

For Your Information

What is the DNG File Format?

The DNG, or Digital Negative, format is an openly published raw file format from Adobe that stores "raw" pixel data captured by digital cameras before it has been converted to another format, such as TIFF or JPEG. In addition, it captures standard 'EXIF' metadata, such as date, time, camera used, and camera settings. Saving raw files in the DNG format provides several advantages. DNG files are smaller than uncompressed TIFFs, and they do not have the artifacts of compressed JPEGs. Many key camera parameters, such as white balance, can be modified even after the image is captured. You have access to 16-bit data for greater detail and fidelity, and the added flexibility of converting a single file using multiple conversion settings. When you convert raw images into the DNG format, you are using a format that is openly published by Adobe and usable by other software and hardware vendors, which makes it a safe format for the long-term storage and archiving of digital images. The raw format used by digital cameras is proprietary to the specific camera (e.g., NEF for Nikon, CR2 for Canon, RAF for Fuji), so the format might not be supported once that camera and its proprietary software is obsolete, which means at some point in the future, you might not be able to open any of your archived raw images. The DNG format solves that problem. To get a free copy of the DNG converter, go to *www.adobe.com* and then search for DNG converter.

Working with Images Using Adobe Bridge

With Adobe Bridge, you can drag assets into your layouts as needed, preview them, and add metadata to them. Bridge allows you to search, sort, filter, manage, and process image files one at a time or in batches. You can also use Bridge to create new folders; rename, move, delete and group files (known as stacking); edit metadata; rotate images; and run batch commands. You can also view information about files and data imported from your digital camera.

Work with Images Using Bridge

① Launch your Adobe product, click the **File** menu, and then click **Browse in Bridge**, or click the **Launch Bridge** button (if available).

② Click the **Folder** path, and then select a folder.

③ Click the **Folders** tab and choose a folder from the scrolling list.

④ Click the **Favorites** tab to choose from a listing of user-defined items, such as Pictures or Version Cue.

⑤ Click an image within the preview window to select it.

⑥ Click the **Metadata** tab to view image information, including date and time the image was shot, and aperture, shutter speed, and f-stop.

⑦ Click the **IPTC Core** arrow to add user-defined metadata, such as creator and copyright information, or captions.

⑧ Click the **Preview** tab to view a larger thumbnail of the selected image. Multiple images appear when you select them.

 ◆ Click the image in the Preview tab to display a Loupe tool for zooming. Drag magnified box to change positions. Click it to deactivate the tool.

⑨ Drag the **Zoom** slider to increase or decrease the thumbnail views.

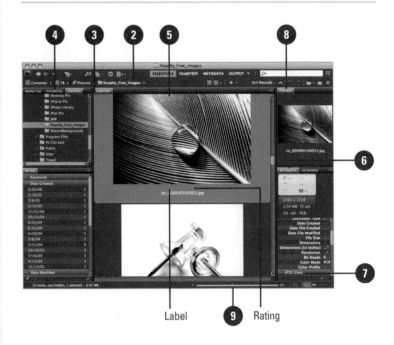

Label   ⑨   Rating

10 Click the preview buttons to select a different view of the workspace you have chosen. If you want to view your images in filmstrip or metadata focus mode, choose that workspace from the Window menu.

◆ **View Content as Thumbnails.** Default view. Displays the images as thumbnails with the file name underneath.

◆ **View Content as Details.** Displays a thumbnail of each image with selected details about the image such as date created, document type, resolution.

◆ **View Content as List.** Displays a small thumbnail of each image with metadata information details, such as date created and file size.

11 Use the file management buttons to rotate or delete images, or create a new folder.

12 To narrow down the list of images using a filter, click the criteria you want to use in the Filter panel.

13 To add a label or rating to images, select the ones you want, click the **Label** menu, and then select the label or rating you want.

14 To group related images as a stacked group, select the images, click the **Stacks** menu, and then click **Group as Stack**.

◆ Use the Stacks menu to ungroup, open, expand, or collapse stacks.

15 Double-click on a thumbnail to open it in the default program, or drag the thumbnail from the Bridge into an open Adobe application.

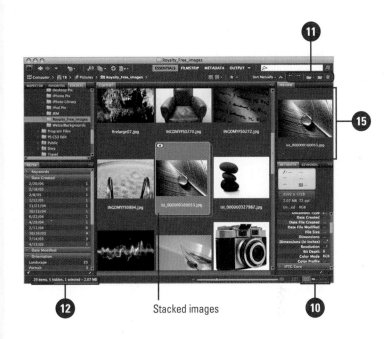

Stacked images

For Your Information

What is Metadata?

Metadata is information about an image file, such as its author, copyright, creation date, size, version, color space, resolution, and searchable keywords. This data is stored in the file or in a separate file known as a **sidecar file**, using a standard format called **Extensible Metadata Platform (XMP)**. Bridge and Version Cue use XMP files to help you organize and search for files on your computer. Metadata is also stored in other formats, such as EXIF (digital camera data), IPTC (photographer and image data), GPS (global positioning system data), and TIFF, which are all synchronized with XMP.

Setting Preferences in Adobe Bridge

Adobe Bridge allows you to set preferences to customize the way you work. The Preferences dialog box is organized into categories—including General, Thumbnails, Playback, Metadata, Keywords, Labels, File Type Associations, Cache, Startup Scripts, Advanced, and Output. You can set specific options within these categories to suit your particular needs. For example, you can choose to display more metadata information with thumbnails, such as dimensions, size, keywords, color mode, label, etc.

Set Bridge Preferences

1. In Adobe Bridge, click the **Edit** (Win) or **Bridge** (Mac) menu, and then click **Preferences**.

2. Click the **General** category.

3. Select the appearance, behavior, and Favorite Items you want.

4. Click the **Thumbnails** category.

5. Specify the performance and details options you want:

    ◆ **Performance and File Handling.** Choose the maximum size of file to be processed (default: 1000 MB).

    ◆ **Details.** Select the metadata details you want to show with the thumbnail.

6. Click the **Metadata** category.

7. Select the check boxes with the metadata you want and clear the ones you don't want.

8. Click the **Labels** category.

9. Enter names for labels you want to be associated with a specific color.

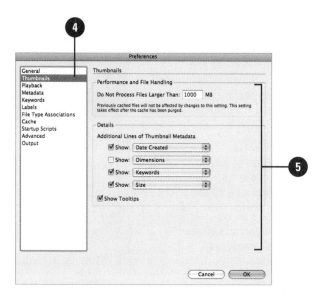

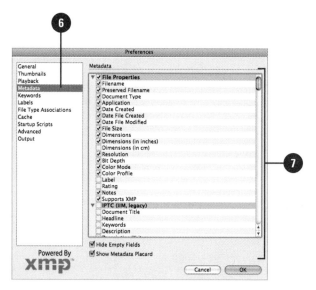

10 Click the **File Type Associations** category.

The left column displays the file type and the right column displays the current program that will open the file by default.

11 To change the default program, click the list arrow next to the file type, and then select a program or choose Browse to locate another application you would like to use.

12 Click the **Cache** category.

13 Choose where to store the cache, choose a cache size, and optimize or purge the cache from here.

14 Click the **Startup Scripts** category.

15 Select the check boxes with the programs you want to enable and clear the ones you want to disable.

16 Click the **Advanced** category, and specify whether to use software rendering and monitor-size previews, and then choose the language and keyboard options you want. You can also choose to have Bridge start automatically at login.

17 Click **OK**.

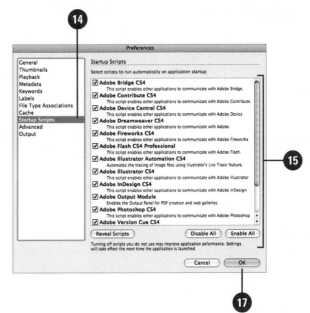

Did You Know?

You can use Photoshop automation commands in Adobe Bridge. You can use the Batch or Image Processor commands on the Tools menu under Photoshop in Bridge to automate the processing of your camera's raw files.

Applying Image Adjustments

Adobe Bridge makes it easy to make adjustments to one image in Camera Raw and then apply those adjustments to other images directly from Bridge without going back into Camera Raw. For instance, you may be correcting the white balance for an image and have many other images that were shot at the same time, under the same lighting conditions. You can use the initial settings to correct the rest of your images right from Bridge. You can also make a preset from your favorite adjustments, which will then be available as a develop setting within Bridge.

Modify Images in Adobe Bridge

1. In Adobe Bridge, display and select the images that you want to adjust.

2. Use any of the following methods to modify an image:

   ◆ **Apply a Preset Adjustment.** Click the **Edit** menu, point to **Develop Settings**, and then select a preset adjustment.

   ◆ **Copy and Paste Settings.** Click the **Edit** menu, point to **Develop Settings**, and then click **Copy Settings**. Select the image(s) to which you want to apply the settings. Click the **Edit** menu, point to **Develop Settings**, and then click **Paste Settings**. Select the options to apply, and then click **OK**.

   ◆ **Apply the Most Recent Adjustment.** Click the **Edit** menu, point to **Develop Settings**, and then click **Previous Conversion**.

Did You Know?

You can use Photoshop automation commands in Adobe Bridge. You can use the Batch or Image Processor commands on the Tools menu under Photoshop in Bridge to automate the processing of your camera's raw files.

Paste Settings

Creating a Web Photo Gallery

Adobe Bridge takes the drudgery out of creating a Web Photo Gallery (**New!**) (thumbnail images on web pages). The pages generated with this command display small thumbnails of a group of images—when you click on an image, a larger version is displayed within another window or section of the page. If your goal is to show the world your photographs, but you don't want to write all the HTML code involved in making that happen, then the Web Photo Gallery is just what you need.

Create a Web Photo Gallery in Adobe Bridge

1. In Adobe Bridge, select a folder with the images that you want to use for the photo gallery.

2. Click the **Workspace** menu, and then click **Output**.

3. Click the **Web Gallery** button.

4. Click the **Template** list arrow, and then select a template.

    ◆ Click the **Refresh Preview** button to view your template choices or click the **Preview in Browser** button to see how it would look on the Web.

5. Use the following panels to customize the Web gallery:

    ◆ **Site Info.** Provide descriptive information about the Web Photo gallery.

    ◆ **Color Palette.** Select custom colors for screen elements.

    ◆ **Appearance.** Specify options to show file names, a preview and thumbnail size, slide duration, and a transition effect.

6. In the Create Gallery panel, enter a gallery name, and then select a creation option:

    ◆ **Save to Disk.** Click **Browse** to specify a location, and then click **Save**.

    ◆ **Upload.** Specify the FTP server location, user name, password, a folder, and then click **Upload**.

Web Photo Gallery

Automating Tasks in Adobe Bridge

The Tools menu provides commands you can use to automate tasks in Bridge. For example, you can automate the process of renaming a group of files using the Batch Rename command. If you use Photoshop, InDesign, or Version Cue, you can use commands on submenus to run automated tasks, such as adding and synchronizing files with Version Cue or processing raw images with Photoshop, or you can create a contact sheet of images in InDesign. You can also use the Tools menu to start other Adobe programs, such as Device Central and Acrobat Connect (Start Meeting) as well as create and edit Metadata templates, which you can use to append or replace metadata in Adobe InDesign or other XMP-enabled programs.

Rename Files Automatically in Adobe Bridge

1. In Adobe Bridge, select the files or folders you want to use.

2. Click the **Tools** menu, and then click **Batch Rename**.

3. Select the Destination Folder option you want: **Rename in same folder**, **Move to other folder**, or **Copy to other folder**, and then click **Browse** to specify a new folder location.

4. Click the **Element** drop-down, and then select options to specify how you want to name the files:

   ◆ Text, New Extension, Current Filename, Preserved Filename, Sequence Number, Sequence Letter, Date/Time, Metadata, or Folder Name.

5. Enter the text you want to use in conjunction with the Element selection to name the files.

6. Select the **Preserve Current File Name In XMP Metadata** check box to retain the original filename in the metadata.

7. Select the check boxes for the operating systems with which you want the renamed files to be compatible.

8. Click **Rename**.

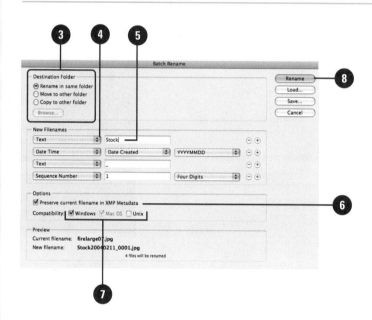

Sharing My Screen

The Share My Screen command (**New!**) on the File menu allows you to connect to Adobe ConnectNow, which is a secure Web site where you can start an online meeting and collaborate on any design project across platforms and programs. You can share and annotate your computer screen or take control of an attendee's computer. During the meeting, you can communicate by sending chat messages, using live audio, or broadcasting live video. In addition, you can take meeting notes, and share files.

Share My Screen

1. Click the **File** menu, and then click **Share My Screen**.

2. Enter your Adobe ID and password.

   ◆ If you don't have an Adobe ID and password, click the Create a Free Adobe ID link, and then follow the online instructions.

3. Click **Sign In**.

   ◆ If prompted, sign in to ConnectNow.

4. To share your computer screen, click the **Share My Computer Screen** button.

5. Use the ConnectNow toolbar to do any of the following:

   ◆ **Meeting.** Use to invite participants, share your computer screen, upload a file, share your webcam, set preferences, end a meeting, and exit Adobe ConnectNow.

   ◆ **PODS.** Use to show and hide pod panels.

   ◆ **Help.** Use to get help, troubleshoot problems, and set account and Flash Player settings.

6. Click the participant buttons at the bottom to specify roles, remove a user, or request control of a user's computer.

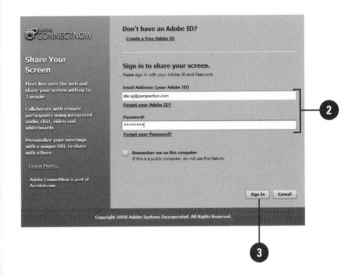

Managing Files Using Adobe Version Cue

With Adobe Drive CS4, you can access Adobe Version Cue CS4, a file versioning program you can use to keep track of changes to a file as you work on it and create projects to keep all your related files together. Version Cue allows you to access and manage Version Cue files and projects. You can use the Inspector panel and buttons in the Content panel to view, navigate, and access information, projects, and files on the Version Cue servers. You can check files in and out to make sure you're the only one making changes and then synchronize the changes.

Before you can start using Version Cue, you need to install and configure the Version Cue Server, create a project to store master copies of files and related information, and assign users to it. The Version Cue Server gets automatically installed on your computer with Adobe Creative Suite 4 Design, Web, or Master Collection. Even though it's installed, you still need to turn it on. Click My Server in the Adobe dialog box or in Adobe Bridge, and then follow the onscreen instructions to complete the initial server administration settings. If you're sharing files and other assets in a workgroup, you should reinstall Version Cue on a dedicated network computer.

Version Cue file management provides access to projects and files. To use file management, you need to enable it. Version Cue is enabled by default in all Adobe Creative Suite programs (except Flash and Acrobat). To turn it on in an Adobe program, open the Preferences dialog box using the Edit (Win) or program name (Mac) menu, and select the Enable Version Cue check box in one of the categories. If you disable Version Cue file management in one Adobe Creative Suite program, you disable it in all others, except Acrobat, Flash, and Bridge.

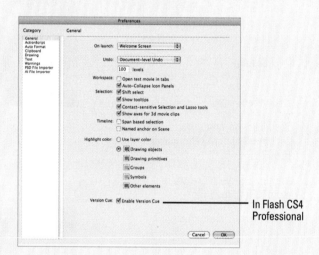

In Flash CS4 Professional

Working with Adobe Drive

Adobe Drive (**New!**) allows you to connect to and use Version Cue servers as if they were a local hard drive or mapped network drive. After you set up a connection, you can work with Version Cue files by using the Open, Import, Export, Place, Save, or Save As dialog boxes, and Explorer (Win) or Finder (Mac). After you start Adobe Drive, you can establish a connection to a Version Cue server, and then work with files on the server like a local or mapped drive. To change Adobe Drive preferences, click Preferences, specify caching and error logging settings, and then click Save.

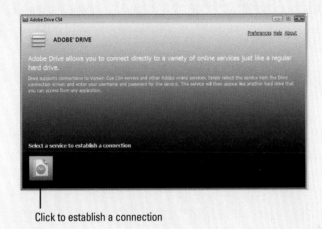

Click to establish a connection

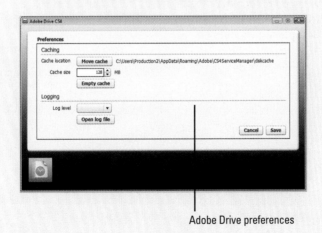

Adobe Drive preferences

Exploring Adobe Device Central

Device Profiles tab
Displays detailed information about devices, including support details for Flash, bitmap, video, and Web.

Emulator tab
Displays a simulation of how content appears on specific mobile devices.

Device Sets panel
Displays sets of devices for testing; availability depends on the content type.

Online Library panel
Downloads specific mobile device specifications.

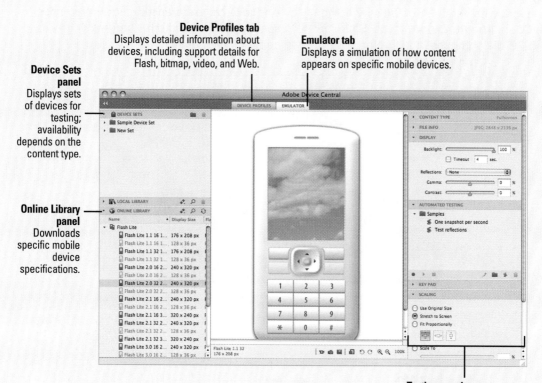

Testing panels
Displays a number of panels for testing content based on the selected options.

Checking Content Using Adobe Device Central

Testing your content on as many different devices as possible allows you to reach a wider audience. Adobe Device Central makes it easy to test your content on a wide variety of different mobile devices in one place. Device Central provides a library of devices from which to choose, and each device includes a profile with information about the device, including media and content support types. Device Central uses an emulator to simulate the way your content will look on a selected device. An emulator is not the same as the real device. However, it allows you to quickly test devices to get initial results.

Check Content Using Adobe Device Central

1. Start Adobe Device Central from the Start menu (Win) or the Applications folder (Mac) or from the File menu in Photoshop and choose Device Central.

   ◆ In Bridge, right-click a file, and then click **Test in Device Central**.

2. From the Welcome screen or the File menu, select the option you want:

   ◆ Open for Testing. Opens a file for testing with the Emulator tab. Use the buttons on the mobile device to test your content.

   ◆ Device Profiles. Displays mobile device profiles. In the Available Devices panel, expand a folder with devices. On the Device Profiles tab, click links to display profile information.

   ◆ Create New Mobile. Creates a new mobile document for Flash, Photoshop, or Illustrator; select a mobile device, and then click **Create**.

3. Select the Online Library panel where you can download specific mobile device specifications.

4. If you're testing, select the options you want in the Testing panels.

5. When you're done, click the **Close** button in the Device Central window.

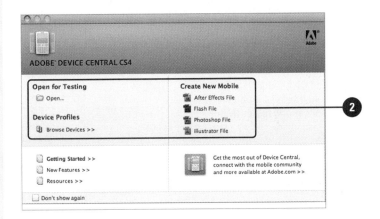

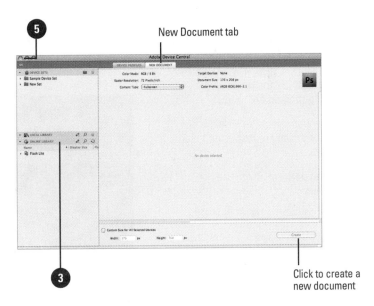

New Document tab

Click to create a new document

Using Adobe Extension Manager

The Adobe Extension Manager CS4 is a program you can use to install and delete added program functionality, known as extensions, to many Adobe programs. The Extension Manager is automatically installed when you install Flash, Dreamweaver, or Fireworks. You can use the Extension Manager to access the Adobe Exchange site, where you can locate, research, and download many different types of extensions. Some are free and some are not. After you download an extension, you can use Extension Manager to install it. Extension Manager only displays extensions installed using the Extension Manager; other extensions installed using a third-party installer might not appear. After you install an extension, you can find and display information about it.

Download and Install an Extension

1 Start Adobe Extension Manager CS4 from the Start menu (Win) or the Applications folder (Mac).

TIMESAVER *In Flash, Dreamweaver, or Fireworks, click the Help menu, and then click Manage Extensions.*

2 Click the **Exchange** button on the toolbar.

3 Select the extension you want to download, and then save it to your computer.

4 In Extension Manager, click the **Install** button on the toolbar.

5 Locate and select the extension (.mxp) you want to install, and then click **Install**.

6 You can perform any of the following:

◆ Sort. Click a column heading.

◆ Enable or Disable. Select or clear the check in the Enabled check box next to the extension.

◆ Remove. Select the extension, and then click **Remove.**

7 Click the **Close** button.

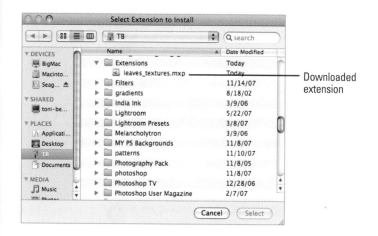

Downloaded extension

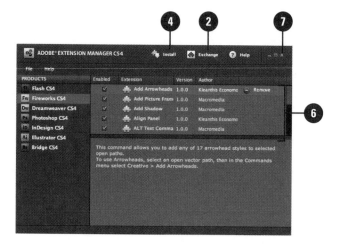

Workshops

W

Introduction

The Workshop is all about being creative and thinking outside of the box. These workshops will help your right-brain soar, while making your left-brain happy; by explaining why things work the way they do. Exploring Illustrator's possibilities is great fun; however, always stay grounded with knowledge of how things work. Knowledge is power.

Getting and Using the Project Files

Each project in the Workshop includes a start file to help you get started with the project, and a final file to provide you with the results of the project so you can see how well you accomplished the task.

Before you can use the project files, you need to download them from the Web. You can access the files at *www.perspection.com* in the software downloads area. After you download the files from the Web, uncompress the files into a folder on your hard drive to which you have easy access from Illustrator.

Project 1: Creating and Using Multiple Artboards

Skills and Tools: Artboards

Artboards are regions of a document that contain printable artwork. You can use artboards as crop areas for printing or placement. You can create multiple artboards (up to 100), which are useful for creating documents at different sizes, creating and organizing artwork elements in different places within the same document, and creating multiple page PDFs. You can view all of your artboards by using Artboard Navigation on the Status bar. Each artboard is numbered so you can quickly switch between them. You can only work on one artboard at a time. After you activate an artboard, you can perform the following artboard operations: change the view (outline or preview), resize, move the artboard with or without its contents, rotate, and delete. In addition, you can also change the display for artboard rulers, center mark, cross hairs, and video safe areas.

The Project

In this project, you'll learn how to create and use multiple artboards to work with multiple art pieces in a document.

The Process

① Open Illustrator CS4, click the **File** menu, click **New**, and then enter a new document name as **multiple_artboards**.

② Change the number of artboards to 2.

③ Select the **Arrange by Column** button.

④ Use the remaining defaults for the New dialog box.

⑤ Click **OK**.

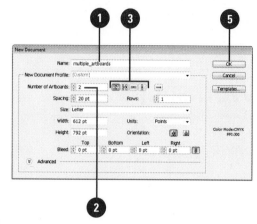

⑥ Save the new Illustrator file with the defaults as **multiple_artboards.ai**.

⑦ Select the **Artboard** tool on the Tools panel.

⑧ Click the bottom artboard, and then click the **Delete Artboard** button on the Control panel.

⑨ Click the **File** menu, click **Open**, and then open the file sea creatures.ai.

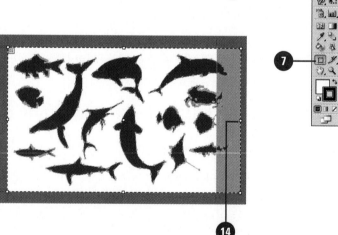

⑩ Select all the objects on the artboard using the Selection tool on the Tools panel.

⑪ Close the file sea creatures.ai.

⑫ Paste the objects on the Clipboard to the artboard.

⑬ Select the **Artboard** tool on the Tools panel.

⑭ Drag the resize handles on the artboard to make the objects fit in the artboard.

⑮ Drag in the workspace (outside an artboard) to create a new artboard.

◆ To create an artboard within an artboard, hold down Shift and then drag.

◆ To use a preset dimension, click the **Preset** list arrow on the Control panel, and then select a preset.

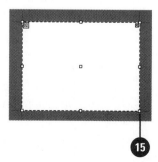

16 Click to select the artboard, click the **New Artboard** button on the Control panel, and then click to place the duplicated artboard.

♦ To create multiple duplicates, Alt-click instead as many times as you want.

17 Select the **Selection** tool on the Tools panel.

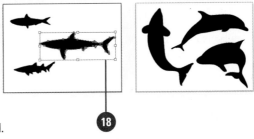

18 Drag the shark objects to artboard number 2 and drag the dolphin objects to artboard number 3.

19 Select the **Artboard** tool on the Tools panel.

20 Click artboard number 3 to select it.

21 Click the **Move/Copy Artwork With Artboard** button to select it (pressed in) on the Control panel.

♦ To show artboard rulers, select the artboard, click the **View** menu, and then click **Show Artboard Rulers**.

22 Drag artboard number down a little bit.

The artboard and the contents of the artboard move together.

23 Click the **Move/Copy Artwork With Artboard** button to deselect it on the Control panel.

24 Drag artboard number down a little bit.

The artboard moves without the contents of the artboard.

25 Click the **Edit** menu, and then click **Undo**.

The artboard moves without the contents of the artboard.

26 To navigate between artboards, use the Navigation buttons on the Status bar.

27 To exit the artboard editing mode, press Esc or click a different tool.

The Results

Finish: Compare your completed project file with the movie in **multiple_artboards_fnl.ai**. ☞

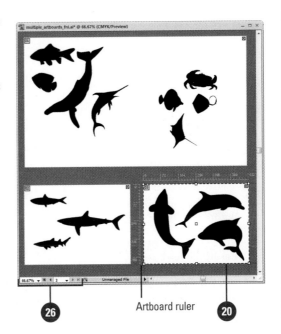

Artboard ruler

Project 2: Using Live Trace and Live Paint

Skills and Tools: Live Trace and Live Paint

If you have a raster graphic, such as a JPEG, TIFF, or PSD file, in your document, you can use tracing options to convert the graphic into editable vector artwork. You can set options to create a close simulation of the graphic or a more artistic rendering of it and then fine-tune your results. The Live Trace command detects and traces the color and shading in a raster graphic to create an editable vector object. You can use tracing presets (recommended for first time users), such as Simple Trace, Hand Drawn Sketch, or Inked Drawing, or set your own tracing options in the Tracing Options dialog box. Tracing options are live, which means that you can apply these options before or after using the Live Trace command. When applied, a traced object is known as a live trace object. You can start a Live Trace in Illustrator or in Adobe Bridge. Live Paint allows you to fill open or closed paths by creating Live Paint Groups. After you create a path using a drawing tool or Live Trace command, you can use the Live Paint command or the Live Paint Bucket tool to convert the paths into a Live Paint Group that you can paint. The Live Paint Bucket tool allows you to click an area formed by intersecting lines to apply fill (known as face) and stroke (known as edges) attributes. As you reshape the Live Paint objects, the paint attributes also change.

The Project

In this project, you'll learn how to create a Live Trace starting from Adobe Bridge and use Live Paint tools to color the artwork.

The Process

1. Open Illustrator CS4, and then click the **Go to Bridge** button on the Applications bar.

2. Navigate to the projects folder to display the project files in Adobe Bridge.

3. Select the sneakers.png file.

4. Click the **Tools** menu, point to **Illustrator**, and then click **Live Trace**.

   The Live Trace dialog box appears.

5. Select **Technical Drawing** from the Tracing Preset.

6. Deselect the **Save and Close Results** check box.

7. Use the remaining defaults for the New dialog box.

8. Click **OK**.

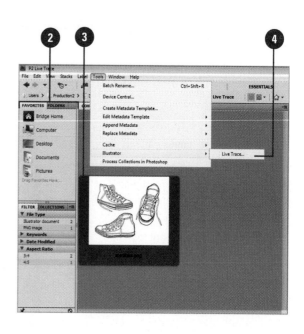

Adobe Illustrator opens, displaying the live Trace object. In Illustrator, you can create a live trace object by selecting the object, and then click the Live Trace button on the Control panel.

9 With the **Selection** tool, resize the sneakers object.

10 Click the **File** menu, click **Save As**, and then save the new document using the defaults with the name **live_trace _paint.ai**.

11 Select all the paths using selection tools on the Tools panel.

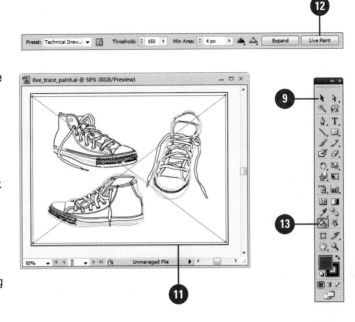

12 Click the **Live Paint** button on the Control panel.

◆ You can also click the **Object** menu, point to **Live Paint**, and then click **Make**.

◆ You can also click the **Live Paint Bucket** tool on the Tools panel, and then click the selected paths.

The paths are nested together into a Live Paint Group, which appears in the Layers panel.

13 Double-click the **Live Paint Bucket** tool on the Tools panel.

14 Select the **Paint Fills** and **Paint Strokes** check boxes to paint fills and strokes with the Live Paint Bucket tool.

15 Click **OK**.

16 Select the **Live Paint Bucket** tool on the Tools panel.

17 Display a Live Paint Group object.

18 Select a fill color on the Swatches (including other libraries), Tools, or Control panels to use with the Live Paint Bucket tool. Select a stroke color, weight, or other attributes on the Strokes, Tools, or Control panels to use with the Live Paint Bucket tool.

◆ If the Cursor Swatch Preview appears above the pointer, you can press the left or right arrow keys to select or display the next or previous color from the Swatches panel.

◆ To remove colors from stroke edges, select **None**.

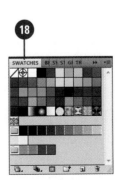

19 Point to the face that you want to fill or the edge that you want to change. The face or edge becomes highlighted.

20 Click an individual face or edge or drag multiple edges.

The Results

Finish: Compare your completed project file with the movie in live_trace _paint_fnl.ai.

Want More Projects

You can access and download more workshop projects and related files at *www.perspection.com* in the software downloads area. After you download the files from the Web, uncompress the files into a folder on your hard drive to which you have easy access from Illustrator.

Get Everything on DVD

Instead of downloading everything from the Web, which can take a while depending on your Internet connection speed, you can get all the files used in this book and much more on a Illustrator CS4 On Demand DVD. The DVD contains task and workshop files, tips and tricks, keyboard shortcuts, and other goodies from the author.

To get the Illustrator CS4 On Demand DVD, go to *www.perspection.com*.

New! Features

Adobe Illustrator CS4

Adobe Illustrator CS4 means superior results faster, with new features and enhancements that help you create and manage your images more easily and efficiently. The indispensable new and improved features help graphic web designers, photographers, and video professionals create the highest quality images, with the control, flexibility, and capabilities that you expect from the professional standards in desktop digital imaging.

Each new release of Illustrator brings with it new features, improvements, and added sophistication. This edition is aimed at the Web designer, interactive media professional, or subject matter expert developing multimedia content, and the application developer.

Only New Features

If you're already familiar with Illustrator CS3, you can access and download all the tasks in this book with Adobe Illustrator CS4 New Features to help make your transition to the new version simple and smooth. The Illustrator CS4 New Features as well as other Illustrator CS3 to Illustrator CS4 transition helpers are available on the Web at *www.perspection.com.*

What's New

If you're searching for what's new in Illustrator CS4, just look for the icon: **New!**. The new icon appears in the table of contents and throughout this book, so you can quickly and easily identify a new or improved feature in Illustrator CS4. The following is a brief description of each new feature and its location in this book.

Illustrator CS4

◆ **Tabbed Document Window (p. 6, 18-19, 26)**   Display multiple documents in a tabbed view or open them side by side so you can easily compare or drag items from one document to another. Simply click a document's tab to open it, or click Close (x) on a tab to close it.

- ◆ **Application Bar and Workspaces Menu (p. 6, 56)** From the application bar at the top of each Creative Suite application, provides menus and options in one easy to access place. Use the workspace switcher to quickly jump to different workspace configurations to meet your specific needs. Also along this bar, you can access Adobe Bridge and the document arrangement panel

- ◆ **Arrange Document Window (p. 18)** Use the intuitive Arrange Documents window to quickly arrange your open documents in a variety of configurations.

- ◆ **Community Help (p. 22-23)** Illustrator Help uses a Community Help site on the web at *adobe.com* (which is updated regularly) to help you find the information you need. When you start Illustrator Help, your browser opens, displaying a web site with Illustrator help categories and topics. Along with help text, some help topics include links to text and video tutorials. In addition, comments and ratings from users are available to help guide you to an answer.

- ◆ **Adobe Product Improvement Program (p. 23)** This is an opt-in program that allows you to test Adobe products and make suggestions for future products. This program enables Adobe to collect product usage data from customers while maintaining their privacy.

- ◆ **Multiple Artboards (p. 34-37)** Create multi-page files containing up to 100 artboards of varying sizes. You can create artboards that overlap, appear side-by-side, or are stacking on top of one another. You can also save, export and print artboards independently or together. Multiple artboards have replaced the Crop Area tool.

- ◆ **Smart Guides (p. 50-51)** Smart guides are now even more practical with unobtrusive appearance and behaviors. Instant pop-ups appear with alignment and measurement information, such as deltas between objects and angles of rotation (that you can specify) and when moving or transforming objects. Of course, objects still snap to any alignment you choose to make it easy to arrange and transform objects exactly how you want.

- ◆ **Key Object Alignment (p. 84)** The Align panel and Control panel now provide quick access to the key alignment option. A key object is the one object that you want other objects to align to. You specify a key object by selecting all the objects you want to align, including the key object, and then clicking again on the key object. When selected, the key objects appears with a thick blue outline, and the Align To Key Object icon appears in the Control panel and Align panel. Simply choose an alignment option, such as Horizontal Align Left or Vertical Align Center, and all the other selected objects align to the key object.

- ◆ **Kuler (p. 106)** Kuler is an extension that provides access to the Kuler online community. The Kuler application is added as a panel in Illustrator. You can add the Kuler color theme to the Swatches panel.

- ◆ **Gradients Panel (p. 134-136)** The Gradient panel now provides a menu of all your saved gradients, directly access color panels, and apply transparency to individual color spots, among other things.

- ◆ **Transparency in Gradient (p. 135)** Create gradients with two to many colors and define the opacity of any or all individual colors. By specifying different opacity values for the different color stops in your gradient, you can create gradients that fade in or out and reveal or hide underlying images.

- **Gradients Tool (p. 137)** Using the enhanced Gradient tool, you can interact with gradients on the object itself by adding or changing color stops, applying transparency to color stops, and changing the direction or angle of a linear or elliptical gradient.

- **Blob Brush Tool (p. 154-155)** Use the Blob Brush to draw paths that merge with existing artwork. The Blob Brush draws paths that are fill only - no stroke - and can merge with existing artwork that has the same fill, and no stroke. The Blob Brush can merge with existing artwork that has complicated appearances (as long as there is no stroke on the artwork and the Blob Brush is set up to paint with the exact same fill and appearance settings. For example, if you've created a yellow filled rectangle with a drop shadow applied, you can set up the Blob Brush with those attributes and then draw a path across the rectangle, and the two paths will be merged. You can easily select and edit the resulting shape. Use the Blob Brush together with the Eraser tool for truly intuitive vector painting

- **Clipping Masks (p. 160-163)** Adobe Illustrator now displays only the masked area while you are moving or transforming a masked object. Double-click the masked object to open it in Isolation mode, where you can view and edit the mask independently of all other objects.

- **Graphic Styles Panel (p. 231, 234-235)** The newly updated Graphic Styles panel provides you with a quick and easy way to view and apply styles to objects in your document. Use the Use Text For Preview option to view a style as it appears on text, or right-click a thumbnail to quickly preview how that style will look on a selected object on the artboard. Effect-only styles now display the outlines of the object on which the style was created, so you can recognize your effect-only styles at a glance. Merge a style with an object's existing style or merge two or more different styles on an object by simply using the Alt or Option key when applying the style.

- **Appearance Panel Editing (p. 236-237)** Select an item in the Appearance panel to view and use the enhanced full-featured controls. Click hyper-links to open option dialog boxes for effects, strokes, and fills. Click a visibility icon for any attribute to easily turn it on or off.

- **Flex Support (p. 360)** Efficiently deliver more editable, workable content to developers for web, interactive, and RIA projects. For instance, use the Flex Skins for Illustrator to create and export vector skins in the Adobe Flex format.

- **Separations Preview Panel (p. 337)** Preview your color separations on your monitor before printing to avoid color output surprises such as unexpected spot colors and unwanted overprinting. The Separations Preview panel lets you easily turn colors on and off so you can see how blending, transparency, and overprinting will appear in color-separated output.

- **Export Multiple Artboards (p. 348, 351, 354, 354-359)** Creating documents with multiple artboards now makes it easy to create multi-page documents for exporting. You can export artboards to any of the following formats: PDF, PSD, SWF, JPEG, PNG, and TIFF. Or import a multiple artboard Illustrator file into Adobe InDesign or Adobe Flash. You can now easily create multiple-page PDFs. When exporting to Flash SWF format, multiple artboards export as multiple files.

- **Adobe ConnectNow (p. 406, 419)** The Share My Screen command on the File menu allows you to connect to Adobe ConnectNow, which is a secure Web site where you can start an online meeting and collaborate on any design project across platforms and programs.

- **Adobe Drive (p. 406, 421)** Adobe Drive is an AIR program that allows you to connect to hosted services, such as Version Cue CS4 servers.

- **Adobe Bridge (p. 407, 409-411, 417)** General improvements include faster asset management and a Quick Search bar, from which you can search keywords, file names, and folder names. You also have a choice of commonly used Workspaces on the Application bar, as well as a "breadcrumb" file path so you can easily link back to the source folder for any file you're viewing. Bridge allows you to create PDF slideshows, contact sheets, PDF layouts for printing, and web galleries.

Adobe Certified Expert

About the Adobe Certified Expert (ACE) Program

The Adobe Certified Expert (ACE) program is for graphic designers, Web designers, systems integrators, value-added resellers, developers, and business professionals seeking official recognition of their expertise on Adobe products.

What Is an ACE?

An Adobe Certified Expert is an individual who has passed an Adobe Product Proficiency Exam for a specific Adobe software product. Adobe Certified Experts are eligible to promote themselves to clients or employers as highly skilled, expert-level users of Adobe software. ACE certification is a recognized worldwide standard for excellence in Adobe software knowledge. There are three levels of ACE certification: Single product certification, Specialist certification, and Master certification. To become an ACE, you must pass one or more product-specific proficiency exams and sign the ACE program agreement. When you become an ACE, you enjoy these special benefits:

- Professional recognition
- An ACE program certificate
- Use of the Adobe Certified Expert program logo

What Does This Logo Mean?

It means this book will prepare you fully for the Adobe Certified Expert exam for Adobe Illustrator CS4. The certification exam has a set of objectives, which are organized into broader skill sets. The Adobe Certified Expert objectives and the specific pages throughout this book that cover the objectives are available on the Web at *www.perspection.com*.

 IL 3.1

Illustrator CS4 ACE Exam Objectives

Objective	Skill	Page
1.0	**Working with Illustrator documents**	
1.1	Given a scenario, choose the correct document options or create a custom document	28-29, 32-33
1.2	Given a scenario, create a document template.	30-31, 362
1.3	Given a scenario, save a document with the appropriate format and options. (Options include: various "Save…" commands, export, file formats)	24-25
1.4	Given a scenario, select the proper settings in the Preferences dialog box.	140, 390-402
1.5	Given a scenario, create Guides, Grids, and use Smart Guides.	48-52
1.6	Manage Illustrator workspace and panels. (Options include opening/closing/docking panels and saving workspaces)	6-9, 56-57
1.7	Build a document structure based on layers. (Options include moving and copying objects to layers)	166-182
1.8	Given a scenario, choose a preview mode to visualize the document.	38-39
1.9	Customize keyboard shortcuts by using the Keyboard Shortcuts dialog box.	403
1.10	Control object size and other options by using the control bar.	11
1.11	Given a scenario, create and use multiple artboards. (Options include create, move, duplicate, and adjust artboard dimensions)	34-37
1.12	Given a scenario, work with multiple documents. (Option include views, tabbed documents, n-up arrangement)	18-19
1.13	View and modify document metadata information.	344-345
2.0	**Drawing and transforming objects**	
2.1	Create and modify a vector object using the Pen tool and bezier controls.	61, 140-153
2.2	Given a scenario, customize the Stroke panel settings to achieve the proper visual appearance.	120-121
2.3	Given a scenario, cut, erase or delete portions of an object by using the appropriate tool.	160-164
2.4	Use Isolation Mode to edit objects, groups, symbols, or layers.	76-77, 162-163
2.5	Given a scenario, create either a clipping mask or layer clipping to hide parts of objects.	160-163
2.6	Given a scenario, use a mix of open/closed path, compound path, and compound shapes. (Options include Pathfinder operations)	156-159, 260
2.7	Align or distribute objects precisely on an artboard.	84
2.8	Select one or more objects and arrange their stacking order.	70-79, 166, 174
2.9	Modify an object with one or more transformation tools.	85-91

Objective	Skill	Page
2.10	Create and apply a pattern swatch.	124-125, 302
2.11	Record steps as a reusable Action.	310-315
3.0	**Managing color and transparency**	
3.1	Given a scenario, set up Color Management settings and proof color on screen.	94-96, 116, 342
3.2	Given a scenario, create or load swatches, organize them, and apply them to objects.	99-110, 118
3.3	Apply transparency options to objects. (Options include Opacity, Color Mode, and Opacity mask)	131-133, 303
3.4	Recolor and fine-tune artwork color by using Live Color.	114-115
3.5	Explore color combinations using Color Guide.	111-113
3.6	Given a scenario, use the appropriate tools to create, modify, save, and apply color gradients to objects.	134-137, 302
4.0	**Using type**	
4.1	Given a scenario, create the appropriate text object. (Options include point type, area text, and text on path)	186-190
4.2	Format type by using character and paragraph attributes.	202-210
4.3	Create and apply character and paragraph styles to text.	212-213
4.4	Use the Glyph and OpenType panels to obtain special characters.	215
4.5	Format a story. (Options include threading text frames and text wrap)	198-199
4.6	Locate or replace fonts inside a document.	200-201, 328-329
4.7	Given a scenario, customize language dictionaries.	201, 325
4.8	Given a scenario, adjust and apply hyphenation.	211
5.0	**Controlling effects, appearances, and graphic styles**	
5.1	Given a scenario, adjust the appearance of objects by using the Appearance panel. (Options include fill, stroke, effect, and transparency)	131, 236-237, 240-247
5.2	Given a scenario, save and apply Graphic Styles.	231-235, 241, 304
5.3	Given a scenario, apply the appropriate Live Effect to an object.	240-247
5.4	Use the Eyedropper to copy attributes between elements.	118, 122-123
6.0	**Building graphic objects**	
6.1	Create and format a graph. (Options include entering data, controlling type options, and design)	322

Illustrator CS4 ACE Exam Objectives *(continued)*

Objective	Skill	Page
6.2	Produce a smooth color mix by using and controlling a gradient mesh.	92, 138
6.3	Given a scenario, adjust the settings for the Blend tool.	129-130
6.4	Given a scenario, choose or create the appropriate brush.	273-283
6.5	Create and use a symbol. (Options include placing it onto the artboard, editing it, and manipulating it with Symbolism tools)	288-304
6.6	Create and edit a Live Paint Group.	262-272
6.7	Apply and edit an object distortion envelope.	92
6.8	Given a scenario, use the Eraser tool or Blob Brush. (Including editing the tool options)	154-155
6.9	Given a scenario, prepare and create artwork by using variables.	320-321
7.0	**Working with images**	
7.1	Import images into your document.	16, 220-223
7.2	Manage assets with the Link panel.	224-227
7.3	Turn an image into a vector object with Live Trace.	228-230
8.0	**Preparing for Web and Flash**	
8.1	Given a scenario, choose the proper settings to save illustrator artwork for Web or mobile devices.	364-388
8.2	Prepare a document for Flash authoring. (Options include Symbols, Flash Text, and Release to Layers)	292, 388
8.3	Given a scenario, export to SWF. (Options include customizing and using SWF presets)	354-355
9.0	**Preparing for print**	
9.1	Analyze the content of a document by using the Document Info panel.	55, 346
9.2	Use the Flattener Preview to preview and create custom settings to control the transparency flattening process.	340-341
9.3	Given a scenario, choose the correct overprinting options. (Options include Preserve, Discard, or Simulate)	337, 340, 401
9.4	Preview and analyze on screen color separations.	337
9.5	Given a scenario, choose the correct print options and create custom print presets.	330-336, 338-340, 343
9.6	Given a scenario, choose the correct PDF presets or customize options.	356-357

Choosing a Certification Level

There are three levels of certification to become an Adobe Certified Expert.

◆ **Single product certification.** Recognizes your proficiency in a single Adobe product. To qualify as an ACE, you must pass one product-specific exam.

◆ **Specialist certification.** Recognizes your proficiency in multiple Adobe products with a specific medium: print, Web, or video. To become certified as a Specialist, you must pass the exams on the required products. To review the requirements, go online to *http://www.adobe.com/support/certification/ace_certify.html*.

◆ **Master certification.** Recognizes your skills in terms of how they align with the Adobe product suites. To become certified as a Master, you must pass the exam for each of the products in the suite.

Preparing for an Adobe Certified Expert Exam

Every Adobe Certified Expert Exam is developed from a list of objectives, which are based on studies of how an Adobe program is actually used in the workplace. The list of objectives determine the scope of each exam, so they provide you with the information you need to prepare for ACE certification. Follow these steps to complete the ACE Exam requirement:

1. Review and perform each task identified with a Adobe Certified Expert objective to confirm that you can meet the requirements for the exam.

2. Identify the topic areas and objectives you need to study, and then prepare for the exam.

3. Review the Adobe Certified Expert Program Agreement. To review it, go online to *http://www.adobe.com/support/certification/ace_certify.html*.

   You will be required to accept the ACE agreement when you take the Adobe Certified Exam at an authorized testing center.

4. Register for the Adobe Certified Expert Exam.

   ACE testing is offered at more than a thousand authorized Pearson VUE and Thomson Prometric testing centers in many countries. To find the testing center nearest you, go online to *www.pearsonvue.com/adobe* (for Pearson VUE) or *www.2test.com* (for Prometric). The ACE exam fee is US$150 worldwide. When contacting an authorized training center, provide them with the Adobe Product Proficiency exam name and number you want to take, which is available online in the Exam Bulletin at *http://www.adobe.com/support/certification/ace_certify.html*.

5. Take the ACE exam.

Getting Recertified

For those with an ACE certification for a specific Adobe product, recertification is required of each ACE within 90 days of a designated ACE Exam release date. There are no restrictions on the number of times you may take the exam within a given period.

To get recertified, call Pearson VUE or Thomson Prometric. You will need to verify your previous certification for that product. If you are getting recertified, check with the authorized testing center for discounts.

Taking an Adobe Certified Expert Exam

The Adobe Certified Expert exams are computer-delivered, closed-book tests consisting of 60 to 90 multiple-choice questions. Each exam is approximately one to two hours long. A 15-minute tutorial will precede the test to familiarize you with the function of the Windows-based driver. The exams are currently available worldwide in English only. They are administered by Pearson VUE and Thomson Prometric, independent third-party testing companies.

Exam Results

At the end of the exam, a score report appears indicating whether you passed or failed the exam. Diagnostic information is included in your exam report. When you pass the exam, your score is electronically reported to Adobe. You will then be sent an ACE Welcome Kit and access to the ACE program logo in four to six weeks. You are also placed on the Adobe certification mailing list to receive special Adobe announcements and information about promotions and events that take place throughout the year.

When you pass the exam, you can get program information, check and update your profile, or download ACE program logos for your promotional materials online at:

http://www.adobe.com/support/certification/community.html

Getting More Information

To learn more about the Adobe Certified Expert program, read a list of frequently asked questions, and locate the nearest testing center, go online to:

http://www.adobe.com/support/certification/ace.html

To learn more about other Adobe certification programs, go online to:

http://www.adobe.com/support/certification

Index

A

accented edges effects, 257
actions
    Actions panel, 308–309
    adding commands to, 314
    adding stops to, 312
    batch file processing, 316–317
    building new, 310
    built-in scripts, 318
    controlling playback of, 311
    deleting commands from, 315
    inserting a non-recordable command in
        an Action, 313
    order of commands in, changing, 314
    recording, 310
    running actions within actions, 310
    saving
        as files, 309
        into sets, 309
    scripts, 318–319
activation, 2
active documents, 19
active windows, 18
Adobe Bridge
    automating tasks in, 418
    browsing documents with, 14
    Camera Raw feature, 410–411
    color settings, 95
    components of, 407
    description of, 406
    editing images in, 416
    Get Photos from Camera command, 409
    opening documents with, 14–15, 408
    placing graphics from, 222–223
    preferences, setting, 414–415
    revealing documents in, 14
    Web Photo Gallery creation, 417

working with images using, 15, 412–413
Adobe ConnectNow, 406, 419
Adobe Device Central
    basic description of, 406, 422
    checking content using, 423
    components of, 422
Adobe Drive, 406, 421
Adobe Extension Manager, 406, 424
Adobe Flex File, saving documents as, 360
Adobe PDF Presets command (Edit menu),
    353
Adobe Product Improvement Program, 23
Adobe Studio Exchange, 2
Adobe Updater, 21
Adobe Version Cue
    basic description of, 406
    file management, 420
Adobe Web site
    Adobe Studio Exchange, 2
    Community Help, 22
advanced print options, 340–341
Advanced tab (File Info dialog box), 345
alignment
    anchor points, 148–149
    objects, 84
    paragraphs, 208
    slices, 383
    stroke, 120
All Objects command (Select menu), 78
All Objects in Active Artboard command
    (Select menu), 78
anchor points
    adding new, 146–147
    alignment, 148–149
    Convert Anchor Point tool, 145
    converting, 144–145
    deleting, 147
    direction lines, 142

anchor point *(continued)*
>   endpoints, 149
>   highlighting, 142
>   moving, 142–143
>   paths and, 61
>   preferences, 142
>   selecting with Direct Selection tool, 72
>   showing and hiding, 61
>   smooth points, converting to corner points, 144

anchors, 393
anti-aliasing, 390
Appearance of Black preferences, 402
Appearance panel, 236–237
Arc tool, 66
arcs, drawing, 66
area graphs, 322
Area Type tool, 189
arranging
>   documents, 18
>   layers, 174–175
>   slices, 382–383

art brushes, 280–281
Artboard tool
>   artboard creation, 34
>   Artboard Options button, 35
>   multiple artboards, 36

artboards
>   within artboards, 34
>   aspect ratio, 35
>   centerpoints, 35
>   deleting, 36
>   display options, 37
>   duplicating, 34
>   exiting editing mode, 34
>   landscape/portrait orientation, 35
>   moving, 36
>   multiple, working with, 36
>   navigating within, 34
>   presets, 34
>   previewing, 36
>   resizing, 36
>   rotating, 36
>   size, 35
>   switching between, 17, 37
>   video safe areas, 35
>   X and Y positioning, 35

artwork, inserting in documents, 16
Assign Profile command (Edit menu), 96
attributes
>   appearance, 236–237
>   stroke, 120–121

Audio Data tab (File Info dialog box), 344
auto slices, 378
AutoCAD drawing format, 349
AutoCAD File format, 349

B

bar graphs, 322
batch file processing, 316–317
Batch Rename command, 418
bend styles, 83
bevel bend style, 83
bevel joins, 121
bitmap, exporting documents as, 350
black appearance options, 402
bleed
>   bleed print option, 335
>   document creation, 32

Blend command (Objects menu), 127–128
Blend tool, 129
blends
>   blending fill colors, 126
>   changing and applying blend options, 128
>   creating automatically, 127
>   creating with Blend tool, 129
>   making and releasing blend objects, 127
>   objects, modifying, 130
>   opacity, 131
>   transformation, 130
>   transparency settings, 132

Bloat tool, 286
Blob Brush tool
>   brush options, setting, 155
>   merging paths with, 154

blur effects, 252
BMP format, 349
bold font, 200
Bounding Box command (View menu), 270–271
Bridge (Adobe)
>   automating tasks in, 418
>   browsing documents with, 14

Camera Raw feature, 410–411
color settings, 95
components of, 407
description of, 406
editing images in, 416
Get Photos from Camera command, 409
opening documents with, 14–15, 408
placing graphics from, 222–223
preferences, setting, 414–415
revealing documents in, 14
Web Photo Gallery creation, 417
working with images using, 15, 412–413
Browse in Bridge command (File menu),
    14–15, 222–223
brushes
    art, 280–281
    Blob Brush tool, 155
    Brushes panel, 273
    calligraphic, 278–279
    deleting, 284
    Paintbrush tool, 274–275
    pattern, 282–283
    scatter, 276–277
    strokes, removing, 284
Brushes panel, 273
built-in scripts, actions, 318

C

calligraphic brushes, 278–279
Camera Data tab (File Info dialog box), 344
Camera Raw feature, 410–411
caps, 121
case, text, 329
Categories tab (File Info dialog box), 344
center mark, 37
centerpoints, 35
Check Spelling command (Edit menu), 324
circles, drawing, 62
clearing
    guides, 49
    objects, 81
clipping masks
    creating, 160
    creating for groups or layers, 161
    editing, 162
    masked object, editing in Isolation
        Mode, 163

release objects from, 161
clipping sets, 163
Close button, 26
Close command (File menu), 26
closed paths, 61
closing
    documents, 26
    Illustrator, 26
    panels, 7
CMYK (Cyan, Magenta, Yellow and Black)
        color mode, 28, 97, 101
collapsing panels, 7
Color Guide panel
    applying color with, 112–113
    color groups, 113
    harmony rules, variations based on, 113
    variation options, selecting, 111
    variation types, displaying, 111
color management print options, 342
color modes. See also colors
    changing, 98
    CMYK, 28, 97, 101
    document creation, 28
    Grayscale, 28, 100
    RGB, 28, 97, 100
    switching between, 97
    working with, 97
Color panel
    Color sliders, 100
    working with, 100–101
colored paper simulation, 33
colors. See also Color Guide panel; color
        modes; Swatches panel
    applying to objects, fills, or stroke, 99,
        118
    applying with Eyedropper tool, 122–123
    Color Guide Panel, 111–113
    Color panel, 100–101
    color profiles, changing or removing, 95
    color settings, changing, 94–95
    converting to grayscale, 109
    crop mark registration color, 54
    gamut warning icon, 101
    global, 108–110
    grayscale images, 109
    grid colors transparency settings, 33
    grids, 52
    guides, 48, 51

colors *(continued)*
  hue, 101
  inverting, 110
  Kuler panel, 106–107
  Live Color feature, 114–115
  luminosity, 101
  nonglobal, 108–110
  proofing, 116
  replacing, 108–109
  saturation, 101
  selecting, 101
  soft proof, 116
  Swatches panel, 102–105
  themes, 106–107
  view box color, 42
  Web-safe, 101
column graphs, 322
commands
  adding to actions, 314
  basic description of, 6
  deleting from actions, 315
  Panel Options menu, 9
Community Help site, 22
compound paths
  creating, 158
  releasing, 159
  reversing object's fill in, 159
condensed font, 200
ConnectNow (Adobe), 406, 419
Constrain Angle general preference, 390
Control panel
  anchor points, converting, 145
  basic description of, 11
  splitting paths using, 153
  tools in, 6
Convert Anchor Point tool, 145
Convert to Shape command (Effect menu), 242
convert to shape effects, 242
converting anchor points, 144–145
Copy command (Edit menu), 197
copying text, 196–197
corner points, 144
Corner Radius general preference, 390
Create New Action button (Actions panel), 309
Create New Set button (Actions panel), 309

crop marks
  creating, 54
  deleting, 54
  general preferences, 391
  registration color, 54
cross hairs, 37
Crystallize tool, 286
cursor preferences, 390
curved segments, 143
curves, drawing, 141
custom dictionaries, spell checking, 325
Cut command (Edit menu), 197
cutout effects, 256

D

dashed stroke, 121
data graphs, 322
data sets
  creating, 320–321
  deleting, 320–321
  renaming, 321
data variables, 320–321
Define Pattern command (Edit menu), 124
Delete button (Actions panel), 309
deleting
  anchor points, 147
  artboards, 36
  brushes, 284
  commands from actions, 315
  crop marks, 54
  data sets, 320–321
  files, 12
  graphic styles, 235
  layers, 171
  objects, 81
  selections, 80
  slices, 380
  symbols, 291
  workspaces, 57
Description tab (File Info dialog box), 344
Deselect command (Select menu), 78
Device Central (Adobe)
  basic description of, 406
  checking content using, 423
  components of, 422
Device Central command (File menu), 39
DICOM tab (File Info dialog box), 345

dictionaries, spell checking, 325
diffuse glow effects, 257
Direct Selection tool
    anchor points, adding new, 146
    anchor points or segments, moving, 143
    deleting anchor points using, 147
    editing patterns using, 125
    end points, connecting, 149
    selecting anchor points and segments
      with, 72
    showing/hiding direction lines, 61
    understanding selections, 70
direction lines
    anchor points, 142
    showing and hiding, 61
Distort & Transform command (Effect
    menu), 90
distributing
    objects, 84
    slices, 383
dithering, 373
dividing paths, 153
DOC format, 193
docking
    documents, 19
    panels, 8
Document Color Mode command (File
    menu), 98, 330
Document Info panel, 346
Document Setup command (File menu), 32,
    133
Document window, 6
documents
    active, 19
    arranging, 18
    bleed and view options settings, 32
    browsing with Adobe Bridge, 14
    closing, 26
    color modes, 28
    creating
      from scratch, 28
      from templates, 30–31
      using presets, 29
    docking/undocking, 19
    exporting
      as bitmap, 350
      Export command, 348
      export file formats, 349

      as Flash Movie, 354–355
      to Photoshop, 352
      with presets, 353
      as TIFF format, 351
    file information, inserting, 344–345
    finding and replacing text and elements
      in, 326–327
    grid pattern, 19
    inserting images in, 16
    language settings, 33
    linking, 16
    measurement units, 32
    opening
      with Adobe Bridge, 14–15
      existing documents, 12
      recently opened, 13
      from Welcome Screen, 13
    printing, 330
    revealing in Adobe Bridge, 14
    rulers, 46–47
    saving, 24–25
      as Adobe Flex File, 360
      as EPS format, 358–359
      as FXG format, 360
      as Microsoft Office, 361
      as PDF format, 356–357
      as template, 362
      for the Web, 364–365
    setting up, 32–33
    spell checking, 324–325
    switching between, 18
    tabbed, 18
    templates, 16
    transparency settings, 32–33
    type options settings, 33
    view size, 17
    viewing information in, 17
    views, 38–41
    windows, 18–19
    working with multiple, 18–19
DOCX format, 193
double quotes, 33
drawing
    arcs, 66
    circles, 62
    curves, 141
    ellipses, 62
    line segments, 65

drawing *(continued)*
  with Pencil tool, 260–261
  polygons, 64, 140
  rectangle grids, 68
  rectangles, 63
  spirals, 66–67
  stars, 64
drawing tablets, 404
Drive (Adobe), 406, 421
drop shadow effects, 245
duplicating
  artboards, 34
  color in Swatches panel, 103
  graphic styles, 233
  layers, 176
  objects, 82–83
  slices, 380
  symbols, 292

E

Edit Colors command (Edit menu), 110, 126
Edit Custom Dictionary command (Edit
    menu), 325
Edit menu commands
  Adobe PDF Presets, 353
  Assign Profile, 96
  Check Spelling, 324
  Color Settings, 94
  Copy, 197
  Cut, 197
  Define Pattern, 124
  Edit Colors, 110, 126
  Edit Custom Dictionary, 325
  Find and Replace, 326–327
  Paste, 196–197
  Paste in Back, 197
  Paste in Front, 197
  Print Presets, 331
  Redo, 58
  Transparency Flattener Presets, 341
  Undo, 58
Edit Selection command (Select menu), 80
Edit View command (View menu), 38
editing
  blend objects, 130
  clipping masks, 162
  color in Swatches panel, 103

colors with Live Color, 114–115
gradients, 136
graphic styles, 234
images in Adobe Bridge, 416
paths within clipping sets, 163
patterns, 125
selections, 80
symbols, 293
Effect menu commands
  Convert to Shape, 242
  Crop Marks, 54
  Distort & Transform, 90
  Effect Gallery, 254–255
  Sharpen, 253
  Stylize, 243
effects
  accented edges, 257
  applying multiple, 254
  blur, 252
  controlling with selections, 255
  convert to shape, 242
  cutout, 256
  diffuse glow, 257
  drop shadow, 245
  dry brush, 256
  Fresco, 256
  gaussian blur, 252
  glass, 257
  glowing edges, 257
  grain, 258
  graphic pen, 258
  Illustrator, 240–241
  inner glow, 244–245
  mosaic tiles, 258
  note paper, 257
  outer glow, 244–245
  panel knife, 256
  Photoshop Effect Gallery, 250–251
  plastic wrap, 258
  previewing, 240
  raster graphics, 248
  scribble, 243
  spatter, 258
  stained glass, 258
  stamp, 257
  text, 192
  3D, 246–247

unsharp mask, 253

vector objects, 249

Ellipse tool, 62

ellipses, drawing, 62

embedded graphics, 226–227

endpoints, 149

Enhanced Metafile format, 349

Envelopes, reshaping with, 92

EPS format, 25, 345, 358–359

Eraser tool, 164

erasing path parts, 164

exiting Illustrator, 26

Expand button (Pathfinder panel), 156

Expand command (Objects menu), 125, 134

expanding

gradients, 134

panels, 7

patterns, 125

exporting

documents

as bitmap, 350

Export command, 348

as Flash Movie, 354–355

to Photoshop, 352

with presets, 353

as TIFF format, 351

export file formats, 349

Extension Manager (Adobe), 406, 424

Extensions command (Window menu), 106–107

Eyedropper tool

applying colors and attributes with, 122–123

color attributes, changing, 123

Save For Web & Devices tool, 366

F

families, font, 200

File Handling & Clipboard preferences, 401

File Info command (File menu), 344

file information, inserting into documents, 344–345

file management, Adobe Version Cue, 420

File menu commands

Browse in Bridge, 14–15, 222–223

Close command, 26

Device Center, 39

Document Color Mode, 98, 330

Document Setup, 32, 133

File Info, 344

New, 28–29

New From Template, 30

Open, 12, 220

Open Recent, 13

Open With, 222

Place, 16, 221, 224, 226

Print, 330, 332

Return to Adobe Illustrator, 14

Revert, 24

Save, 24

Save a Copy, 25

Save As, 25, 31

Save For Web & Devices, 364–366

Scripts, 318–319

files

deleting, 12

saving actions as, 309

fills

applying color to, 99, 112, 118

blending fill colors, 126

patterns as, 124–125

Find and Replace command (Edit menu), 326–327

Find Font command, 328

Fit All In Window command (View menu), 44

Fit Artboard In Window command (View menu), 44

Flare tool, 63

Flash format, SWF, 349, 365

Flash Movie, exporting documents as, 354–355

Flattener Preview command (Window menu), 39, 341

flattening layers, 182

fonts

bold, 200

condensed, 200

families and styles, 200

Find Font command, 328

finding, 201

italic, 200

replacing, 201

reusing recent, 200

size, 202

Free Transform tool, 86–87
Fresco effects, 256
full screen mode, 43
FXG format, 25, 360

G

gamut warning icon, 101
Gap options, 272
gaussian blur effects, 252
General preferences, 390
Get Photos from Camera command
    (Adobe), 409
GIF documents, optimizing, 372–373
GIF format, 345
glass effects, 257
global colors, 108–110
glowing edges effects, 257
glyphs, 215
Go to Bridge button, 14–15
Gradient tool, 137
gradients
    applying to objects, 134
    creating, 135
    editing, 136
    expanding, 134
    Gradient tool, 137
    linear type, 135
    mesh, 92, 138
    radial type, 135
grain effects, 258
graphic pen effects, 258
graphics
    embedded, 226–227
    linked, 226–227
    linking, 224–225
    opening graphic images, 220
    placing, 221–223
    print options, 336
    raster
        interpolation and, 60
        tracing, 228–230
        understanding raster graphics, 60
    styles
        applying, 231
        breaking links to, 235
        creating, 232

        deleting, 235
        duplicating, 233
        editing, 234
    graphs, 322
Grayscale color mode, 28, 100
grayscale images, 109
grid colors transparency settings, 33
grid patterns, 19
grid size transparency setting, 32
grids. *See also* guides
    color, 52
    displaying in back of artwork, 52
    Polar Grid tool, 69
    preferences, 52
    Rectangle Grid tool, 68
    showing and hiding, 52
    Snap to Grid command, 52
    styles, 52
    subdivisions, 52
    Transparency, 133
Group command (Objects menu), 76
Group Selection tool, 70
grouping objects, 76–77
groups, creating clipping masks for, 161
guides. *See also* grids
    clearing, 49
    color, 48
    converting vector objects to, 49
    creating, 49
    locking, 48
    preferences, 48
    ruler, 47
    showing and hiding, 48
    smart guides
        object transformation, 87
        preferences, 51
        turning on/off, 50
        working with, 50–51
    snap to point, 48
    style, 48
    switching, 49

H

Hand tool
    moving elements around with, 53
    quick access to, 53
    Save For Web & Devices tool, 366

handles, 393

hanging indents, 209

hardware, Illustrator CS4 system requirements, 3

Help menu commands
Adobe Product Improvement Program, 23
Illustrator Help, 22–23
Updates, 21
Welcome Screen, 13

help options
Community Help site, 22
searching topics, 23

Hide Edges command (View menu), 61

Hide Panels command (Window menu), 18

hiding
anchor points, 61
direction lines, 61
grids, 52
guides, 48
layers, 178
panels, 8, 43
rulers, 47
slices, 380–381
Transparency grid, 133

highlighting anchor points, 142

histograms, 411

History tab (File Info dialog box), 345

HSB color slider (Color panel), 100

HTML text, adding to slices, 386

hue, 101

hyphenation, 211, 397

I

icons, collapsing and expanding panel sets between icons and panels, 9

Illustrator Help command (Help menu), 22–23

Illustrator tab (File Info dialog box), 345

images
inserting in documents, 16
replacing, 16
working with images using Bridge, 15

importing text, 193

indentation
hanging indents, 209
paragraphs, 209

Info panel

color fill and stroke information, 55
uses for, 55

inner glow effects, 244–245

installing Illustrator CS4
in Macintosh, 3
in Windows, 2

Internet, checking for updates from, 20

interpolation, 60

Inverse command (Select menu), 78

inverting colors, 110

IPTC tab (File Info dialog box), 344

Isolation Mode, 163

italic font, 200

J

joining anchor endpoints, 149

joins, 121

JPEG documents, optimizing, 370–371

JPEG format, 345, 349

K

kerning type, 204

Keyboard Increment general preference, 390

keyboard shortcuts, 403

Knife tool, 152

Knockout Group option, 132

Kuler panel, 106–107

L

landscape/portrait orientation, 35

language settings, document creation, 33

Lasso tool
selecting objects with, 73
understanding selections, 70

layers. *See also* Layers panel
arranging, 174–175
creating clipping masks for, 161
creating top level layers, 168–169
deleting, 171
deselecting, 170
duplicating, 176
flattening, 182
hiding, 178
locking, 177
merging, 179
moving, 174–175

layers *(continued)*

    moving objects to, 180–181

    naming, 169

    releasing objects to, 181

    selecting, 170

    selecting objects with, 172–173

    showing and hiding, 178

    sublayers, 168–169

Layers panel. *See also* layers

    accessing, 166

    components of, 166

    locating objects in, 183

    options, setting, 167

layouts, workspace, 56

leading text, 203

line graphs, 322

Line Segment tool, 65

line segments, drawing, 65

linear gradient type, 135

linked graphics, 226–227

linking

    documents, 16

    graphics, 224–225

    slices, 381

Liquify tools, 289

Live Color feature

    applying color groups to objects with, 114–115

    editing colors with, 114–115

Live Paint Bucket tool

    paint fills, 266

    preferences, setting, 265

    selecting options to paint fills or strokes with, 264

    stroke edges, changing, 267

Live Paint Groups

    adding paths to, 271

    converting traced objects to, 263

    creating, 262–263

    Gap options, 272

    reshaping or moving paths in, 270–271

Live Paint Selection tool, 268–269

    locking

    guides, 48

    layers, 177

lossy compression, 373

lowercase text, 329

luminosity, 101

M

Macintosh

    Illustrator CS4 system requirements, 3

    installing Illustrator CS4 in, 3

    starting Illustrator CS4 in, 5

Macintosh PICT format, 349

Magic Wand tool

    selecting objects with, 74–75

    understanding selections, 70

marks print options, 334–335

Measure tool, 55

measurement

    distance between objects, measuring, 55

    measurement units, document creation, 32

menus, 6

merging

    layers, 179

    paths, 154–155

mesh, 92, 138

metadata, 345

Microsoft Office, saving documents as, 361

miter bend style, 83

miter joins, 121

Mobile SWF tab (File Info dialog box), 344

mosaic tiles effects, 258

Move tool, 50

moving

    anchor points, 142–143

    artboards, 36

    document elements with Hand tool, 53

    layers, 174–175

    objects, 81

    objects to layers, 180–181

    segments, 142–143

    slices, 382

    text, 191, 196–197

    between tools, 53

N

naming

    layers, 169

    selections, 80

    workspaces, 56

navigation

    artboards, 37

    within artboards, 34

Navigator panel
    customizing, 42
    view area, 41
    view box color, 42
    view size, 40
New command (File menu), 28–29
New From Template command (File menu),
    30
New View command (View menu), 38
Next Object Above command (Select
    menu), 78
Next Object Below command (Select
    menu), 78
nonglobal colors, 108–110
normal screen mode, 43
note paper effects, 257

O

objects
    alignment, 84
    applying color to, 99, 112, 118
    clearing, 81
    deleting, 81
    distributing, 84
    duplicating, 82–83
    grouping, 76–77
    measuring distance between, 55
    moving, 81
    moving to layers, 180–181
    reflecting, 85, 89
    rotating, 85–86, 88
    scaling, 85, 88
    selecting
        with Lasso tool, 73
        with Magic Wand tool, 74–75
        similar objects, 78–79
        using Direction Selection tool, 72
        using Select menu, 78–79
        using Selection tool, 71
    transforming, 85–87
Objects menu commands
    Blend, 127–128
    Clipping Mask, 160
    Compound Path, 158
    Expand, 125, 134
    Group, 76
    Text Wrap, 216

    Transform, 90
    Ungroup, 76
offsetting paths, 83
opacity, blends, 131
Open command (File menu), 12, 220
open paths, 61, 147
Open Recent command (File menu), 13
Open With command (File menu), 222
opening
    documents
        with Adobe Bridge, 14–15
        existing documents, 12
        recently opened, 13
        from Welcome Screen, 13
    graphic images, 220
    panels, 7
Origin tab (File Info dialog box), 345
outer flow effects, 244–245
Outline view, 38–39
outlines, 217
output print options, 338–339
output slice settings, 385
overflow, text, 198–199
Overprint Preview command (View menu),
    39, 337

P

Paintbrush tool, 151
painting
    art brushes, 280–281
    Brushes panel, 273
    calligraphic brushes, 278–279
    Live Paint Bucket tool, 264–267
    Live Paint Groups
        adding paths to, 271
        converting traced objects to, 263
        creating, 262–263
        Gap options, 272
        reshaping or moving paths in,
            270–271
    Live Paint Selection tool, 268–269
    Paintbrush tool, 274–275
        pattern brushes, 282–283
        scatter brushes, 276–277
    panel knife effects, 256
    Panel Options menu, 7, 9

panels
    adding, 8
    closing, 7
    collapsing, 7
    displaying hidden, 43
    docking/undocking, 8
    expanding, 7
    hiding, 8, 43
    opening, 7
    Panel Options menu, 9
    sets, collapsing and expanding between icons and panels, 9
    subtracting, 8
paragraphs
    alignment, 208
    indentation, 209
    spacing, 209
Paste command (Edit menu), 196–197
Paste in Back command (Edit menu), 197
Paste in Front command (Edit menu), 197
Pathfinder panel, 156
paths
    anchor points and, 61
    clipping mask, 160–163
    closed, 61
    compound, 158–159
    dividing, 153
    erasing parts of, 164, 260
    merging, 154–155
    offsetting, 83
    open, 61, 147
    reshaping, 150–151
    segments and, 61
    Shape Mode command, 156
    shape of, changing, 61
    splitting, 152–153
pattern brushes, 282–283
patterns
    applying to objects, 124
    editing, 125
    expanding, 125
    as fills, 124–125
PDF format, 25, 345, 356–357
Pen tool
    anchor points, adding, 147
    drawing curves with, 141
    drawing polygons with, 140

Pencil tool
    preferences, 261
    reshaping paths with, 151
    working with, 260–261
Photoshop Effect Gallery, 250–251
Photoshop, exporting to, 352
Photoshop format, 349
pie graphs, 322
Pixel Preview command (View menu), 39
pixels, 35
Place command (File menu), 16, 221, 224, 226
placing graphics, 221–223
plastic wrap effects, 258
Play button (Actions panel), 309
playback, action, 311
plug-in preferences, 398
PNG format, 345, 349
PNG-8 document, 374–375
PNG-24 document, 376
point type, 187
point/pica size, 46
points, anchor
    adding new, 146–147
    alignment, 148–149
    Convert Anchor Point tool, 145
    converting, 144–145
    deleting, 147
    direction lines, 142
    endpoints, 149
    highlighting, 142
    moving, 142–143
    paths and, 61
    preferences, 142
    selecting with Direct Selection tool, 72
    showing and hiding, 61
    smooth points, converting to corner points, 144
Polar Grid tool, 69
Polygon tool, 64
polygons, drawing, 64, 140
portrait/landscape orientation, 35
preferences
    Adobe Bridge, 414–415
    anchor points, 142
    Appearance of Black, 402
    cursor, 390
    File Handling & Clipboard, 401

General, 390
grids, 52
guide, 48
hyphenation, 397
keyboard shortcut, 403
Live Paint Bucket tool, 265
Pencil tool, 261
plug-in, 398
ruler, 46
Scratch Disk, 399
Selection & Anchor Display, 392–393
slices, 397
smart guides, 51
text, 394–395
Transparency grid, 133
type, 394–395
Units & Display Performance, 396
updates, 20
user interface, 400
presets
    artboard, 34
    creating new documents using, 29
    exporting with, 353
    list of, 29
    printing with, 331, 340
Preview view, 38–39
Preview View command (View menu), 260
previewing
    artboards, 36
    color separations, 337
    effects, 240
Print command (File menu), 330, 332
Print Presets command (Edit menu), 331
printing
    advanced print options, 340–341
    bleed options, 335
    color management settings, 342
    color separations, previewing, 337
    documents, 330
    general print options, 332–333
    graphics print options, 336
    marks options, 334–335
    number of copies, specifying, 333
    output options, setting, 338–339
    Overprint preview, 337
    overprints, 340
    presets, 340
    with presets, 331
    Print command, 330
    print problems, checking for, 343
    print tiling, 333
    reverse order, 332
    Separations preview, 337
    summary print options, 343
Product Improvement Program (Adobe), 23
Proof Colors command (View menu), 116
Proof Setup command (View menu), 39
proofing colors, 116
PSD format, 345
Pucker tool, 286
punctuation, 214

Q

Quit Illustrator command (Illustrator menu), 26
quotes, 33

R

radar graphs, 322
radial gradient type, 135
raster graphics
    effects, 248
    interpolation and, 60
    tracing, 228–230
    understanding raster graphics, 60
Raw Data tab (File Info dialog box), 345
Record button (Actions panel), 309
recording actions, 310
Rectangle Grid tool, 68
Rectangle tool, 63
rectangles, drawing, 63
Redo command (Edit menu), 58
Reflect tool, 89
reflecting objects, 85, 89
registration, 4–5
releasing
    compound paths, 159
    objects from clipping masks, 161
    objects to layers, 181
renaming
    data sets, 321
    selections, 80
    workspaces, 57

rendering intent color management print
      option, 342
replacing
    colors, 108–109
    fonts, 201
    images, 16
Reselect command (Select menu), 78
Reshape tool, 150
reshaping paths, 150–151
resizing
    artboards, 36
    slices, 382
resolution preset transparency setting, 33
Return to Adobe Illustrator command (File
      menu), 14
reverse order printing, 332
Revert command (File menu), 24
revolving 3D effects, 247
RGB (Red, Green, Blue) color mode, 28, 97,
      100
Rotate tool, 88
rotating
    artboards, 36
    objects, 85–86, 88
    text, 207
round bend style, 83
round joins, 121
Rounded Rectangle tool, 63
RTF format, 193
rulers
    artboard display options, 37, 47
    displaying, 46–47
    document, 46–47
    guides
        alignment, 51
        changing, 47
        clearing, 49
        color, 48
        converting vector objects to, 49
        creating, 49
        locking, 48
        preferences, 48
        ruler, 47
        showing and hiding, 48
        smart guides, 50–51
        snap to point, 48
        style, 48
        switching, 49

hiding, 47
origin, changing, 47
preferences, 46

S

safe area, artboard display options, 37
Same command (Select menu), 79
saturation, color, 101
Save a Copy command (File menu), 25
Save As command (File menu), 25, 31
Save command (File menu), 24
Save For Web & Devices command (File
      menu), 364–366
Save Selection command (Select menu), 80
Save Workspace command (Workspace
      menu), 56
saving
    actions
        as files, 309
        into sets, 309
    documents, 24–25
        as Adobe Flex File, 360
        as EPS format, 358–359
        as FXG format, 360
        as Microsoft Office, 361
        as PDF format, 356–357
        as template, 362
        for the Web, 364–365
    selections, 80
    slices for Web, 384–385
    symbols, 291
Scale tool, 88
scaling
    objects, 85, 88
    type, 206
Scallop tool, 286
scatter brushes, 276–277
scatter graphs, 322
Scissor tool, 152
Scratch Disk preferences, 399
screen modes, 43
scribble effects, 243
scripts, actions, 318–319
searching
    fonts, 201
    for help information, 23
segments

curve, 143

moving, 142–143

paths and, 61

selecting with Direct Selection tool, 72

Select menu commands, 78–79

Edit Selection, 80

Same command, 79

Save Selection, 80

Selection & Anchor Display preferences, 392–393

Selection tool. *See also* selections

aligning and distributing objects using, 84

duplicating objects with, 82–83

moving objects with, 81

reflecting or shearing objects, 89

rotating and scale objects with, 88

selecting objects with, 71

transforming objects with, 85

understanding selections, 70

selections. *See also* Selection tool

anchor points, 72

controlling effects using, 255

deleting, 80

editing, 80

examples of, 70

inverting color of, 78

layers, 170

naming, 80

renaming, 80

reselecting, 78

saving, 80

selecting next object above/below current, 78

slices, 380–381

type, 194–195

understanding selections, 70

sentence case, 329

Separations Preview command (Window menu), 39

Shape Mode command (Pathfinder panel), 156

Share My Screen command, 419

Sharpen command (Effect menu), 253

Shear tool, 89

shortcuts

starting Illustrator CS4, 4–5

tool, 11

Show Bounding Box command (View menu), 85

Show Edges command (View menu), 61

Show Panels command (Window menu), 18

Show Print Tiling command (View menu), 38

Show Text Threads command (View menu), 198

Show Transparency Grid command (View menu), 133

single quotes, 33

size

artboard, 35

font, 202

views, 40

Slice Selection tool, 366

slices

alignment, 383

arranging, 382–383

auto, 378

deleting, 380

distributing, 383

duplicating, 380

hiding, 380–381

HTML text, adding, 386

linking, 381

moving, 382

output option settings, 385

preferences, 397

resizing, 382

saving for Web, 384–385

selecting, 380–381

showing, 380–381

stacking, 383

subslices, 379

unlinking, 381

URL links, adding, 387

user, 378

viewing slice options, 380–381

working with, 381

smart guides

object transformation, 87

preferences, 51

turning on/off, 50

working with, 50–51

Smart Punctuation, 214

smooth points, converting to corner points, 144

Snap to Grid command, 52
Snap to Point command, 48, 392
soft proof colors, 116
software, Illustrator CS4 system requirements, 3
spacing paragraphs, 209
spatter effects, 258
spell checking, 324–325
Spiral tool, 66–67
spirals, drawing, 66–67
splitting paths, 152–153
stacked bar graphs, 322
stacked column graphs, 322
stacking slices, 383
stained glass effects, 258
stamp effects, 257
Star tool, 64
stars, drawing, 64
Start menu, opening documents using, 13
starting Illustrator CS4
    in Macintosh, 5
    shortcuts, 4–5
    Welcome screen, 4
    in Windows, 4
status bar, 17
Stop button (Actions panel), 309
stops, adding to actions, 312
stroke
    alignment, 120
    applying color to, 99, 112, 118
    attributes, changing, 120–121
    caps or joins, changing, 121
    dashed, 121
    weight of, changing, 120
styles
    font, 200
    graphic
        applying, 231
        breaking links to, 235
        creating, 232
        deleting, 235
        duplicating, 233
        editing, 234
    grids, 52
    guides, 48
    type, 212–213
Stylize command (Effect menu), 243

sublayers, 168–169
subscript text, 33
subslices, 379
subtracting panels, 8
summary print options, 343
superscript text, 33
SVG format, 25, 365
Swatches Library
    copying swatches between libraries, 104
    customized swatch panels, saving, 105
    displaying, 104
    gradient library, 134
Swatches panel
    creating color groups in, 103
    deleting colors from, 102
    display of, changing, 102
    editing or duplicating color in, 103
    sorting colors in, 102
    swatches, displaying by type, 102
    Swatches Library, 104–105
SWF format, Flash, 349, 365
symbols
    creating, 290
    deleting, 291
    duplicating, 292
    editing, 293
    links, breaking, 294–295
    saving, 291
    sets, expanding instances of, 305
    Symbol Libraries, 289
    Symbol Screener tool, 303
    Symbol Scruncher tool, 299
    Symbol Shifter tool, 298
    Symbol Sizer tool, 300
    Symbol Spinner tool, 301
    Symbol Sprayer tool, 296
    Symbol Strainer tool, 302
    Symbol Styler tool, 304
    symbolism tool options, setting, 297
    Symbols panel, 288
system requirements, 3

T

tab stops, 210
tabbed documents, 18
tabs, 210
Targa format, 349

templates
  creating documents from, 30–31
  document, 16, 30–31
  saving documents as, 362
text
  case, 329
  copying, 196–197
  effects, 192
  fonts, 200–202
  glyphs, 215
  hyphenation, 211
  importing, 193
  kerning, 204
  leading, 203
  moving, 191, 196–197
  outlines, 217
  overflow, 198–199
  paragraphs, 208–209
  preferences, 394–395
  rotating, 207
  scaling, 206
  selecting, 194–195
  styles, 212–213
  subscript, 33
  superscript, 33
  tabs, 210
  threads, 198–199
  tracking, 205
  typing new, 187–188
  wrapping, 216
Text Format, 349
Text Wrap command (Objects menu), 216
themes, color, 106–107
threads, text, 198–199
3D effects, 246–247
thumbnail views, 41
TIFF format, 345, 349, 351
Tolerance selection option, 392
tool tips, 391
tools
  accessing in Tools panel, 10
  accessing multiple, 10
  Control panel, 6
  moving between, 53
  shortcuts to, 11
Tools panel
  accessing tools in, 10

  contents of, 6
tracing raster graphics, 228–230
tracking type, 205
transformations
  applying multiple, 90–91
  blends, 130
  Distort & Transform command, 90
  repeating, 90
  Transform Each command, 90
transforming objects, 85–87
Transparency Flattener Presets command
    (Edit menu), 341
Transparency grid, 133
transparency settings
  blends, 132
  colored paper simulation, 33
  controlling transparency effects, 132
  document creation, 32–33
  grid colors, 33
  grid size, 32
  resolution preset, 33
turning on/off smart guides, 50
TXT format, 193
type
  Area Type tool, 189
  copying, 196–197
  fonts, 200–202
  kerning, 204
  leading, 203
  moving, 196–197
  outlines, 217
  overflow, 198–199
  paragraphs, 208–209
  preferences, 394–395
  rotating, 207
  scaling, 206
  selecting, 194–195
  styles, 212–213
  threads, 198–199
  tracking value, 205
  Type on a Path tool, 190
  Vertical Area Type tool, 189
  Vertical Type on a Path tool, 190
  Vertical Type tool, 187
  wrapping, 216
Type on a Path tool, 190
Type tool, 186
typographer's quotes, 33

Twirl tool, 286

U

Undo command (Edit menu), 58
undocking
    documents, 19
    panels, 8
Ungroup command (Objects menu), 76
Units & Display Performance preferences, 396
unsharp mask effects, 253
Updater (Adobe), 21
updates
    checking for, 20–21
    preferences, 20
Updates command (Help menu), 21
updating, from previous versions, 2
uppercase text, 329
URL links, adding to slices, 387
user interface preferences, 400
user slices, 378

V

variables, data
    creating, 320–321
    deleting, 320–321
    renaming, 321
vector objects
    converting to guide, 49
    effects, 249
    understanding vector graphics, 60
Version Cue (Adobe)
    basic description of, 406
    file management, 420
Vertical Area Type tool, 189
Vertical Type on a Path tool, 190
Vertical Type tool, 187
Video Data tab (File Info dialog box), 344
video safe areas, artboards, 35
View menu commands
    Bounding Box, 270–271
    Edit View, 38
    Fit All In Window, 44
    Fit Artboard In Window, 44
    Hide Edges, 61
    New View, 38
    Overprint Preview, 39
    Pixel Preview, 39
    Preview View, 260
    Proof Colors, 116
    Proof Setup, 39
    Rulers, 46
    Show Bounding Box, 85
    Show Edges, 61
    Show Print Tiling, 38
    Show Text Threads, 198
    Show Transparency Grid, 133
    Smart Guides, 50
    Soft Proof, 116
view size, documents, 17
views
    box color, 42
    changing, with Zoom tool, 44–45
    display view, changing, 38–39
    document, 38–41
    fit in window, 44
    Outline, 38–39
    Preview, 38–39
    ruler options, 46
    size, 40
    thumbnail, 41

W

Warp tool, 286
WBMP document, optimizing, 377
Web
    file formats, 368–369
    GIF documents, optimizing, 372–373
    images, optimizing to file size, 367
    JPEG documents, optimizing, 370–371
    PNG-8 document, optimizing, 374–375
    PNG-24 document, optimizing, 376
    saving documents for, 364–365
    saving slices for, 384–385
    WBMP document, optimizing, 377
Web-safe color, 101
Welcome screen, 4, 13
Welcome Screen command (Help menu), 13
Window menu
    Extensions, 106–107
    Flattener Preview, 39
    panel display, 7–8
Window menu commands
    Flattener Preview, 341

Hide Panels, 18
Separations preview, 39
Show Panels, 18
Windows
Illustrator CS4 system requirements, 3
installing Illustrator CS4 in, 2
starting Illustrator CS4 in, 4
windows
active, 18
document, 18–19
Windows Metafile format, 349
Workspace menu commands, 56
workspaces
creating, 56
deleting, 57
displaying, 56
layouts, 56
naming, 56
renaming, 57

wrapping text, 216
Wrinkle tool, 286

X

X and Y positioning, 35
XMP format, 344
XMP Software Development Kit, 345

Z

zoom
in/out, 45
using Navigator thumbnail, 41
view size, 40
Zoom tool
changing view with, 44–45
Save For Web & Devices tool, 366